A Reader's Guide to Charles Dickens

Other titles in the Reader's Guide Series

A Reader's Guide to Charles Dickens

Philip Hobsbaum

SYRACUSE UNIVERSITY PRESS

First Syracuse University Press Edition 1998

98 99 00 01 02 03   6 5 4 3 2 1

Originally published in 1972. Reprinted by arrangement with Farrar, Straus & Giroux.

The paper used in this publication meets the minimum requirements of American
National Standard for Information Sciences—Permanenceof Paper for Printed
Library Materials, ANSI Z39.48-1984. ∞™

Library of Congress Cataloging-in-Publication Data

Hobsbaum, Philip.
      A reader's guide to Charles Dickens / Philip Hobsbaum. — 1st
Syracuse University Press ed.
            p.   cm.
      Originally published :   New York   :   Farrar, Straus and Giroux, c1972.
      Includes bibliographical references (p.   ) and index.
      ISBN 0-8156-0475-0 (pbk. : alk. paper)
      1. Dickens, Charles, 1812–1870—Criticism and interpretation—
Handbooks, manuals, etc.   I. Title
PR4588. H54   1998
823'.8—dc21   97-44984

For the wisest and most
wonderful of women,
Patricia

. . . All the more honour to you then
If, weaker than some other men,
You had the courage that survives
Soiled, shabby, egotistic lives,
If poverty or ugliness
Ill-health or social unsuccess
Hunted you out of life to play
At living in another way;
Yet the live quarry all the same
Were changed to huntsmen in the game,.
And the wild furies of the past,
Tracked to their origins at last . . .

W. H. AUDEN

Contents

Preface

My deepest thanks are due to Tom Rosenthal, who originally suggested that I write this book; to my friend and partner, the American poet Anne Stevenson, who helped and encouraged me throughout its composition; to Alice Rutherford, who typed the manuscript with the precision and care of friendship; and to Kate McManus.

No words can express my sense of indebtedness to my research assistant and amanuensis, Miss Julia Hawkins. Without her ability to resuscitate buried facts and to analyse the findings of other workers in the field, this book would have been flimsier and far less accurate. Needless to say, if any inaccuracies remain, I am answerable for them.

I cannot convey my affection for the dedicatee, friend of many years, other than by inscribing to her this King Charles's Head in the hope that she will see fit to set it alongside those of James I, James II and the Old Pretender.

Introduction

The reputation of Charles Dickens is in no danger. His books have headed the list of best-sellers for 130-odd years. Among popular classics he ranks behind only the King James Bible and Shakespeare. He is one of the most widely translated of authors, and the one most disseminated over the globe. His work has been edited, criticized, interpreted, re-interpreted, researched into – indeed, Dickens is the centre of a thriving academic industry. He has figured in more theses and dissertations than any other Victorian, and the activity seems to be growing. In any given year of the 1960s, twice as many books and articles on Dickens appeared than was the case in the 1930s, and the publication explosion exceeded all previous bounds in the centenary year of 1970. Moreover, those who have traversed this range of research will testify to the quality as well as the quantity of the contribution. It is as though an interest in Dickens were a guarantee of intelligence. Given the volume and tone of the general chorus, what need for an additional voice?

But the area of attention is seriously bifurcated. Work upon Dickens falls into two different categories. One of these includes the writings of critics; and for books with such titles as *The Quintessential Boz* or *The Social Vision of Dickens* (I am inventing) we should, I suppose, be grateful. They tend, characteristically, to deal with some half-dozen of the major novels, and fulfil a need in pushing one up a notch or two in the canon or in throwing light on an unusual angle of another. But the critics give little indication of how the books came to be written; they do not trouble to imply a social context. The point will be clear if I say that one would hardly gather from the usual treatment of Dickens that he was, throughout his life, a busy editor and journalist. A third of the works published by him were articles, essays and reportage, and we are still waiting for the first adequate study of his non-fictional prose. In other words, the literary critics who put forward accounts of Dickens are mostly far more limited in their survey than they will ever admit.

The other distinct category into which comment on Dickens falls is that of research. One looks through the endless shelves of periodicals in the secure hope of turning up the most recondite information. The legal aspects of Dickens, the theatrical aspects, items of social or economic history, buried biographical details – all are unearthed in one specialist paper or another. Every Dickensian is a scholar in his little field, but the hedgerows have been left to grow, and communication between the different workers is difficult. There is a case for a synthesis between the various areas of research; there is, farther, a case for research informing criticism. The literary critic does his readers no service by failing to tell them that areas of research exist.

One must attempt a synthesis. It will not affect the fact that the great novels will be in the forefront of the survey. But attention to background and conditions of publication will help to show why these novels are the shape they are. Nor need we exclusively concentrate on work that is major. A study of the lesser writings may expose the reasons for relative failure; it may even turn up a codicil in the dust. This is especially true of the uncollected prose and the Christmas Stories.

One must also determine upon an approach to the work. And here the claims of the reader must be especially considered. There can be no doubt that useful work has been done (for instance) in characterizing Dickens's symbolism. But at times the sense of plot has been lost in the process. When odd bits of imagery are lifted from context and analysed, it may only be the exceptional reader who can be certain of putting them back into place. Most readers are not exceptional. The critic must allow for the person who has imperfect acquaintance with the text.

Such a reader may wish to be introduced to a book he has not yet read. Or he may have difficulty with the author and be seeking a line on his work. He may simply feel that a point of view other than his own would sharpen his understanding. All these are legitimate needs, and the critic must take them into account. However much we respect Dickens, we are not living in a world of Dickensians. There is also the fact that our cultural habits are continually changing. The bulk of our fiction reaches us, in neatly shot snippets, through the medium of the television screen. In an age of economical and straightforward plot, the massive complex of the Victorian novel is becoming harder to grasp. To take into account such changes as these is not necessarily to condone them; but it is a bad lecturer who fails to recognize the previous experience of his audience. It seems to me that, if we are to help people to understand Dickens, our basic concern must be with the structure of his novels.

The aspect of Dickens that is all too often left out of consideration is the shape and function of his plots. One would think, from the way in which some critics talk, that the plots of his novels were irrelevant. If that were true, Dickens would be the first major author of whom such a thing could be said. One would not attempt to discuss Lear's Fool aside from his function in the total fabric of the play; if old Krook is an integral part of *Bleak House* and Mrs Gamp an irrelevance in *Martin Chuzzlewit*, so much the worse (we may say) for *Martin Chuzzlewit*. It seems to me that we have underestimated Dickens's sophistication in this respect. *Our Mutual Friend* will seem labyrinthine only if we fail to consider that a large part of the action has taken place before the book officially begins, and comes across to us in the form of retrospect and flashback. Old Harmon, the miser, is a subterranean presence throughout the book, and emerges from time to time in the recollections of witnesses and through the weight of his dead hand upon the hopes of the living.

Therefore my present purpose in this book is to provide a structural survey of Dickens's fiction. The term 'fabric' or 'structure' is used to indicate the complex of plots that forms a novel. 'Plot' itself is taken to refer to a main line of action; if it has reference to the activity and development of character, it is called a 'strand'. In a book that has, relatively speaking, failed, one or another of its plots or strands will be detachable from its total structure. In a book that has succeeded, all the plots will be seen to work together towards one common end; and this I term the Theme.

There can be no doubt that, in the earlier novels of Dickens, plot coincides with Theme only by chance. We see glimpses in *Pickwick Papers* of a ghost-novel that assures us, in the teeth of its hero's optimism, that virtue does suffer, that the life of man is not so much like the road to Dingley Dell as a long period of confinement in the cellars of the Fleet Prison. *Oliver Twist* begins with a hero who is an emblem of all waifs ground in the mill of society; it ends with a smug young bourgeois reinstated in his inheritance. After the first eleven chapters, the plot detaches itself from the Theme, and the children who are left in the workhouse are forgotten. In *Nicholas Nickleby* the theme emerges only as Dotheboys Hall; otherwise we have a routine melodrama, dashing hero, wicked uncle and all. Most fascinating of all these early works is *Martin Chuzzlewit*: a monstrous farrago of plots, tending in at least five different directions, any one of which has interest; but the novel is devoid of theme or total structure capable of containing them all.

One would be inclined to say that, before Dickens could devise any such structure, he had to get rid of a good deal of autobiography. The great catharsis of *David Copperfield* released him for more important work. At last he was able to put his childhood troubles in perspective, if not to sublimate them, and attribute their working to some kind of source; even though the source was grotesquely over-simplified. In the later novels, the Theme stands out clear: it shows the fight of the individual against the System.

The Theme is intermittently present, though not so clear, in the earlier novels. In *Oliver Twist* the System is the Workhouse; in *Nicholas Nickleby*, it is Dotheboys Hall; in *Martin Chuzzlewit*, it is America; in *David Copperfield*, it is Mr Murdstone, Creakle and the Firm. All these are by way of being personifications – Society as Ogre, one might say – and they lack the impetus to take them through their respective books. One could go farther, and say that they stand as targets for Dickens's anger: the anger of a deprived child unable directly to blame his parents for his misfortunes. Dickens's parents were not wicked; they were weak. They broke off his schooling and put him to work labelling bottles in a blacking warehouse, it is true; but this was not the result of malice but of helpless improvidence. And, since there was no Mr Murdstone in Dickens's own life, to justify his anger he had to create one in *David Copperfield*. But the amount of personal rancour released in this book allowed Dickens to depersonalize his theme. It was not an Ogre now but Society who stood in place of father; and a barren and neglectful Father it turned out to be. Thus, the theme of *Bleak House* is the individual in the toils of the Law; in *Hard Times,* he is imprisoned by Industry; in *Great Expectations* by Class; in *Our Mutual Friend* by Money; while in *Little Dorrit* the Theme is imprisonment itself – prison as a society, and all Society as a prison. In these novels, incidents, characters, strands of plot, lines of action, the pattern of symbolism and the evocative prose all subserve and act out the great Dickens theme: the individual against the System. It is no coincidence that we may have some confidence in claiming these as Dickens's greatest works.

Of course there are various subsidiary themes throughout the Dickens oeuvre. His work has at times an hallucinatory, a phantasmagoric, quality which we associate with exhaustion and nightmare. It comes out strongly at points where the organization of the novel is under stress: the 'Tale of the Queer Client' is one such example in *Pickwick Papers;* the murder of Nancy in *Oliver Twist* is another; the eruption of the Madman in *Nicholas Nickleby* and the ogreish clutchings and babblings of Charley the Pawnbroker in *David Copperfield* are also cases in point. Related to these are the functionless machinations of Quilp in *The Old Curiosity Shop* and the free-association ramblings of Mrs Gamp. It is worth pointing out that much of the life in these characters depends upon their being seen intermittently and in a strongly marked attitude. The effect is of their going through a limited but highly individual repertory of motions all the time we are elsewhere in the script. Thus Mr Micawber appears only at intervals throughout *David Copperfield*; but, every time we see him, he is making a gesture, verbal or physical, which we recognize as highly characteristic. The result is that, quite factitiously, he appears to be a 'living' character; even though, when we consider, the number of his gestures is few, and his relation to the later developments of the plot questionable. It is noticeable that we experience Mr Dorrit in quite different terms: in *Little Dorrit* he is an integral part of an inexorably developing structure. But he, unlike Micawber, cannot be called a 'Dickens character'; the term is best applied to those figures who belong to the subsidiary themes in Dickens's work.

Such fantasy, melodrama and farce as appear in the early novels remained with Dickens throughout his life; though this may not be evident to those who have not studied the various Christmas Stories.

These partly collaborative ventures came out year by year as extra numbers of Dickens's magazine *Household Words*, and they canalized much of the wild imagining instinct in Dickens's nature. It seems to have helped clear the serious vision of the great novels; at any rate, they are far less bedevilled by irrelevant death-bed scenes and outbursts of farce. Over the years, however, Hyde trespassed upon Jekyll; Dickens's fancy made inroads, not upon his vision, but upon his time. The public readings up and down the country gave such fantasy free rein; they also took up energy. In these readings, Dickens spent himself on work which we should now consider inferior: *A Christmas Carol,* 'Boots at the Holly Tree Inn', 'Mr Chops the Dwarf'. The more he read, the less he was able to write. The interval after his first tour allowed him to compose *Great Expectations*; the disappointment following the administrative crises of the second tour impelled him to stay at home writing *Our Mutual Friend*; his collapse in the middle of the last tour compelled him to begin *Edwin Drood*. And, in this last work, phantasmagoria breaks loose. Brilliantly executed though it is, it is a fragment; and, even if it had been completed, it is unlikely that we should have been able to say what it was about in the way we can talk of Theme in *Little Dorrit,* say, or *Our Mutual Friend*. Dickens's career, had it continued, is all too likely to have been an extension into infinity of Christmas Stories. The objection to those eerie fancies is not altogether on the grounds of writing; rather, they tap ancillary experience and leave the minds of mature readers untouched.

The superiority of the great novels over the Christmas Stories is a superiority not of social criticism only but of symbolic drama. The world of these novels seems more solid, more referential to adult environment, than the world of Scrooge or Chops. Yet it draws to no small extent on Dickens's own personal substance. His range in certain respects is more limited than has been recognized. Certain topics recur with the force of obsession: the substitute or inadequate father, the debtors' prison, the deprived child, the buried past, the Calvinist heritage: these are familiar properties throughout the books. And much else is omitted: Dickens does not go deeply into politics, and scarcely touches the world of work or art; he is in no sense a novelist of ideas; he has little to say worth hearing about sex, though much that deserves note about frustration. His main complaint is that the society that should protect the individual in fact neglects him. But even this apparently dramatic theme draws upon deeply personal experience. In his critique of the money-system, *Our Mutual Friend*, Dickens himself appears in various guises. Old Harmon educates his son on the system adopted by Dickens himself – a cheap schooling abroad. This son, in his turn, suppresses his own earlier life, as Dickens did the blacking factory. The most paranoid aspect of Dickens, his jealousy and uncertainty, vitalizes the unhappy figure of Bradley Headstone. The wiles and moods of his mistress, Ellen Ternan, impel the petulant and wayward Bella Wilfer. Dickens's attempt to gain knowledge and distinction is dramatized in the slow-learning Charley and Lizzie Hexam. While the fine gentleman, Wrayburn, completely at ease in the world, is very much Dickens's beau ideal. One could go on, through Boffin, through Veneering, through a host of minor characters; but the point is plain. Whenever a detached and eloquent critique of society is called for, nine times out of ten Dickens is depicting himself. Nevertheless, this expenditure of personal substance in no way impugns the artistic integrity of the books. It is rather as though, once the lyrical phase is past, the great author proceeds, more cautiously, through empathy.

Dickens's personality was a complex and not always engaging one. The rheumatic fever which left him much alone as a child exposed him to the horror-stories of an incompetent nursemaid. His highly escapist reading – *Arabian Nights, Roderick Random* – also helped to build up certain areas of sensitivity to experience. Dickens was certainly vulnerable to the assault upon his sensibility represented by the blacking factory long before any such assault was delivered. The subsequent humiliation of his failure in courting Maria Beadnell, wounding though it was to his feelings, was hardly necessary: the damage had already been done. Often a situation in adult life re-produces an infantile syndrome and so brings about neurosis. It was Dickens's misfortune that this happened to him in early adolescence. At the age of twelve, the blacking factory was his 1984, his dark night of the soul, his street of shame. The only way out was by willed and deliberate over-compensation.

As a man, Dickens was gay, extrovert, the centre of numerous friends. It was only when crossed that his steely will struck out, as Mark Lemon found when he befriended the estranged Mrs Dickens.

Dickens protected himself by mixing with intellectual inferiors. His company included cartoonists and writers, none of the highest calibre; one can hardly imagine him being at home (for instance) in the George Eliot circle. He could not brook the smallest criticism, the faintest hint at failure, as publishers and colleagues found. The deprived child survived into a man who could bear no word of warning or advice: his quarrels with Hall, with Bradbury, with Thackeray and Lemon show that. He drove his friends, as he drove himself, without mercy; and they were docile: happy to act in his plays, to attend his social gatherings, to contribute to his magazines, to be ordered about, rewritten, abridged and brightened. His frantic appeals to his friends to keep him company when inspiration flagged show all too clearly the nature of his ruthless drive: when Dickens was not active, he did not exist.

All this points to a personality, through experience rather than heredity, distinctly paranoid. This meant that, deep down, Dickens nourished a distrust of himself. Hence the over-compensation, the impulse to dominate, the assertion of the will. This, in effect, turned people into extensions of his personality. But once a person became such an extension, they were liable to bear the weight of this self-distrust. And any resultant unease on their part increased Dickens's quotient of anxiety. His rage was founded upon fear; his fear was born from the cry of an anxious child in the night.

Whatever the world did for Dickens, it could never do enough. Famous and caressed, his mind never ceased to wander back to the blacking factory and all the horrors beyond. His marriage was dust and ashes to him; from what we can gather, his affair with Ellen Ternan brought him no peace; his children ceased to interest him once they developed minds of their own. Though he had been a runaway success with *Pickwick Papers* at the age of twenty-four, still he sought a closer relation with his public. First he courted them through the week-by-week media of his magazines; later, he achieved direct contact through his ever popular Readings. Through all this activity raged his relentless will.

But nothing could satisfy him: his books show a darkening world. This is why we must not spend too much time in laying stress upon his antecedents. Looked at in perspective, Fielding, Smollett, Goldsmith, Sterne, seem of limited interest now. It is worth remarking that their great contemporary was Gibbon, and, while he was chronicling the fall of an empire, they were modelling in clay. Dickens may, indeed, have had his feet set in that engaging substance; but he refined it throughout his working career and emerges, as none of them do, as a colossus. He remained, indeed, immune from the counter-influence of contemporaries other than Carlyle and Wilkie Collins; but he learned an immense amount from blue-books, factory reports and his own personal experience – much the same pabulum as that of Marx and Engels, whose vision is similar, though their conclusions are very different. But to relate Dickens to Marx is effectively to dissociate him from Smollett. Smollett exercised his talents in a mode deriving from *Don Quixote* and domesticated in this country by Fielding. Here, characteristically, a young man is sent out on the road to find his fortune, meeting many adventures on the way. Dickens may have begun by sending his characters on the road, but it was never long before they landed in prison. Indeed, the main legacy from the picaresque tradition discernible in the mature novelist is his retention of the essentially passive hero of Sterne, Fielding and Smollett. His principal figure characteristically endures experience rather than shapes it. It is not with his predecessors or with most of his contemporaries that Dickens can be identified; it is rather with the great writers, comparatively few of them English, who were, in every sense, his successors.

The Great Tradition in some ways passed Dickens by. His people have no place in the polite drawing-rooms of Hartfield, of Tipton, of Gardencourt. This is a mode that rarefied itself into the fiction of Ivy Compton-Burnett and Anthony Powell. Dickens has no affinities with drawing-room comedy or with the education of young ladies. Rather he is redolent of the confining chamber of Raskolnikov; the gloomy isolation of Razumov; Joseph K's meaningless trials and Rubashov's prison cell; the barren interdependence of Smith and O'Brien; the claustrophobic humours of the prison at Mavrino. Dickens's personal sense of crisis, dramatized in his novels, is a foreshadowing of crises yet to come. The twentieth century in which we take such pride has more than its share of disaster. What Dickens forecast is embodied in Dostoievsky, Conrad, Kafka, Koestler, Orwell, Solzhenitsyn and beyond – in Ka-Tsetnik, who wrote from Auschwitz, say, or Peter Redgrove, poet of nightmare and grotesquerie.

Personal premonition of a general crisis will not in itself ensure contemporaneity. But Dickens sets his crisis so massively before us, structures it into so convincing an artefact of emotion, extends it so forcefully into the context of our present-day world, that we have to take notice in order to survive. Wherever the innocent are condemned, the weak tormented, the free spirit cast into a confining dungeon, there the great poet of claustrophobia reigns and has his being. Dickens's fiercest relevance appears where Law defaults upon justice; where class takes over from character; where the cash-nexus stands in place of co-operation between man and man; wherever, in short, Society becomes a prison. The voice of Dickens is that which speaks for the individual caught in the mechanism of System.

I Sketches by Boz (1835-36)

At the age of seventeen Dickens became a freelance journalist. He began by making shorthand notes of cases in the now defunct court of Doctors' Commons. By 1832, partly through family influence, he was working as a political reporter for *The True Sun* and *The Mirror of Parliament*; before long, the latter gave him permanent employment. Between 1833 and 1834 he wrote a few police reports for *The Morning Chronicle*, and became in the latter year a member of the regular staff of this important paper. His first major assignment was the report of a reception given to Earl Grey in Edinburgh. It is one of the few pieces of early journalism by Dickens that we can identify, and it has more than a foretaste of his characteristic exuberance. The guest of honour was late, and one gentleman, overcome by

the cold fowls, roast beef, lobster and other tempting delicacies . . . appeared to think that the best thing he could possibly do, would be to eat his dinner, while there was anything to eat. He accordingly laid about him with right good-will, the example was contagious, and the clatter of knives and forks became general. Hereupon, several gentlemen who were not hungry, cried out 'Shame!' and looked very indignant; and several gentlemen who were hungry cried 'Shame!' too, eating nevertheless, all the while, as fast as they possibly could. In this dilemma, one of the stewards mounted a bench and feelingly represented to the delinquents the enormity of their conduct, imploring them, for decency's sake, to defer the process of mastication until the arrival of Earl Grey. This address was loudly cheered, but totally unheeded; and this is, perhaps, one of the few instances on record of a dinner having been virtually concluded before it began. (*Morning Chronicle*, 18 September 1834).

During these years, Dickens had begun to compose fictitious sketches based on shabby-genteel *moeurs* in and about London. These owed much to his observation in a solicitors' office where he had worked before his spell at Doctors' Commons, and on journalistic assignments. But an immediate working model may have been the now forgotten stories of John Poole. There is more than a passing resemblance between Poole's 'The Pic-nic', which appeared in *The Monthly Magazine* in October 1829, and 'A Dinner at Poplar Walk' (later re-entitled 'Mr Minns and his Cousin'), which appeared in the same magazine in December 1833. Dickens followed his first story up with 'Mrs Porter Over the Way', 'Horatio Sparkins', 'A Bloomsbury Christening' – in fact, ten of his contributions appeared in *The Monthly Magazine* between December 1833 and February 1835. The young author even had the doubtful pleasure of seeing himself plagiarized in rival periodicals.

But *The Monthly Magazine*, run by the Liberal, Captain Holland, was primarily a political magazine, and in spite of his growing reputation, Dickens was not paid for his services. So, from early 1835 onward, he concentrated on writing for *The Morning Chronicle*, by which he was already employed and for which he had already done some descriptive pieces. And when the proprietors inaugurated an *Evening Chronicle* Dickens was asked to write sketches for that, too: no less than twenty of them appeared between January and August 1835. Dickens's salary was raised and his prospects improved accordingly. But they were not considered good enough by the father of Miss Maria Beadnell, whom the young author was courting at the time. So he turned his affections to the daughter of George Hogarth, his editor on *The Evening Chronicle*, and, with his fellow-Scotsman, John Black of *The Morning Chronicle*, one of Dickens's earliest backers.

Other periodicals to which Dickens contributed were *The Carlton Chronicle*, to which he gave a couple of realistic documentaries, and *Bell's Life in London*, to which he contributed twelve 'scenes and characters'. For *Bell's* he used the pseudonym 'Tibbs', derived from the essays of Oliver Goldsmith; for *The Monthly Magazine* he used the much more famous pseudonym of Boz – also a Goldsmith derivation, this time from *The Vicar of Wakefield*.

The publisher Macrone, who had already successfully backed

Dickens's acquaintance, Harrison Ainsworth, decided to collect the various pieces into two volumes. Macrone agreed to pay £150 for the copyright of the first edition and undertook to bring it out in 1836. Thus was *Sketches by Boz* born, and Dickens married Catherine Hogarth on the strength of this and of the impending *Pickwick Papers*.

As we have them now, the *Sketches* are a collection of fifty-six descriptive pieces and anecdotes. Some attempt to impose order on articles that had appeared quite separately was made by grouping them, for publication in book form, into four categories: Sketches, Scenes, Characters and Tales. The latter stand a little apart from the rest, since they have plots which direct their humour and observation. But there is scarcely one piece in the collection without vivacity and freshness. Their ultimate source, as Dickens's pseudonyms imply, was Oliver Goldsmith. It does not take much percipience to relate 'The Streets – Night' to Goldsmith's 'A City Night Piece' which also appears as Letter CXVII in *The Citizen of the World*. A nearer influence still is the currently unread essayist, Leigh Hunt.

Now blinds are let down, and doors thrown open, and flannel waistcoats left off, and cold meat preferred to hot, and wonder expressed why tea continues to be so refreshing, and people delight to sliver lettuces in bowls, and apprentices water doorways with tin-cannisters that lay several atoms of dust . . .
Now clerks in offices do nothing but drink soda-water and spruce-beer and read the newspaper. Now the old-clothes man drops his solitary cry more deeply into the areas on the hot and forsaken side of the street; and bakers look vicious; and cooks are aggravated; and the steam of a tavern kitchen catches hold of one like the breath of Tartarus . . . (Leigh Hunt, 'Description of a Hot Day', *The Indicator*, 28 June 1820).

. . . the dust flies in clouds, ginger-beer corks go off in volleys, the balcony of every public house is crowded with people, smoking and drinking, half the private houses are turned into tea-shops, fiddles are in great request, every little fruit-shop displays its stall of gilt gingerbread and puny toys . . . servants of all-work, who are now allowed to have followers, and have got a holiday for the day, make the most of their time with the faithful admirer who waits for a stolen interview at the corner of the street, every night, when they go to fetch the beer . . . (Dickens, 'Greenwich Fair').

One can see why some contemporary reviewers attributed the *Sketches* to Hunt. But the prose of Dickens, even at this early stage, is more varied and vigorous than that of the older man.

One can say, however, that the early Dickens belongs to a recognizable tradition of the essay. Along with Hunt, one can detect the influences of Hazlitt and Lamb, and behind all these are the eighteenth-century belles-lettrists, Goldsmith, Addison and Steele. But Dickens has a sharper eye than that of his predecessors; his humour is less gentle; he has more social concern.

The last drunken man, who shall find his way home before sunlight, has just staggered heavily along, roaring out the burden of the drinking song of the previous night: the last houseless vagrant whom penury and police have left in the streets, has coiled up his chilly limbs in some paved corner, to dream of food and warmth. The drunken, the dissipated, and the wretched have disappeared; the more sober and orderly part of the population have not yet awakened to the labours of the day, and the stillness of death is over the streets; its very hue seems to be imparted to them, cold and lifeless as they look in the grey, sombre light of daybreak. The coachstands in the larger thoroughfares are deserted; the night-houses are closed; and the chosen promenades of profligate misery are empty.

Already the prose, with its variety of cadences, is that of a master. It is strange that Dickens throughout his life underrated these *Sketches by Boz.* Many of the leading themes which he was to work out in future novels are to be found here. We have a foreshadowing of Oliver Twist's Bumble in the pompous beadle whom Dickens delineates in 'Our Parish': 'See him again on Sunday in his state-coat and cocked-hat with a large-headed staff for show in his left hand and a small cane for use in his right. How pompously he marshals the children into their places! and how demurely the little urchins look at him askance as he surveys them when they are all seated, with a glare of the eye peculiar to beadles.' The Artful Dodger is prefigured in the anonymous Boy who appears before the 'Criminal Courts': ' "Have you any witnesses to speak to your character, boy?" "Yes, my lord; fifteen gen'lm'n is a vaten outside, and vos a vaten all day yesterday, vich they told me the night before my trial was comin' on." ' And Bill Sikes slouches through 'Monmouth Street', 'a stout, sturdy-chested man [who] seldom walked forth without a dog at his heels'. There are hints, too, of *Martin Chuzzlewit*. In the rather strained and eccentric story of 'The Four Sisters' there is a first glimpse of Sarah Gamp in action: 'We were very much alarmed by hearing a hackney-coach stop at Mrs Robinson's door, at half-past two o'clock in the morning, out of which there emerged a fat old woman, in a cloak and nightcap, with a bundle in one hand and a pair of pattens in the other, who looked as if she had been suddenly knocked up out of bed for some very special purpose.' Mr Tigg, the confidence trickster from the same book (*Martin Chuzzlewit*), makes a lightning appearance in 'Our Next Door Neighbour', even down to his pseudo-military get-up – only to vanish abruptly, accompanied by the bed-linen and the spoons.

There is a preliminary draft, too, for Mrs Rouncewell, the housekeeper of Chesney Wold in *Bleak House*, based on a neighbour remembered from Dickens's childhood in Chatham. She appears as the Old Lady of the 'Parish Sketches'.

She has a son in India, whom she always describes to you as a fine handsome fellow – so like the profile of his dear father over the side-board, but the old lady adds, with a mournful shake of the head, that he has always been one of her greatest trials, and that indeed he almost once broke her heart; but it pleased God to enable her to get the better of it, and she would prefer your never mentioning the subject to her again.

In contrasting mood, another vignette prefiguring *Bleak House* may be found in 'The Streets – Night': 'That little round-faced man, with the small brown surtout, white stockings and shoes, is in the comic line; the mixed air of self-denial and mental consciousness of his own powers is particularly gratifying'. This surely anticipates Little Swills, the red-nosed comedian who parodies the Coroner and the Inquest.

Dickens is able to satirize and caricature so adeptly because often he fears that which he observes. This is seen most clearly in the impressions of prison and prison life that intersperse the *Sketches*, most especially in the one entitled 'Newgate'. So far from being a picaresque novelist, Dickens has always seemed to me at his best as a poet of claustrophobia, and his great gift is to render the sense of oppression with sharp particularity.

On either side of the school-yard is a yard for men . . . . Huddled together upon two opposite forms by the fireside sit twenty men perhaps; here a boy in livery, there a man in a rough great-coat and top-boots; further on, a desperate-looking fellow in his shirt sleeves, with an old Scotch cap upon his shaggy head; near him again, a tall ruffian, in a smock-frock, and next to him a miserable being of distressed appearance, with his head resting on his hands; – but all alike in one respect, all idle and listless: when they do leave the fire, sauntering moodily about, lounging in the window, or leaning against the wall, vacantly swinging their bodies to and fro . . . . The press-yard . . . is a long, narrow court of which a portion of the wall in Newgate Street forms one end, and the gate the other. At the upper end, on the left-hand – that is, adjoining the wall in Newgate Street – is a cistern of water, and at the bottom a double grating (of which the gate itself forms part) similar to that before described. Through these gates the prisoners are allowed to see their friends, a turnkey always remaining in the vacant space between, during the whole interview . . .

One cannot exaggerate the part prison and the sense of imprisonment plays in Dickens, from the debtors' prison in *Pickwick Papers* to Harmony Jail in *Our Mutual Friend*; and indeed one novel, *Little Dorrit*, is entirely given up to the idea. That it was deeply ingrained in Dickens, no doubt as a result of his father's improvidence in his unhappy childhood, is clear enough. It is the dynamic in many of the *Sketches*.

But it was early yet for this idea to achieve dramatization on the level of narrative. That is why prisons appear as documentation rather than drama; and they scarcely appear at all in that section of the *Sketches* known as Tales. These are most remarkable for their observation of shabby-genteel idiosyncrasies. The jumped-up Maldertons of 'Horatio Sparkins' collectively fall in love with a Byronic young gentleman who turns out – to their horror – to be an assistant in a cut-price draper's shop. This theme – social snobbery – is a determinant also in 'The Tuggs's at Ramsgate', where a shy young man is jockeyed into a compromising position by adventurers playing upon his social aspirations. Here, however, the theme goes along with a representation of sexual repression. This is where the Tales are at their most interesting. It is a theme that goes underground in Dickens's middle period, only to emerge, formidably, in the shy and repressed bachelors of the final phase. Needless to say, it is touched upon lightly here; but Dickens seems to find in frustration opportunities for endless – though rather sadistic – mirth. One of the best Tales is, in fact, the earliest, 'Mr Minns and his Cousin'. The central figure is sketched with precision and economy.

Mr Augustus Minns was a bachelor, of about forty as he said – of about eight-and-forty as his friends said. He was always exceedingly clean, precise, and tidy; perhaps somewhat priggish and the most retiring man in the world. He usually wore a brown frock-coat without a wrinkle, light inexplicables without a spot, a neat neckerchief with a remarkably neat tie, and boots without a fault: moreover, he always carried a brown silk umbrella with an ivory handle.

Such obsessional neatness goes along with a hatred of spontaneity and the unexpected, localized in his detestation of children and dogs. Mr Minns's cousin has one of each, and the old bachelor's encounter with them both leads him to embarrassment and exposes weaknesses in his limited personality. The tale is slight, but, in its revised version, flawless. Comic though it is, the loss of Mr Minns's umbrella, which directly leads to the disruption of his ordered life, is a symbolic dismemberment; and his extreme tidiness prefigures that whited sepulchre, Bradley Headstone of *Our Mutual Friend*.

The same sadistic humour is found in a rather more complex tale, 'A Passage in the Life of Mr Watkins Tottle. Chapter the First'. Disconcertingly, there is no chapter the second; the wretched man's life ends with the story. Its protagonist acts out the paradox, familiar through the corpus of Dickens's work, of having sexual aspirations without oneself being a desirable sexual object. The description of Mr Tottle is cutting, and not made less so by the verbal wit in which it is couched.

Mr Watkins Tottle . . . was about fifty years of age; stood four feet six inches and three-quarters in his socks – for he never stood in stockings at all – plump, clean, and rosy. He looked something like a vignette to one of Richardson's novels, and had a clear, cravatish formality of manner, and kitchen-pokerishness of carriage, which Sir Charles Grandison might have envied. He lived on an annuity which was well adapted to the individual who received it, in one respect – it was rather small. He received it in periodical payments on every alternate Monday; but he ran himself out about a day after the expiration of the first week as regularly as an eight-day clock, and then, to make the comparison complete, his landlady wound him up, and he went on with a regular tick.

The smartness of that last pun is typical of the way in which the whole tale is written: Tottle is a small, precise, mechanical person, and it is no accident that he is compared with the most sexless of Richardson's heroes. He is deflected from his routine by the un-angelic and irreligious Gabriel Parsons. This worthy persuades him to pay court to a lady of some property. The plot proceeds in a series of misunderstandings, activated by the genuine shyness of Tottle and the sham propriety of the lady in question; so that the old bachelor becomes the uncomprehending instrument by which his Intended becomes espoused to another. Like so much of Dickens's work, this is sadistic, but there is no denying the sharpness with which it is achieved. And this tale is less slight than the others; including, among other things, an enforced visit to a sponging-house and one of Dickens's best marital disputes – the prototype of many.

So one can say of *Sketches by Boz* that they look forward to an exceedingly bright future. But this is not to deny the actuality of their present. Essays such as 'The Streets – Morning', 'The Streets – Night', 'Astleys', 'Criminal Courts', 'A Visit to Newgate', and 'The Hospital Patient' are of permanent interest as observation enshrined in precise and particular prose. The Sketches proper represent that documentary realism that was to underpin even the wildest of Dickens's subsequent creations. There is no doubt that he actually saw much of what he later fictionalized. And if the very latest phase is hardly that of a realist, it may be that it was Dickens's splendid powers of observation, exemplified in the Sketches, that enabled him to break out of the constricting conventions of the so-called 'naturalistic' novel.

Of the Tales, the ones we have discussed here mark out a line of their own in shabby-genteel humour. More urgently, they expose, however humorously, flaws and oddities in the make-up of those who appear to be almost preternaturally ordered in their lives. Dickens as novelist is always going to be more exciting than Dickens as essayist and story-teller; his powers of conceptual thought were limited. Still, there is much in *Sketches by Boz* that deserves serious study, even if their ultimate significance is that of a dress rehearsal for the pageant to come.

II Pickwick Papers (1836-37)

The sketches appearing in *The Monthly Magazine* attracted the attention of a new publishing house called Chapman and Hall. They had already produced a little book called the *Squib Annual*, and this had plates by the well-known artist, Robert Seymour. Chapman and Hall thought it would be a good idea if they followed this up with a series of stories, published monthly to serve as a vehicle for Seymour's sporting prints. Their original conception was that of a Nimrod Club – a bunch of Cockneys who would go out into the country, shooting and fishing, and getting themselves into difficulties through their ludicrous want of skill. 'Boz' seemed to them the ideal author for such an enterprise.

Now clearly there was a great deal wrong with this conception. First of all, it put the writer in a position very much junior to the illustrator of the series. And secondly – as Dickens himself protested – since he was neither a countryman nor a sportsman, it was unsuited to his interests. Rather he would have preferred the illustrations to arise out of the narrative and the whole to encompass a wider range of English character than that envisaged in the publishers' plan. His ideas were agreed to, and the series was started in monthly numbers on 31 March 1836; the basic means of publication Dickens used for subsequent novels.

Fortunately for *Pickwick Papers*, as the enterprise came to be called, the artist Seymour died by his own hand between the first and second issues. It is unlikely that he would have contributed much to the success of the series: even his original conception of Pickwick as a tall thin man had to be countermanded by the senior partner of Chapman and Hall, who wanted him modelled on a fat old beau called John Foster. Seymour's successor, Hablôt Browne, proved more amenable, and, as Phiz, was Dickens's lifelong – though very much subordinate – collaborator.

Nevertheless, this unpropitious start left its mark on *Pickwick Papers* as a whole. For one thing, it made for notable instability in the work. Dickens's true interests, in the vagaries of the law and the bitterness of imprisonment, pulled very strongly against the explicit plan of four gentlemen at large, touring the country. And this plan, in its turn, made him curiously vulnerable to the literary influences of his youth, particularly his childhood reading of Tobias Smollett. Now there is no doubt that this eighteenth-century novelist had his merits, but they were not akin to those of Dickens. His books mostly concern peripatetic heroes who meet with a variety of eccentric characters in a succession of bizarre situations. However, without richer experience to organize, there can hardly be much of subtle interest in his fiction. The linear progression of the picaresque novel has proved an inadequate vehicle for serious literature. All is external action; human motivation concerns Smollett not at all. This writer may very well have enlivened the weary hours of a neglected child, but he could hardly do much for the mature man. Indeed, the career of Dickens the novelist may very well be typified as a development away from the ramshackle harness of the picaresque novel.

F.D. Wierstra has painstakingly traced the influence of Smollett on *Pickwick Papers*, and the result is not too encouraging. The plot of *Humphry Clinker* concerns the perambulations of Matthew Bramble about the country accompanied by three myrmidons; the ground-plan of *Pickwick Papers* shows the central figure meeting all sorts and conditions of men, one quite separate from another, in company with Tupman, Winkle and Snodgrass. Just as the elderly, irascible and kindly Matthew Bramble is followed everywhere by his youthful servant, Humphry Clinker, so Mr Pickwick has, as *his* lackey, the indefatigable Sam Weller. Both Bramble and Pickwick meet with plausible villains on the highway, in the shape of, respectively, Martin and Jingle. Both are befriended by jovial country squires: Bramble by Dennison, and Pickwick by Wardle. Many other parallels – comic duels, gentlemen surprised in nightclothes – assert themselves; and it may be said that the influence of Smollett is most strongly felt in the weakest sections of *Pickwick Papers*.

No doubt it was the basic familiarity of the plot and properties that ensured *Pickwick's* success. The public are most eager to greet that which they already know. We have no reason to suppose that what we now value in *Pickwick Papers* was the source of its popularity in the 1830s. And there can be no doubt that, well before Dickens, the picaresque novel enjoyed a long innings; through Smollett, Fielding and Defoe, back to Le Sage, and beyond, to Cervantes – the idealistic, though elderly, Quixote accompanied by his earthy and low-born Sancho Panza.

But if the traditional elements of *Pickwick* were all that needed to be discussed, we should hardly be giving it our attention at the present time. On the contrary, the picaresque character of the book is less in evidence as it proceeds. Those episodes that live longest in the memory have little to do with Smollett and his predecessors. After all, Dickens himself begins to fade out the Pickwickians proper quite early on in the book. The poetical Snodgrass leads only a shadowy existence: we are spared his romantic effusions. Tupman, the elderly lover, retires to the background after only two harmless flirtations; while Winkle's couple of sporting episodes hardly intrude at all on the main action of the book. *Pickwick Papers* is an extraordinary example of a novel outgrowing its original conception. The very Pickwick Club that gives the book its name has a real existence in the first chapter only, as a satire on the newly founded British Association for the Advancement of Science. There is really no need for its formal dissolution in the last chapter of all.

The interest of the novel builds up very much with the development of Pickwick himself. At first he is one of a number of eccentrics who go careering round the countryside, and is only differentiated from his associates by being less given to a prevailing humour. But, with the introduction of Sam Weller, his stature increases – a demonstration that the central figure of a novel benefits greatly through being seen through the eyes of an ancillary character. It was not simply the appearance of Sam in the fourth number of *Pickwick* that caused the sales to go up, nor yet the superior quality of the engravings of 'Phiz'. Rather its increasing popularity was due to an all-round tightening and sharpening of the writing, and this could easily be demonstrated by a comparison between the quality of the prose in the earlier episodes with that in the later ones. Dickens had already given evidence of his command over cockney idiom in such sketches as 'Seven Dials' and 'The Omnibus Cad'; it goes with his understanding of cockney character. In Sam Weller he was able to concentrate this into a single figure, and to use it as a satirical commentary upon middle-class *moeurs* thereafter.

Sam Weller is first introduced to us as a lower servant in a suburban inn. From the first he is sharply realized in 'a coarse-striped waistcoat, with black calico sleeves, and blue glass buttons'. And his speech has the same distinctness of quality. Almost his first remark, when requested to give priority to a particular guest's boots, is 'Ask number twenty-two vether he'll have them now, or vait till he gets 'em'. His objection is a democratic one: he shines the shoes according to the time people have asked to be woken up in the morning. 'No, no,' he goes on, 'reg'lar rotation, as Jack Ketch said, ven he tied the men up' – Jack Ketch being the public hangman. And this sturdy independence, together with macabre undertones, is a characteristic of his speech throughout – unparaphrasable, as Dickens's first Russian translator was to find. These 'Wellerisms', as they came to be called, are very much a part of Sam's utterance on each appearance: 'Business first, pleasure arterwards, as King Richard the Third said ven he stabbed the other King in the Tower, afore he smothered the babbies'. The mode of utterance is at once comic and macabre, Sam is attractive and charming, as is shown by his success with the ladies, and physically formidable, as witness his combats with beadles, constables, and other emblems of authority. Altogether he becomes a symbol of the sturdy, independent workingman – 'footman, groom, gamekeeper, seedsman, or a sort of compo of every one of 'em'.

But Sam Weller does not stand alone. Pickwick himself, once the early caricature episodes are over, emerges as a representative of a settled middle class – 'retired, and of considerable independent property'. We must beg the question of how this was acquired. Pickwick shines as an example of what every good rich man should be: defiant to villains, courteous to ladies, understanding towards the young, magnanimous to his enemies. It is no accident that the novel is dedicated to Thomas Noon Talfourd, the kindly judge and amateur author who went out of his way to befriend young aspirants such as Dickens himself. Only in the earlier episodes does Pickwick act out a stupendous ignorance of the world – hotels, law-courts, politics – as though he had been·born, full-grown, in 1827 or there-abouts, without any discernible past. It is near the beginning of the book, also, that he is found drunk in a wheelbarrow. But his character progressively develops; it is noticeable that his generous behaviour towards Jingle occurs near the end.

This character, Jingle, is one of the elements designed to stiffen the plot. At first he is introduced as just another counter in the ap-parently random permutations of *Pickwick Papers*. But Dickens evidently saw his future possibilities as a trickster. From the first, like Sam Weller, he has a remarkable style of speech: proceeding in jerks, apparently by free association. Of Spain he remarks,

'Conquests! Thousands. Don Bolaro Fizzgig – Grandee – only daughter – Donna Christina – splendid creature – loved me to distraction – jealous father – high-souled daughter – handsome Englishman – Donna Christina in despair – prussic acid – stomach pump in my portmanteau – operation performed – old Bolaro in ecstacies – consent to our union – join hands and floods of tears – romantic story – very.'

This utterance has some odd antecedents. We may reject suggestions that Jingle's disjointed phraseology derives from eccentric characters in Smollett or Hook. Rather he would appear to have, like so many Dickensian figures, his origin in real life, or real life as presented in Dr Johnson's hastily written account of his travels in France: 'There we waited on the ladies to Monville's. – Captain Irwin with us. – Spain. County towns all beggars. – At Dijon he could not find the way to Orleans. – Cross roads of France very bad. – Five soldiers. – Woman. – Soldiers escaped. – The Colonel would not lose five men for the sake of one woman. – The magistrate cannot seize a soldier but by the Colonel's permission, etc., etc.' It is impossible to decide whether this is a transcript of the Captain's speech or simply John-son's mode of recording impressions; certainly the rest of the nar-rative is similarly jerky. But, as it stands, it resembles the manner of Jingle more than any other prototype that has been suggested. This manner, like the more circumstantial mode of speech in the utterance of Sam Weller, affords ample opportunity for far-fetched anecdote; and such anecdote, in every sense of the word, is the life of both these characters.

And both, so to speak, give Pickwick his chance to live. If Sam acts as a perpetual protector to his master, then Jingle is an intermittent gadfly. He first elopes with a maiden aunt and has to be bought off; later he is found inveigling his way into the social circle of the Mayor of Ipswich. He is, after Weller, the second of the linchpins that support what continuous action *Pickwick* has.

The third is the breach of promise case centring on Mrs Bardell. This action is based on a kind of misunderstanding familiar in early Dickens. Mr Pickwick, in announcing his intention of hiring a manservant, is taken by his landlady to be making her a proposal of marriage. The main merit of this event is that it culminates in the comic set-piece of *Pickwick Papers*, the trial of Bardell v. Pickwick. Like a great deal else that seems far-fetched in Dickens, this is based upon a collocation of ascertainable facts, and on characters in real life. The judge in the case, Mr Justice Stareleigh, is all too close to his original, Sir Stephen Gazelee. Even more remarkable is the basis for the prosecuting attorney. The Serjeant Buzfuz of the case was based on a Serjeant Bompas – described by one of his contemporaries as stout, sandy, and forceful in his efforts to press his point upon a jury. The plot-material derived from a different but equally usable source: the celebrated Norton-Melbourne case, which Dickens himself had reported in twenty-six columns the month before he wrote his fictional version. Mr Norton had brought an action against the Prime Minister, Lord Melbourne, for 'criminal conversation' (namely, adultery) with his wife. The evidence was so trivial and the testimony so corrupt that the jury returned an acquittal without leaving the box. The prosecution in this case, as in that of Bardell v.Pickwick, cited incriminating letters: '"I will call about half past 4. Yours. Melbourne"' . . . The style and form of these notes, Gentlemen, seems to import much more than they contain. Cautiously, I admit, they are worded; there are no professions of love . . . but still they are not the letters of an ordinary acquaintance.' The colour and verve of the trial in *Pickwick* comes from Dickens's remarkable combination of the Melbourne facts with the Bompas manner:

'They are covert, sly, underhanded communications, but, fortunately, far more conclusive than if couched in the most glowing language and the most poetic imagery . . . "Garraway's, twelve o'clock. Dear Mrs B. – Chops and Tomata sauce. Yours, Pickwick." Gentlemen, what does this mean? Chops and Tomata sauce. Yours, Pickwick! Chops! gracious heaven! and Tomata sauce! Gentlemen, is the happiness of a sensitive and confiding female to be trifled away by such shallow artifices as these?'

Needless to say, the jury finds against Pickwick, and his refusal to pay damages and costs lands him in a debtors' prison. This is by far the grimmest part of the book. Here, again, Dickens's early experiences – as distinct from his reading – come into play. Weeds like Mivens the Zephyr and Smangle the Rake flourish happily in the close atmosphere of the Fleet Prison; while the cobbler, ruined by his legacy, sleeps under a table to remind himself of the four-poster bed he will never be able to occupy again. Characters such as these have a satire and poignancy we shall look for in vain in Smollett. In this episode, though not in the rest of *Pickwick*, we have intimations of Dickens's later powers of symbolism. 'A bird-cage, sir,' says Sam, 'Veels within veels, a prison in a prison.' Or 'a lean and haggard woman, too – a prisoner's wife – who was watering, with great solicitude, the wretched stump of a dried-up withered plant, which, it was plain to see, could never send forth a green leaf again; – too true an emblem, perhaps, of the office she had come there to discharge.' In this episode, we have the power of observation associated with the greater Dickens:

Here, four or five great hulking fellows, just visible through a cloud of tobacco-smoke, were engaged in noisy and riotous conversation over half-emptied pots of beer, or playing at all-fours with a very greasy pack of cards. In the adjoining room, some solitary tenant might be seen, poring, by the light of a feeble tallow candle, over a bundle of soiled and tattered papers, yellow with dust and dropping to pieces from age, writing, for the hundredth time, some lengthened statement of his grievances, for the perusal of some great man whose eyes it would never reach, or whose heart it would never touch . . . . Near him, leaning listlessly against the wall stood a strong-built countryman, flicking with a worn-out hunting-whip the top-boot that adorned his right foot; his left being thrust into an old slipper. Horses, dogs, and drink had brought him there pell-mell. Poor wretch! He never rode a match on the swiftest animal in his costly stud, with half the speed of which he had torn along the course that ended in the Fleet. On the opposite side of the room, an old man was seated on a small wooden box, with his eyes riveted on the floor, and his face settled into an expression of the deepest and most hopeless despair. A young girl – his little grand-daughter – was hanging about him, endeavouring, with a thousand childish devices, to engage his attention; but the old man neither saw nor heard her. His limbs were shaking with disease, and the palsy had fastened on his mind.

Dickens himself testified that, when he went to prison to see his parents, he was always keen to hear from his mother what she knew about the histories of the debtors in the place. It is clear both observation and narrative had deeply penetrated his youthful mind.

Curiously enough, both of Pickwick's adversaries, Jingle and Mrs Bardell, end up in this prison, and Pickwick has a chance to show his magnanimity by being the instrument of their release. It is here that the ghost-novel which runs· throughout the apparently random episodes of *Pickwick* asserts itself, and shows us what could have been done with a sounder concept, a little forethought, and some resistance to an over-simple tradition. As it is, the second half is, at once, grimmer than the first and far more unified in action. It is not a coincidence that this was written after the sudden death of Dickens's much-loved sister-in-law, Mary Hogarth. This first of many crises in his adult life brought the realities of existence to the foreground at the expense of existing literary conventions.

Certainly the earlier part of *Pickwick Papers* has little to do with the remainder of the book. One feels embarrassed by the hobble-dehoydom of the manoeuvres at Chatham, the Rochester duel, and the Eatanswill election. Crude, also, is the device of the interpolated tales. Seven of the nine occur in the first half of the novel, where there is comparatively little plot and the character is that of miscellany. They succeed only in dissipating what sustained interest the action has. One cannot put them on the level of the anecdotes told by Jingle or by Sam Weller, for the characters that tell these tales exist only as mouthpieces. Nor is there any thematic connection: the juxtaposition of the Madman's Manuscript with the episode of Bill Stumps's mark serves only to establish the versatility of 'Boz'; and neither does much to show his genius. It may be that the tales in *Pickwick* were originally composed for independent publication, but were incorporated into the main enterprise when the latter showed itself to be far more profitable. It is noticeable that this practice of interpolation was dropped thereafter, with the exception of two tales in *Nicholas Nickleby* – and even there their insertion was determined by the fact that he had, in a particular number, several pages spare.

Enough should have been said by now to establish that *Pickwick Papers* exists on a number of different levels, not all of them related. One is almost driven to conclude that the book is best read as a collection of short stories that happen to be about the same characters. Some of the best episodes, indeed, have little to do with what centrality of focus the book can boast. The splendid scene of the medical students' party, a set-piece for Dickens's future readings, ranks only a little below Bardell v. Pickwick. Its wealth of detail would bear a fair amount of examination: one thinks of Orwell's remarks on the subject in his essay on Dickens in *Inside the Whale*. The whole scene turns on the perennial need of homeless young bachelors to live in the houses of people who are middle-aged and staid. The rent of these tenants is welcome, but it goes along with habits that are incompatible with the settled ways of their hosts. This particular episode is decked out with macabre anecdote and drunken squabble and still farther enriched by the inclusion of a landlady with unparalleled gifts of invective. Mr Pickwick is present, but merely as a spectator. Like so much else in *Pickwick Papers*, Bob Sawyer's party could very well stand as a sketch on its own. And the other appearances of Sawyer and his friends have similar virtues.

In the end, we do not care so much about Pickwick and his three friends gallivanting about the countryside. Rather it is the set-pieces of the Pickwick trial and the Sawyer party that have prior claim on our attention. Moreover, the shadowy lineaments of another novel, to do with the fall of pride and one man's compassion for another, assert themselves at certain turning-points of the total action. There is, after all, a grim side to this book; one which deals with imprisonment, poverty, the checks and blights of existence. No doubt *Pickwick Papers* is rightly considered the funniest of Dickens's novels. Yet what is most noticeable about this achievement of Dickens's youth is what leads on to the great work of his maturity: a feeling, between bouts of frenetic escapism, of claustrophobia; a sense, among all the oases of hospitality and benevolence, of the expanse of waste even in the most successful of lives.

III   Oliver Twist (1837-38)

By the fifth number of *Pickwick Papers*, it was clear to the publishing trade that they had a genius and a money-spinner in their midst. Dickens seems to have been much of their opinion. Exhibiting an audacity equalled by few young authors, he made arrangements with a rival publisher to edit a monthly magazine for which he himself would supply a new serial. In other words, while month by month Dickens was writing the last half of *Pickwick Papers*, concurrently he was producing for *Bentley's Miscellany* the first half of *Oliver Twist*.

The whole book was written at a furious rate. Dickens spoke of the impossibility of keeping his hands off the characters, and his recently-made acquaintance, Forster, testified that he never knew him work so concentratedly or so late into the night. From the first, the author seems to have been possessed by his theme.

I say theme advisedly, because the theme can only marginally be said to coincide with the plot. The latter belongs to a recognizable species of tale; containing a wronged woman, a dispossessed heir, a wicked brother, a missing will, a death-bed secret; and, finally, happiness all round. But the theme is something else again.

The first eleven chapters of the book move with a speed and certainty which Dickens was only once, in *David Copperfield*, ever again to equal. These chapters enact the progress of innocence through a world in itself totally corrupt. The wanderings of Oliver Twist, the workhouse boy, are highly patterned; the characters he encounters exist in social relationship one with another. If this early part seems picaresque, that is merely external illusion. Oliver remains separate both from the official world, which fails to protect him, and the underworld which seeks to take him in.

It is important to remember that we do not identify with Oliver in the ordinary sense of the word. He is not, strictly speaking, a hero. Rather he is the embodiment of goodness; a means of setting society in perspective. He acts as emblem rather than character, and the distancing effect is achieved by an irony that, in the earlier chapters, hardly ever lets up. Take the new-born Oliver, for instance.

What an excellent example of the power of dress, young Oliver Twist was! Wrapped in a blanket which had hitherto formed his only covering, he might have been the child of a nobleman or a beggar; it would have been hard for the haughtiest stranger to have assigned him his proper station in society. But now that he was enveloped in the old calico robes that had grown yellow in the same service, he was badged and ticketed and fell into his place at once – a parish child – the orphan of a workhouse – the humble, half-starved drudge – to be cuffed and buffeted through the world – despised by all, and pitied by none. Oliver cried lustily. If he could have known that he was an orphan, left to the tender mercies of churchwardens and overseers, perhaps he would have cried the louder.

The irony owes something in tone, as well as subject-matter, to the recently serialized novel, *Sartor Resartus*, by Thomas Carlyle, who was to become Dickens's lifelong friend and influence. The prose is, however, less frenetic, more distanced and controlled, than that of Carlyle; it needed to be, if it was not to burst forth in torrents of indignation.

This is not to deny that *Oliver Twist* is securely based in reality. On the contrary, it is a composite of sharp, perceived particulars. Volumes have been written on the social philosophy of its background: from Walter Crotch to Philip Collins, workers in the field have defined the exact relationship between Dickens's observation and the progress of social reform. Much of the description of slum and workhouse could have come with very little alteration out of the pages of the sociologist, Mayhew, and the political economist, Engels. The novel is, very topically, an attack both upon Malthus's principles of rationalizing population control and on the Poor Laws of 1834. Humphry House quotes No. 1 Dietary approved by a Poor Law Commission: like that favoured by Oliver's workhouse, it consists mostly of gruel diversified by the odd ounce of cheese and pound of potatoes. Nevertheless, though Dickens was writing about the Workhouse laws and the iniquity of the Parish's refusal to give relief outside its walls, we lose a great deal if we consider *Oliver Twist* simply as documentation.

The Workhouse in this novel is considerably more than one specific workhouse, keenly observed though it is; it is more, even, than a representative of its class. It is, as Dickens says, a conglomeration of churchwardens and overseers, the instigators and perpetuators of a bad system. Here the human spirit is systematically ground and punished into subjection in a manner described by writers as far apart as Engels and Blake.

The embodiment of Authority is seen in the Board. It appears to be perpetually in session. A sign of the Board's unyielding blockishness is that Oliver, called up for interview, is uncertain whether to bow to the table or to the gentlemen sitting about it. But the gentlemen in question condemn themselves out of their own mouths.

'Boy,' said the gentleman in the high chair, 'listen to me. You know you're an orphan, I suppose?' 'What's that, Sir?' inquired poor Oliver. 'The boy *is* a fool – I thought he was,' said the gentleman in the white waistcoat . . . And to be sure it was very extraordinary. What could the boy be crying for? . . . . 'Well! You have come here to be educated, and taught a useful trade,' said the red-faced gentleman in the high chair. 'So you'll begin to pick oakum to-morrow morning at six o'clock,' added the surly man in the white waistcoat.

Representative of the Board, and their instrument, is Bumble, the beadle. We see him always in company with his cocked hat and his cane – emblems, also, of authority, and, like the Board's table and high chair, helping to distance the irony and so tending towards dehumanization. Bumble is not one beadle or even a class of beadle; it is appropriate that he should have given his name to a species of unimaginative bureaucracy that has passed into the language as Bumbledom. Even his button is emblematic. 'Yes, I think it is rather pretty . . . The die is the same as the porochial seal – the Good Samaritan healing the sick and bruised man. The board presented it to me on New-Year's morning, Mr Sowerberry. I put it on, I remember, for the first time to attend the inquest on that reduced tradesman, who died in a doorway at midnight.' Bumble is a summation of impersonal officialdom. The fact that a jury brought in a verdict condemning the Board and its instrument for its handling of this matter has no effect upon events at all. Dickens is treating the official world of Parish and Charity as criminal, and unconvictably criminal at that. The language which Dickens uses to describe them is that of a prosecuting attorney grimly convinced of his cause's justice. 'For the next eight or ten months Oliver was a victim of a systematic course of treachery and deception.'

But nature has a way of asserting itself even against the most systematic oppression. This is emblematized in the most famous incident of the whole book; one that has passed into folklore.

The gruel disappeared; the boys whispered each other, and winked at Oliver; while his next neighbours nudged him. Child as he was, he was desperate with hunger, and reckless with misery. He rose from the table; and advancing to the master, basin and spoon in hand, said: somewhat alarmed at his own temerity: 'Please, Sir, I want some more.'

The episode, brief as it is, is presented as emblem, not mere particular: Oliver is asking for more gruel, not for himself alone but also for his fellows. The image we retain is that of a small slight child thrusting out his empty bowl in supplication to the burly workhouse master. The impact of the episode owes much to the effect it has on its witnesses. The boy's modest request is treated as a major insurrection.

The assistants were paralysed with wonder; the boys with fear . . . The master . . . shrieked aloud for the beadle.
The board were sitting in solemn conclave when Mr Bumble rushed into the room in great excitement, and addressing the gentleman in the high chair, said, 'Mr Limbkins, I beg your pardon, Sir! Oliver Twist has asked for more!' There was a general start. Horror was depicted on every countenance . . . 'That boy will be hung,' said the gentleman in the white waistcoat.

Subtler than this, Dickens was later able to be; never more direct and emblematic. It is this quality that gives the incident its character of legend.

And this sense of emblem continues throughout these early chapters. Each succeeding chapter shows authority to be blockish, like the Board, or bumbling, like Bumble, or half-blind, like the magistrates, or brutal, like the chimney-sweep who tried to apprentice Oliver, or powerless like Sowerberry, the undertaker who offers to apprentice him to his trade. This latter is tall and gaunt, like a yew tree rising from a grave. His servant, Claypole, the charity-boy, is delighted that he at last has encountered someone in a situation of life even lower than himself –

for he could trace a genealogy all the way back to his parents, who lived hard by; his mother being a washerwoman, and his father a drunken soldier, discharged with a wooden leg, and a diurnal pension of twopence-halfpenny and an unstatable fraction . . . But, now that fortune had cast in his way a nameless orphan, at whom even the meanest could point the finger of scorn, he retorted upon him with interest. This affords charming food for contemplation. It shows us what a beautiful thing human nature sometimes is; and how impartially the same amiable qualities are developed in the finest lord and the dirtiest charity-boy.

Again, events are retailed through the distancing irony which relates immediate particulars to a far 'greater world outside. It is not one specific charity-boy that is being condemned, but society in action: snobbery, genealogy, station, privilege and all.

What we have to notice is that, up to and including his apprenticeship, Oliver is neither fed nor instructed. Evidently the official world has failed him. It is after an altercation with his employers that Oliver runs away, and so – in Chapter VIII – encounters the underworld. Here again, we have a pattern in events; this is no random journey of a picaro; the current of irony continues while the theme appears to reverse itself. The connection is plain: the world has treated Oliver harshly and taught him nothing, while the underworld takes him in, feeds him, and begins the process of his education. As we might expect, this is directed against the society from which he has been rejected.

The first representative of the underworld is encountered by Oliver on the road to London. This representative calls himself the Artful Dodger, and is a precocious lad dressed up in the clothes and manners of a remarkably knowing man; a Sam Weller gone wrong, in fact. He buys Oliver a meal and takes him to a place where he can sleep.

It is noticeable that the Artful Dodger and his close associate, Charley Bates, regard themselves as professional men and talk in highly professional terms.

Dodger What a pity he isn't a prig.
Charley Ah! he don't know what's good for him.
Dodger (to Oliver) I suppose you don't even know what a prig is?

Oliver I think I know that. It's a th –; you're one, are you not?
Dodger I am, I'd scorn to be anything else . . .
Charley Why don't you put yourself under Fagin, Oliver?
Dodger And make your fortun' out of hand?
Charley And so be able to retire on your property and do the gen-teel; as
          I mean to, in the very next leap-year but four that ever comes, and
          the forty-second Tuesday in Trinity-week.

The mock-precise tone here is a parody of two young stockbrokers
calculating the possibilities of an assured future. It serves to remind
us that the underworld is a mirror image of the world itself: capitalistic, acquisitory, self-aggrandizing.

   The dominant figure in this underworld is Fagin. He has many
of the characteristics of a benevolent employer. We see him with
great care grounding his boys in the elements of their trade –

The merry old gentleman . . . trotted up and down the room with a stick,
in imitation of the manner in which old gentlemen walk about the streets
any hour in the day . . . All the time the two boys followed him closely about
. . . At last, the Dodger trod upon his toes, while Charley Bates stumbled up
against him behind; and in that one moment they took from him, with the
most extraordinary rapidity, snuff-box, note-case, watch-guard, chain, shirt-
pin, pocket-handkerchief, even the spectacle-case. If the old gentleman felt
a hand in any one of his pockets, he cried out where it was; and then the game
began all over again.

This 'game' is considerably more serious than any previous efforts
at apprenticeship; and it is noticeable that over and over again Oliver's
relationship with Fagin is presented in educational terms.

'You've been brought up bad,' said the Dodger . . . 'Fagin will make something out of you, though, or you'll be the first he ever had that turned out
unprofitable' . . .

The wily old Jew . . . was now slowly instilling into his soul the poison which
he hoped would blacken it, and change its hue for ever . . .

'Once fill his mind with the idea that he has been a thief; and he's ours . . .
With this boy, properly managed, my dears, I could do what I couldn't with
twenty of them.'

This voice is that of Fagin himself, and his character will bear a fair
amount of attention. His real-life antecedents are clear enough,

and have been categorized by Harry Stone, among others. In the summer of 1830, a Jewish fence called Isaac or Ikey Solomons was convicted of possessing stolen goods – like Fagin he dealt chiefly in jewellery and clothing – and sentenced to be transported. The case was sufficiently notorious for a play of the period, *Van Diemen's Land*, to be rechristened *Ikey Solomons*, and a minor character, Barney Fence, to be transformed into Ikey himself and promoted to the role of chief villain.

Fagin's antecedents are, however, a little more complex than this would suggest. We know from a letter of 3 November 1837, that at the same time as he was writing *Oliver Twist*, Dickens was reading Defoe's *History of the Devil*. And a cant name for the devil, repeatedly conferred upon Fagin by the narration, is 'the old gentleman'. So it may be more than a coincidence that Fagin's associates apostrophize him in terms usually reserved for the Father of Lies. Nancy, the prostitute, calls him 'Devil . . . and worse than Devil.' Sikes, the robber, demands of his dog, 'Don't you know the devil when he's got a great-coat on?' And, later in the book, Sikes suggests that Fagin came straight from the 'old 'un' without any intermediary in the shape of a father between them.

Fagin's appearance bears this influence out – 'a very old shrivelled Jew, whose villainous-looking and repulsive face was obscured by a quantity of matted red hair'. In the miracle plays, Judas was ascribed hair of this colour, and the acting tradition carried the connection on: both Garrick and Macklin played Shylock in red wig and beard. By extension from this, Jews in more modern plays were similarly made up; and it would seem natural for Dickens to make the application to Fagin. The striking description of Fagin at his first appearance continues as a motif through the book. We usually see him garbed in a greasy dressing-gown, frying sausages with the help of that impish article, a toasting-fork. And he achieves extraordinary ascendancy over the boys and young women with whom he seems always to be surrounded. His sinister quality is reinforced by the peculiar fact that his various hideouts are always to be found at the top of labyrinthine flights of unlit stairs.

Ironic as *Oliver Twist* is in its early chapters, it acquires a special note when dealing with Fagin. The treatment of this character derives, as Thackeray declared, from Henry Fielding's Newgate satire, *Jonathan Wild the Great*. Dickens has, of course, a greater range and variety of character. Nevertheless, the two modes of prose have this much in common: that they present their respective personae as emblematic, stylized representations of a general reality, rather than point-by-point transcripts of experience.

Mutual interest, the greatest of all purposes, was the cement of this alliance, which nothing of consequence, but superior interest, was capable of dissolving . . .

'How vain is human greatness! What avail superior abilities and a noble defiance of those narrow rules and bounds which confine the vulgar, when our best-concerted schemes are liable to be defeated! How unhappy is the state of priggism . . . A prig is more unhappy than any other; a cautious man may, in a crowd, preserve his own pockets by keeping his hand in them; but while the prig employs his hands in another's pockets, how shall he be able to defend his own?'

In something of the same way, Fagin is always presented with ironic courtesy. He is spoken of as a respectable old gentleman, a merry old gentleman, a playful old gentleman, and so forth; and he himself always speaks in terms of irreproachable idealism. Of the Dodger he remarks to Oliver: 'He'll be a great man himself and will make you one too, if you take pattern by him.' Bumble and Sowerberry can exchange sly anecdotes about people they have maltreated and buried; not so Fagin. 'Oliver was rendered the more anxious to be employed by what he had seen of the stern morality of the old gentleman's character. Whenever the Dodger or Charley Bates came home at night, empty-handed, he would expatiate with great vehemence on the misery of idle and lazy habits; and would enforce upon them the necessity of an active life by sending them supperless to bed. On one occasion, indeed, he even went so far as to knock them both down a flight of stairs; but this was carrying out his virtuous precepts to an unusual extent.'

Here we have the climax of Dickens's ironic reversal of values. It would be a great mistake to regard Fagin and his associates as representing, in any sense, a rebellion. Rather, it could be said that they play the social world at its own game. The virtues of industry and competition are invoked by the leader of a gang devoted to undermining a capitalist society. So it is the irony of ironies that, as Nancy and the other criminals remark, theirs proves to be the most viable road for Oliver to travel.

However, it is hard to see how this irony could continue throughout the book: *Oliver Twist* is not so great a novel as *Huckleberry Finn*. Both works, indeed, are rooted in that blackest of beliefs, that the world offers no purchase to human goodness; but it is Dickens who lacks a moral fable capable of sustaining so tough an attitude. The pattern of his earlier narrative is that of the waif striving for some foothold upon existence, only to find himself rejected by society and befriended by thieves. But it proved impossible for the young Dickens to keep this up. And so the book drastically changes direction after Chapter XI. The point is superbly made by Arnold Kettle. 'Until Oliver wakes up in Mr Brownlow's house he is a poor boy struggling against the inhumanity of the state. After he has slept himself in to the Brownlow world he is a young bourgeois who has been done out of his property.'

The state which oppressed Oliver now becomes his servant. The Benevolent Old Gentleman adopts him, the Lady Bountiful fosters him, the Good Doctor heals him, the Good Angel watches over him, and an alliance of them all foils the thieves and awards him his inheritance. But all this raises the question which even Professor Kettle does not ask. What happens to all the boys whom Oliver left behind in the workhouse? In losing his emblematic significance, Oliver becomes the chance young gentleman picked out of a ruck of unfortunates. He, even more than Noah Claypole, proves to be blessed in his heredity; in other words, the author has begun to operate upon a false set of values. Oliver's sorrow in the first eleven chapters is representative and stylized; his happiness in the remainder of the book is highly individual in just the wrong way – a sort of Victorian success story. As the moral fable diminishes into a mere tale, so we gradually lose the sense of theme. And the plot as a whole is poor compensation.

One cannot get excited about Mr Brownlow, surely the dullest of Dickens's good rich men, whose heavy hints at a tragic past are most boringly explained in the grand finale. One can only compare his adoption of Oliver with the odd couplings of old men and youths in Fielding and Smollett; not the most encouraging of parallels. One cannot, either, work up much enthusiasm for the life and love

of Miss Rose Maylie, even though she was the first of the virgin
heroines inspired by the death of Mary Hogarth. Rose gets ill, it
is true, but quite irrelevantly; and, anyhow, she recovers. As a nameless orphan she is not good enough to be affianced to a rising young
politician; but her lover gains great éclat by renouncing his career
and becoming a clergyman instead; apparently in the Church
illegitimacy does not matter.

And the action itself creaks with circumstance. It is a striking
coincidence that the only two crimes in which Oliver is involved, the
theft from Brownlow and the robbery of Mrs Maylie, are both directed
at close connections of his dead mother. The wicked brother, Monks,
is a monstrous absurdity: it is crude indeed for Dickens to make him
recognize Oliver during the first piece of thievery and so persuade
Fagin to associate him with the second; this has all the appearance
of being thrust in as motivation. Fagin has ample incentive and
opportunity to corrupt Oliver without such extraneous prompting.
But the prompting is necessary because of the claims of the plot.

Needless to say, Dickens being Dickens, the theme asserts itself
against the plot, though with decreasing frequency as the book wears
on. The triangular relationship of Fagin, Sikes and Nancy temporarily redeems the action, in Chapters XIII-XV, after the Brownlow
episode; the kidnapping of Oliver, especially, is imaginatively done.
And the trial of the Artful Dodger in Chapter XLIII is a return to
the invention and conciseness of the early pages. The young thief
seizes, as Oliver never does, the initiative against a lackadaisical
court: the watch-word is 'this ain't the shop for justice'. One could
even make a case for such melodrama as the murder of Nancy and
flight of Sikes, which Dickens so loved acting out to his audiences
in later years.

But the later part of the book necessarily exists as fragments. There
simply is no way of sustaining the theme against the plot once the
latter takes Oliver over as a dispossessed gentleman. The thinness
is seen in the use Dickens makes of Bumble and Claypole as mere
adjuncts to the narrative: they, like Oliver, lose their emblematic
significance. The failure is not merely local. That it is organic and
widespread is indicated by various loose ends: the incident of the
hunchback in Chapter XXXII serves no purpose, nor does the sudden
appearance in Chapter XXXIV of Fagin during Oliver's dream at

the Maylies' house. What we wanted was a schematized fiction or fable after the manner of *Pilgrim's Progress*, or *Gulliver's Travels*; what, finally, we get is an aesthetic and moral yielding to the set presentation of a nineteenth-century tale.

And for years to come Dickens lost his way. Suggestions of the emblematic power manifest in the early chapters of *Oliver Twist* appear from time to time in subsequent novels, and often such moments are most striking in works that have grave deficiencies of formal organization. But it was necessary for Dickens to get rid of some submerged autobiography before he could come to terms with Victorian realism. And only after that necessary purgation was he able to launch out on the symbolic dramas of his later years, the books by which he best deserves to be known.

IV   Nicholas Nickleby (1838-39)

The enormous sales of his work had impressed upon Dickens the
need to have some control over copyright. So, when the serial publication of *Pickwick Papers* came to an end, Chapman and Hall
allowed him a share in future proceeds. This concession was made
on 19 November 1837. And on the same day, Dickens signed a
further agreement with his publishers: to write a new work of a
size and scope similar to *Pickwick*. Thus the later chapters of *Oliver
Twist* witnessed the beginning of *Nicholas Nickleby*.

But we may infer from Dickens's friend Forster that *Nicholas
Nickleby* never took the hold over the author's imagination that
the earlier books had. It was Bumble and Fagin that drove him still,
not his new bunch of characters. Nevertheless, the public was in
favour. Now they had, for the first time from Dickens's pen, a dashing
hero, a pathetic heroine, a picaresque plot, all spiced with melodrama.
These were the ingredients they had been waiting for: previous heroes
had been, respectively, an old man and a little boy. Trevor Blount
remarks that the book 'is a sentimental variant of the picaresque
form as practised by Smollett'. Its antecedents are obvious. A
courageous hero followed by a feeble-minded friend, the thrashing
of a cruel schoolmaster in front of his pupils, a weak-minded fop
in tutelage to a buck of many seasons – all these have their roots
in such novels as *Roderick Random* and *Launcelot Greaves*. But,
as we saw in *Pickwick Papers*, Dickens fell back on Smollett only
when his interest was not seriously engaged.

The book is picaresque, then, in outline. But there are other
elements. Most notable is that of the melodrama which Dickens
so loved – not only to see, but to act in. One often parodies what

one enjoys, and *Nicholas Nickleby* is full of send-ups. It contains melodramas performed by actors as well as ludicrous people who behave melodramatically. Unfortunately there is no great gap between effects such as these, used for comedy, and the serious passages in the book. Nicholas actually tells his wicked uncle that he will never darken his door again, and this same uncle dies a most melodramatic death, cursing his fill. The weakness can be seen when I say that these two are the positive and negative dynamics of the action. The point has been made epigrammatically by Irving Kreutz: while Nicholas wanders the country, Uncle Ralph stays home and minds the plot. So that even the various elements do not form a homogeneous whole.

Uncle Ralph, as I have implied, is a stage villain. Therefore it falls to Nicholas and his sister Kate to push the action along against his will. This is done mostly in terms of the jobs they are compelled to take. Kate is successively milliner, ladies' companion, and house keeper to her brother; Nicholas becomes in turn schoolmaster, tutor, actor and clerk. But neither Kate nor Nicholas develops as a result of their various changes of employment: these serve mostly as a way of bringing in new groups of characters – Mantalinis, Wititterleys, Kenwigses, Cheerybles. And, as soon as Nicholas encounters the last-named, the picaresque element stops. From being a free agent, he is imprisoned in a counting-house. For some reason, Dickens represents this as the highest happiness possible. 'There ain't such a young man as this in all London . . . and I shall have the satisfaction of knowing that there never were such books . . . as the books of Cheeryble Brothers!'

Nicholas settles down in the counting-house and his sister in a cottage at Bow; all this in Chapter XXXVII. The action has effectively ceased to move forward. Unfortunately, before the book comes to an end, there are twenty-eight chapters to go. These are eked out with the highly unconvincing betrothal of Nicholas's beloved to a decrepit friend of Uncle Ralph's. We saw that in *Oliver Twist* the theme was eventually buried under the plot; is it possible to disinter some similar theme from *Nicholas Nickleby*?

I have not yet mentioned the episode in this novel that has attracted the greatest attention: Mr Squeers and Dotheboys Hall. It is, in fact, possible to summarize the action of *Nicholas Nickleby* without touching upon what should have been its central feature. The school occurs in the plot merely because Dickens happened to send Nicholas there. He might – and it has been suggested that he nearly did – have sent Nicholas with equal propriety to the factories of the industrial North. So that here, far more than in *Oliver Twist*, the crucial moments are detached from the basic plot.

Further: unlike the Workhouse and the Thieves' Kitchen, Dotheboys Hall does not transcend its merits as documentation. Authenticity it certainly has: the Yorkshire schools served a purpose, and it was a vicious one. They were cheap depositories for unwanted children, and in those days of slow travel it was difficult for the boys to pay or receive visits. The researches of Philip Collins, among others, have established that these schools were institutions of long standing. They were advertised as early as 1749; magazines and novels were satirizing them by the later eighteenth century; and at least one case of cruelty was recorded in 1776. In 1807 they were written up by Robert Southey in his *Letters from England*: apparently the boys were a useful source of cheap labour on their master's farm. There are first-hand descriptions, too, from those who suffered in such institutions. John Abernethy claimed that his clothes were taken away from him as soon as he arrived; Richard Cobden recalled that he was ill-fed and ill-taught; while Sir Joshua Walmsley tells of a parent who refused to pay fees for his son when the boy returned home ill from malnutrition. Now, a good deal of this must be regarded as direct source-material for Dickens's novels.

Dickens himself, in his 1848 Preface, assures us that his interest in the subject was no sudden fancy. It was in his childhood at Chatham that he had met a boy from one of these same schools who claimed that he had been operated upon for an abscess with a penknife. This was itself to serve as an anecdote in *Nicholas Nickleby*. And this childhood impression never left Dickens. 'I was always curious about Yorkshire schools – fell, long afterwards and at sundry times, into the way of hearing more about them – at last, having an audience, resolved to write about them.'

Just before starting *Nicholas Nickleby*, Dickens went up to Yorkshire, together with his illustrator, Hablôt Browne. This journey appears to have been undertaken chiefly as a refresher to the author's memory. Nevertheless he picked up information, relayed back to his wife in letters home, which proved of service to the narrative. And several schoolmasters took this to be the occasion he had made them sit for the portrait of Squeers; though it turned out that most of them had little in common with that figure apart from his brutality. But, when all the literary sources, hearsay and observation have been taken into account, there can be no question that the prototype of Squeers is William Shaw.

Shaw may very well have attracted Dickens's notice by reason of two notorious cases brought against him in 1823 for gross neglect. During the trial, it came out that the boys were given maggoty food and slept in overcrowded, flea-infested beds, and that ten boys had previously lost their sight there. Not surprisingly, the jury found Shaw guilty; the damages, legal fees and medical fees proved heavy. Yet he was able to continue in business; which therefore must, as Professor Collins remarks, have been very profitable. Dickens explicitly mentions meeting Shaw near Greta Bridge, and the research that has been done as a result of this chance remark suggests that he was a very bad teacher indeed. Contemporary witnesses aver that he was very like Squeers in physique, even to having only one eye, and V.C. Clinton-Baddeley has discovered one of Shaw's advertisements which were very little less sinister than the claims made by Squeers himself 'no extras, no vacations, and diet unparalleled'. The more that comes up about Shaw, the worse he seems to be; and the worse he gets, the more he seems like Squeers.

What is the difference, then, between documentation, on the one hand, and Dickens's fiction on the other? Partly it is a matter of selection: the most striking attitudes of Shaw may be put before us, but not the doldrums in between. Moreover, those particulars that are included are played up by an analogical method very peculiar to Dickens. It is not enough to say of Squeers that he had one eye; it has to be 'greenish-grey, and in shape resembling the fan-light of a street door'. It is not enough for Squeers to be brutal: he has to cover up his real nature under an affected jocosity, as when he tastes the milk he has watered down for his young charges, smacking his lips and commenting eulogistically 'Here's richness'.

This sets off the intense moral passion which supervenes when Dickens comes to contemplate the boys directly. The 'young noblemen', whom Nicholas has been led to believe he will teach, turn out to be pale, haggard, emaciated and shackled with every deformity. The tone is that of Macaulay describing the Siege of Derry or Marx on the subject of the Working Day: its emotional pressure and power of observation raise documentary to the level of literature. It is, however, far from the controlled irony of *Oliver Twist*.

Such a rhetoric of indignation would be intolerable if it were not interspersed with the Jonsonian humours of the schoolmaster's hypocrisy.

'Now then, where's the first boy?'
'Please, sir, he's cleaning the back parlour window,' said the temporary head of the philosophical class.
'So he is, to be sure,' rejoined Squeers. 'We go upon the practical mode of teaching, Nickleby; the regular educational system. C-l-e-a-n, clean, verb active, to make bright, to scour. W-i-n, win, d-e-r, der, winder, a casement. When the boy knows this out of book, he goes and does it. It's just the same principle as the use of the globes. Where's the second boy?'
'Please, sir, he's weeding the garden . . .'

It is often forgotten how small a compass Dotheboys Hall takes up. In its pristine state it occupies no more than two chapters of a very long book indeed. For I take the farce of Fanny Squeers's infatuation with Nicholas to be a thinning-out; as the very Smollett-like tone of her letter to Uncle Ralph complaining of Nicholas's conduct would suggest. And the thrashing of Squeers is worse back to melodrama again: 'Wretch, touch him at your peril! . . . My blood is up, and I have the strength of ten such men as you.' Later on, as with Bumble in *Oliver Twist*, Squeers becomes reduced to a mere instrument, serving the needs of a mechanical plot. But in his own kingdom, Squeers swells to major proportions, and Dotheboys Hall remains one of the great creations of all time.

Arbitrary though the novel may seem, this Yorkshire school has a necessary balancing factor. After thrashing the schoolmaster, Nicholas sojourns briefly in London, and then goes off and joins a troupe of travelling actors led by Vincent Crummles. The relationship between the world of Squeers and the world of Crummles has been analysed in some detail by John Archer Carter. Nicholas meets Crummles, as he met Squeers, at an inn accompanied by children; but Crummles feeds his children generously and teaches them their trade – in this instance, fencing. Nicholas is able to make use of his education with Crummles, as he could not with Squeers, in instructing Smike – 'never had master a more anxious, humble pupil' – and in writing a play. Unlike the violence of Squeers and his wife, that of the actors is merely make-believe and arouses the audience's sympathy. In contrast to that of Squeers, this environment is fanciful and, in its odd way, life-enhancing. Crummles's troupe belongs to a series of entertainments in Dickens, from Astleys in *Sketches by Boz* to Sleary's Horseriding in *Hard Times*. All represent escapes from reality – welcome, though not permanent. The tradition led on to the circuses that play such a prominent part in both E.M. Forster and D.H. Lawrence.

It is worth mentioning that Crummles's theatre is as soundly documented as Squeers's school. According to Malcolm Morley, Crummles himself is based on T.D. Davenport, an actor weighing 280 pounds with powerful lungs and a face of alarming fatness which he was in the habit of contorting into horrible but unconvincing grimaces. He always took lodgings in such a position that people could not fail to remark himself and his little daughter, Jean, on their way to church. She was the most celebrated juvenile of her time, according to James Ollé, and would be seen playing with an outsize doll to attract the notice of potential playgoers. Circumstances such as these remind us irresistibly of Crummles and his Infant Phenomenon.

As with Squeers, Dickens selects and points up his factual details; for instance, Crummles's amazing production technique. When Nicholas bids him goodbye, he wants to organize a farewell benefit in which the young man stands with the Phenomenon on a pair of steps, stage centre, and nine people in the wings let off a dozen and a half squibs simultaneously between them – 'awful from the front, quite awful.' Nicholas prefers to depart more quietly, but finds himself balked even in this when Crummles seizes him at the coachstand, crying 'Farewell, my lion-hearted boy' for the benefit of a crowd of spectators. Nevertheless, genuine kindliness shines through all this extravagance, and a sense of craft learned and work done balances Dotheboys Hall. It is with a pleasing sense of fitness that we note the novel is dedicated to the actor, Macready, who, however, resembled Crummles in his kindness to a young writer.

There are, indeed, other memorable moments in the novel. The shabby-genteel Kenwigses read like one of the better Sketches. While Mrs Nickleby, based on Dickens's mother, is a comic figure remarkable chiefly for her power of free-association. She launches into a monologue concerning the Thirsty Woman of Tutbury and the Cock Lane Ghost – one of which, she forgets who, went to school with her great-grandfather – shortly before a madman tumbles down her chimney. But the rambling is not so random as it may seem: the Thirsty Woman and the Cock Lane Ghost were, in their time, famous frauds, and, like the old madman, were closely associated with beds. Indeed, he is the biggest fraud of the lot. His rhetoric has a logic of its own – he refers to the Aldgate Pump and the Statue at Charing Cross walking together arm-in-arm at midnight by the Royal Exchange. But these two figures were famous landmarks – the statue was that of Charles I – and were used in juxtaposition by Dickens as early as *Sketches by Boz*. The madman – 'all is gas and gaiters' – is one of those hallucinatory creations Dickens went in for when his sober invention was beginning to fail. In real life this creature was, according to his keeper, a skinflint very similar to Nicholas's Uncle Ralph; which shows a ghostly connection with the main plot that could have been made effective if Dickens had had, at this stage, sufficient energy and control.

As it is, the main action of *Nicholas Nickleby* judders along in an arbitrary manner. Theme is almost absent, except in his two inspired documentaries, and fantasy is in danger of taking hold. How could it be otherwise? Dickens's boyhood experiences certainly put him in sympathy with the rejected children, but had nothing to do with the exploits of a vigorous young hero upon the road. One may remark here that Dickens was never at his best with extrovert heroes. In this, as in his next novel, he chose plots with which he could not possibly be seriously engaged. Clearly he was using fiction as a way out of a reality he had his own reasons for refusing to face. And it is not paying Dickens's subsequent work a compliment to say that all too large a proportion must be discussed in terms of hallucination and fantasy.

V   The Old Curiosity Shop (1840)

Master Humphrey's Clock (1840)

Dickens found his relations with Bentley deteriorating as those with Chapman and Hall improved. Therefore he sought to bind himself more closely to the latter. He persuaded them to sponsor a new periodical, to be modelled on Addison's *Spectator* and Goldsmith's *Bee*, containing satire, stories and descriptive sketches. He wished to receive a regular salary *and* take half the profits; while the publishers would pay all the costs of printing and advertising and stand the loss, if any. Their acceptance of this proposition shows what an impregnable position Dickens thought he was in – heads I win, tails you lose.

Neither Dickens nor his publishers, in this, took sufficient account of the public mind, and, in the event, the latter risked a heavy loss. It is true that the first number of *Master Humphrey's Clock*, as the periodical was called, sold seventy thousand copies. But this was because the public had mistaken the miscellany for a new Dickens novel. Sales fell off sharply; by the third issue, the enterprise was in danger. And indeed it is difficult to see how Dickens could have thought it would ever succeed.

The focus of the periodical was an old recluse who invited his friends around once a week to read stories which were deposited in his clock; it is fitting that the work in its collected edition should have been dedicated to the elderly litterateur, Samuel Rogers. One story from the Clock opens out of another in bewildering fashion. We are introduced to Master Humphrey and he tells us a tale of an encounter between the Lord Mayor of London and an old schoolmate who falls asleep in the Guildhall and hears the giants who guard it indulging in dialogue which gives way to a story of Elizabethan times. . . Such a farrago could never have commanded public attention. Author and publishers held a hasty editorial conference. The result was that Dickens agreed to develop one of the tales he had projected for the periodical into a full-scale novel. In the meantime Mr Pickwick and Tony Weller were revived and thrown into the breach. They jerked about with none of their former animation, and looked decidedly odd in company with Master Humphrey and his fusty associates. But at least they prevented any farther readers seeping away before *The Old Curiosity Shop* got fairly started.

In form, the novel is a picaresque. As I have already hinted, this form never really suited Dickens's temperament. The great poet of claustrophobia and the prison cell was never really at home on the open road. Little Nell and her grandfather are escaping into the country from the city streets and the city's greed. But it is the condemnation of what they leave behind that makes the novel interesting.

The old man keeps a curiosity shop, but seeks to better his fortunes by gambling. The result is that his goods are seized by a rascally dwarf called Quilp. His little grand-daughter, Nell, persuades him secretly to decamp. They fall into the company of various travellers – a Punch-and-Judy show, a Waxworks Museum – but, because of the old man's gambling mania, they have to keep moving on. Finally they reach a village where they find some peace. The place appears to be full of dead children and moribund ancients. Little Nell herself has been exhausted by all her wanderings, and, at the end of the book, is found dead in a scene that moved to tears such men as O'Connell, the Irish statesman, Jeffrey, the Scottish critic, and Macready, the Shakespearian actor.

'Master!' he cried, stooping on one knee, and catching at his hand. 'Dear master. Speak to me!'

The old man turned slowly towards him; and muttered, in a hollow voice, 'This is another! – How many of these spirits there have been tonight!'

'No spirit, master. No one but your old servant. You know me now, I am sure? Miss Nell – where is she – where is she?' . . .

'She is asleep – yonder – in there.'

'Thank God!'

'Ay! Thank God . . . Hark! Did she call? . . . She has called to me in her sleep before now, Sir; as I sat by, watching, I have seen her lips move, and have known, though no sound came from them, that she spoke of me . . . She is sleeping soundly, but no wonder. Angel hands have strewn the ground deep with snow, that the lightest footsteps may be lighter yet; and the very birds are dead, that they may not wake her. She used to feed them, Sir. Though never so cold and hungry, the timid things would fly from us as they never flew from her!'

It is plain that most of the work is being done by *King Lear*. The old man's failure to recognize his faithful servant, his inability to distinguish spirits from people, his refusal to believe Nell dead – the whole scene takes place in a solemn hush of literary reminiscence. And we may believe that Macready's famous production of 1838 was not far away from the author's mind: contemporary accounts, such as that of John Forster, assure us that it concentrated upon pathos.

But *King Lear* is a tragedy. Cordelia's death scene is worked towards. Lear splits the kingdom and dismisses his daughter; the heavens themselves revolt at such unnatural conduct; the King goes mad raving against the thunder. In contrast, all Dickens can offer us is an old man afflicted with gambling mania whose ceaseless travels wear his grand-daughter to death. There is not much here to justify the portentous tone Dickens adopts.

What is wrong with Little Nell is that she has no function. Cordelia represented all that was good in a world all too open to evil; her death is a condemnation of that world. Even Oliver Twist, that stylized representative of the oppressed, is a standing reproach to society. Whereas the wanderings of Little Nell have neither purpose nor meaning; her death exists merely on the level of sensation. It is a trigger to spark off emotions already existing in the reader's breast.

We must remember that Macready had a daughter who died in infancy: this may explain both his production of *King Lear* and his reaction to Little Nell. Dickens, too, was in the grip of emotions that he could neither judge nor control.

It is a matter of fact that his wife's young sister lived with them both in the early months of their marriage and died in Dickens's arms; this was in 1837. What Mary Hogarth was really like we cannot know, but she became the cult-object of Dickens's mystique for the next twenty years. She – or Dickens's idealization of her

– served as the model for Rose Maylie, Little Nell, Mary Graham, Florence Dombey, and possibly others. Smike, the foundling in *Nicholas Nickleby*, Paul Dombey and Jo the sweeper picked up various of her traits, and she synthesizes even with unlike characters in their death-scenes; consider the solemnizing of Dora Copperfield. It is not, however, Mary Hogarth with whom we are concerned, but what she became in Dickens's mind.

The epitaph he wrote for her could have come from *The Old Curiosity Shop* itself: 'Young, beautiful, and good, God in his mercy numbered her with his angels.' But it was beyond Dickens to distance the emotion he undoubtedly felt. It bursts out in the wildness of his letters concerning her – 'I cannot bear the thought of being excluded from her dust'. The result is that, while Dickens's pathos is more complex than is commonly thought, it suffers by comparison with his satire and humour in being inadequately placed in context and charged with meaning.

The way out from such emotionalism was in flights of macabre fancy. We have already seen that, when invention flagged in *Nicholas Nickleby*, Dickens launched out on the extraordinary figure of the madman. This hallucinatory quality never left him; indeed, it grew stronger with the years. Its light in this novel flickers mainly around the person of Daniel Quilp.

Now, Edward Fitzgerald made himself a kind of saga of Little Nell by cutting out from *The Old Curiosity Shop* all that did not immediately concern her. I would propose that the modern reader pick up what Fitzgerald discarded and fashion himself, as far as he can, a saga of Daniel Quilp: a Quilpiad.

As in *Nicholas Nickleby*, the good people take to the road while the villain stays home and minds the plot. But, in the case of *The Old Curiosity Shop*, there isn't much plot to mind. All Quilp succeeds in doing is to fix a false suspicion of theft on an honest working-lad; this is ingeniously based on a notorious case of the seventeenth century. Nell is not Quilp's victim but her grandfather's; Quilp can't even find out where she is. So, in the absence of more serious business, he has ample space in which to expand his personality. The result is a good deal of posturing for its own sake.

Quilp first comes into his own in Chapter IV, when we see him in domestic circumstances. His wife is having a tea-party and Quilp overhears a conversation of her friends. It is mostly critical of him as man and husband. Suddenly they see him in their midst.

'Go on, ladies, go on,' said Daniel. 'Mrs Quilp, pray ask the ladies to stop to supper, and have a couple of lobsters and something light and palatable.'

'I – I – didn't ask them to tea, Quilp,' stammered his wife. 'It's quite an accident.'

'So much the better, Mrs Quilp; these accidental parties are always the pleasantest,' said the dwarf, rubbing his hands so hard that he seemed to be engaged in manufacturing of the dirt with which they were encrusted, little charges for popguns. 'What! Not going, ladies, you are not going, surely!'

Quilp's mocking charm seems to imply a deep and abiding malice. The dichotomy is conveyed by contrast between the inappropriate geniality of his speech and the extreme violence of the gestures accompanying it – in this case, 'rubbing his hands so hard that he seemed to be engaged in manufacturing . . . little charges for popguns.' The tone of his comedy is so peculiar that it has lent itself to the language which otherwise would have had no term to cover so odd a range of conduct. Rather more sinister than Shakespeare's Puck as he is, the behaviour of Dickens's dwarf is best termed 'Quilpish'.

Quilp manages to dominate everyone he meets. Partly this is a matter of sex-appeal. Though he is ugly, he is certainly the most erotic figure in Dickens. Mrs Quilp testifies to his irresistible charm, and Gabriel Pearson has pointed out the sexual nature of the images through which he is presented.

'Now, Mrs Quilp,' he said, 'I feel in a smoking humour and shall probably blaze away all night'. . . . The room became perfectly dark and the end of the cigar a dark fiery red.

The imagery is not just sexual but sadistic; it extends even to the acts of eating and drinking.

He ate hard eggs, shell and all, devoured gigantic prawns with the heads and tails on, chewed tobacco and water-cresses at the same time and with extraordinary greediness, drank boiling tea without winking, bit his fork and spoon till they bent again, and in short performed so many horrifying and uncommon feats that the women were nearly frightened out of their wits, and began to doubt if he were really a human creature.

Much of Quilp's psychic energy is expended in activity such as this;

he seems to live to astonish those with whom he comes into contact.
Part of his dynamic is his unappeasable vanity – natural over-compensation in one so misshapen and dwarfish. Here his mother-in-law,
under the impression he is drowned, dictates a highly unflattering
description of the supposed corpse to Sampson Brass, his attorney.
Quilp tries to overhear everything but can't contain his impatience.

'Respecting his legs now – ?'
   'Crooked, certainly,' said Mrs Jiniwin.
   'Legs crooked,' said Brass, writing as he spoke. 'Large head, short body,
legs crooked –'
   'Very crooked,' suggested Mrs Jiniwin. . . .
   'A question now arises in relation to his nose.'
   'Flat,' said Mrs Jiniwin.
   'Aquiline!' cried Quilp, thrusting in his head, and striking the feature with
his fist. 'Aquiline, you hag. Do you see it? Do you call this flat? Do you?
Eh!'

But this same vanity proves to be his undoing. Quilp overestimates
his ascendancy over Brass, who finally betrays him to the authorities.
The last we see of Quilp, after an impotent dance of rage round his
counting-house, is him floating down the river until his corpse –
drowned in earnest this time – fetches up against a sand bank, the
wind playing Quilpishly with his hair.
   Quilp's behaviour is directed at all around him, and, paradoxically,
is paraded for their benefit; but the minor grotesques of *The Old
Curiosity Shop* are in no sense his equals. Shrinking Mrs Quilp,
censorious Mrs Jiniwin, fawning Sampson and masculine Sally
Brass, jolly Dick Swiveller, even the Marchioness, the minuscule
servant-drudge whom Quilp himself can look down upon – these
are poor adversaries for his wit. So Quilp's speech tends towards
the condition of monologue, and he himself has the appearance of
capering round a rather deserted stage. This was a tendency which
grew upon Dickens in the books of his middle period, so that the
epic personae of *Martin Chuzzlewit* and *David Copperfield* have
things very much their own way.
   But such a tendency itself testifies to the lack of an urgent theme.
We may choose to prefer Quilp's demonology to Little Nell's fairy-
land, but both are alike irrelevant to serious concerns.

VI   Barnaby Rudge (1841)

The first of all Dickens's novels to be conceived was *Barnaby Rudge*. It was originally meant to be called *Gabriel Varden, the Locksmith of London*. The novel should have appeared as a three-volume work at the end of 1836; such was the agreement made in May of that year with Macrone, publisher of *Sketches by Boz*. But the success of Pickwick encouraged Dickens to seek a better bargain than Macrone was able to concede. Macrone himself does not seem to have understood this. At any rate, as soon as the news of Dickens editing *Bentley's Miscellany* got out a year later, Macrone began to advertise *Gabriel Varden* as forthcoming under *his* imprint.

This first of several disputes concerning the novel was only settled when Dickens sold Macrone the rights in *Sketches by Boz* for £150 less than he had originally asked; this in consideration of his failure to fulfil the initial agreement. The new plan was that *Gabriel Varden* would be published by Bentley, and delivery was promised for October 1838. Once more it was advertised as 'forthcoming', this time in the first edition of *Oliver Twist*. But the venture was postponed repeatedly. Dickens felt that the production of *Barnaby Rudge*, as by now it was called, concurrently with the serials *Oliver Twist* and *Nicholas Nickleby*, would be beyond even his powers.

Therefore he suggested to Bentley that *Barnaby Rudge* should succeed *Oliver Twist* as his serial contribution to the *Miscellany*, and be published in three volumes after its course was completed. But Bentley insisted on dealing with Dickens's *Miscellany* contributions quite separately from *Barnaby Rudge*. Once more the much-delayed novel was advertised as imminent—this time, in the pages of the *Miscellany* itself.

However, in January 1839 Dickens begged Bentley to allow him a further postponement of six months – 'and but for you, it should stand over altogether'. Bentley would only agree if Dickens refused to work for any other publisher in the future. But Dickens was not the man to accept an ultimatum. He immediately resigned from the *Miscellany* as editor and postponed his delivery-date a further three months. Moreover, as yet another sign of dissociation from Bentley, he contracted to undertake *Master Humphrey's Clock* for Chapman and Hall.

By September 1939, the new date for delivery, only two chapters of *Barnaby Rudge* had been completed, and Chapman and Hall were advertising *Master Humphrey's Clock* as a periodical with Dickens as principal contributor. Bentley threatened legal proceedings, but eventually he was persuaded to assign Dickens rights over the unwritten *Barnaby Rudge,* together with *Oliver Twist* which had already appeared, in return for a payment of £1,500. This meant that, for the immediate future, Dickens was able to make Chapman and Hall – 'the best of booksellers' – his sole publishers.

Master Humphrey's Clock was still running, so Dickens devised some link passages to take the reader from the concluding chapters of *The Old Curiosity Shop* to the beginning of *Barnaby Rudge*. The latter got under way at long last on 13 February 1841.

But so many delays had considerably changed Dickens's plans for the novel. Originally, as the first title would suggest, Gabriel Varden was to have been at the centre of events. The action would have shown a sturdy English yeoman of the previous century protecting his family at a time of riot. The crucial incident would have been the old locksmith's refusal to open the doors of Newgate Prison to the mob. One is irresistibly reminded of the storming of the Tolbooth in *The Heart of Midlothian* by Walter Scott.

However, continual reading in the period affected considerably Dickens's view of his subject-matter. He seems to have used as source material such works as Robert Watson's life of his master, Lord George Gordon; Thomas Holcroft's narrative of the riots; Frederick Reynolds's reminiscences; the letters of Horace Walpole; and verbatim accounts of contemporary witnesses. A good deal of the narrative – the old man seeing his son's execution in Chapter 77 is one example – derives very much from newspaper accounts of the time. And such matters as the mob's visit to parliament are virtually direct quotations; heightened, however, by the author's imagination, and by his acquisition of a narrative technique learned from a major historian.

Scott had given place, as a literary influence, to Thomas Carlyle. *The French Revolution* had decisively influenced Dickens between his conceiving the novel and his writing it. The result was that the emphasis shifted from the individual lives disrupted by the Gordon Riots to the Riots as social phenomena in themselves.

Therefore *Barnaby Rudge* is hard to discuss as a novel. The characters do not live, move or generally have their being in the fabric of events. There are too many strands of action, and they are not satisfactorily interwoven. Much of the earlier part of the book is concerned with the attempt of the Protestant, John Chester, to circumvent the romance between his son and the Catholic, Emma Haredale. But the point is lost by Chester's display of unmeaning wickedness; derived, no doubt, from Dickens's misunderstanding of the letters of the eighteenth-century politician, Lord Chesterfield. If the old man is objectlessly villainous, we get no flavour of his sense that union between Protestant and Catholic is miscegenation. Thus, that particular line of plot is taken too far away from the centre of the book.

Another disconnected strand is the effort of Emma's uncle, Geoffrey Haredale, to discover the murderer of her father. This he might easily do, since the villain in question sneaks, breathes and judders through the novel in a manner calculated to draw the utmost attention to himself. Even so, his pursuit by the relentless Haredale has nothing to do with the Protestant-Catholic riots.

This murderer is, in fact, the steward, Mr Rudge, long since thought to be murdered himself. He is recognized only by his wife, who flees with her idiot son, Barnaby. The latter gets caught up fairly purposelessly in the riots, and father and son land in the same cell in Newgate. But we cannot say that this takes Barnaby nearer the centre of the book. At best, he is a mere adjunct to the striking descriptions of a mob out of control. One has to concede, moreover, that he, more than most of what goes on in the novel, is an uneasy recollection of Scott: with his ravings and snatches of song, a kind of male Madge Wildfire.

Yet another line of action is the love of Joe Willet for Dolly Varden.

This connects up two aspects of England, the Maypole Inn in the country and the London home of the sturdy City locksmith. There are, indeed, good moments concerned with each. Fatheaded John Willet with his dull cronies in the bar night after night outstares the boiler that hangs suspended above the fire; he represents the insensate John Bull of rural England. Varden, on the other hand, an honest citizen in himself, is beset with a shrewish wife, a wayward daughter, a vain apprentice, and a comic serving-maid; all this to give us some idea of a bygone London town. Mr Varden's breakfast in Chapter IV gives us some savour of the original concept of the book.

It was a substantial meal; for over and above the ordinary tea equipage, the board creaked beneath the weight of a jolly round of beef, a ham of the first magnitude, and sundry towers of buttered Yorkshire cake, piled slice upon slice in most alluring order. There was also a goodly jug of well-browned clay, fashioned into the form of an old gentleman, not by any means unlike the locksmith, at the top of whose bald head was a fine white froth answering to his wig, indicative, beyond dispute, of sparkling home-brewed ale. But better far than fair home-brewed, or Yorkshire cake, or ham, or beef, or anything to eat or drink that earth or air or water can supply, there sat, presiding over all, the locksmith's rosy daughter, before whose dark eyes even beef grew insignificant, and malt became as nothing.

It is this personal vein that Dickens's reading of the riot literature and subjection to the influence of Carlyle's historical writing was bound to erode. Varden's importance in the book is not what the detail of this early chapter would suggest. And this is true of the other characters I have mentioned: John Chester, Geoffrey Haredale, Joe Willet, Dolly; especially, Barnaby Rudge himself.

There are some glimpses of fictive possibility – one or two in connection with Lord George Gordon, the half-mad instigator of the riots. This nobleman attempted to bring a petition to parliament intended to proscribe the civil rights of Catholics and so created a very ugly situation. Dickens has a moving passage in Chapter LVII where Gordon dimly recognizes himself in the lineaments and behaviour of the idiot, Barnaby Rudge. And the converse situation is seen in Chapter XLIX, when Barnaby believes himself to be in actual fact a leader. But this Doppelgänger effect – superbly used in the later novels – is momentary here; too brief to make an effect.

Such odd glimpses as this count for little in the total narrative of the book.

Rather, the quality of *Barnaby Rudge* resides in Dickens's epic descriptions of riot. It is hard to relate these to fluctuations of plot, especially since the individual set-pieces tend to blur together in the memory. We are, in fact, not so much conscious of several different outbreaks of violence as of one continuous revolt. The mob murmurs, builds up, bursts out in a frenzy, and finally dies away.

Here Dickens is writing as historian rather than novelist; and writing, moreover, under the spell of Carlyle. If he had even more limited powers of conceptualization than his master, he had considerably more taste and restraint: in *Barnaby Rudge,* we are spared the frantic appeals to an audience, the apostrophes and ejaculations, that characterize *The French Revolution.*

Meanwhile, the faster, O ye black-aproned Smiths, smite; with strong arm and willing heart. This man and that, all stroke from head to heel, shall thunder alternatively, and ply the great forge-hammer, till stithy reel and ring again; while ever and anon, overhead, booms the alarm-cannon – for the City has now got gun-powder. Pikes are fabricated; fifty thousand of them, in six-and-thirty hours; judge whether the Black-aproned have been idle. Dig trenches, unpave the streets, ye others, assiduous, man and maid; cram the earth in barrel-barricades, at each of these a volunteer sentry; pile the whinstones in window-sills and upper rooms. Have scalding pitch, at least boiling water ready, ye weak old women, to pour and dash it on Royal-Allemand, with your old skinny arms: your shrill curses along with it will not be wanting!

Dickens may be even less interested in causes and consequences than Carlyle – there is singularly little before and after in any of his work – but his prose has a flow that the older man was never able to manage. We may judge that Dickens learned from Carlyle the technique of making the generalizations of history immediate and particular, but he had far more sense of the natural run of the English prose sentence.

The burning pile, revealing rooms and passages red hot, through gaps made in the crumbling wall; the tributary fires that licked the outer bricks and stones, with their long-forked tongues, and ran up to meet the flowing mass within; the shining of the flames upon the villains who looked on and fed them; the roaring of the angry blaze, so bright and high that it seemed in its rapacity to have swallowed up the very smoke; the living flakes the wind bore rapidly away and hurried on with, like a storm of fiery snow; the noiseless breaking of great beams of wood, which fell like feathers on the heap of ashes, and crumbled in the very act to sparks and powder. . . .

Although the glass fell from the window-sashes, and the lead and iron on the roofs blistered the incautious hand that touched them, and the sparrows in the eaves took wing, and rendered giddy by the smoke, fell fluttering down upon the blazing pile; still the fire was tended unceasingly by busy hands, and round it, men were going all ways. They never slackened in their zeal, or kept aloof, but pressed upon the flames so hard, that those in front had much ado to save themselves from being thrust in; if one man swooned or dropped, a dozen struggled for his place, and that although they knew the pain, and thirst, and pressure to be unendurable. . . .

The gutters of the street and every crack and fissure in the stones, ran with scorching spirit, which being dammed up by busy hands, overflowed the road and pavement, and formed a great pool, in which the people dropped dead by dozens. They lay in heaps all round this fearful pond, husbands and wives, fathers and sons, mothers and daughters, women with children in their arms and babies at their breasts, and drank until they died. While some stooped with their lips to the brink and never raised their heads again, others sprang up from their fiery draught, and danced, half in a mad triumph, and half in the agony of suffocation, until they fell, and steeped their corpses in the liquor that had killed them. . . .

Perhaps I should say that these are various manifestations of the riot: though they cohere as a single narrative, they are, in fact, dispersed throughout the book. The burning of The Warren in Chapter LV, the storming of Newgate in Chapter LXIV and the burning of the Distillery (Chapter LXVIII) are separate occasions, yet there is no difference in the tone with which Dickens recounts these individual events. I have suggested an affinity between such passages merely by leaving the fictional characters out. The continuity thus achieved suggests that perhaps the fiction was not necessary in the first place. A judicious abridgement would leave us with a brief history in the romantic manner of *The French Revolution*. The shrinking murderer, the jolly locksmith, Sweet Dolly Varden, the idiot boy – all are in the way. The true hero of *Barnaby Rudge* is the mob.

Dickens used similar energy of denunciation in describing the ill-

treatment of the children in *Dotheboys Hall,* and there reached a
kind of sublime documentation. Here he moves into historiography
of a remarkably dramatic kind: the simplicity of his subject-matter
allowed him to spread himself. The mode would not do for events
more intricate and subtle, and we must remember that what is documented here was quite a trivial affair seen in the context of English
history. The Gordon Riots do not have the centrality of the French
Revolution. And, even if we allow that *any* riot is serious, Dickens
makes no attempt to sound the various causes. What we have here
is no more than a vivid rendering of external events. Dickens was
never at his best on political motivation, and he mars even what
pattern he achieves by an attempt to whitewash the wretched Gordon.
He provides him with a remarkably unconvincing Secretary who dogs
Gordon's footsteps, whispering and flattering and generally acting
as an evil genius. There is no historical warrant for this: Robert
Watson, from whom Dickens takes much of his information, was an
altogether different character. The substitution of a real spy for a
misguided follower deprives Gordon of the little free-will he has been
credited with.

If we are to enjoy *Barnaby Rudge,* then, it seems to me we have to
make a bonfire of its fictive semblances. Gone are Gordon's moti-
vations, the love interest, the murder hunt, the homely life of the
Locksmith of London. Gone, too, is the comedy – forced and shrill
here, even though Chester looks like a first sketch for Pecksniff and
Miggs, the handmaid, may be said to anticipate some aspects of
Gamp. What is left is an historical set-piece: the portrait of a mob.
And here Dickens stands clear from the wreckage of his book. He
is not, in this instance, a novelist of anything like genius, but, without
question, he has proved himself a sensationally talented historian.

VII   American Notes (1842)

Martin Chuzzlewit (1843-44)

CHAPTERS XV–XVII, XXI–XXIV, XXXIII–XXXIV

During the run of *Barnaby Rudge*, it had been decided that Dickens would discontinue *Master Humphrey's Clock* in November 1841, and start publishing a new serial month by month from March onwards. But this would have been to continue at what was already a killing pace, and Dickens managed to persuade Chapman and Hall to let him have some time off. He argued that not only he but the public would soon be exhausted. The example in his mind was that of Scott, who had satiated his readers by over-production.

There was nothing much that the publishers could do but agree. Dickens had therefore won himself a year's respite, to November 1842, at which time he promised to begin another novel. But so far from resting, on an impulse almost as sudden as that taken by Martin Chuzzlewit himself, Dickens decided to go to America.

True, the notion had been forming as far back as the early days of *Master Humphrey's Clock*. But it was like Dickens to spring it on his friends without warning. He wrote to Forster: 'Now to astonish you. After balancing, considering and weighing the matter in every point of view, I HAVE MADE UP MY MIND (WITH GOD'S LEAVE) TO GO TO AMERICA.' He promised Chapman and Hall to bring back a journal for publication in volume form. But, in effect, *American Notes* is based on the letters home to his friends, Maclise, Beard, Mitton, Fonblanque and Forster himself.

It is the letters to this last that mostly survive. They have qualities as raw material, but display, as letters will, a certain instability of form. At times they are splendid documentary: the author is here performing as historian, setting down whatever happened to come within his purview. But also in the Letters we have the author as autobiographer; quirkily individual, picking up and projecting the specific instance. It is this mode that gets developed into the fiction of *Martin Chuzzlewit* with its highly personal bias. So it does not really make sense to regard the novel as a fictionalized version of the documentary *American Notes*. Rather they are different compositions refined from the same ore.

This can be seen in so apparently small an example as that of the American newspapermen who besiege the ship as it comes into port.

I was standing in full fig on the paddle-box beside the captain, staring about me, when suddenly, long before we were moored to the wharf, a dozen men came leaping on board at the peril of their lives, with great bundles of newspapers under their arms; worsted comforters (very much the worse for wear) round their necks; and so forth. 'Aha!' says I, 'this is like our London-bridge': believing of course that these visitors were news-boys. But what do you think of their being EDITORS? And what do you think of their tearing violently up to me and beginning to shake hands like madmen? Oh! If you could have seen how I wrung their wrists! And if you could but know how I hated one man in very dirty gaiters, and with very protruding upper teeth, who said to all comers after him, 'So you've been introduced to our friend Dickens – eh?' There was one among them, though, who really was of use; a Doctor Palmer, editor of the Boston *Transcript*. He ran off here (two miles at least), and ordered rooms and dinner. . . .

This is chatty and inconsequential, and it contains both the historian's report of actual fact and the autobiographer's eye for odd detail. It is the former element, that of hard fact, that is brought out in *American Notes*; the individual circumstance is kept in abeyance.

Neither will I more than hint at my foreigner-like mistake, in supposing that a party of most active persons who scrambled on board at the peril of their lives as we approached the wharf, were newsmen, answering to that industrious claim at home; whereas, despite the leathern wallets of news slung about the necks of some, and the broad sheets in the hands of all, they were Editors, who boarded ships in person (as one gentleman in a worsted comforter informed me), 'because they liked the excitement of it'. Suffice it in this place to say, that one of these invaders, with a ready courtesy for which I thank him most gratefully, went on before to order rooms at the hotel. . . .

It is clear that the letter already quoted was the original source for all this. What has been dropped, however, is the sharp delineation of individual traits. The man with the protruding teeth disappears in the general ruck of editors, and the specific Doctor Palmer becomes generalized into 'one of these invaders'.

Quite the reverse procedure is adopted for *Martin Chuzzlewit*. Here, the man with the teeth is not only built up into a forbidding character, but also synthesized with Doctor Palmer himself – except that in this case, he runs errands for gain. And he has acquired a formidable amount of context, chiefly political.

These good-humoured little outbursts of the popular fancy . . . found fresh life and notoriety in the breath of the newsboys, who not only proclaimed them with shrill yells in all the highways and byeways of the town, upon the wharves and among the shipping, but on the deck and down in the cabins of the steam-boat; which before she touched the shore, was boarded and overrun by a league of those young citizens. . . .

'Here's the New York Sewer, in its twelfth thousand, with a whole column of New Yorkers to be shown up, and all their names printed! Here's the Sewer's article upon the Judge that tried him, day afore yesterday, for libel, and the Sewer's tribute to the independent Jury that didn't convict him, and the Sewer's account of what they might have expected if they had! . . .'

'It is in such enlightened means,' said a voice, almost in Martin's ear, 'that the bubbling passions of my country find a vent.'

Martin turned involuntarily round, and saw, standing close at his side, a sallow gentleman, with sunken cheeks, black hair, small twinkling eyes, and a singular expression hovering about in that region of his face, which was not a frown, nor a leer, and yet might have been mistaken at the first glance for either. Indeed it would have been difficult, on a much closer acquaintance, to describe it in any more satisfactory terms than a mixed expression of vulgar cunning and conceit. . . .

'It is in such enlightened means, that the bubbling passions of my country find a vent.'

As he looked at Martin, and nobody else was by, Martin inclined his head, and said:

'You allude to –'

'To the Palladium of rational Liberty at home, sir, and the dread of foreign oppression abroad,' returned the gentleman, as he pointed with his cane to an uncommonly dirty newsboy with one eye.

The editor with the protruding teeth – a mere detail in the original letter – is here personalized as Colonel Diver, Editor of the *Rowdy Journal*. His unprepossessing appearance and evasive rhetoric proves to be Martin's first direct contact with the New World. He emblematizes its whole apparatus of communication: its bluster, cant, vulgarity and meretriciousness. In other words, the mode of the American press is that of propaganda, not of information. Colonel Diver proves to be an emissary from the Father of Lies himself. He first defends in the name of freedom his paper's attacks on personalities, then applauds them because of the number of copies they sell. He has become the embodiment of all the reviewers who attacked *American Notes*, a diver into the muddy well of scandal, a rowdy who intimidates those whom he cannot buy. From the incident of the newsboys, observed in his letter, Dickens builds up a satire upon a debased press, itself the symbol of a breakdown in communication among men, and in its turn an institution all too representative of America itself.

The American chapters of *Martin Chuzzlewit* amount in size and scope of character to a fair-sized book. They are extraordinarily independent of the novel as a whole, both in their internal coherence of structure and in their consistency of form. The satire is remarkably sour: normally Dickens could approach Swift only through the intermediary humour of Henry Fielding, especially the Henry Fielding of *Jonathan Wild*. But here we are in a world akin to the Ireland of Swift's *Modest Proposal* or the Laputa of *Gulliver's Travels*: folly, greed, vainglory are alike mocked in this urbane prose – 'the friends of the disappointed candidate had found it necessary to assert the great principle of Purity of Election and Freedom of Opinion by breaking a few legs and arms, and furthermore pursuing one obnoxious gentleman through the streets with the design of slitting his nose,' etc.

A series of repellent external traits is exhibited in the harshest possible light. It is as though the worst qualities of a nation that could become known to a traveller were treated in terms of its whole history. The ugliest of all the various details touched on in the Letters are picked out and played up into caricature to satisfy Dickens's rankling bias.

The dynamics of the situation are plain to see. *American Notes*, as we may observe in the snippets previously quoted, is an unpretentious book which does not seek to be a political or economic treatise. An introductory chapter explaining it as the impressions of an individual tourist was suppressed at the suggestion of the

officious Forster; the only conciliatory sign is in the dedication to
Dickens's friends in America. These could not have been many,
for the book received the worst press Dickens had experienced in
his life. The Americans, particularly, were uninhibited in their
disapproval. They vilified Dickens as a 'penny-a-liner', a 'conceited
cockney', a 'low-bred scullion' who had spent his life 'in the stews
of London' and was 'fit only to associate with dancing monkeys'.

Opposition, even of a trifling kind, was apt to arouse Dickens's
fiercest passions; we have already seen this in his dealings with various
publishers. What, then, are we to make of the fury with which he
reacted to mud-slinging of this type? He had, as he thought, written
American Notes in good faith; and a comparison with the Letters
shows that, on many occasions, he played down some of the more
unwholesome traits he had seen. There is therefore every indication
that he was enraged by the American reviewers' complaints that he
had scourged them with whips. Certainly in *Martin Chuzzlewit*
he went on to flay them with scorpions. Even mere hints, such as
that of the newspapermen overrunning the incoming boat, were
developed into a scarifying attack upon America and all its institutions. It forms the frontage or exposition of the American chapters.

Looked at carefully, it will be seen that the muddy characters of
Colonel Diver, his war correspondent and his landlord circle about
one central idea: the fact that an atrocious piece of double-dealing
could be thought of as being 'smart'. And this word 'smart' Dickens
strongly objects to, in the Letters as elsewhere. In *American Notes*
he defines it as signifying perverse admiration of any successful
piece of scoundrelism. But in *Martin Chuzzlewit* the word runs the
entire gamut, from the Colonel cajoling Martin into staying at his
sleazy ordinary, to the remarkable confidence trick by which the
wretched immigrant becomes owner of a particularly insalubrious
piece of his adopted country.

The embodiment of 'smartness' in this latter context is the truly
amazing figure of Zephaniah Scadder, agent for the Eden Land
Corporation. 'Scadder' suggests a sort of snake, a phenomenon
in which Eden is richer even than its biblical archetype, and also a
mode of scanning for victims or clients. 'Zephaniah', of course,
was an Old Testament prophet who predicted universal destruction:
'And I will bring distress upon men, that they shall walk like blind

men . . . and will make Nineveh desolation . . .' Scadder is as good as his namesake's word. He has to be flattered and persuaded into selling Martin the least concession, and represents Eden as anything but desirable – requesting him to call back in a fortnight, assuring him he won't like it when he gets there, and requiring not to be blamed if the territory shouldn't happen to fit. In one sense, then, Zephaniah is not a false prophet; though the whole thing is an elaborate confidence trick whereby a would-be dupe actually talks himself into making a purchase. And so Martin leaves Mr Scadder in his temporary-looking office, with his empty desk and rusted files, quietly rocking his time away as he waits – like a Bad Samaritan – for another victim to fall into his clutches. I ought to add that Scadder has the face of Janus; one profile turned towards the world in an expression of paralytic gravity, the other independently set in a lasting sneer. Janus, of course, was the god of doorways; and this one guards the gate to Eden.

For the rendering of this settlement, Dickens used his experiences of Cairo, which he had seen in a boat-journey along the Mississippi. Unlike the letter about the newsboy incident, Dickens's original note is by no means heated upon its subject. The traveller is pained by the blight he sees around him; but, still, the settlement is no more than a point on his journey.

I have not seen six cabins out of six hundred, where the windows have been whole. Old hats, old clothes, old boards, old fragments of blanket and paper, are stuffed into the broken glass; and their air is misery and desolation. It pains the eye to see the stumps of great trees thickly strewn in every field of wheat; and never to lose the eternal swamp and dull morass, with hundreds of rotten trunks, of elm and pine and sycamore and logwood steeped in its unwholesome water. . . .

This, in *American Notes*, is worked into a description that formalises the scene. It is, in fact, moralised as a warning to the reader. But the indignation is somehow abstract; that of the recording angel rather than the satirist.

A dismal swamp on which the half-built houses rot away: cleaned here and there for the space of a few yards; and teeming, then, with rank unwholesome vegetation, in whose baleful shade the wretched wanderers who are tempted hither, droop and die, and lay their bones; the hateful Mississippi circling and eddying before it, and turning off upon its southern course a slimy monster hideous to behold; a hotbed of disease, an ugly sepulchre, a grave uncheered by any gleam of promise; a place without one single quality on earth or air or water, to commend it: such is this dismal Cairo.

That last cadence sounds as though it was thought out too carefully; and the paragraph, as a whole, piles phrase upon phrase in an effort to reach a climax of denunciation. Carlyle, we may feel, rides again. But the prose is too stylized to be moving. We miss the personal vision. Details are certainly recorded, but they have no organic connection, one with another. This is decent documentary, but a little too rhetorical for its purpose.

However, between this passage and its fictional parallel in *Martin Chuzzlewit* intervened the reviewers who had called Dickens a conceited cockney. The rage that informs what amounts to a massive rewriting of the Letters had that personal anguish at its root. The result is that the language in which Dickens describes Eden burns with an indignation so hot that the details observed by the traveller fuse into one composite image of decay. The particulars are anthropomorphized all in the same direction; so that everything growing in that wilderness is seen metaphorically as humanoid, indeed, but irretrievably malformed and crippled.

A flat morass, bestrewn with fallen timber; a marsh on which the good growth of the earth seemed to have been wrecked and cast away, that from its decomposing ashes vile and ugly things might rise; where the very trees took the aspect of huge weeds, begotten of the slime from which they sprang, by the hot sun that burnt them up; where fatal maladies, seeking whom they might infect, came forth at night, in misty shapes, and creeping out upon the waters, haunted them like spectres until day; where even the blessed sun, shining down on festering elements of corruption and disease became a horror; this was the realm of Hope through which they moved.

The fallen trees prefigure the collapse of many who venture into this settlement. And the trees that still are able to grow malfunction like weeds and so suggest the diseases that will warp and sap the physique of such adventurers as survive. Moreover, the diseases themselves are anthropomorphized – they creep out in misty shapes like ghastly caricatures of the live things they seek to infect. So far, the difference in technique between this, on the one hand, and the letters from which it derives, is fairly clear. But there is one further difference, and it is crucial. The people who shudder with the agues of Eden are not tourists passing through, but settlers, doomed to remain there.

Eden is the climax of the American chapters: the wilderness behind the show of civilization. It is the unsound backing of American society; the Big Lie festering quietly, behind the garish frontage that lures the immigrant into the New World.

Zephaniah Scadder, Colonel Diver, Jefferson Brick, Major Pawkins, La Fayette Kettle, General Choke, the Mother of the Modern Gracchi, Hannibal Chollop, Elijah Pogram – the very names suggest the fantastic menagerie of noise, dirt and brag exposed by these American chapters. The characters, unlike those in the rest of *Martin Chuzzlewit*, stay very much within their frame of reference; cannot, indeed, be separated from it. And behind the noisy bars and spittoons of the town rise the sluggish mists of Eden.

This is the most advanced writing Dickens had achieved so far. The American chapters are far more than an indictment of one country, whatever the personal rancour that proved their dynamic. It is hard to discern a genuine theme through the fantasy and euphoria that characterize the rest of *Martin Chuzzlewit*. But in the American episodes we have a battle in Dickens's incessant war against the dehumanizing tendency of institutions. And what is satirized as 'Bumbledom' in *Oliver Twist* and 'Wiglomeration' in *Bleak House*, Dickens has chosen here to call 'America'.

VIII   Martin Chuzzlewit (1843-44)

Dickens seems to have had unusual difficulty in getting *Martin Chuzzlewit* started. Neither title nor story had been determined in America. And in the autumn of 1842, when he had promised to start the novel, Dickens went with a party of his friends on an expedition to Cornwall. He may have been seeking inspiration; if so, it came grudgingly. The first concrete mention of the book appears in a letter to Forster dated 12 November, and the uncertainty is manifest. Dickens knew that his hero was to be called Martin, but whether Sweezleback, Chuzzletoe or Chubblewig – among other possibilities – had not decided itself. Later he drafted a title which is also indicative of the projected ground-plan of the book: 'The Life and Adventure of Martin Chuzzlewig, his family, friends and enemies. Comprising all his wills and his ways. With an historical record of what he did and what he didn't. The whole forming a complete key to the house of Chuzzlewig.'

It is clear from this that the finished novel differs from the original conception in more than the choice of the hero's name. The early chapters as we have them conform, in part, to the ground-plan. Scenes such as the family gathering of the Chuzzlewits show in some detail characters who may originally have been intended to play an important role in the novel, but who have to wait till chapter the last before they reappear. In much the same way, the plot of the novel shifts in emphasis after the first couple of chapters from Old Martin, his wills and his ways, to young Martin's wanderings in the Old and New Worlds.

The scope of the novel is therefore broadened considerably from its ground-plan. In bulk alone it is among the largest of Dickens's works, and it has more variety of scene and character than any. In a way, this proves to be its undoing. There is writing in *Martin Chuzzlewit* as brilliant as any achieved by Dickens, but it would be very difficult to say what, as a whole, the book is about.

From his various letters and comments, Dickens seems to have had the idea at first of exhibiting the vice of selfishness as manifested through all the branches of a large family. The scheme foundered in its very detail. Selfishness is an abstract concept, and any attempts to make it concrete will take on many different forms. Moreover, the more compelling of those forms are liable to take over, in the shape of individual characters, and assert their independence vigorously. Therefore we can see, in Dickens's act of writing the novel, the fiction refining itself away from its original mould.

The trouble is that this refinement takes place in ways so various that no structure could possibly bring them all together. The strands of plot each have their individual atmosphere and in tone, as well as in action, diverge from each other; the characters are in themselves highly individual, which means that their relationships, one with another, are mostly tenuous; so that, while full of striking scenes and distended humours, the novel is amorphous.

One problem was that Dickens as a man was developing rapidly, and that his technique could not keep up with him. Some parts of his vision already anticipated Dostoevsky, Kafka and Orwell, yet the framework of *Martin Chuzzlewit* is still based on the old-style picaresque novel. This is particularly true of the main strand of the plot.

Young Martin Chuzzlewit antagonizes his grandfather by falling in love with the latter's ward. He joins his grandfather's cousin, Seth Pecksniff, as an architectural student. But Pecksniff, in his turn, joins forces with the grandfather, and rejects the young man. Therefore the young man goes off to America. So far all this is conventional enough: grandfather's will, lovely but penniless ward, scheming villain, and even America – which had proved a convenient dumping-ground for characters long before those of Dickens.

One has to admit that the American episode speaks with a life of its own. But the tone has changed, drastically, from quasi-realistic fiction to satire and allegory. Young Martin is no longer the picaresque hero, but rather a Pilgrim, a Gulliver, an Alice in Blunderland, a passive consciousness whose reactions index the evils and failures of a corrupt society. The whole episode stands by itself as a book in its own right.

When Martin returns to England, the tone of the picaro resumes, but not his wanderings. On the contrary, he fetches up in much the same manner as Nicholas Nickleby in the counting-house. After a brief period, during which it is not clear how he earns his bread, he is taken back – quite literally – to grandfather's bosom; acquiring the ward, of course, as well. Nobody is going to get very excited about that.

But, in intention at least, this is the book's main strand of action, and its dependence upon this strand brings about much of its structural incoherence. The trouble is that Young Martin doesn't represent anything very much, not even selfishness. Characters far more compelling than he pursue their schemes at home; and so we have the pattern of the villain minding the plot, with which *Nicholas Nickleby* and *The Old Curiosity Shop* have familiarized us.

In this case, the villain is Mr Pecksniff. He it is who poisons the old man's mind against his grandson and seeks to humour him into a state of imbecility so that he can take control of the Chuzzlewit fortunes. But this gives no idea of the magnitude of the character. Pecksniff's schemes are relatively ineffective; the personality himself is sublime.

At first the comedy is a little heavy-handed: Pecksniff warms his back 'as if it were a widow's back, or an orphan's back, or an enemy's back, or a back that any less excellent man would have suffered to be cold'. But, as the book goes on, Pecksniff becomes a presence existing in his own right. We first see him in his glory presiding over the Chuzzlewit gathering, and it is quite apparent why the family at large cannot be the subject of a book: Pecksniff will not let them. Sketched out indeed they are, some in detail, but, when one of them calls him a hypocrite, Pecksniff sets him down superbly, speaking through his daughter to do so:

Charity, my dear, when I take my chamber candlestick tonight, remind me to be more than usually particular in praying for Mr Anthony Chuzzlewit; who has done me an injustice.

The family gathering achieves nothing, does nothing; simply acts as a foil for Pecksniff's eloquence. His very hesitation has an unction of its own –

Why, the truth is, my dear, that I am at a loss for a word. The name of those fabulous animals (pagan, I regret to say), who used to sing in the water, has quite escaped me.

That 'pagan, I regret to say' is a clue to the quintessential Pecksniff. He develops his utterance throughout the book from the hint afforded here: something which combines a religiose rhetoric with the odd lapse into bathos.

You find me in my garden-dress . . . Primitive, my dear Sir; for, if I am not mistaken, Adam was the first of all our calling. *My* Eve, I grieve to say, is no more, Sir; but I do a little bit of Adam still.

The magniloquence of his speech is that of a melodious snore, and is a remarkably dramatic use of an insensitivity to the nuances of language. He tends very much to monologue – an index at once of his lack of response to human beings and of the moral failings of his character. But the monologue is reinforced by the narrative's passing descriptions of his physique and attitude. His manner is soft and oily, he himself sleek, though not corpulent, the breath of slander passes from him as from a polished surface, he suffers tears of honesty to ooze out of his eyes, his very embrace is that of an affectionate boa-constrictor, and, even when he shouts, he does so with stentorian blandness. However, there are times when he dwindles – as when he is rejected indignantly by Old Martin's ward, and seems to be trying to hide himself within himself. But, paradoxically, his physical presence is even more thoroughly set before us on such occasions. So one can truthfully say that, aesthetically speaking, Pecksniff is never deflated. As a dramatic figure, he dominates almost every scene he enters: the Tartuffe of nineteenth-century fiction. Poor Tom Pinch discovers his star, Pecksniff, to be a mass of putrid vapour; but he is not allowed to have his tragedy out. Counting up the meagre earnings in lieu of notice, Pecksniff remarks outrageously 'I wouldn't have believed it, Mr Chuzzlewit, if a fiery serpent had proclaimed it from the top of Salisbury Cathedral'. And even when Tom leaves the house, a pathetic figure clutching a carpet-bag, his thunder is stolen by the spectacle of Pecksniff, standing at the top of the steps, his hand stretched out as though to say 'Go forth!'

However, Pecksniff has altogether too much elbow-room to make
very much sense of the action as a whole. Structurally, he ought to be
an adjunct to the main plot: a scheming villain to set the two Martins
at loggerheads. But his feel and presence are so great that he attracts
all the interest to himself, thus rendering the plot lop-sided. Even
in the denouement, when he is publicly exposed and denounced, the
attention is on him: his gloss visibly fading, his voice, however, no
less resonant –' "I have been struck this day with a walking-stick (which
I have every reason to believe has knobs upon it) on that delicate and
exquisite portion of the human anatomy, the brain. Several blows
have been inflicted, Sir, without a walking-stick, upon that tenderer
portion of my frame; my heart." ... and gave himself two or three
little knocks upon the breast ... as if he were answering ... the tinkling
hammer of his conscience.' What attention can get we give Old
Martin, Young Martin, Mary, Tom Pinch et al. in such a presence?
Pecksniff exists for his own sake, and not to advance the plot. We
welcome his presence as comic relief because the main plot of *Martin
Chuzzlewit* is something we can well bear to be relieved of. And it is
very appropriate that a mock benefactor should occur in a book
dedicated to the great philanthropist, Dickens's friend, Angela Burdett-
Coutts. But it must be admitted that Pecksniff's more limited counterpart, Chadband in *Bleak House,* serves a dramatic function better.

More inherently interesting than the main plot of *Martin Chuzzlewit* is what may be termed the sub-plot. It was resented by the early
readers of the book on the grounds of its containing such sordid characters as Jonas Chuzzlewit and Montague Tigg. More to the point,
its exploration of human morbidity leaves out a good deal of human
potential. But the insight into the psychology of the criminal which it
manifests anticipates some crucial developments in the twentieth
century.

Nothing is more symptomatic of the way in which *Martin Chuzzlewit* grew under Dickens's hands than the power and momentum
gathered by this sub-plot as it moves forward. At first Jonas is just
another Chuzzlewit, a sketch for a griffin, a mere miser's son. He
has not gained much in complexity when we find him, some chapters
on, taunting his father, in the old man's dusty counting-house, for
lingering too long in the world. He attempts to hasten his father's
departure, and indeed thinks he has done so; and, once master of

the estate, gets himself engaged to Pecksniff's daughter, Mercy. But Jonas is a man without mercy himself and on whom mercy is wasted. Tantalized by the young girl during their engagement, he terrifies her into subjugation after they are married. The tone in which the relationship is conveyed implies the classic partnership of sadist and masochist. The whole action is accompanied by the choric refrain of his father's old clerk: first in imbecile admiration, 'your own son, sir', then, the same words in the third person, 'his own son', forming a persistent reproach.

Jonas is indeed his father's son, and has inherited or learned the old man's rapacity and cunning. This brings him into contact with another villain who is his polar opposite. From then on both Jonas and the sub-plot gain in interest and complexity. Jonas is physically unattractive, socially ill-at-ease, and takes his revenge upon the world he fears in ceaselessly aggressive behaviour; when thwarted, he retreats into depression. Tigg, on the other hand, believes himself to be sexually irresistible, invents all manner of exhibitionistic roles for himself, and despises the society that Jonas fears. Neither of them can understand the psychology of the other; in that lies their respective weakness, which in its turn brings about the crisis of their plot.

The whole saga of Tigg is masterly. We see him first as the raffish confidence-man of the early chapters; later, as the bejewelled and dandified Chairman of the Anglo-Bengalee Life Insurance Company. Literally, he has turned himself inside-out; from Montague Tigg to Tigg Montague – a new name to go with his new appearance and status. Yet the resemblances are kept clearly before us. His later image, like his earlier one, has an air of disguise, of play-acting, about it. Of the unregenerate Tigg, a servant remarks 'Yes, I see *him*! I could see him a little better, if he'd shave himself, and get his hair cut'. And of the transformation, Tigg Montague, Esquire, another servant says – this time in admiration – 'You can't see his face for his whiskers, and you can't see his whiskers for the dye upon 'em'. Either way, you can't see him, but what is despicable at one stage is thought admirable at another. And both comments, moreover, turn upon the definition of what is a gentleman; a theme to be taken up, crucially, in *Great Expectations*. It is not accidental that Tigg is compared, in passing, with Peter the Wild Boy – a savage discovered

in the woods of Hanover, and brought across to England, but never
civilized. It would take more than a hairdresser and tailor to civilize
Tigg the mountebank into an aristocratic Montague; he is still a
wild man in society, but pursues his ends in a larger way. It is true
that his vocabulary has gone up a notch or two in the social scale,
and he cajoles rather than bludgeons; but his credit is illusory, his
speculations fraudulent, his entire frontage an irresponsible bluff.

Montague comes to grief in failing to estimate Jonas correctly.
He can bamboozle the miser's son into buying shares in his company,
and blackmail him with the charge of poisoning his father; what he
cannot do, as a persistent fantasist, is to anticipate Jonas's aggression. The stratagem by which Montague prevents Jonas leaving the
country seals his own fate, too.

From then on, the relationship between Jonas and Montague is
that between murderer and victim. The association sensitizes both
characters in a manner never foreshadowed in the original conception, or even the early chapters. There is, for one thing, the extraordinary richness of their respective dream imagery. Montague
dreams that he is barricading a door against some nameless horror,
helped by an old school-friend whose name he has forgotten. The
unknown helper, is, of course, called Tigg – the name Montague has
buried – and the bloody smear on his head betokens a premonition
of danger. Behind the door in real life is Jonas, plucking up courage
to come in and commit murder.

Jonas, too, has a dream which includes an alter ego; in this case,
it is not a defined character but one that fluctuates and alters in personality. The dream is full of anxiety symbolism: streets, identified
by signs in a language he cannot understand, so precipitous that he
can only bridge them by descending ladders much too short for the
purpose or by climbing ropes that swing and set off warning bells.
His clothes are all wrong for the occasion, and the occasion is felt
to be the Day of Judgment. In Montague's world, one has a helper,
even if it is only a projection of oneself; in the world of Jonas, even
the self is accused.

The whole sequence is worth careful study. It tends to detach
itself, in narrative technique and tone, from the rest of the book:
as Chapter XXVII-VIII; XXXVIII; the latter half of XL to XLII;
XLIV; the latter half of XLVI; XLII; XLIV; the latter half of XLVI;

XLVII; and LI. Certain characters from other strands of the novel tend to intervene, and one cannot claim for the sub-plot the self-substantive quality of the American chapters. But it gains in cohesion towards the end, and is best read as a more subtle rendering of the Sikes-Nancy situation; or, if you like, a foreshadowing of *Crime and Punishment*, the Headstone chapters of *Our Mutual Friend*, and *The Mystery of Edwin Drood*.

But, in giving free rein to so dark a vision of the world, Dickens, in effect, took leave of his novel. There is no theme in common between Martin's wanderings and the murder of Montague. Invoking a concept such as 'selfishness' will not do here; it cannot bridge the gulf in tone between extrovert picaresque and psychological drama.

I have said that characters from other strands of the novel intertwine themselves into the sub-plot: Pecksniff and Old Martin, in particular, make decisive appearances. But the most extraordinary intervention is made by a character who hardly belongs to the book at all, if you think in terms of plot, and yet who is the best remembered person in it.

The role of Sarah Gamp in the novel is basically that of a nurse who is brought in to look after Old Chuffey, Jonas's imbecile clerk, and who, by a coincidence, also nurses Lewsome, the man who compounded the drug that Jonas bought as poison for his father. She therefore has in her hand a considerable body of information about this murder, or attempted murder as it turns out, though of course has no idea what to do with it. Those who know Lewsome and who are determined to bring Jonas to book use her as a means of getting at Chuffey; her role in the novel is as peripheral as that.

But her character is blown up to the most startling dimensions. If the euphoria that went into the making of Pecksniff blurred any chance of a theme in *his* part of the novel, what are we to say of Sarah Gamp? Even Pecksniff, who dominates all else, shrinks before her. She is based upon a sufficiently odd character who nursed a companion of Dickens's friend, Miss Coutts. This person had the remarkable habit of rubbing her nose along the fender, as well as other such Gampish habits as drinking gin, taking snuff, and supping up vinegar with a fork. But these details, odd though they are, don't add up to the quintessential Gamp. To believe Dickens's Preface, he had a social purpose in creating this portrait of a sickroom attendant before the age of professional nursing. But in a letter to Forster he was perhaps more frank – 'I mean to make a mark with her'. The result was a projection from an assemblage of realistic details into sheer fantasy; surely, the greatest comic character Dickens ever created.

The effect is only partly one of physical presence. Mrs Gamp is represented as being elderly, fat and snuffy, with a red nose and a moist eye constantly turning itself up by way of emphasis. But she is really created in her accessories – a rusty black gown, shawl similar, bonnet, bundle, a pair of pattens, and an umbrella. This latter, especially, has a life of its own.

It was a troublesome matter to adjust Mrs Gamp's luggage to her satisfaction; for every package belonging to that lady had the inconvenient property of requiring to be put in a boot by itself, and to have no other luggage near it, on pain of actions at law for heavy damages against the proprietors of the coach. The umbrella with the circular patch was particularly hard to be got rid of, and several times thrust out its battered brass nozzle from improper crevices and chinks, to the great terror of the other passengers.

Mrs Gamp, then, is an assemblage of properties. More than that, though, she is always in action. See her, for example, in attendance upon one of her patients.

She moralized in the same vein until her glass was empty, and then administered the patient's medicine by the simple process of clutching his windpipe to make him gasp, and immediately pouring it down his throat.

She is thus at an advantage compared with Pecksniff, for her professional avocations are of an active character. They provide her, too, with a wealth of anecdote, projecting her beyond the immediate present.

I never see a poor dear creetur took so strange in all my life, except a patient much about the same age, as I once nussed, which his calling was the custom-'us, and his name was Mrs Harris's own father, as pleasant a singer, Mr Chuzzlewit, as ever you heard, with a voice like a Jew's harp in the bass notes, that it took six men to hold at such times, foaming frightful.

It will be seen that this utterance is distinctive; speech rather than prose; consisting of long sentences unravelling through clauses tenuously associated both in syntax and meaning and full of floating ambiguities; usually, moreover, ending – as here – with unexpected abruptness. They exhibit, too, a perverse delight in circumstances that to non-professionals would seem revolting.

Don't I know as that dear woman is expecting of me at this minnit, Mr Westlock, and is a lookin' out of winder down the street, with little Tommy Harris in her arms, as calls me his own Gammy, and truly calls, for bless the mottled little legs of that there precious child (like Canterbury Brawn his own dear father says, which so they are) his own I have been, ever since I found him, Mr Westlock, with his small red worsted shoe a gurgling in his throat, where he had put it in his play, a chick, wile they was leavin' of him on the floor a looking for it through the ouse and him a choakin' sweetly in the parlour!

This Mrs Harris who keeps recurring is a fiction of Sarah's own, usually brought into the conversation as a booster to her ego and uttering encomia greatly to her advantage – '"Mrs Gamp," she says, "if ever there was a sober creetur to be got at eighteen pence a day for working people, and three and six for gentlefolks – night-watching being an extra charge – you are that inwalable person."' As all this will show, Mrs Gamp, like Mr Pecksniff, tends towards monologue; and monologue which brings in, like his, a great deal of ludicrously misplaced biblical allusion – for instance, 'Rich folks may ride on camels, but it ain't so easy for them to see out of a needle's eye.' Necessarily, this reduces other characters to foils or stooges, and in this way she floats herself even farther out of context. In a sense, then, Pecksniff and Mrs Gamp come from the same mould – perhaps modelled on the solo turns of the actor Charles Mathews – and exhibit a similar sense of euphoria. But it is not a good thing for the architecture of a novel when its two most distinctive characters are gargoyles.

Some symptoms of structure there are, certainly, and in one or two instances they prefigure developments in later novels. For instance there is, as A.E. Dyson has pointed out, a persistent dualism throughout *Martin Chuzzlewit*. There are two Martins, of course, old and young, Montague Tigg is paralleled by his other self, Tigg Montague; while Jonas Chuzzlewit is so divided a personality that, when he comes back from murdering this same Tigg, he half expects to find himself asleep in his own bed.

Or again: some of the plot-links are forged with commendable skill. Young Bailey, the boy at Todgers's boarding house, is a means of drawing together a number of threads in the action. He leaves

Todgers's to serve Montague, and so in one move links up the Pecksniffs, Jonas and the Anglo-Bengalee company; and, by a rather more laboured connection, relates to Poll Sweedlepipe, the hairdresser, who in his turn is the landlord of Sarah Gamp. Doctor Jobling, too, attends Anthony Chuzzlewit, meets Pecksniff at his funeral, and recommends Jonas to Montague. Rather more forced is the matter of Nadgett, Montague's secret agent, who proves to be the landlord of Tom Pinch, Pecksniff's former assistant and Jonas's enemy. And sometimes Dickens himself despairs of making essential connections: as in the unsatisfactory jolt from the knocking at Mr Pecksniff's door at the end of Chapter XX to the noise of an American railway train which begins Chapter XXI. This, moreover, together with the two chapters immediately following, is very much an American interpolation, since Chapter XXIV starts exactly where Chapter XX left off, as though the American episode had never happened. It gives the American chapters a cohesion of their own, as I remarked earlier, but badly disrupts the narrative in England.

More than in any previous novel, Dickens seems to have been under the control of his readers; or, at least, sensitive to the sales graphs of his serial, which amounts to the same thing. Thus, when the circulation began to drop, he sent Young Martin off to America; the decision was fortunate, so far as the episode was concerned, though not especially happy for the novel as a whole. More of a lift to circulation was given by Mrs Gamp: her evident popularity may have led Dickens to overplay her in his hand, so far as the total conduct of the novel was concerned.

Martin Chuzzlewit, then, is an anthology just as much as *Pickwick*; except that here the stories run parallel to one another, rather than in succession. The structure is not conceivable that could contain not only the picaresque wanderings of Young Martin and the psychological sub-plot of Jonas and Montague, but also the sour satire of the American chapters, the monologues of Pecksniff, and the irrepressible farce of Mrs Gamp and her friends. No residual theme can be distilled from so various a spread of humour, incident and atmosphere.

Certain familiar Dickens properties are missing. *Martin Chuzzlewit* is almost the only novel without a prison, though the choking claustrophobia of Jonas's room makes up for that. It is – more mercifully

– the only one of the earlier novels without a Mary Hogarth figure, though the unearthly goodness of Tom Pinch and Mary Graham in part supplies that want. It does not, either, sport a pathetic death-scene; that of Anthony Chuzzlewit is, rather, a masterpiece in the grotesque. No wonder the early readers were lukewarm; they were certainly not getting the mixture as before. There are fewer 'positive' characters in this book than in any except the still gloomier *Hard Times*. Instead of Mr Cheeryble or Mr Brownlow, we get obstinate Old Martin, grasping Old Anthony, oily Pecksniff, sullen Jonas and glittering Montague. For all its faults of structure, *Martin Chuzzlewit* must be accounted a major work. It triumphantly exhibits a range of villainy and duplicity hardly to be equalled, outside Balzac, in nineteenth-century fiction.

IX   Christmas Books

A Christmas Carol (1843)

The Chimes (1845)

The Cricket on the Hearth (1846)

The Battle of Life (1847)

The Haunted Man (1848)

The sales of *Martin Chuzzlewit* had not increased sufficiently to meet Dickens's growing commitments. Not just his wife and by now four children, but his father and brothers were dependent upon him; and his sister-in-law, Georgina, kept house. What he had wanted to do was to fade away from the public eye and live abroad for a year. As it was, he launched himself into a fresh enterprise: the first of what came to be known as his Christmas Books.

A Christmas Carol was the work of such time as Dickens had spare from writing two numbers of *Martin Chuzzlewit*. Though it was undertaken for cash, the daemon took over and the work was prosecuted with remarkable intensity. It was instantaneously popular: the entire edition of six thousand copies sold out on the first day, and two thousand more were bespoken by the trade before the tale was even reprinted. But for Dickens's insistence on a high quality of production and illustration, it would have netted its author a small fortune.

And there can be no doubt that *A Christmas Carol* is a remarkable work. One can see why it has always appealed so widely: its wish-fulfilment has something in common with that perennial fantasy, *Cinderella*. The story of a grim old miser turned into a fairy god-father corresponds to so many childish dreams; based, like so much else of Dickens, on a child's conception of his parent in moments of wrath, as ogre. The tale has so often been lambasted for its senti-mentality that perhaps one should point out there is some very good writing in it. The opening is characteristically brilliant – a splendidly off-hand rendering of speech rhythm.

Marley was dead: to begin with. There is no doubt whatever about that. The register of his burial was signed by the clergyman, the clerk, the undertaker, and the chief mourner. Scrooge signed it: and Scrooge's name was good upon 'Change for anything he chose to put his hand to. Old Marley was as dead as a door-nail.

Right away, we are given the theme, which, oddly enough, was to prove central to Dickens's later work; the gap between institution, on the one hand, and personal sympathy, on the other. We have seen instances of this theme in the early chapters of *Oliver Twist*; from now on it is to become increasingly a dominating concern in Dickens.

One should not, therefore, think of Dickens as a crypto-Marxist. Many of his perceptions were those of Marx, and his community of vision with that of the Engels of *The Condition of the Working Classes* is really quite startling. But his attitude towards what he saw was quite different. As George Orwell remarked, it was beyond Dickens to realize that, given the existing form of society, certain evils *cannot* be remedied. The fact that he acted as adviser to a host of Miss Coutts's private charities should establish this, and it is certainly acted out over and over again in his books. To some extent it is an abiding weakness: what happened to those without a fairy godfather to rescue them from prison or the workhouse? This question, never satisfactorily answered, accounts at once for the strength and the weakness of *A Christmas Carol*.

Scrooge as curmudgeon is brilliantly done. His utterance is not just harsh: he is a greatly superior Ralph Nickleby, with a sour humour of his own. He says to his nephew, indignantly, 'If I could work my will, every idiot who goes about with "Merry Christmas" on his lips, should be boiled with his own pudding, and buried with a stake of holly through his heart'. He stands up valiantly to the ghost of his partner, Marley: 'You may be an undigested bit of beef, a blot of mustard, a crumb of cheese, a fragment of an under-done potato. There's more of gravy than of grave about you, whatever you are'.

But he is intimidated by the awful howl that the ghost sets up at this – mere bullying, we may think it – and farther by the Spirits that wait upon him in the night. Each focuses upon Christmas: past, present and future. The past is psychologically convincing: Scrooge is shown as a neglected child with a brutal father. The spirit also shows him as an adult though there is an awkward gap between the gay young apprentice of his early years and the businessman whose fiancée gives him up because of his fondness for money. The second spirit shows him what other people are doing at Christmas, notably his wretched clerk, Bob Cratchit, whose scanty dinner is enhanced by the affection of his family; and his nephew, Fred, who throws a party and drinks the old man's health in his absence. The third spirit shows the sordidness of Scrooge's death – his laundress selling his clothes, his acquaintance in the city remarking 'Old Scratch has got his own', and the only people feeling emotion about his death being a couple of debtors who see this as a reprieve. But the conversion of Scrooge, as a result of all this, is rather thin: the characteristics which made him distinctive are lost, and he turns into another of Dickens's benevolent old gentlemen, substitute fathers, rushing up and down, half smiles and half tears, seeking whom they can succour.

The fable, perhaps because of this, has a built-in appeal to the public: for this moral vision, possibly, but also for its gross and earthy evocation of Christmas parties and Christmas shops. These give full scope to Dickens's gifts for anthropomorphizing inanimate objects –

The fruiterers were radiant in their glory. There were great, round, potbellied baskets of chestnuts, shaped like the waistcoats of jolly old gentlemen, lolling at the doors, and tumbling out into the street in their apoplectic opulence. There were ruddy, brown-faced, broad-girthed Spanish Onions, shining in the fatness of their growth like Spanish Friars; and winking from their shelves in wanton slyness at the girls as they went by, and glanced demurely at the hung-up mistletoe.

What is good in the story is this hallucinatory fancy of Dickens, often a symptom of incipient exhaustion, which invades and irradiates a weary reality. What is bad is the tendency to sketch in an archetype – the death of Cratchit's son, Tiny Tim, is one such example – as a means of triggering off an emotion already set up in us.

The need created by *A Christmas Carol* was fed by four subsequent stories written between *Martin Chuzzlewit* and the early stages of *Dombey and Son*. Although they were popular enough in their day, they have not worn well. Their main interest is that they show certain subterranean themes in Dickens attempting to reach the surface.

The social consciousness that had been exposed in *Oliver Twist* and in the Dotheboys Hall sequence of *Nicholas Nickleby* is very definitely to the fore in *The Chimes*. He wrote this in Genoa in 1844, and had some trouble in beginning the story: the trigger, in fact, proved to be the bells of the churches which clanged in a high wind one night. Unfortunately the story is something of a mess. The least convincing bit of *A Christmas Carol* was the passage where Scrooge looks into the future and sees doom impending over the Cratchit family; a doom which, however, turns out to be illusory. Now it is upon just such an idea as this that *The Chimes* is built. Toby Veck, a porter, meets some uncommonly nasty capitalists and utilitarians in the course of his work, and, falling asleep, conceives that their worst predictions have come true. The vision is one of a world where poor people cannot afford to marry and when the weakest must either go to the wall or have their lives completely run for them. There is some strong incidental satire: Alderman Cute says 'I am a plain man, and a practical man; and I go to work in a plain and practical way.... There's a great deal of nonsense talked about Want – "hard up", you know: that's the phrase, isn't it? ha! ha! ha! – and I intend to Put It Down. There's a certain amount of cant in vogue about Starvation, and I mean to Put It Down! That's all! Lord bless you ... you may Put Down anything among this sort of people, if you only know the way to set about it.' This was based upon Alderman Peter Laurie, who wanted to legislate against suicide, and who was made the subject of an article Dickens wrote for Forster's paper, *The Examiner* (22 April 1848). It looks forward to the ferocious satire of Gradgrind and Bounderby, and shows Dickens's increasing awareness of misery in industrial conditions. Kathleen Tillotson has pointed out the crucial influence upon Dickens of Hengist Horne's *Second Report on Children's Employment in Mines and Factories*, but this and similar blue books took a little time to be imaginatively absorbed. So there is a tremendous gap between the social satire and the sentimentally-comic figures of Trotty, his daughter and his prospective son-in-law; to say nothing of the obtrusive imagery of the bells – they may have sparked the story off, but they are not intrinsically related to its theme. The setting is intermittently powerful; the figures, however, do not belong to the stage Dickens has dressed for them. There is nothing in *The Chimes* that is not much better done in *Bleak House* and *Hard Times*.

The Cricket on the Hearth, 1845, which came next, was rescued from the conception of a magazine – *The Cricket* – which never materialized. Here Dickens made the crucial mistake of developing the sentimental rather than the social side of his vision. With unconscious irony, Dickens dedicated the little volume to Lord Jeffrey, the uncritical admirer of Little Nell. It outsold all the other Christmas books, however, and one can see why. Powerful stock responses are elicited by the steady repetition of words like 'snug', 'hearth', 'cosy', 'home'; and the emblem of the chirping cricket as a household god is something which the Victorian reader was unaffectedly eager to worship. But the story is evanescent: the middle-aged carrier thinks his wife is carrying on an intrigue with a stranger. He is wrong, of course: the stranger has only come home in disguise to claim his bride – a quite different girl – from the elderly toymaker to whom she has been affianced. The only moment in the story that has a glimpse of Dickens's vision is the passage when the toymaker's assistant reveals to his blind daughter the fact that he has been deceiving her all the while with tales of false glamour – that their home, which he depicted as a palace, is a hovel, their furniture, sticks, and he himself, a tired old man. Underlying the apparent euphoria is, once more, a deep and abiding weariness.

The Battle of Life was begun under peculiar difficulties at the same time as *Dombey and Son*: in 1846. It was written in Switzerland and is dedicated to Dickens's English friends there. But none of his works gave him more trouble. He had difficulty in realizing his original fancy, a battlefield playing an integral part in a realistic story. When he started writing, he had to do what he had never done before – cancel a first scene. At times he thought of abandoning the venture altogether; and even when it was two-thirds finished, dreamed of it as 'a series of characters impossible to be got to rights or got out of'. And when it had been completed, Dickens told Lytton that he had not seen the full capacity of his theme until it was too late to think of another plot. He meant, perhaps, that the basic idea would have done well for a full-length novel.

Certainly the underlying theme fails to align itself with the sentimental love story here unfolded. The sisters, Grace and Marion, are in love with the same man, Alfred; but Grace, who does not tell her love, loves him the more deeply. Marion herself becomes conscious that she inclines towards another man, and she disappears, ostensibly with him. After a time her sister marries Alfred; and, after another lapse of time, Marion comes back in maiden white – not having eloped at all, it appears. But she ends up, like her sister, marrying the man she loves. A great deal of suffering, it would seem, to little end.

But the underlying theme is far more interesting, albeit it can be seen only intermittently. The conception is of life as a ceaseless battle, never to be won, which leaves indelible marks that can never be healed. This is done in terms of a battlefield turned to cultivation, where green patches in the growing corn still hint at heaps of past heroes buried with their horses and enriching the ground with their clay. This theme is counterpointed by the cynicism of the girls' father, Doctor Jeddler, who regards life as a struggle devoid of meaning, each relationship as a joke, each event as an absurdity. But there is no way of mating this with the love story I have already described, and *The Battle of Life* must be accounted one of Dickens's most notable failures.

In aesthetic terms, perhaps *The Haunted Man* is no better. Dickens envisaged the theme as far back as 1846, at the same time as *The Battle of Life*, though the story was not written until the winter of 1848 – a time of great introspection on Dickens's part. The story suffers badly from structural incoherence and an imperfectly realized central character. The action, also, is too cerebral truly to be called dramatic. A learned Professor of Chemistry, whose life has been a wilderness, is visited by a phantom who is his mirror image. When reminded of his life by this phantom, he begs for oblivion, so that he can shut out his past wrongs. This gift is granted to him, together with the concomitant: that he will pass it on to those whom he meets. The only people proof against it are a waif from the streets, a wholly evil product of society, and the angelic serving-maid, Milly. The effect upon Redlaw is said to be a freezing-up and a deadening of his sympathies; since commonly we only sympathize with others from the knowledge of our own past sufferings.

A great deal of what I have said here is no more than an attempt to surmise the author's probable intention. Redlaw, for instance, does not seem much altered by this truncation of his faculties: he still goes around, dispensing charity, reprieving fallen women, visiting death-beds, and the like. This lack of contrast may be a result of imperfect realization of his character in the first place. What does come over as a difference is that the people Redlaw sees now exhibit themselves in their worst guises, though this need not be a result of the Phantom's gift. In fact, one does not see the connection between Redlaw losing his memory, others losing theirs, the general failure in sympathy, and the sudden exposure of everyone's least pleasant traits. It may follow logically, though I doubt it, but there is no imaginative link-up here. The main reason why we are likely to take an interest in the story now is that it affords clues to the welter of conflicting emotions in Dickens's mind at that time.

I am he, neglected in my youth, and miserably poor, who strove and suffered, and still strove and suffered, until I hewed out knowledge from the mine where it was buried, and made rugged steps thereof, for my worn feet to rest and rise on . . . No mother's self-denying love, no father's counsel aided *me* . . . My parents, at the best, were of that sort whose care soon ends, and whose duty is soon done; who cast their offspring loose, early, as birds do theirs; and, if they do well, claim the merit; and, if ill, the pity.

It is impossible not to feel, as Edgar Johnson has suggested, that behind this looms the blacking factory where Dickens worked as a boy. No wonder he allegorizes his unconscious conflict about suppressing his childhood experience into a bargain compounded with a ghost. The problem is clear: memories torment, but they alone teach; and to lose them may be to lose one's powers of empathy. As Dickens wrote in his fragment of autobiography, 'all these things have worked together to make me what I am'. The sentence might almost have come from *The Haunted Man* itself. It is therefore best seen as an allegory of the artist, who has not only to undergo suffering but to relive it in order to understand the sufferings of others and embody them in art.

Collectively, the Christmas Books amount to a brilliantly whimsical parable, an incipient social satire, two sentimental love stories – one with resonant undertones – and, finally, an imperfectly allegorized piece of autobiography. As literature, only *A Christmas Carol* can be said to have lasting merit. And, henceforward, Dickens chose to write Christmas stories on a much smaller scale and in collaboration with others. Yet these fictions have their place in Dickens's development: they show Dickens was beginning to separate off personal from dramatic elements. *The Haunted Man* is perhaps best seen as a stage on the progress to *David Copperfield*.

X   Letters on social questions (1846-50)

Pictures from Italy (1846)

In one sense or another, Dickens was a journalist all his life. Apart from his early work on the *Morning Chronicle*, he contributed to Forster's *Examiner* until 1850, when he founded his own magazine, *Household Words*. Farther than that, for a brief and lurid period, Dickens was the first editor of the *Daily News*.

The idea of founding a liberal newspaper had been in Dickens's mind for some time. His interest in social questions could be seen as early as 1836, when he published a pamphlet against Sabbath Observance, *Sunday Under Three Heads*. Though he had rejected three offers of parliamentary seats, he at one point entertained hopes of being a stipendiary magistrate. And the political climate of the time, with Peel's reluctance to repeal the Corn Laws and ameliorate industrial conditions, impelled Dickens into an enterprise for which he was ill-equipped. The editor of the *Morning Chronicle* had already asked him to be a staff contributor on that paper, but Dickens consulted Forster and the printing firm of Bradbury and Evans to see whether a new daily newspaper could not be started instead.

The *Daily News* began with a high-minded editorial by Dickens, saying that the newspaper would advocate 'Principles of Progress and Improvement, of Education, Civil and Religious Liberty, and Equal Legislation; Principles such as its Conductors believe the advancing spirit of the time requires, the Condition of the Country demands, and Justice, Reason and Experience legitimately sanction'.

But the paper ran into difficulties right away. The failure of one of its backers nearly wrecked the enterprise; and the fact that two others (Paxton and Walmsley) were financially interested in railways gave the paper an unsuitable bias towards railway news. Moreover, the printers were not used to the work of producing a daily paper; there was delay over the first number, and, when it came out, it proved to be badly put together. Still worse, one of these printers, Bradbury, persisted in interfering in Dickens's editorial functions. Dickens was not the man to brook opposition of any sort; after only seventeen days in the editorial chair, he resigned.

Dickens lived up to his ideas less as an editor than as the newspaper's star contributor. He began a series of 'Travelling Letters written on the Road' in the first issue. These, like *American Notes*, were based upon letters written chiefly to Forster. They were published in volume form as *Pictures from Italy*.

Taken as literature, they now seem rather flimsy. Dickens had little understanding of the visual arts, and, as far as natural beauties were concerned, he was happier painting the backcloth for a human drama than designing a landscape meant to stand in its own right. There is too much of this sort of writing.

The Villa Bagnerello: or the Pink Jail, a far more expressive name for the mansion: is in one of the most splendid situations imaginable. The noble bay of Genoa, with the deep blue Mediterranean, lies stretched out near at hand; monstrous old desolate houses and palaces are dotted all about; lofty hills, with their tops often hidden in the clouds, and with strong forts perched high up on their craggy sides, are close upon the left; and, in front, stretching from the walls of the house, down to a ruined chapel which stands upon the bold and picturesque rocks on the sea-shore, are green vineyards, where you may wander all day long in partial shade, through interminable vistas of grapes, trained on a rough trellis-work across the narrow paths.

The heavy dependence on the verb 'to be' and the predominance of the passive voice indicate slack and unfelt writing. The prose is littered with such conventional adjectives as 'splendid', 'noble', 'picturesque' which succeed in defining nothing. However, *Pictures from Italy* certainly has its moments. Some of the live bits look forward to *Little Dorrit*: one thinks of the quarantine at Nice or Dickens's description of Neapolitans gesticulating as they converse. The book is at its most entertaining, however, when it vouchsafes us a glimpse of the Englishman abroad.

Mr Davis always had a snuff-coloured greatcoat on, and carried a great green umbrella in his hand, and had a slow curiosity constantly devouring him, which prompted him to do extraordinary things, such as taking the covers off urns in tombs, and looking in at the ashes as if they were pickles – and tracing out inscriptions with the ferrule of his umbrella, and saying with intense thoughtfulness, 'Here's a B you see, and there's an R, and this is the way we goes on in; is it!'

One remembers this; and the farcical description of the confrontation of Napoleon with the governor of St Helena as enacted in a marionette show; and the portrait of a gentleman who was consumed with curiosity about the ritual portraying the Last Supper – 'Can any gentleman, in front there, see mustard on the table? Sir, will you oblige me! *Do* you see a Mustard-Pot?' It is as if Dickens had himself brought urban mannerisms abroad, and was happiest when he could indulge them. The uncommercial traveller only understood his home from which he started.

Far more worthy of attention are the 'Letters on Social Questions' Dickens wrote for the *Daily News*; on 'Capital Punishment', 'The Ragged Schools', and 'Crime and Education'. His views on the first of these are very progressive, and his comments upon the risk of executing innocent men anticipate the twentieth century, while the papers on education carry some harrowing descriptions of London's poverty.

Huddled together on a bench about the room, and shown out by some flaring candles stuck against the walls, were a crowd of boys, varying from mere infants to young men; sellers of fruit, herbs, lucifer-matches, flints; sleepers under the dry arches of bridges; young thieves and beggars – with nothing natural to youth about them: with nothing frank, ingenuous or pleasant in their faces; low-browed, vicious, cunning, wicked; abandoned of all help but this; speeding downward to destruction; and UNUTTERABLY IGNORANT. . . . This was the Class I saw at the Ragged School. ('Crime and Education')

The Ragged Schools were run by high-minded volunteers as a desperate stop-gap against the viciousness and ignorance of the working-classes. But Dickens points out how makeshift they were; for instance, they dared not even trust their pupils with books! Subjects such as this increasingly engaged Dickens's attention. After he had severed his connections with the *Daily News*, similar papers from his pen appeared in Forster's *Examiner*. His earlier pieces for this magazine had been mostly on literary topics, but the papers of the late 1840s have a different tone, taking over and deepening the social protest of the *Daily News*.

'Ignorance and Crime' (22 April 1848) relates lack of educational opportunity to criminal statistics, and is powerfully backed up by 'Ignorance and its Victims' (29 April 1848) – for the identification of which we are indebted to Alec Brice. Mr Brice also found for us a satiric piece entitled 'A Truly British Judge' (19 August 1848), showing a particularly unfeeling specimen of the judiciary vacillating between flogging, transporting and imprisoning a child aged ten who had stolen a purse containing five and threepence. And the hero of this piece, Mr Baron Platt, by a fortuitous coincidence was to figure largely in a remarkable group of four articles Dickens wrote about the Drouet case.

Bartholomew Drouet was, in his way, even more extraordinary a phenomenon than the prototype Squeers, William Shaw. On his 'farm' – a place where pauper children were boarded out from the workhouse – no less than 150 children died of cholera – so many that 'Tooting churchyard became too small for the piles of children's coffins that were carried out of this Elysium every day'.

On Drouet's appalling 'farm' Dickens expends his most scarifyingly ironic description.

The dietary of the children is so unwholesome and insufficient that they climb secretly over palings, and pick out scraps of sustenance from the tubs of hog-wash. Their clothing by day, and their covering by night, are shamefully defective. Their rooms are cold, damp, dirty, and rotten. In a word, the age of miracles is past, and of all conceivable places in which pestilence might – or rather *must* – be expected to break out, and to make direful ravages, Mr Drouet's model farm stands foremost.

This is from 'The Paradise at Tooting' (*Examiner*, 20 January 1849), the first of his essays on the subject. They form a running commentary upon the original complaint and the consequent hearings, and so make up a formidable narrative in their own right. Here we have Dickens pouring scorn upon the ineffectual Poor Law inspector, haphazard and lackadaisical in the pursuance of his duties.

He considers the dietary a fair dietary IF *proper quantities were given where no precise quantity is specified*. He thinks that, with care, the premises might have been occupied without injury to health, IF *all the accommodation on the premises had been judiciously applied.* As though a man should say he felt he could live pretty comfortably on top of the monument, IF a handsome suite of furnished apartments were constructed there expressly for him, and a select circle came to dinner every day! ('The Paradise at Tooting')

The ferocious show of geniality, the scalding analogies, once more mark out Dickens as the true successor of Swift – and on a peculiarly Swiftian topic, too. It is clear that he has far more grasp of this domestic issue than of the Italian landscape. The facts alone lend themselves to drama.

The matter went up before the enlightened coroner, Thomas Wakeley, who called for a verdict of manslaughter. This meant a hearing by the Recorder of the Central Criminal Court, to decide whether there was a case to answer. Finding that there was, the Recorder (Ewan Law) nevertheless suggested that cholera was a dispensation of providence. Finally the issue was resolved into a criminal trial, conducted by Justice Vaughan Williams and the egregious Mr Baron Platt.

Dickens describes the testimony and conduct of this trial with the vigour of Dotheboys Hall and the irony of *Oliver Twist.* A nurse at Gray's Inn Hospital recalled that one of the boys was unable to eat the food she gave him, which made the judge suggest this indicated that at least he wasn't starving. Dickens is scathing on the subject: this is the mode of Tiny Tim put to ironic use with a vengeance.

'Oh, nurse!' says the poor little fellow, with an eager sense that what he had longed for had come too late; 'what a big bit of bread this is!' Yes, Mr Baron Platt, it is clear that it was too much for him. His head was lifted up a moment, but it sank again. He could not but be full of wonder and pleasure that the big bit of bread had come, though he could not eat it. An English poet in the days when poetry and poverty were inseparable companions, received a bit of bread in somewhat similar circumstances which proved too much for him, and he died in the act of swallowing it. The difference is hardly worth pointing out. The pauper child had not even the strength for the effort which choked the pauper poet.

That comes from 'The Verdict for Drouet', a comment upon the criminal trial made all the more trenchant by its restraint. For it turned out that Drouet was acquitted! The grounds were, in Dickens's

words, that 'there had been no evidence adduced to show that the
child was ever, at any time, in such a state of health as to render it
probable he would have recovered from the malady but for the treatment of the defendant'. So the case went by default; and all Dickens
could do was write the matter up with all the eloquence at his dis-
posal.

These four pieces from *The Examiner*, the two I have quoted
together with 'The Tooting Farm' (27 January 1849) and 'A Recorder's
Charge' (3 March 1849), tell the story of the pauper's farm with a
mordant savagery that looks forward to the great attack upon the
legal system in *Bleak House* and to the powerful reportage of Dickens's
essays in *Household Words*. There can be no doubt that these inves-
tigations into social matters quickened Dickens's sensitivity and
made him aware that such disasters were the responsibility not of
the wicked individual but of society itself. They amount to a rejection of the existing system. Notice, though, that Dickens at no point
makes any attempt to put forward a substitute. The demand is for
a change in heart rather than a change in society itself.

These essays, therefore, are an essential bridge between Dickens's
earlier and later period. It is an extraordinary fact that *Pictures
from Italy* is reprinted with every edition of Dickens, while the work
we have been considering remains, to all intents and purposes, unknown. Indeed, but for the dedicated research of Mr Brice, three
of these would remain unidentified in the close-packed anonymity
of an excessively rare magazine. One could make an impressive
volume out of these Drouet articles together with their forepiece,
'A Truly British Judge', and the essays on education written for
The Examiner. Bound up with the *Daily News* essays and called
by their generic title, *Letters on Social Questions*, this would not be
the least striking work in the Dickens canon. It seems almost as if,
for the journalist travelling at large in Italy, Dickens had grimly
and deliberately indicted a portrait of England in the 1840s.

XI Dombey and Son (1846-48)

In spite of his difficulties with Bradbury and Evans over the *Daily News*, Dickens allowed them to publish *Dombey and Son*. Publish in a sense, that is, for he now controlled half of his copyrights. This represented something of a triumph, because he had spent the previous years of his working life wrangling with various intermediaries between himself and his beloved public. His sensitivity on the matter can be seen in three remarkable articles he wrote for *The Examiner* on the subject of Scott and his publishers. Once he had trusted Chapman and Hall, but had been furious when the junior partner had shown signs of bringing into action the repayment clause on *Martin Chuzzlewit* – which would, in effect, have docked Dickens of a quarter of his earnings. The breach was further exacerbated by the failure of *A Christmas Carol* to realize the profits its sanguine author had anticipated. And so Chapman and Hall – once 'best of booksellers', now 'scalyheaded vultures' – were informed that their issue of *Martin Chuzzlewit* in bound volumes marked the end of a prosperous relationship.

Dickens had arranged with Bradbury and Evans to write a novel in twenty monthly parts. *Dombey and Son* was begun in Switzerland, continued in Paris and finished in his own home, at Devonshire Terrace. The book was carefully planned: if *Martin Chuzzlewit* had been meant to act out selfishness in all its guises, the dominant theme of *Dombey and Son* was to be pride. Needless to say, things didn't go as smoothly as that. Dickens had trouble in fitting all the necessary incidents in, and there were marked changes of emphasis, even of plan, as the novel proceeded. The finished work does not strike us as a play of humours; it does not even, in any true sense, represent the life of a businessman. The mode is not sustained throughout the book, and some of the plot-ramifications seem willed, if not perverse. But, in the earlier chapters at least, Dickens's exposition is masterly. For the first time in his work we have the authoritative selection of particulars to be used as poetic drama.

The basic situation of *Dombey and Son* is the simplest Dickens ever achieved. The merchant prince, whose son and heir dies, leaving him with an unwanted daughter – this is medieval in its simple dignity, and lends itself, therefore, to complex symbolism.

Dombey is always represented in terms of snow, ice, marble; freezing into stone those who seek contact with him. Even the fire which is lit to warm his infant son retreats into distant feebleness in his presence. He represses emotion on all issues but one: his icy nature thaws for a moment to admit his son, then freezes with him into an unyielding block.

The brilliance of these opening chapters is seen at its best in Chapter V, 'Paul's Progress and Christening' – one of Dickens's finest serio-comic scenes. The very weather of the christening is an extension of Dombey: hard, cold, iron-grey, autumnal. And it is the same as the climate within the house: books drawn up in ranks like soldiers, fire-irons as stiff and stark as their starched and buttoned-up master. The guests stand around with blue noses, frosty faces and chattering teeth. They all set off for the church in a procession which, but for its colours, might be that of a funeral. And the church itself seems the more disposed towards the end of life than its beginning, with its shrouded pulpit, dreary pews, cold stone slabs, clergyman white and ghost-like. Mr Dombey is the cold centre of this shivering world: he seems even to have power to freeze the water in the font. Back from Church, a cold collation awaits them, with freezing champagne that chills the teeth. The christening party gradually becomes as congealed as the corpse of a dinner around which they sit; always with the exception of Mr Dombey, who alone is native to this element, and who, Dickens says, might have been hung up for sale at a Russian fair as a frozen gentleman. The baby cries piteously. 'What's the matter with the child?' 'He's cold, I think,' replies the nurse.

The images associated with little Paul are, predominantly, those of falling leaves and premature withering. He has precociously aged mannerisms and likes old people about him. It is as though the cold of his christening had struck through to his bones. The boarding house where he is sent is run by a frosty old lady, Mrs Pipchin; and, in his preparatory school, 'every description of Greek and Latin vegetables were got off the driest twigs of boys, under the frostiest circumstances . . . And then, with an aching void in his young heart, and all outside so cold, and bare, and strange, Paul sat as if he had taken life unfurnished, and the upholsterer were never coming'.

But there is another current of imagery in the book, and it is distinctly warm, not to say wet. At the birth of Paul, the neglected little girl had wept on her mother's breast. Mr Dombey called it 'a feverish proceeding'. And certainly the mother dies – 'clinging fast to that slight spar within her arms, the mother drifted out upon the dark and unknown sea that rolls around all the world.' It seems as though Florence has a tearful mystique from which Mr Dombey is excluded. The image of that death-scene recurs in a later chapter. 'He could not forget that closing scene. He could not forget that he had no part in it. That, at the bottom of its clear depth of tenderness and of trust, lay those two figures clasped in each other's arms, while he stood on the bank above, looking down a mere spectator – not a sharer with them – quite shut out.'

Of all Dickens's heroines, Florence is the most lachrymose. It has been calculated that she weeps in the book eighty-eight times, or more than twice for each appearance. It is not being facetious to suggest, as Julian Moynahan does, that her tears are associated with tidal waves and engulfing seas. Her part in the novel is to rain tears on the icy Mr Dombey in an effort to melt him down – so that he can, so to speak, drift with her tide.

At first, Mr Dombey is able to subjugate her with a glance. 'The tears that stood in her eyes as she raised them quickly to his face were frozen by the expression it wore.' Or again: 'The warm light vanished from the eyes of little Florence, when, at last, they happened to meet his'. But, as the book proceeds, the tides of Florence continue to rise. The little boy, Paul, is a powerful associate in all this because he alone has a hold over his sister. He is recommended sea-air for the good of his health. This sends him to Brighton, which puts him in Florence's sort of country, with the salt waves rolling in. Over and over again, we see them on the beach, the child asking questions about the sea.

'I want to know what it says,' he answered, looking steadily in her face. 'The sea, Floy, what is it that it keeps on saying?'

She told him that it was only the noise of the rolling waves.

'Yes, yes,' he said. 'But I know that they are always saying something.'

This not only associates Paul in the present with Florence, but looks backwards to his mother's death-scene, and forwards to his own.

His fancy had a strange tendency to wander to the river, which he knew as flowing through the great city; and now he thought how black it was, and how deep it would look, reflecting the host of stars – and more than all, how steadily it rolled away to meet the sea. . . .

'Why, will it never stop, Floy?' he would sometimes ask her. 'It is bearing me away, I think!' . . .

How many times the golden water danced upon the wall; how many nights the dark dark river rolled towards the sea in spite of him; Paul never counted, never sought to know. . . .

'Remember Walter, dear Papa,' he whispered, looking in his face. 'Remember Walter. I was fond of Walter!' . . .

Sister and brother wound their arms around each other, and the golden light came streaming in, and fell upon them, locked together.

'How fast the river runs, between its green banks and the rushes, Floy! But it's very near the sea. I hear the waves. They always said so!'

Presently he told her that the motion of the boat upon the stream was lulling him to rest. . . .

The scene gets more and more out of control as it goes on. The river image is well enough, but the passionate clinging of sister to brother – a repetition of her clinging to their mother – has an unpleasant undercurrent, as though she is enjoying his dissolution. Indeed, their being 'locked together' in the 'golden light' has an underlying implication of sexuality. As they hug each other, the little child clasps his hands in prayer at the back of her neck, and this religiosity is carried to an excruciating extreme when he sees his mother – that same mother who is almost a comic figure in Chapter I – as an angel waiting for him on the far shore. The old critic, Jeffrey, cried and sobbed over this death-scene at night and again at morning with a fervour worthy of Florence herself, and felt his heart purified by those tears. The Victorian world melted alongside him.

Florence and all her associates yield too much. The Walter referred to in Paul's death-scene – the name itself is a pun – is Florence's suitor and protector, and holds some humble clerkship in Dombey's firm. Uncomplainingly, he leaves Florence behind when Dombey sends him away to sea, leaving her to be looked after by a number of sentimentally-comic guardian angels: Mr Toots, Susan Nipper, Captain Cuttle and the dog, Diogenes; all of whom are susceptible to being wept over, if not to actual tears. Diogenes, indeed, seems to shrink in the process: from being big enough to knock over a man in the earlier chapters he diminishes into being quite a toy creature, who can be set on a window sill.

The character, Walter, was necessary because of the claims of the plot. The Dombey situation, as created in the early chapters, is notably static. Any possibility of movement from within is taken away with the death of Dombey, junior. But to get the book going in terms of ordinary plot was to sacrifice certain advantages. The aloofness of Dombey had to give way to realistic detail, and this meant that his loftiness carried a taint of absurdity: the language of an absolute monarch is unsuitable to a city gentleman seen at close quarters. Possibly it was some sense of vulgarity in this pseudo-aristocrat that led Dickens to dedicate the book to the Marchioness of Normanby – whose husband, as Lord Mulgrave, had been Dickens's fellow-traveller on his first trip to the States. The concomitant of Dombey's reduction in stature is that his freezing autumnal symbolism had to be played down into a mere statement of coldness. This, in its turn, benefits the Florence current of imagery. By and large, one can argue that the book gains in realistic detail, but thins out in significance.

An indication of this thinness is seen in the whole conception of Walter as a sort of Dick Whittington. At first Dickens had intended him to go to the bad, and provided a broken exemplar (John Carker) to act as dramatic foreshadowing. But it is hard to see how this would have helped the book: what would have been done with Florence, for example? As it was, Forster talked Dickens out of this, rendering John Carker an unnecessary detail in the process. Instead, Walter is thought to have foundered in the symbolically named *Son and Heir*.

In Walter's absence, relations between Florence and her father get worse. She overhears people talking about her as though she were already an orphan, and the flowers she holds fall from her trembling hands as the withered leaves fell at Paul's christening. She begins to wonder whether her father would relent at her bedside if she were dying, and at this thought the 'golden water' imagery of Paul's death-scene returns. There is even a late hint (more naturalistic, this time) that she resembles her brother in appearance and may well be suffering from the malady that took him away (Chapter XLVII). She tosses on a sea of doubt and hope; all the more, since Walter is by now thought to be beneath the waves.

But, with Walter's absence, the plot would have come to a halt yet once more, so Dickens has Mr Dombey marry again. The choice falls on a penniless widow called Edith. She is proud and beautiful, and ought to have been a successful character. On one level she is consistently presented. Her imagery is that of picture-frames and mirrors, as befits one who appears to be a determined solipsist. But she sacrifices a good deal of sympathy by entering into a marriage with Dombey that she declares to be loveless. She loses even more when she runs away with Dombey's manager (a stage villain called James Carker) on the second anniversary of their wedding. And it is difficult to know what to think of her when she reveals to Carker that she has been using him merely as a catspaw in order to discredit him and to heap coals of fire on her husband.

Another weakness in this character is her close alliance with Florence: even this proud beauty melts before Florence's tears. In this, a good deal of authority is sacrificed; it is worth mentioning that Edith has scant tenderness for her own mother. But Florence wins her over right away. In congratulating her father – 'Oh, Papa, may you be happy all your life' – Florence embraces her stepmother – who presses her hand as if to reassure and comfort her. And she passes the night before her wedding in vigil by the side of Florence's virgin couch.

But just as she clasped her mother and brother in their dying moments, so Florence's dreams seem to aim towards drowning her remaining associates on earth.

She dreamed of seeking her father in wilderness, of following his track up fearful heights, and down into deep mines and caverns; of being charged with something that could release him from extraordinary suffering – she knew not what, or why – yet never being able to attain the goal and set him free. Then she saw him dead, upon that very bed, and in that very room, and knew that he had never loved her to the last, and fell upon his cold breast, passionately weeping. Then a prospect opened and a river flowed, and a plaintive voice that she knew, cried, 'It is running on, Floy! It has never stopped! You are moving with it!' And she saw him at a distance stretching out his arms towards her, while a figure such as Walter's used to be, stood near him, awfully serene and still. In every vision, Edith came and went, sometimes to her joy, sometimes to her sorrow, until they were alone upon the brink of a dark grave, and Edith pointing down, she looked and saw – what! – another Edith lying at the bottom.

In view of Edith's fate – a living grave, retirement from the world – Florence's dream is unpleasantly symptomatic of her own general malaise: a death-wish, a recessive tendency towards the womb, a general anxiety that is nourished only when there is something to be anxious about – hence this character's marked tendency to meet trouble half-way, as with the death of Walter, or to create trouble for herself, as in her incessant importuning of her father. The tear-and-water imagery assumes considerable force in the later stages of the novel compared with the ice imagery of Dombey – who can only summon up a 'cold breast' to protect him from Florence's overwhelming emotionalism. There is no check to her imagery: Florence's dream shows that she wants to drown the world in her sorrows, but the neurotic drift of her imagining, asleep or awake, is never evaluated by the author in dramatic terms.

Dombey makes a strong fight against all this, and it is not until he has been deserted by Florence as well as by his wife, and his firm is in ruins and he himself contemplating suicide, that he finally gives in. Florence's reappearance is prefigured by the rain falling on Dombey's roof: it sets up patterns of memory that finally melt him into tears. And, once he starts crying, he is lost in Florence's embrace – 'Papa! Dearest Papa! Pardon me! Forgive me! I have come back to ask forgiveness on my knees. I never can be happy more without it.' Walter has conjoined with Florence, of course – native to the element, he avoided drowning at sea – and joins all her protectors in a final celebration at which Dombey is an incongruous presence, a little like a reformed Scrooge. We catch a last glimpse of him, on the seashore, weeping over his little grandchild: another Florence.

So much of the later part of the book is merely movement of plot, without action of any significance, that a good deal of one's analysis has to be privative. The grinning Carker, with whom Edith decamps, is (apart from Monks) the least interesting of Dickens's villains. Some of his activity is mere bustle: such as his planting a spy on Solomon Gills's shop, or first humouring, then badgering, Captain Cuttle. He has neither antecedents nor motivation, and the clichés in which he is described have no connection with the prevailing currents of imagery. But he is a local manifestation of a general failure in the book.

Far more impressive as a character is the one flight of fancy Dickens does allow himself in *Dombey and Son*: the truly mephistophelean figure of old Joe Bagstock, old Joey Bagstock, old J. Bagstock, Josh Bagstock, Joey B., old J. B., etc., etc., as the blue-faced Major, who has seen too much service in India, variously terms himself. This figure is built around its distended stomach, the repository of devilled grills, savoury pies, dishes of kidneys, to say nothing of private zests and flavours with which its owner daily scorches himself. Clearly life has lost its savour; perhaps its potency, too. Prawn-eyed, with the complexion of a Stilton cheese, and an alarming propensity to swell and turn black when laughing or coughing – he does a good deal of both – the Major chokes and gasps his way through the book, and carries most of its comic emphasis. He attaches himself to Dombey in the capacity of performing bear – he is highly circumspect, so calls himself in public 'tough and blunt' and in private 'dev'lish sly' – and is the instrument of Dombey's meeting his second wife. Otherwise he appears to exist mainly for the purpose of comic relief: indulging himself in the role as surely as Quilp or Pecksniff. And he contrasts splendidly with his neighbour and enemy, sad Miss Tox, who nurtures a hopeless passion for the remote Dombey from her squeezed-up little house.

Otherwise we have the general spectacle of characters drifting away from Dombey, and, the majority of them, attaching themselves to Florence. And one has to admit that, aesthetically speaking, Dombey is by far the most impressive figure in the book. But we must not allow this artistic effect to enlist us on his side, morally speaking. He is an obstinate and repressed individual, and nearly all his decisions turn out for the worse. At the same time, it is a pity that he has no more respectable figure to contrast with than Florence.

However, there is a third line of imagery, not associated either with ice or with salt water. A new feature – new to Dickens, anyway – is the railway that runs through the book. Dickens had presumably become aware of the possibilities of this mode of transport when editing the *Daily News*, financed by railway magnates. We are first affected by this in the smoky presence of Mr Toodles, whose wife fortuitously becomes Paul's wet-nurse.

'You were going to have the goodness to inform me, when we arrived at the door, that you were by trade, a –'
   'Stoker,' said the man.
   'A choker!' said Miss Tox, quite aghast.
   'Stoker,' said the man. 'Steam ingine. . . . I'm a going on one of these here railroads when they comes into full play.'

And later we see the railway uprooting the old-fashioned allotments and stagnant cottages of Staggs's Gardens.

Where the old rotten summer-houses once had stood, palaces now reared their heads, and granite columns of gigantic girth opened a vista to the railway world beyond. The miserable waste ground, where the refuse-matter had been heaped of yore, was swallowed up and gone; and in its frowsy stead were tiers of warehouses, crammed with rich goods and costly merchandise. The old by-streets now swarmed with passengers and vehicles of every kind; the new streets that had stopped disheartened in the mud and waggon-ruts, formed towns within themselves. . . . The carcasses of houses, and beginnings of new thoroughfares, had started off upon the line at steam's own speed, and shot away into the country in a monster train.

This is the force of progress, beside which Dombey's firm is a survival from the dark ages. In its occasional eruptions through the novel, the steam engine affords us glimpses of what could have been an effective countertheme. But it may be doubted how far Dickens's heart was in industrial development. The railway in *Dombey and Son* exists in terms of sensations, as an element of thrill: there is, however, an undercurrent of criticism regarding its dirt and noise. So the railway could never have been morally weighty enough to represent a challenge to the Firm even in the sense that Florence does. It is, however, significant that Dombey instantaneously dislikes Toodles, and later resents 'this presumptuous raker among coals and ashes' wearing mourning for Paul. In his various train rides,

all Dombey is conscious of is ruin and desolation; he has no idea
that the railway has let the light of day in on these things. It is noticeable that Carker, Dombey's manager, in his turn fails to understand
the trains by which he seeks to travel, even up to the one that eventually
runs him down. It seems that he does not recognize the two red lights
which were the usual headlamps of a train running on a single track;
instead they appear to him to belong to an avenging monster. Clearly,
the firm of Dombey and Son stands in active opposition to the growth
of industry; that much is plain from its old-fashioned City ways
and class-conscious reliance upon nouveau-riche aristocracy.

But it is unfortunate that we cannot see more of the workings
of this firm. We are never told precisely what it is that Dombey
and Son do. This strikes me as being, not a subtlety, but a weakness.
It is unfortunate that Dickens had done no routine job outside
journalism, and therefore was limited in his understanding of the
world of work. The result is that the Firm is rather nebulous –
certainly in contrast to the railway – and indeed, for long stretches
in the novel, it does not manifest itself at all.

So *Dombey and Son* is far more a book about family relations
than about business. And the stark simplicity of the basic scheme
is, in any case, hardly suited to a setting of commerce and industry.
The naturalistic detail that keeps the novel going cannot rise to the
symbolic power of the early chapters. The result is that, the more
plot it tries to relay, the more conventional the novel becomes.

Dombey and Son is, more than any other of his novels, Dickens's
King Lear. But, occurring where it does in his work, as the first
novel of his maturity, it suggests that he was seeking to run before
he could walk. There was much in Dickens's makeup he had not
admitted, even to himself. And, having attempted the impersonal
theme of a major tragedy, it was necessary for him to step back a
little, in technical terms, and try his hand a little nearer home. If
Dombey and Son is a failure at being *King Lear*, *David Copperfield*
is very nearly a success as Dickens's *Hamlet*.

XII David Copperfield (1849-50)

Forster told Dickens, in April 1847, that a mutual acquaintance used to recollect him working, as a young boy, in a warehouse near the Strand. Dickens made no reply at the time; but, some weeks later, placed in his friend's hands the fragment of an autobiography provoked by what had proved to be a painful question.

In this autobiography, we have facts of Dickens's early life that otherwise might have remained suppressed for ever. In 1822, his father, a clerk in the Navy office, had been transferred from Chatham to London. In the process, the whole family moved from precariously shabby gentility to abject poverty. They had taken a house too imposing for their means, in Gower Street, but Mrs Dickens tried to retrieve their fortunes by opening a school. Nobody came. Shortly afterwards, John Dickens was thrown into the Marshalsea Prison for debt. In the interim period, a relative procured the young Dickens a job in a blacking factory. For the next five months, he washed out and labelled blacking bottles twelve hours a day, six days a week. This, all too soon in life, was the dark night of his soul. The agony comes out in the prose of this autobiographical fragment.

It is wonderful to me how I could have been so easily cast away at such an age. It is wonderful to me that, even after my descent into the poor little drudge I had been since we came to London, no one had compassion enough on me – a child of singular abilities, quick, eager, delicate, and soon hurt, bodily or mentally – to suggest that something might have been spared, as certainly it might have been, to place me at any common school. Our friends, I take it, were tired out. No one made any sign. My father and mother were quite satisfied. They could hardly have been more so, if I had been twenty years of age, distinguished at a grammar-school, and going to Cambridge.

The agony is genuine, and it did a great deal to form Dickens's character. The man, who reacted to opposition like a steel spring unleashing itself, was the child who felt himself wickedly put upon because he had to work with common labouring boys.

No words can ever express the agony of my soul as I sunk into this companion-ship; compared these every day associates with those of my happier child-hood; and felt my early hopes of growing up to be a learned and distinguished man, crushed in my breast. The deep remembrance of the sense I had of being utterly neglected and hopeless; of the shame I felt in my position; of the misery it was to my young heart to believe that, day by day, what I had learned and delighted in, and raised my fancy and my emulation up by, was passing away from me, never to be brought back any more; cannot be written. My whole nature was so penetrated with the grief and humiliation of such considerations, that even now, famous and caressed and happy, I often forget in my dreams that I have a dear wife and children; even that I am a man; and wander desolately back to that time in my life.

An agony of the spirit such as this can never be allayed. Any set-back will revive it in its pristine force, and all that the victim can do is compensate for it. Dickens's entire career was an attempt to make sure that no one was going to put him back into the blacking factory of his nightmares. The effort involved some powerful repressions. He never spoke of this episode to his wife or friends, or anyone until Forster's painful question; and it is significant that this, his best-beloved book, was dedicated not to Forster but to the Richard Wat-sons, two of his friends in Switzerland. Dickens's secret had escaped only in obsessive reference to blacking bottles in his work – for example, *Oliver Twist*, Chapter V, and *Nicholas Nickleby*, Chapter XL, where they occur in close association with stories of human misfortune.

It might be argued that Dickens was exaggerating the situation. His condition, after all, was temporary; his father was making every effort to sort out his affairs, and, ultimately, he was himself set free from the house of bondage. But for a child, even one of twelve, time is not structured as for an adult. To the young Dickens, his hell seemed interminable. However exaggerated his complaints seem to us, they reflect a situation very real to him.

As the autobiographical fragments suggest, even in childish days

Dickens had set his heart on fame and dignity. The robust extroversion of adult years was an overlay, mere role-playing. He had been a sickly child, inclined to introspection; watching healthier boys at their play, but finding solace in dreams and in the fictions of Sterne, Fielding, Goldsmith and Smollett. All this may have left him unduly open to experience. Something like the blacking factory was lying in wait along his path, even though it might not have manifested itself in those precise terms. But one could hardly expect a child to see this, and it was the agony of the child that formed the man.

As it stands, the pain exposed in the autobiography seems in excess of the ascertainable facts. But the blacking factory must have seemed like this to Dickens. How, then, was he to justify the agony it caused him? for, once he had told the story to Forster, he had an urge to share it with his readers. He had, therefore, to find a means of redeeming his lamentations over his young self from being self-pity, that least communicable, though most sincere, of feelings.

The answer lay in abandoning the autobiography and taking up a fiction which would allow him to provide an adequate correlative for his pain. This proved to be *David Copperfield*. It was not enough for circumstances alone to bring about the hero's incarceration in the factory: he had to be driven there by the death of a mother and the wickedness of a stepfather. Chapters I to XIV of this work are a dramatization, not only of the autobiography, but of the sense of desolation in Dickens's early life.

The word 'dramatization' must be used with some caution here. Unlike Shakespeare, in *Hamlet*, Dickens has provided a good deal of motivation to explain the sense of loss that is David Copperfield's central core. If we scan the autobiography for elements transmuted in the novel, we come across statements like these following.

No advice, no counsel, no encouragement, no consolation, no support, from any one that I can call to mind, so help me God . . .

I know that, but for the mercy of God, I might have been, for any care that was taken of me, a little robber or a little vagabond. . . .

I saw my father coming in at the door one day when we were very busy, and I wondered how he could bear it . . .

I do not write resentfully or angrily: for I know how all these things have
worked together to make me what I am: but I never afterwards forgot, I never
shall forget, I never can forget, that my mother was warm for my being sent
back . . .

Overtly expressed in that last quotation is the resentment against
his mother. Submerged deeper beneath the surface is a consuming
rancour against the weakness of his father. The dynamics, not just
of *David Copperfield* but of many other Dickens novels, is a condemnation of father images; and, beyond that, of social institutions,
for their failure to act on behalf of those who most stood in need.
This is why it makes no sense to talk of Dickens as an incipient so-
cialist. Private charity, the interference of the strong on behalf of
the weak – this was Dickens's panacea for the ills he saw all around
him. And this, too, explains why only certain forms of distress
sparked off his righteous indignation: Oliver Twist, the helpless
foundling; the outcast children of Dotheboys Hall; the sickly paupers
on Drouet's farm; Florence, neglected by her unfeeling father; and,
later, Jo in *Bleak House*, Little Dorrit, Pip, in gilded adulthood,
seeking to conceal his labouring past.

Behind all this is the feeling that fathers *ought* to be a protection
against the world and that mothers ought to be a solace for its in-
justices. In the case of *David Copperfield*, it was necessary to dramatize
this feeling in terms of external menaces to the vulnerable child.
These menaces take the following forms: mothers who are charming
but ineffectual; mothers who are effective but odd; Bad Fathers,
who can extend into ogres; and Boon Companions, who include
boys and fathers who act like boys, failing in their responsibility to
advise and provide. Most of these manifest themselves as characters,
but Odd Mothers and Bad Fathers can as easily appear as places or
institutions. The first fourteen chapters of *David Copperfield* are
no arbitrary set of rambles: they can be interpreted entirely in terms
of the young David staving off Bad Fathers, relying temporarily on
Boon Companions, but seeking a satisfactory Mother.

The annoyance of Dickens with his mother is dramatized in the
curiously ambiguous device whereby David Copperfield appears
to have two of his own. The natural one has all the skittish mannerisms of a girl, and is probably Dickens's childhood recollection
of his own mother in her feckless youth. Indeed, he seems to have

received a strong imprint from her in his infancy, since this was the image which he wooed as Maria Beadnell in life and as Dora in fiction. But it was only in fiction that he married her; nevertheless, the foundation for David Copperfield's desire for the girl who became his wife is laid down in his early chapters of the story. He also has a surrogate mother in Peggotty, the serving-maid, who performs the unglamorous duties of washing the child and mending his clothes. The point is made by Dickens giving both these 'mothers' the same Christian name: Clara. It is noticeable that, under stress, little David will turn away from the unalluring maid-of-all-work and cling to the glamorous object of his infantile sexuality. This is an exact parallel to the famous psychological experiment of the young monkeys and their substitute mother. The monkeys would go to wire substitutes for the milk they provided, but would return to cloth substitutes – who were warm and cuddly – for affection. Dickens is quite explicit on the whole matter: Peggotty's hard red arms and roughened fingers are in vivid contrast to Mrs Copperfield's pretty hair and youthful shape.

An extension of Peggotty, as mother-surrogate, is the house where her brother lives, in Yarmouth. David is sent there for a holiday in order to give his real-life mother the chance to get married behind his back. The house, like all the more successful mother-surrogates in the book, is distinctly odd. For one thing, it is not really a house at all, but a black barge, pulled up high and dry on the ground, with a black chimney smoking 'very cosily' on top. It therefore combines association of salt sea or amniotic fluid with the apparent safety of land; but not without a certain incongruity, as if for David maternal affection must always necessarily be off-key. The Boat is best thought of as a womb. Here one is cosseted and comforted, like a roc's egg in Aladdin's palace. This palace, it is true, is small, but in a comfortably circumscribing way. An image corresponding to so deep-seated an archetype accounts for this chapter's popularity with generations of readers, especially children.

There was a delightful door cut in the side, and it was roofed in, and there were little windows in it; but the wonderful charm of it was, that it was a real boat that had no doubt been on the water hundreds of times, and which had never been intended to be lived in, on dry land. That was the captivation of it to me. If it had ever been meant to be lived in, I might have thought it small, or inconvenient, or lonely; but never having been designed for any such use, it became a perfect abode.

It was beautifully clean inside, and as tidy as possible. There was a table, and a Dutch clock, and a chest of drawers, and on the chest of drawers there was a tea-tray with a painting on it of a lady with a parasol, taking a walk with a military-looking child who was trundling a hoop. The tray was kept from tumbling down, by a bible; and the tray, if it had tumbled down, would have smashed a quantity of cups and saucers and a teapot that were grouped around the book. On the wall there were some common coloured pictures, framed and glazed, of Scripture subjects; such as I have never seen in the hands of pedlars without seeing the whole interior of Peggotty's brother's house again, at one view. Abraham in red going to sacrifice Isaac in blue, and Daniel in yellow cast into a den of green lions, were the most prominent of these. Over the little mantel-shelf was a picture of the *Sarah Jane* lugger, built at Sunderland, with a real little wooden stern stuck on to it; a work of art combining composition with carpentry, which I considered one of the most enviable possessions that the world could afford. There were some hooks in the beams of the ceiling, the use of which I did not divine then; and some lockers and boxes and conveniences of that sort which served for seats and eked out the chairs.

All this, I saw in the first glance after I crossed the threshhold – child-like, according to my theory – and then Peggotty opened the little door and showed me my bedroom. It was the completest and most desirable bed-room ever seen – in the stern of the vessel; with a little window, where the rudder used to go through; a little looking-glass, just the right height for me, nailed against the wall and framed with oyster shells; a little bed, which there was just enough room to get into; and a nosegay of seaweed in a blue mug on the table. . . .

Most people have found this enchanting, but let us consider why. The smallness of the place is stressed, but also its closeness; underlying this, is a sense of the oddity of one's being there at all; like an embryo in the womb. One may aspire to return – there is a delightful door cut in the wall – and one's pleasure might even be enhanced by the persistence of some residual childlike idea to the effect that it was never designed for any such use in the first place. But, either way, it is a temporary residence.

The paintings and household images within Mr Peggotty's Boat are highly significant. They act out the sense of a womb seen in terms of family and home. There is, for example, a tea-tray, familiar domestic object, showing a mother taking her child (evidently a boy) out for a walk; father is in evidence only as a phallic symbol, her parasol, and the boy is trundling a hoop reminiscent of the female genital organ. It is not a father but a Bible that prevents the tray from crashing down and breaking up farther familiar home properties (cups, saucers, teapot) which are gathered around the book. The inference is that not father but God (a father-substitute) keeps this house going. Significantly, Mr Peggotty is a bachelor looking after his nephew (Ham), niece (Little Em'ly), the widow of an old friend (Mrs Gummidge), and, by extension, his sister Peggotty and the fatherless David. One may also remember the cry from the heart in the Autobiographical Fragment: 'But for the mercy of God, I might have been . . . a little vagabond'. Fathers let one down; only God is merciful. Hence the picture on the wall of the Bad Father (Abraham) sacrificing his little son; we remember it was God who intervened and saved the boy. Or Daniel being cast into the lion's den, as Dickens had been, in the Blacking Factory. The bright colours (Abraham is red, lions painted green) draw some of the sting out of what are, after all, passing images. But their very presence shows the power of the emotion infusing the passage, looking back to Dickens's desolate boyhood and forward to the events in the life of David. The picture of the *Sarah Jane*, also on the wall, is ambiguous as the mother images are: either drowning at sea or immersion in the womb.

The womb imagery contracts farther, the more we explore Mr Peggotty's boat. It circumscribes itself into the 'desirable' bedroom: here is a grown man recollecting sexual pleasure – partly sadistic ('a little window where the rudder used to go through', 'a little bed, which there was just enough room to get into') and narcissistic ('a looking-glass framed with oyster-shells'). The whole amounts to a complex group of symbols, signifying a 'positive' in terms of a cosy womb to which the boy is temporarily admitted, as a man may feel himself to be, in the act of love; but which clearly (the boat is grounded, but may drift out to sea) embodies certain dangers. Its foreshortening and oddity have their counterparts in mother-surrogates throughout the book.

One must, as a grown man, eventually withdraw from the opening of one's pleasures; as a boy, one takes leave of a glorious holiday-place; as a baby, one has to be born. David finds himself delivered into a very terrible life when he goes back to what had been his home. The house had previously been described in terms similar to those of the Boat – one thinks of a garden, fenced off, padlocked, secret – and it was all the better for not having a father in charge. Dickens had killed him off before the book started, and the baby David's only fear is in case he rises again, like Lazarus, from the grave. But now there is a Father living there, and a very bad one he turns out to be.

Mr Murdstone has no prototype in Dickens's life; he is simply the repository of hatred against the failure of a real-life father to fulfil his obligations. John Dickens was not wicked but weak. This did not affect the force of Dickens's rage. Since it could not be checked or repressed, it had to be directed, and directed against a fitting object; one that was not weak, but wicked. Hence the creation of an ogre, together with a Wicked Sister, to fulfil the role of Bad Father between them. They are built on the same scale, with black hair and deep voices, except that the sister has eyebrows in lieu of whiskers. They are aggressively masculine, and this is a challenge to the young David, who feels their physical superiority in terms, almost, of a threat against himself, of impending castration.

'David,' he said, making his lips thin, by pressing them together, 'if I have an obstinate horse or dog to deal with, what do you think I do?'

'I don't know.'

'I beat him.'

I had answered in a kind of breathless whisper, but I felt in my silence, that my breath was shorter now.

'I make him wince, and smart. I say to myself, "I'll conquer that fellow"; and if it should cost him all the blood he has, I should do it. What is that upon your face?'

'Dirt,' I said.

He knew it was the mark of tears as well as I . . .

The little boy will not own up to the feminine weakness of crying. Child as he is, he wants to assert his manhood against that of the Bad Father who has taken his mother away from him. Gone are the good old days when reading lessons were paths of flowers – an image of his Forsaken Garden. He is confronted by impossible problems such as this: 'If I go into a cheese-monger's shop, and buy five thousand double-Gloucester cheeses at fourpence-halfpenny each, present payment'. The old reading book could turn crocodiles into vegetables, but Murdstone is capable of turning cheeses into canes. Unimaginative work, unconnected with domestic reality, is erected into a positive, and will is assumed to be under personal volition.

'I can't learn while you and Miss Murdstone are by.'
  'Can't you indeed, David? We'll try that.'

The young David bites this threatening Goliath, and is flogged to a jelly for his pains. Further, Mr Murdstone extends himself into a School where he sends David for this act of defiance; itself based upon Dickens's experiences, after the Blacking Factory, at Wellington House Academy, under the sadistic headmaster, Jones. This institution in *David Copperfield* manifests itself as a grosser, coarser and atrophied development of Murdstone's personality. There is something wrong with everybody there: the boys are low-spirited, the second master is shabby and epileptic, the first master has a wig, the porter, Tungay, has a wooden leg, and the headmaster has no voice and so is called Mr Creakle. Like the Murdstones, the last two together form a team, the one loudly echoing the other; a composite Father to carry on the Murdstone work – 'If I have an obstinate dog . . . I beat him'.

Mr Creakle came to where I sat, and told me that if I was famous for biting, he was famous for biting, too. He then showed me the cane, and asked me what I thought of *that*, for a tooth? Was it a sharp tooth, hey? Was it a double tooth, hey? Had it a deep prong, hey? Did it bite, hey? Did it bite? At every question he gave me a fleshy cut that made me writhe. . . .

David is, quite literally, treated like a dog – he has a placard put on his back, 'Take care of him. He bites'. But a child *should* be taken care of, and not in the Murdstone-Creakle sense. These Goliaths, however, are secretly afraid of David: their aggression rooted in fear, and it is powered – indirectly with Murdstone and blatantly with Creakle – by a greedy sadism. Like Dickens's own schoolmaster at Wellington House, the ignorant and vicious Jones, Creakle physically enjoys cutting at boys who are fleshy.

Such are the vessels into which Dickens pours his resentment against his father. Paradoxically, because his father was weak, he creates Bad Fathers against whom he can rage because they are strong.

A passing mother-substitute is, indeed, found in Mrs Creakle, but she combines Peggotty's failure as a sex-symbol with Mrs Copperfield's failure as efficient solace. Unable to protect him against Creakle's cane, she even – though with the best intentions – makes a mess of breaking to David the worst news he can hear: that of his mother's death. 'I had already broken out into a desolate cry, and felt an orphan in the world'. Temporarily, at any rate, the mother-surrogates are taken from him. His house is infested with Murdstones, the barge is no longer an easement, and even Peggotty is carried off to a home of her own by, appropriately enough, the carrier. The only book he can find to read in her house is Foxe's *Book of Martyrs.* 'I had lost Peggotty.'

Now, at last, David is sacrificed; he is thrown to the lions. Murdstone has not exhausted his capabilities in extending outwards to Creakle, Tungay and the School. His much-vaunted firmness extends still further, *to* a firm, the firm of Murdstone and Grinby. Dickens confronts the Factory at last.

'I now approach a period in my life, which I can never lose the remembrance of, while I remember anything; and the recollection of which has often, without my invocation, come before me like a ghost, and haunted happier times.' Dickens is at pains to motivate David's sense of desolation as strongly as possible. Therefore he reduces his age from twelve in his own history to eight in the novel, and represents the little labouring hind as totally orphaned and alone in the world. Yet much of this section is taken verbatim from the Autobiographical Fragment. Given circumstances as dire as these, the intense pity Dickens felt for his own plight falls naturally into place as appropriate and inevitable.

I was so young and childish, and so little qualified – how could I be otherwise? – to undertake the whole charge of my own existence, that often, in going to Murdstone and Grinby's, of a morning, I could not resist the stale pastry put out for sale in the pastry-cook's doors, and spent in that, the money I should have kept for my dinner. Thus I went without my dinner, or bought a roll or a slice of pudding. I remember two pudding-shops, between which I was divided, according to my finances. One was in a court close to St Martin's Church – at the back of the Church, – which is now removed altogether. The pudding at that shop was made of currants, and was rather a special pudding, but was dear, two-pennyworth not being larger than a pennyworth of more ordinary pudding. A good shop for the latter was in the Strand – somewhere in that part which has been rebuilt since. It was a stout pale pudding, heavy and flabby, and with great flat raisins in it, stuck in whole at wide distances apart. It came up hot at about my time every day, and many a day did I dine off it.

It is clear that this passage is about a great deal more than its overt subject-matter. The exact description of minutiae, the agonizing decision between one pudding and another, shows a state of depression and evokes the sense of grinding penury. The large statement about unguarded youth has great force in its local application: the temptation – only tempting to a child – of half-price pastry at the expense of a decent dinner. The rhetoric of the autobiography is pinned down to precise detail, and the detail is that of a life without spark, without hope. Passages such as these, which touch obliquely upon his predicament, carry most of his sense of degradation, and save him from acting out the relationship of David to the other boys in the factory in detail.

Even so, the desolation is not complete. There are one or two faint simulacra of substitute mothers: for example, the publican's wife who returns his beer-money and gives him a womanly kiss. But, in the main, David is thrown upon what I have termed boon companions.

Chief among these are the startling figures of the Micawbers. These were, of course, based upon Dickens's own father and mother. It is interesting to see that he removes them from any such intimate connection and puts them forward, instead, as mere chance acquaintances. This is partly because, in real life, they failed as parents; partly because their weakness cannot be represented as being wicked; partly because, for the sense of the book, David had to be shown as an orphan. So the rancour against the elder Dickens is deflected on to various ogre-figures, and the feckless parents are distanced in relationship and allowed to go relatively free from condemnation.

Mr Micawber is so powerfully set before us in these early chapters that it is hard to remember he occupies, in most of the editions, no more than 14 or 15 pages of the text. Partly this is a matter of physical appearance: he is a Humpty Dumpty, with his egg-like head totally

bald, stout body, imposing shirt-collar, quizzing-glass and stick.
It is partly, also, a matter of speech: an orotundity that loses itself
mid-way and lapses into a not unpleasing colloquialism.

'Under the impression,' said Mr Micawber, 'that your peregrinations in this
metropolis have not yet been extensive, and that you might have some difficulty in penetrating the arcana of the Modern Babylon in the direction
of the City Road – in short,' said Mr Micawber, in another burst of confidence, 'that you might lose yourself – I shall be happy to call this evening,
and instal you in the knowledge of the nearest way.'

Pecksniff, it is true, had similar traits; but his rhetoric is religiose
and his colloquialism not homely but vulgar. Moreover, Micawber's
rhetoric is a mode of compensating for shabby surroundings; a
method of cheering himself up. He is a distinct individual with his
manic-depressive gamut of violent emotions. He can begin an evening with a flood of tears, and end it with a comic song; go into prison
striking a tragic attitude, and be found playing a lively game of
skittles an hour or so later. He redeems himself from being anti-
social by his endless, life-giving optimism: this Humpty-Dumpty
is always putting himself together again, in the hope, as he says,
that 'something will turn up'. As well, remarks Dickens in the next
book (*Bleak House*, ch.XX), might a madman exist in the hope of
the world turning triangular. But the sting is taken out of Micawber's
improvidence and Mrs Micawber's reminiscences by the genuine
charm of their presentation. Improvident or not, they are gallantly
loyal to each other. And their appeal to the reader is the fact that
they are always in trouble: creditors, pawnbrokers, the debtors'
prison, Plymouth – adventures swarm round them like bees. The
odds are heavily against them. People so incapable of ordering their
own lives can hardly be blamed for failing to order other people's.
How can the Micawbers be seen as parents – bad, good, odd or
whatever? And so they stand in relation to David as school-friends,
playmates or Boon Companions. Mr Micawber always addresses
David as though he were only a couple of years his junior, while Mrs
Micawber – after so many heart-rending confidences – only when
he kisses her goodbye on the Plymouth coach recognizes what a
little fellow he is, after all.

With these last companions gone, David is anybody's prey. His decision to leave the Factory and seek out the last of his mother-surrogates, Aunt Betsey Trotwood, takes him through dangerous territory. On the road to Dover, like bad fathers run mad, he meets all kinds of Ogres. A man with a cart drives off with his box and his money, leaving him stranded. Two successive pawnbrokers, a mad Murdstone and a mad Creakle, defraud him of his jacket and waistcoat – the last of these pawnbrokers, old Charley, ceaselessly gibbering 'Oh, my lungs and liver, what do you want? Oh, goroo'. There is a tinker on the road, too, who bullies him and steals his neckerchief. Box, money, jacket, waistcoat, neckerchief all gone, David is systematically deprived of the outward signs of station in the world.

But the ultimate mother-surrogate is Aunt Betsey, and her home is another substitute Womb. David arrives, footsore, stripped and penniless, and is promptly adopted as one of the 'family'. This consists of old Mr Dick, who has the intellect and habits of a young boy David's age, and a young girl called Janet, whom Betsey is training to forswear the world of men. It has a tell-tale garden – fronted by a plot of green grass forbidden to men and donkeys, from which the Murdstones, when they arrive, are speedily and ignominiously routed. While Father retires defeated, back into the adult society whence he came, David is spoon-fed, coddled and bundled in swaddling-clothes. He has found himself at last.

It is clear, then, that much of the book is a protest at facing life. The protest is made respectable by a rendering of adult life in the most ogreish of terms possible. No doubt this fear is powered by the blacking factory, but life is not a wilderness of blacking factories, and Dickens seems reluctant to admit this. Instead, his positive emerges as the split image of the Glamorous Mother and the Practical Mother; or as the high-and-dry Boat with its attendant genii. These are recessive symbols, and it is no accident that David ends up being fed from a bottle. The father is only present in the masculine mannerisms of the essentially kind Aunt Betsey. Men have no place in this world of aunts, lunatics, virgins, boys and gardens.

Needless to say, the book goes on. But, as John Jones remarks, it ceases to be *The Trials of David* and turns into *The Portrait of an Artist*. And an excessively dull artist David turns out to be; it is a blessing that we don't have to read *his* novels. He has nothing what-

soever to do with his own young self. The Factory, that extension
of the Father, has been rooted out of his life. His weakness is in
failing to resemble Dickens at all. As distinct from that life of struggle
for power, the only real event in his career is marriage. Even this
has an air of being put in to eke out the plot.

David chooses a skittish little thing called Dora, with a skittish
little dog just like herself. Let us grant the psychological truth of
this: the son has chosen a mate in the image of his mother. But a
book is more than applied psychology: *The Trials of David* would
not be the great masterpiece it is if its obsessional images were not
dramatically functional. Dora's skittishness has nothing like the
relevance of Mrs Copperfield's: with her, the story loses what point
it might have. David's courtship is mere clowning compared (say)
with the real-life agonies of Dickens in tow to Maria Beadnell, or
Pip dancing attendance upon Estella in *Great Expectations*. In
contrast, though we are supposed not to get weary of Dora, it is
perfectly evident that David does. More, we are asked to continue
in sympathy with David, even though we see him hovering over
Dora's housekeeping accounts like an incipient Murdstone. The
morality wanders all over the place, and the attention of the reader
wanders with it. Either David is right to be irritated by Dora or he
is wrong in reproving her: the author blurs his picture by losing
perspective. And an oddly parallel case is that of Agnes: while Dora
is married to a substitute father, Agnes is 'married' to her real-life
father, a kind of substitute husband. After David's child-wife dies,
he eventually marries this wife-child. There is no indication that
the relationship will ever graduate to intercourse between adults,
and it is an insult to the reader to expect him to give it his blessing.

What else happens in the book happens well away from David.
There is a melodramatic sub-plot involving the schemes of Uriah
Heep. This is a Carker-like individual, fawning and slinky, who
seeks to marry Agnes and ruin her father. His downfall is brought
about by the resuscitated Mr Micawber, who enmeshes him in a web
of intrigue. But this Micawber resembles the great original only
in name. The action is pushed on with Micawber, according to his
role, affecting changes of dress; but it is all mechanical. Like Bumble
in *Oliver Twist* or Squeers in *Nicholas Nickleby*, these late chapters
see Micawber reduced from character to agent, becoming no more

than the function of a line of plot inorganically dissociated from the novel's focus of action.

The only other strand in the later chapters of *David Copperfield* that requires explication is the seduction of Em'ly. Thackeray claimed that Dickens had learned from *Vanity Fair*, and it may well be this that was in his mind. There are real inventions here, like the soft-footed valet, Littimer, the discarded mistress, Rosa, the stony Mrs Steerforth, the light-hearted seducer, Steerforth himself, and the storm scene that drowns him. Decent Victorian novel-writing, one may suggest, without depth or meaning; from which we turn back to the phantasmagoric symbolism of *The Trials of David*. The difference between the boy David and the mature man is that between the torments of Mr Creakle's academy and the translation to the torpid paradise of Doctor Strong's. The one is precisely imagined, a savage indictment of the flames of hell; the other is polite and febrile, conforming in a conformist world.

In the early part of the book, the picaresque shape allows for motive. It provides a correlative to Dickens's own sense of desertion. The first chapter infallibly reminds us of *Tristram Shandy*, and he is forever comparing his young hero with Robinson Crusoe, Tom Jones and Roderick Random. It is true that Dickens was not left an orphan, nor blocked by his relatives, nor even beaten by pedants (though his schoolmates were); though all this happens to Roderick, and, beyond him, to David. However, so great a rage as that of Dickens can only be justified by the paranoid creation of enraging circumstance. The young David is not a passive hero reacting to obstacles across his path, though this might be said of Robinson Crusoe, Roderick Random *et al.*, to say nothing of his grown-up self. Rather the obstacles are all the more keenly apprehended because of their effect upon him as a character. They frighten or enrage him, and he is therefore all the more aware of them; and we are aware of them, too, because we see them through his eyes.

The young David is sharply individual, as earlier heroes of Dickens are not. He is as representative as Oliver, but far more personalized; as oppressed as the children of Dotheboys Hall, but informed with the author's own feeling. He is at once an archetypal waif upon the road and a projection of his author's own psyche. At last Dickens was able to inform social criticism with personal emotion; or, what comes to the same thing, he projected his personal emotion into a critique of society, and so erected realistic details into symbolic drama.

The picaresque wanderings, then, are not, like those of Roderick, at random. There is very little in the earlier *Copperfield* that does not relate to the respective roles of parent and child. Dickens's paranoid sense of rejection is made precise and dramatic by creating a boy-hero who survives against dreadful odds. And the odds are made real enough; genuine horrors of an unheeding Society. In this way, Dickens escapes the charge of subjectivism. But he survives only at the cost of regression. His positives – motherhood, sexuality – show a personality in retreat from maturity. The young David may stay with Betsey Trotwood; we cannot.

But all this had to be got out of Dickens's psyche before he went on to write his greatest books. Hence, perhaps, the retrospective technique, invoking those same novels that were the solace of his own childhood as well as that of his hero. It indicates, too, the struggles and backslidings of Dickens's development. If *Dombey and Son* was the first novel of Dickens's maturity, then *David Copperfield*, its successor, is the last novel of his apprenticeship.

XIII Household Words (1850-59)
Reprinted Pieces (1858)
All the Year Round (1859-70)
The Uncommercial Traveller (1860-69)

As a boy, Dickens had read collected volumes of Addison's magazine *The Spectator* and Goldsmith's magazine, *The Bee*. As a young man, he had been influenced by the essays that Leigh Hunt published in *The Indicator*. And, in maturity, he had, several times, tried to run a periodical himself.

At the first attempt, *Bentley's Miscellany* (1837), he found himself unable to get on with the proprietor. At the second, *Master Humphrey's Clock* (1840), he found that it was the public he was at loggerheads with. And his editorship of the *Daily News* (1846) lasted a matter of days: the printers' interference in editorial policy may have been only one of the reasons for his resignation.

But, long before *David Copperfield* had run its course, Dickens was formulating the project of a magazine designed to appeal to the family. After rejecting such titles as *The Holly Tree* and *The Household Guest*, and having his concept of The Shadow as conductor and guide heavily sat upon by Forster, Dickens began on 30 March 1850 the weekly periodical known as *Household Words*.

This was a curiously personal venture. Though none of the articles or stories was signed, every page carried at the top this legend: 'Conducted by Charles Dickens'. Some readers were under the impression that Dickens not only edited the magazine but wrote the entire contents himself. In some ways, they were right: Dickens was an editor of the extrovert variety. For example, he gathered around him an inner circle of regular contributors with the happy gift of being able to write to some extent after the model of their Chief, though, for the most part, they pick up his mannerisms without the impetus behind them. The key figure among these was H. W. Wills, with whom Dickens collaborated very happily throughout his working life. Wills had been his secretary on the *Daily News* and later became one of the original staff of *Punch*, from which magazine he was garnered to be manager, factotum and generally deputy editor of the new periodical. He could write, more than most, in the manner of Dickens, and scholars are still attempting to sort out the fruits of their collaboration. One essay, 'A Plated Article', seems to be very much a joint venture: at least it appears both in Dickens's selection from his essays, *Reprinted Pieces*, and in Wills's *Old Leaves: Gathered from Household Words* (1860). From internal evidence alone, it would be impossible to say whether this is bad Dickens or good Wills. And Wills became Dickens's alter ego, the day-to-day manager of the magazine, completely happy in subsuming his personality in that of his master. Without his attention to routine matters beneath the notice of the Inimitable, *Household Words* never could have survived.

Other writers, while less indispensable, caught and promulgated the *Household Words* manner. R. H. Horne, whose social insight had impressed Dickens in the 1840s, was on the staff for the first couple of years; he was much in demand as a scientific popularizer. Another popularizer was the elderly hack, Charles Knight, whose version of Faraday's lectures on combustion appeared on 3 August 1850, and helped to fertilize Dickens's conception of Krook blowing himself up in *Bleak House*. It does not present the facts as bare bones, but shows a small boy explaining to an indulgently sceptical uncle the chemistry of burning a candle. This approach served as the pattern for informative articles in boys' magazines for a century afterwards, and out of that tradition came the familiar BBC Schools Broadcasts of today. Dickens's great cry to his editors and contributors was 'Brighten it, brighten it'. And so, enormous pains were taken, not just with the facts in *Household Words*, but with the presentation of those facts. It was not easy to appear in its pages: in 1854, the rate of acceptance was one article in every eighty; and the eleven articles from 'outside' contributors that did appear in *Household Words* were all extensively rewritten. To be one of the inner circle an author had to share much of Dickens's approach, in style as well as idea. George Augustus Sala achieved entry into the magazine in 1851 with a piece called *The Key of the Street* (itself a quotation from *Pickwick*) which bears ample evidence that this aspiring twenty-four-year-old had studied his market. It is an account of the homeless vagrants that sleep out at night in London, and it fictionalizes, dramatizes and 'brightens' the facts much in the manner of the Inimitable himself. Naturally, Dickens was delighted, and wrote to Wills that the article would have been placed first in the magazine – a position normally occupied by Dickens – if it were not that such an honour would go to the young man's head! And Sala remained a regular contributor for some years thereafter. Other contributors were equally pliable. Henry Morley was used for the more routine documentary work, being a notable digester and retailer of fact. Wilkie Collins supplied melodramatic fiction and collaborated with Dickens on several of the stories that came out as supplements at Christmas time; his role in the magazine and in Dickens's life was to increase as time went on. And a lot of the general hackwork was done by James Payn, Percy Fitzgerald and John Hollingshead; journalists whose work has receded into the general ruck of the magazine and is virtually indistinguishable from the general house style.

Not one of these writers can be regarded as being in the top flight. And of the luminaries who contributed serials – Charles Lever, Bulwer Lytton, Collins again – there is not one whose radiance has not faded. Though George Eliot was invited to send in work, she refused to be tempted; judging, no doubt rightly, that she would sacrifice artistic integrity in submitting her own very different genius to the direction and guidance of Boz. So far as we can make out, Thackeray wasn't even asked. Indeed, it would be true to say that the only writer of real distinction who could be termed any sort of regular contributor was Mrs Gaskell. And she was the only one whose work was free from the abridgment, tightening and brightening of Dickens's editorial hand.

For his constant pleas to contributors, sustained and reinforced by the detailed sub-editing of Wills, was 'Keep *Household Words* imaginative!' And this meant that a good many of the contributors had to allow their articles to be reworked, interpolated and added to by the Conductor and his indefatigable factotum. Harry Stone, in a monumental piece of research, has identified a good many of these composite articles, and it is amazing how many of them could have come from the hand of the Master himself in an off-period.

One would not imagine present-day writers putting up with this form of dictatorship. The nearest equivalent in our own time is perhaps Kingsley Martin of the *New Statesman*; but, though journalists such as Crossman, MacCarthy, Mackenzie and Pritchett may have picked up or adopted a house style, they certainly weren't rewritten and brightened into one.

Household Words, therefore, was a unique phenomenon. Its policy was to educate and entertain at the same time; its contributions included fiction, verse, social documentary, politics of the radical Dickens variety, popular science and straight reportage. Dickens seems marvellously to have caught the public mood. His insistence upon style of presentation meant that all kinds of subjects were rendered palatable to his readers: dockyards, markets, even snails. Sometimes the emphasis on presentation means that obvious and simple facts are burnished and dressed up to the extent that their brightness does not so much illuminate as dazzle.

Dickens eventually published a selection of his own writing for *Household Words* under the title, *Reprinted Pieces*. This volume has become quite famous through being included in all subsequent collected editions of his work. But, if one considers that he appeared in over two hundred issues, it will be seen that the thirty *Reprinted Pieces* give only the slightest indication of what he was doing.

There is every case for considering this collection of essays as a book in its own right. The astringency of selection indicates care and planning on the part of the author. The manner is related to that of Leigh Hunt, Goldsmith and Addison: relaxed, easy and gentle in tone. Typical of such periodical essays are 'Our English Watering Place', 'Our French Watering Place' and 'Out of the Season'. This last, a good specimen of its kind, shows a holiday town with half the houses shut up and the other half to let, and business generally at low ebb. It is an example of the essayist's gift for the deft notation of mundane events. But a form of writing that derives from Leigh Hunt's descriptive sketches and leads on to (say) J. B. Priestley's *The Balconinny* is hardly going to stun us at this point in time.

Fortunately, Dickens the essayist was also Dickens the reporter, and, if nothing else, the *Reprinted Pieces* show how rooted in fact are the fictional recreations of the major novels. 'On Duty with Inspector Field' anticipates the nightmare journey into Tom-all-Alone's of Bucket and Snagsby in *Bleak House*. 'Down with the Tide', even more prophetically, foreshadows the river imagery of *Our Mutual Friend*. But, for the most part, Dickens sought to eschew the topical and the political; and, to that extent, the *Reprinted Pieces* are untypical of his work for *Household Words* as a whole. We have only one or two glimpses of the radical Dickens of the novels. One is the story of a Poor Man's Patent: agonizing in fact, genuinely comic in presentation; and, once more, a documentary foreshadowing of an event that was to take place in Dickens's fiction – in this instance, the awful experiences in *Little Dorrit* of the inventor, Doyce, at the Circumlocution Office. The poor man is pushed from the Home Secretary to the Attorney-General, to the Patent Office, the Engrossing Clerk, the Lord Chancellor, the Lord Chancellor's Purse-Bearer, the Clerk and the Deputy Clerk of the Hanaper, and the Deputy Chaff-wax. No man in England, he declares, could patent an india-rubber band without feeing the lot of them. 'Note. I should like to see the Deputy Chaff-wax. Is it a man, or what is it? My opinion is . . . that the whole gang of Hanapers and Chaff-waxes must be done away with, and that England has been chaffed and waxed sufficient.'

This, in little, is how Dickens kept *Household Words* imaginative. The basis of this article is a quite factual explanation of the tedious procedure that had to be gone through in order to secure a patent. But the whole piece is dressed up so that we have an actual inventor, very strongly characterized, and the whole story is told in his own, highly specific, terms.

But of the central Dickens, who was a writer of non-fictional prose fit to be set above Carlyle, at the side of Ruskin and only marginally below Macaulay, there is scant sign in the *Reprinted Pieces*. The only hint of his true greatness comes in 'A Walk in the Workhouse' which is really biting satire, infused with a pervading compassion for the poor and weak. The description of the old men's ward looks forward to the evocation of Nandy, which is one of the finest things in *Little Dorrit*.

As we have seen, however, Dickens chose for the most part not to collect in volume form his most disturbing prose. The job was done for him by B. W. Matz in 1908 and was incorporated into the Gadshill and Nonesuch editions of Dickens's work. But this collection of *Miscellaneous Papers*, though it is of the first importance, has never been anything like as easy to come by as the *Reprinted Pieces*. And, to judge from the paucity of comment upon it, the work in these volumes would seem to have remained comparatively unfrequented. This is a pity, for it includes writing as achieved, though not as complex and subtle, as that of the great novels. I shall have occasion to deal with 'On Strike' (*Household Words*, 11 February 1854) when speaking of *Hard Times*: and, similarly, the Carlylean rhetoric of 'Nobody, Somebody and Everybody' (*Household Words*, 30 August 1856) has its proper place in the discussion of *Little Dorrit*. The reader will have, therefore, to assume the presence of these essays in the present chapter.

Germane to any consideration of Dickens's non-fictional prose are his excursions into reportage, especially that concerned with social issues. Hence the keen observation is powered by radical anger. Allied with the one essay in the *Reprinted Pieces* to exhibit this are several that had to wait for Matz to collect them: notably another article on the ragged schools, 'A Sleep to Startle us' (*Household Words*, 13 March 1852); 'Home for Homeless Women' (23 April 1853); and 'A Nightly Scene in London' (26 January 1856). This last shows the pitiful degradation of human beings not inside but, perforce, outside an overcrowded workhouse.

Crouched against the wall of the Workhouse, in the dark street, on the muddy pavement-stones, with the rain raining upon them, were five bundles of rags. They were motionless, and had no resemblance to the human form. Five great beehives covered with rags – five dead bodies taken out of graves, tied neck and heels and covered with rags – would have looked like those five bundles upon which the rain rained down in the public street. . . .

We went to the ragged bundle nearest to the Workhouse-door, and I touched it. No movement replying, I gently shook it. The rags began to be slowly stirred within, and by little and little a head was unshrouded. The head of a young woman of three or four and twenty, as I should judge; gaunt with want, and foul with dust; but not naturally ugly. . . .

'What have you had to eat?'
   'Nothing.'
   'Come!' said I. 'Think a little. You are tired and have been asleep, and don't quite consider what you are saying to us. You have had something to eat today. Come! Think of it!'

'No I haven't. Nothing but such bits as I could pick up about the market. Why, look at me!'

She bared her neck, and I covered it up again. . . .

This is documentary raised to the level of art. The clarity of vision rivals that which had already seen and described Tom-all-alone's in *Bleak House*, and its truth to fact makes for a stark simplicity precluding the kind of emotionalism that tends to hang about Jo, the crossing-sweeper. The sentence 'she bared her neck, and I covered it up again' – no doubt, a description of fact – tells us more about the plight of the young vagrant than paragraphs of adjectival description and chapters of denunciation à la Carlyle. Denunciation there certainly is in the article, but it is given root in reality by such specific description as this. So that when, in the end, Dickens cries out upon the promulgators of laissez-faire who think poverty is part of the natural order of things, he does so backed by the certainty that he has seen and felt for himself the degradation that he pities. 'I know that the unreasonable disciples of a reasonable school, demented disciples who push arithmetic beyond all bounds of sense . . . can easily prove that such things ought to be, and that no man has any business to mind them . . . I utterly renounce and abominate them in their insanity; and I address people with respect for the spirit of the New Testament, who do mind such things, and who think them infamous in our streets.'

Such essays in social documentation as this do not have quite the focus of the series on Drouet and his cholera-ridden child-farm, but they certainly demand circulation in some popular form. Even if he cannot qualify as a political philosopher, Dickens has no rival in describing the plight of human beings in distress. His genius is to empathize and so inform reported example with personal feeling. He could specify and particularize as Carlyle could not; so that behind even his lapses into rodomontade is the pressure of many particular instances.

Naturally, it is harder for Dickens's brand of social concern to emerge in writings that are composite, and most of these latter are descriptive in character and, hence, lower in intensity. Some of them caused Dickens considerable distress: a contribution from Morley went against one aspect of the *Household Words* ideology – that the prevention of crime mattered more than the cure of the criminal –

and therefore had to be rewritten into orthodoxy by Wills and the result still further 'brightened' into literature by Dickens. The final version saw the light on 14 May 1853, but bears all too many marks of the months of labour preceding.

The best of the composite articles are undoubtedly those that Dickens wrote in collaboration with Wills. Dickens sometimes began these and often ended them, and put in the odd paragraph wherever he felt the interest begin to slacken. Thus, in a descriptive piece on Epsom (7 June 1851), Dickens entrusts to Wills the run-of-the-mill reportage, but comes in on the last five columns to whip the descriptive prose into a fine foam of poetry.

Now, the gentleman who is accustomed to public driving gets into astonishing perplexities. Now, the Hansom cab whisks craftily in and out, and seems occasionally to fly over a wagon. Now the postboy on a jibbing or a shying horse, curses the evil hour of his birth, and is ingloriously assisted by the shabby ostler out of place, who is walking down with seven shabby companions, more or less equine, open to the various chances of the road. . . .

The description continues in this vein; but, vivacious though it is, the structure of this essay is less advanced than that of Dickens's social documentaries and suggests that in composite writings Dickens was unable to travel far from the simple 'Now' formula patented after Goldsmith by Leigh Hunt and adopted for several of the Sketches by Boz.

So even the best of the articles that Dickens wrote with Wills are of comparatively minor stature in the body of his work. He made some powerful interpolations in Wills's 'The Heart of Mid-London' (*Household Words*, 4 May 1850), but this is an essay not about people but animals; Smithfield Cattle Market, in fact. Wills gives us facts carefully documented and certainly personalized – 'brightened' in their presentation after the approved manner of *Household Words*. But, every now and then, Dickens himself comes in, and the effect is galvanic. Wills says, of the cattle,

Across their horns, across their backs, across their hocks, across their haunches, Mr Bovington saw the heavy blows rain thick and fast, let him look where he would.

But Dickens goes on to vitalize that picture in all its frenetic detail:

Obdurate heads of oxen, bent down in mute agony; bellowing heads of oxen lifted up, snorting out smoke and slaver; ferocious men, cursing and swearing, and belabouring oxen; made the place a panorama of cruelty and suffering. By every avenue of access to the market, more oxen were pouring in: bellowing, in the confusion, and under the falling blows, as if all the church-organs in the world were wretched instruments – all there – and all being tuned together.

Wills was an acceptable prose writer, but he could never have managed the controlled ambiguities contained in such phrases as 'heads of oxen' and 'wretched instruments'. Here the literal and metaphorical senses play upon each other and interact. This is not the letter on Drouet or the essay about the overcrowded workhouse, but it is certainly impressive.

In a different vein, when Wills has given us a useful description of a night at a Central London police station ('The Metropolitan Protectives', *Household Words, 26* April 1851), Dickens comes in for five really funny columns, taking Wills's documentation to heights well beyond that modest functionary, and creating two fine comic characters in the process: the formidable Mrs Megby, of Drury Lane, and a 'very stupid little gentleman', so incapably drunk that he cannot be convinced that his watch has been stolen.

'Now, sir, your name, if you please?'

'Ba – a.'

'*That* can't be your name, sir What name does he say, Constable?'

The second Constable 'seriously inclines his ear'; the gent being a short man, and the second constable a tall one. 'He says his name's Bat, sir?' (Getting at it after a good deal of trouble.)

'Where do you live, Mr Bat?'

'Lamber.'

'And what are you? – what business are you, Mr Bat?'

'Fesher,' says Mr Bat, again collecting dignity.

'Profession, is it? Very good, sir. What's your profession?'

'Solirrer,' returns Mr Bat.

'Solicitor, of Lambeth. Have you lost anything besides your watch, sir?'

'I am nor aware – lost – any – arrickle – prorrery,' says Mr Bat.

The Inspector has been looking at the watch.

'What do you value this watch at, sir?'

'Ten pound,' says Mr Bat, with unexpected promptitude.

'Hardly worth so much as that, I should think?'

'Five pound five,' says Mr Bat. 'I doro how much. I'm not par-TICK-ler,'
this word costs Mr Bat a tremendous effort, 'abow the war. It's not my war.
It's a frez of my.'
  'If it belongs to a friend of yours, you wouldn't like to lose it, I suppose?'
  'I doro,' says Mr Bat, 'I'm nor any ways par-TICK-ler abow the war.
It's a frez of my;' which he afterwards repeats at intervals, scores of times.
Always as an entirely novel idea. . . .

No doubt, from what we know of Dickens's methods, Mr Bat had
his prototype, and this prototype was there for Wills, equally as for
Dickens, to write up. But it is Dickens who has the art to pick out
and play up the salient trait, the odd distinguishing detail, the fact
that the Inspector – as we cannot – interprets drunken obscurity
into intelligible speech; and thus he turns reportage into recreation.

  Household Words continued, year after year, to be found compulsively readable by its Victorian audience, although we may consider it – especially in relation to Dickens's novels – a little inclined to
underestimate the intelligence and education of its readers. However,
suddenly the whole enterprise was brought to a halt.

  For some years Dickens had been living less and less easily with
his wife. In 1857 he vacated the matrimonial chamber in favour of his
dressing-room, and directed that a barricade be erected between the
two. In a matter of months after that, he took up temporary residence
in the *Household Words* office, and remained there until Kate Dickens
left their home at Gad's Hill – as it turned out, for ever. With a rash-
ness that now seems inconceivable, Dickens published in the *Household Words* of 12 June 1858, a statement marked Personal, emphasizing
that he and his wife had parted amicably, and that no other woman
was in question. But he quarrelled furiously with Bradbury and
Evans for not reprinting the statement in *Punch* which they also
published; this, in spite of the fact that *Punch* was a comic paper
and that he had made no request to them to do so. And, after a
reading tour covering Ireland and the North of England, he broke
off relations with his printers. For the future publication of his novels
he returned to Chapman and Hall, who had been rendered inoffensive
to him by the death of Hall and the imminent retirement of Chapman
– the firm being effectively run by the latter's cousin, Frederic. More
difficult was the ousting of Bradbury and Evans from *Household
Words*. The financial arrangements were so inextricably entangled

that finally Dickens withdrew from the editorship, blocked the attempts on the part of the printers to continue the magazine, and – most crucially – started another of his own. That was how, in 1859, *All the Year Round* was born.

Dickens took his staff and regular contributors with him; and the faithful Wills continued to manage affairs from day to day for the new magazine. But the second temple was not like the first. Though Dickens now had sole control, as he never did with *Household Words*, he was more and more content to leave the running of the magazine – and the 'brightening' of articles – to Wills, with Collins as the most important ancillary contributor. No longer do we have the frenetic interplay of editor and writers that we saw, uniquely, in the earlier magazine; nor is there so violent a cascade of articles from the editor's own pen. He published two serials in the pages of the magazine: *A Tale of Two Cities* (1859) and *Great Expectations* (1861), and wrote a number of essays that appeared under the generic title of *The Uncommercial Traveller*. Apart from this, the periodical writing Dickens did during eleven years on *All the Year Round* was ephemeral: obituaries of Leigh Hunt, the prototype of Skimpole, and Walter Savage Landor, the prototype of Boythorn, both in *Bleak House*; the odd correction of fact, or note on a controversy; the occasional squib or blow-off. So that when we consider Dickens's later non-fictional prose, it is to *The Uncommercial Traveller* we must turn.

This has all the appearance of being intended as a group of essays, as clearly as Addison's *Spectator* or Goldsmith's *Citizen of the World* which seems to be its immediate prototype. The attitude is struck in the very first essay, published in *All the Year Round* on 28 January 1860. The words have become famous: 'I am both a town traveller and a country traveller, and am always on the road. Figuratively speaking, I travel for the great house of Human Interest Brothers, and have rather a large connection in the fancy goods way.' The conception is clearly related to that of the Shadow who, until dissolved by Forster's scorn, was to have permeated *Household Words* as general guide and conductor. The figure of the Uncommercial Traveller is unspecific enough to allow for flexibility of stance and subject-matter and still provide focus sufficient for the thirty-six essays finally collected to appear something of a unity. Indeed, not a few of Dickens's earlier essays could fall into something of the same category: the interested outsider entering a workhouse, say, or observing a market.

The essays of *The Uncommercial Traveller* were published as three separate series. Chapters 1–17 appeared in *All the Year Round* between 28 January and 13 October 1860. They are the most rapidly and fluently composed, and bear all the evidence of an editor's excitement in launching a magazine as well as the author's natural zest for a new form. This first series was published as a collection in 1861. Both as individual essays and as a book, *The Uncommercial Traveller* was successful enough to take the road again on 2 May 1863. He travelled continuously through that year, winding himself up on 24 October (Chapters 18–29). Then there was a long gap, only partly filled by the writing of *Our Mutual Friend* and seemingly part and parcel with Dickens's reluctance to begin a new novel thereafter. The time was filled with reading tours and lectures. Even when Dickens did resume his uncommercial travels, he did so a little tentatively. Chapters 30–34, beginning with 'Aboard Ship', came out as 'New Uncommercial Samples' between 5 December 1868 and 27 February 1869. Chapter 35 stands a little apart from the others, on 5 June 1868; while Chapter 36, the last to come from Dickens's pen, appears in the body of the magazine, albeit attributed to the Uncommercial Traveller. And one, markedly depressive piece, in which Dickens sees himself as Merdle, the swindler pictured in *Little Dorrit*, was published on 22 May 1869, as one of the Uncommercial Samples, but was never reprinted.

Most of these essays resemble the *Reprinted Pieces*, although the concept of the Traveller renders them more unified in subject-matter and form. But – 'what can I but enumerate old themes?' The best among these essays concern the ill-treatment of sailors on board ship; emigrants going out to America; schools where the pupils split their lives between factory and classroom; alms-houses; ruffians. And there are several of Dickens's town sketches, the most attractive of which is 'Shy Neighbourhoods' with its humorous divagation concerning dogs.

The Traveller, in other words, does not range quite far enough out of Dickens's now well-known territories. This is not quite the same as accusing him of failing powers: the merest comparison between Sala's Dickensian imitation. 'The Key of the Street', and the Inimitable himself in 'Night Walks' would persuade us otherwise, and there is no doubt that the eye is as keen as ever, and the ear. Nor has Dickens's gift for evoking character out of reportage deserted him. Here is one of the inhabitants of 'Titbull's Almshouses'. Notice how the old man's battle with the recalcitrant pump is prepared for.

I take the ground to have risen in these parts since Titbull's time, and you drop into his domain by three stone steps. So did I first drop into it, very nearly striking my brows against Titbull's pump, which stands with its back to the thoroughfare just inside the gate, and has a conceited air of reviewing Titbull's pensioners.

'And a worse one,' said a virulent old man with a pitcher, 'there isn't nowhere. A harder one to work, nor a grudginer one to yield, there isn't nowhere!' This old man wore a long coat, such as we see Hogarth's Chairmen represented with, and it was of that peculiar green-pea hue without the green, which seems to come of poverty. It had also that peculiar smell of cupboard which seems to come of poverty.

'The pump is rusty, perhaps,' said I.

'Not *it*,' said the old man, regarding it with undiluted virulence in his watery eye. 'It never were fit to be termed a pump. That's what's the matter with *it*.'

'Whose fault is that?' said I.

The old man, who had a working mouth which seemed to be trying to masticate his anger and to find that it was too hard and there was too much of it, replied, 'Them gentlemen.'

'What gentlemen?'

'Maybe you're one of 'em?' said the old man, suspiciously.

'The trustees?'

'I wouldn't trust 'em myself,' said the virulent old man.

'If you mean the gentlemen who administer this place, no, I am not one of them; nor have I ever so much as heard of them.'

'I wish *I* never heard of them,' gasped the old man: 'at my time of life – with the rheumatics – drawing water – from that thing!' Not to be deluded into calling it a Pump, the old man gave it another virulent look, took up his pitcher, and carried it into a corner dwellinghouse, shutting the door after him.

This is a flawless vignette, beautifully conceived and executed – notice the old man's 'working mouth which seemed to be trying to masticate his anger and to find that it was too hard and there was too much of it'. Such humorous recreation of salient traits renders

Dickens essentially inimitable even by the best of his contributors. Yet there is something a little unnerving about the easy assurance with which Dickens handles his themes in *The Uncommercial Traveller*. One can't help feeling that he is making artistic capital out of other people's misery. Not that the social indignation isn't there: it is burning at its most furious in what is, perhaps, the best of all the Travels: 'A Small Star in the East', which reports the poverty rampant in Dockside London. But, one begins to feel, Dickens has done so much reporting of this nature, so consummately well for so many years, that by now we are entitled to ask for rather more positive approaches to criticism. It is true that he approved such attempts at alleviating poverty and ignorance as the part-time schools, but he never seems to see the specific instances he describes in any larger context. And we may be aware of a certain unction in reporting these instances; as though the Traveller were able to pass through such scenes, fortunate man, and not be scathed by them; as though poverty, malnutrition, disease and ignorance at one level of society did not affect them all. In brief, the social criticism of (say) *Oliver Twist* or the Dotheboys Hall episode in *Nicholas Nickleby* was informed by personal feeling. In those early tracts, Dickens saw himself as waif. Here, in the flood tide of success, famous and caressed, he could not. He is, as regards misfortunes of poverty and neglect, at last on the outside looking in.

What we may notice that is new in *The Uncommercial Traveller* is a tendency to slip into moments of autobiography, sometimes only tenuously related to the subject in hand. There is a prefiguration of this in 'One Man in a Dockyard', an evocation of his childhood Chatham, written in collaboration with R. H. Horne (*Household Words*, 6 September 1851). We find such autobiographical detail, tenderly touched upon, in 'Travelling Abroad', 'Dullborough [i.e. Chatham] Town', 'Nurse's Stories' with its marvellous retelling of the grotesque tale of Captain Murderer, 'Birthdays', and 'At a Dockyard' (Chatham, again). Here we have hints towards the autobiography that Dickens was destined never to write. But, like his earlier essays, the distinction of *The Uncommercial Traveller* rests upon its evocation of poverty, disease, workhouses, and the lower echelons of society generally. Had it been less mellow in its evocation, the writing would have been that much more distinguished.

The case I would make out for Dickens here is that he was a truly great essayist whose non-fictional work has been obscured by the greater glory of the novels. Earlier chapters of this book have pointed to individual Sketches and letters on social questions which deserve promulgation; it is arguable that Dickens did nothing better in this kind than the articles on Drouet, hard of access though they are. Much of the best journalism from 1850 onward has also remained virtually inaccessible to the general public. Some twenty essays, at least, could be selected from the outpouring of twenty years, and they would show Dickens not only as a social critic and inspired reporter but as a great writer of non-fictional prose. It is not Dickens's fault if the form of the periodical essay gave his genius less scope for range and profundity than the infinitely superior form of the novel as dramatic poem. But the latter was not achieved without various alarms and excursions on the way.

XIV   Christmas Stories (1852-67)

Every Christmas, from 1850 onwards, Dickens issued an extra number of *Household Words*. The first issue was a miscellany of stories by regular contributors; the second consisted of essays; but, after this, the Christmas numbers were invariably fictional in character. And the practice of producing a collection of stories by various hands at Christmas time ran on into the succeeding periodical, *All the Year Round*, and was discontinued in 1868 – a result, Dickens said, of too many cheap imitations from other publishers.

At first, these compilations were very much a random harvest. Dickens wrote to the Reverend James White on 19 October 1852, 'We are now getting our Christmas extra number together, and I think you are the boy to do, if you will, one of the stories. I propose to give the number some fireside name, and to make it consist almost entirely of short stories supposed to be told by a family sitting round the fire. I don't care about their referring to Christmas at all; nor do I design to connect them together otherwise than by their names, as: The Grandfather's Story, The Father's Story, The Daughter's Story,' etc.

But the idea grew upon Dickens that the stories could, in fact, be interconnected, and this gave him a chance to use his extrovert skill as editor to bind together what became an essentially collaborative enterprise. From 1854 onwards he designed a fictive framework that would bring into contact various characters, each with a story to tell. The instructions to prospective contributors become more elaborate. Those for *The Holly Tree Inn*, which was the number for 1855, at once show the nature of Dickens's editorship and the form which, basically, most subsequent issues took.

A traveller who finds himself the only person staying at an Inn on Christmas Day, is at his wits' end what to do with himself; the rather as he is a timid and reserved character, and, being shut up in his solitary sitting-room, doesn't well know how to come out of it and speak to anybody. The general idea of the Number is, that he overcomes this feeling, finds out the stories of the different people belonging to the Inn – or some curious experience that each has had – and writes down what he discovers.

Both for the sake of a variety between this No and previous Christmas numbers, and also for the preservation of the idea, it is necessary that the stories should *not* be in the first person, but should be turned as if this traveller were recording them. Thus the Headings will not be The Waiter's Story, The Cook's Story, The Chambermaid's Story, etc., but simply The Waiter – The Cook – The Chambermaid – and under each head the traveller himself is supposed to tell whatever he heard from, or fancied about, or found out about, that particular person. Thus the person to whom the story belongs may be described, if necessary, as pretty or ugly – of such an age – of such a bringing up – and what is related about him or her may have happened at that Inn, or at another Inn, or at no Inn; and may belong to that person's present condition in life, or to some previous condition in life and not only to himself or herself but (if necessary) to other persons encountered in life.

In the resultant collection, Dickens himself writes up the Guest and the Boots and finishes off the issue by presenting the Bill. Wilkie Collins does the Ostler, the Landlord and the Poor Pensioner, while Adelaide Anne Procter provides a sentimental poem put into the mouth of the Barmaid.

Dickens chose the contributors and supplied, sometimes in collaboration with Collins, head and tail links. But there was a good deal of discussion beforehand. Percy Fitzgerald, a *Household Words* regular, has recorded the sense of expectancy, indeed excitement, that built up as another Christmas number was prepared. 'It was the object for all to have a seat in a vehicle which travelled every road and reached the houses of a quarter of a million persons.' *The Queen* for 21 December 1861 has a caricature showing Dickens and his staff gathered around a table debating their respective ideas in various stages of enthusiasm, doubt and anxiety.

It was an eccentric venture, but it met with great public success. Dickens was aiming for an audience even wider, and consequently less literate, than that which welcomed his major novels. Once set up, the pattern of Christmas stories hardly ever varied. *The Seven*

Poor Travellers (1854) has a narrative framework whereby several strangers come into fortuitous contact at a hospice founded by a charitable will. The general narrator, written up by Dickens himself, says, 'Shall we beguile the time by telling stories, in our order as we sit here?' Well, of course, they do. Dickens supplies the tale of Richard Doubledick, a Waterloo veteran founded upon one of his relatives; G. A. Sala tells the Shipwright's and Watchmaker's stories; Adelaide Procter gives us (in verse) stories from a Sailor Boy and a Book Pedlar; Mrs Lynn Linton, the Widow's Story; Wilkie Collins, in a startling anticipation of *Great Expectations*'s Mr Jaggers, the Lawyer's Story; while Dickens winds the whole thing up himself in a brief epilogue.

The Wreck of the Golden Mary (1856) is mostly an adventure story written by Dickens and Collins somewhat after the model of Captain Marryat. But the castaways in the open boats beguile their time in telling stories by Percy Fitzgerald, Harriet Parr, Adelaide Procter and the Rev. James White. *A House to Let* (1858) simply records the fortunes of its various inhabitants within a narrative framework embodying an old lady, her absurd beau, and her manservant. The collaborators on this occasion included, as well as the usual team of Wilkie Collins and Adelaide Procter, Mrs Gaskell with a story in her Manchester vein. However, the pièce de resistance was Dickens's saga of the rise and fall of Mr Chops, the circus dwarf: a comic-pathetic effort that was to enliven not a few of his future recitals. And the formula succeeded equally well in *All the Year Round,* with *The Haunted House* (1859), *A Message from the Sea* (1860), *Tom Tiddler's Ground* (1861); with much the same group of people contributing their various pieces, though Charles Collins and Amelia Edwards were new recruits to the regular corps.

It cannot be said that much of this was very distinguished. One can sometimes make an exception for Dickens himself, as in his contribution to *A House to Let.* But, by and large, he went down to meet his contributors half way rather than, as in the non-fictional collaborations of *Household Words* proper, raising them nearer his own level. Possibly this was due to the enforced absence of Wills as a direct participant: whatever his talents on the administrative side of collecting material, the ability to write fiction was not among them. The melodramatic daemon of Wilkie Collins counted for infinitely more, and seems to have induced Dickens to embrace what became a common stock of utterance. As well as the occasional bout of brisk action or wild humour in these Christmas Numbers of *Household Words*, there is a good deal of sentiment, much reliance on hearty coincidence, and a certain amount of markedly stagey posturing. At best, what these extra numbers represent is pleasant and conventional light reading for the holiday season.

But the later Christmas numbers, in *All the Year Round*, are different. The framework becomes far more that of monologue, and comic monologue at that. With Sam Weller and Sarah Gamp behind him, Dickens had no rival in Cockney humours. So that we find that, characteristically, the plodding sentiment of Charles Collins, Amelia Edwards, Rosa Mulholland, Hesba Stretton – the casting favours lachrymose authoresses as the years wear on – is enclosed by a running commentary which, at moments, rises to the topmost flight of Dickensian extravaganza.

The new tone is set by *Somebody's Luggage* (1862). Here the stories are found in various articles of clothing left behind by a mysterious guest in an hotel. The stories themselves are of no especial interest, even when they come from the hand of Dickens himself; one of his contributions is the sentimental tale of a middle-aged Englishman adopting a small child in France. But the framework, especially the introductory section, is a different matter altogether. Here we have a Waiter descanting upon the trials and torments of Waiting, especially the disrupted family life it entails. The monologue is done with humour, insight and a wealth of descriptive detail put across with superbly inventive grotesquerie.

You were conveyed, by surreptitious means, into a pantry adjoining the Admiral Nelson Civil and General Dining Rooms, there to receive by stealth that healthful sustenance which is the pride and boast of the British female constitution . . . your innocent mind surrounded by uncongenial cruets, dirty plates, dish-covers and cold gravy; your mother calling down the pipe for veals and porks, instead of soothing you with nursery rhymes. . . .

In later Christmas numbers, other remarkable figures were added to the language: all in this same post-Weller mode, for Dickens had an extraordinary ear for certain forms of Cockney intonation. We are introduced to *Mrs Lirriper's Lodgings* in 1863. They indeed become a little oppressive when dealing with the plight of a deserted wife and positively claustrophobic when the usual assortment of sentimental tales is confided by sundry lodgers to Mrs Lirriper's perpetual (and non-paying) tenant, 'Major' Jemmy Jackman. But of Mrs Lirriper herself, expounding the trials of her vocation, there can be scant criticism.

Girls as I was beginning to remark are one of your first and your lasting troubles, being like your teeth which begin with convulsions and never cease tormenting you from the time you cut them till the time they cut you, and then you don't want to part with them which seems hard but we must all succumb or buy artificial, and even when you get a will nine times out of ten you'll get a dirty face with it and naturally lodgers do not like good society to be shown in with a smear of black across the nose or a smudgy eyebrow. . . .

This is all one sentence – rambling, but only on the surface inconsequential. At the least, it gets in a life-time's experience of employing slaveys; at most, it shows the intimate connection of events – teeth and maidservants alike being symptoms of the gradual attrition of life – which to the rational mind seem unconnected. But Mrs Lirriper is very far from being rational: her very feminine and untutored garrulity produces effects that are at once comic and poetic. Mrs Lirriper herself was successful enough to warrant a sequel in 1864: rather damaged by too much sentiment in relation to too little of the comedy of her stream of consciousness. But definitely the best of the Christmas Stories is *Doctor Marigold's Prescriptions* (1865).

Doctor Marigold is a cheapjack, driving round the country selling his wares in a species of mock auction. Dickens was always fascinated by mountebanks, and quite likely the astonishing line of patter adopted by Doctor Marigold is a cento of many encounters with his kind, raised to a zany inventiveness by its reporter's selectivity and heightening of detail. This is Sleary's Horseriding, from *Hard Times*, on a more imaginative plane. The implied comparison is of monologue. One can see why this was one of Dickens's favourite political 'dearjack' who cozens them with fabulous promises.

Now here, my free and independent woters, I'm a going to give you such a chance as you never had in all your born days, nor yet the days preceding. Now I'll show you what I am a going to do with you. Here's a pair of razors that'll shave you closer than the Board of Guardians; here's a flat-iron worth its weight in gold; here's a frying-pan artificially flavoured with essence of beefsteaks to that degree that you've only got for the rest of your lives to fry bread and dripping in it and there you are replete with animal food; here's a genuine chronometer watch in such a solid silver case that you may knock at the door with it when you come home late from a social meeting, and rouse your wife and family, and save your knocker for the postman; and here's half-a-dozen dinner plates that you may play the cymbals with to charm the baby when it's fractious. Stop! I'll throw you in another article, and I'll give you that, and it's a rolling-pin; and if the baby can only get it well into its mouth when its teeth is coming and rub the gums once with it, they'll come through double, in a fit of laughter equal to being tickled. Stop again! I'll throw you in another article, because I don't like the looks of you, for you haven't the appearance of buyers unless I lose by you, and because I'd rather lose than not take money to-night, and that's a looking-glass in which you may see how ugly you look when you don't bid. What do you say now? Come! Do you say a pound? Not you, for you haven't got it. Do you say ten shillings? Not you, for you owe more to the tallyman. Well then, I'll tell you what I'll do with you. I'll heap them all on the foot-board of the cart – there they are! razors, flat-iron, frying-pan, chronometer watch, dinner plates, rolling-pin, and looking-glass – take 'em all away for four shillings, and I'll give you sixpence for your trouble!

This is beautifully organized, from the address at the beginning, through the description of the articles offered for sale, to the demand for bids from the customers. Notice the résumé of the goods in the last sentence, so that we never lose for a moment the sense of context. Each claim for the virtue of Doctor Marigold's trash is put in such a way as to prevent our taking it seriously, and counterbalanced by good-humoured gibes directed at the crowd: an easy relationship between showman and audience is established through such devices of monologue. One can see why this was one of Dickens's favourite and most popular recital pieces. But the best things in it have to do with the persona's occupation rather than with the plot. There are moments like Marigold's father on his death-bed auctioning himself off into the grave – 'Here's a working model of a used-up old Cheap Jack, without a tooth in his head, and with a pain in every bone' – that touch greatness in a curious mixing of black comedy and luminescent compassion. More lurid in colour, but startling enough, is Dickens's version of 'on with the motley': the cheapjack standing with his dying daughter in his arms, raking the crowd with the patter desperately necessary if he is to auction off his goods is a bad season.

But, much as one would like to, it is impossible to recommend *Doctor Marigold* wholeheartedly as a masterpiece. It wears a little thin as it proceeds; Marigold's adoption of a deaf and dumb girl is less compelling than the freaks of his verbal imagination in pursuit of his craft.

And this is the trouble with even the later and better *Christmas Stories*. Granted that one can ignore the dolorous tales that cumber *Mrs Lirriper* or *Doctor Marigold* – 'How or where could Coll Dhu find an opportunity to put the charm round the neck of the colonel's proud daughter' – it is not possible to get rid of the claims that even the surrounding framework has on our tears.

There is some difficulty, too, in deciding on how to present the *Christmas Stories* to the public. The casual reader of these volumes – the first was collected in 1859 – must be sorely puzzled by the gaps left in Dickens's work through the excision of material properly belonging to his collaborators. No sense can be made of the earlier stories, and little enough of *Somebody's Luggage* and *Mugby Junction* as at present printed. So that one could say that a critical edition of *Christmas Stories* is highly in requisition. It could either take the form of a ruthless selection from the cumbrous text of the key monologues, based on Dickens's reading-versions when they were used in recitals; or else (and worse things have happened) a reprint of the entire Christmas numbers of *Household Words* and *All the Year Round*, to give an idea of what Dickens's work looked like in its original setting.

For obvious reasons it is difficult to take his Stories as satisfactory wholes. The analogy is with the incidental music Purcell wrote for so many dead Restoration dramas. But it would be a pity to miss the astonishing empathy Dickens has with certain figures of the submerged classes – the Waiter, the Lodginghouse Keeper, the Cheapjack, the boy in the railway refreshment room. Their presentation is alight with the lunatic exuberance that Dickens – in writing, as in life – used as an escape from incipient depression and weariness. But *Doctor Marigold* could only be written when *Our Mutual Friend* was done, and perhaps the *Christmas Stories* are best seen as flights away from the social realism and symbolic drama of the novels.

XV   Bleak House (1852-53)

David Copperfield placed in perspective the desolation of Dickens's childhood. Nothing in the world could compensate him for what he had lost, but, after that book, he was able to direct his angst at targets of more interest to adults. Targets of more interest, at any rate, than the ogre-figures he had set up in lieu of the father who had failed to protect him. Instead of the individually and inexplicably Wicked Man, he indicted the universe that had made him – to use his own words in *Bleak House*, Chapter VI – rather an indifferent parent.

In the early Dickens novels, we are conscious of a Theme asserting itself, intermittently, against the claims of the plot. Dickens's plots vary, but the Theme is consistently an attack upon a System that refuses to take account of human needs. The System appears as the Workhouse in *Oliver Twist*, Dotheboys Hall in *Nicholas Nickleby* and America in *Martin Chuzzlewit*. This is in contradistinction to the conventional, and often sentimental, plots of those novels.

Dickens himself seems to have been aware of this dichotomy between theme and plot. But in the early novels he saw the matter as chiefly one of focus, and his attempts at remedy were consequently rather simple-minded. He sought to curb his picaresque sprawl of character and incident by arranging it around a single vice. Thus, in conception, *Martin Chuzzlewit* is an acting out of Selfishness, and *Dombey and Son* of Pride. But such concepts are too abstract to admit of satisfactory formulation in dramatic terms, and much that happens in these novels is unconnected with what was supposed to be their governing concept. Moreover, a good deal that was crying to be expressed was kept back as a result of Dickens's inhibitions about his background. One cannot repress a key circumstance of one's life without repressing a good deal else besides.

That was why *David Copperfield* was necessary, even though, technically speaking, it is a regression. Dickens went back to a familiar position, the waif astray in the world, but this time he defined it in terms of his own life. Perhaps it is always necessary for a novelist to purge himself of autobiography. At any rate, from this time on, Dickens was able to move forward; in a direction different from that of his early novels, and one, I would say, far more relevant to what we need to know of the world.

The technical advance from *Copperfield* to *Bleak House* is that between the Zeppelin and the Apollo; its dedication to Dickens's companions in the Guild of Literature and Art has thus a certain appropriateness. Here, indeed, we have technique, but it cannot be defined as an external grouping of facts. Rather, the critic extrapolates the theme from symbolism that precipitated into fictional form. The Dickens 'character' virtually disappears in favour of a figure who is, like symbol, a function of Theme; plot, too, can now be discussed in terms of thematic expression rather than melodramatic or sentimental 'story'. The series of social novels begun by *Bleak House* is superior to the early work, not only in the observation of the facts presented, but in their relevance to society. It is not that *Bleak House* is less realistic than its predecessors, but the events it portrays are more carefully selected and more precisely judged. So that the literal plot acted out before us resonates well beyond the confines of Dickens's stage. Thus, it makes sense to talk of *Bleak House*, not as the tragic story of Lady Dedlock and her illegitimate daughter, but as a crushing indictment of the failure of Law to observe the human need for justice.

Personal elements – characters, that is to say, existing for their own sake – do persist; but really they have lost their battle. Such elements as there are in *Bleak House* unconnected with the theme can readily be separated off as irrelevant to the total structure.

An incipient uncertainty in Dickens's own mind is suggested by the fact that this novel – uniquely in his work – employs two quite distinct techniques of narration. Thirty-two of the chapters are told in the third person, invariably using a highly dramatic present tense, while thirty-three chapters are a narrative in the past tense told in the first person by a girl called Esther.

Esther herself appears to be founded upon Georgina Hogarth,

Dickens's sister-in-law, who for twenty-eight years kept house for the family. There is a close identity of tone between the presentation of Esther and the way in which Dickens always speaks of Georgina. For example, in his will, he says 'I solemnly enjoin my dear children . . . never to be wanting in a grateful and affectionate attachment to her, for they know well that she has been, through all the stages of her youth and progress, their ever useful self-denying and devoted friend'. In some ways, it is a pity that Dickens overrated devotion at the expense of personality, and associated human goodness with self-effacement. This is not only true of Esther but of earlier heroines based on Georgina's elder sister, the dead Mary. But Esther is less ethereal than Rose Maylie or Little Nell; she is an embodiment of the homely virtues. And so we never seem to see her without her little household basket and bunch of household keys.

Esther has been strongly objected to, and certainly some of her mannerisms are annoying. For example, she continually speaks of herself in the third person with a curious kind of mock-irritability. This manner was ruthlessly parodied by Lewis Carroll in *Alice in Wonderland*, where it has its place as part of a general send-up of Victorian commonplaces. But in *Bleak House* Esther's manner stands apart from the predominant satiric mode, and has the effect of mere complacency.

I said to myself, 'Esther, Esther, Esther! Duty, my dear!' and gave my little basket of housekeeping keys such a shake, that they sounded like little bells, and rang me happily to bed. (Chapter VII)

I said to myself, 'Esther, my dear, you surprise me! This is really not what I expected of you!' and it had such a good effect that I folded my hands upon my basket and quite recovered myself. (Chapter VIII)

I am sure when I find myself coming into the story again, I am really vexed and say, 'Dear, dear, you tiresome little creature, I wish you wouldn't!' (Chapter IX)

This last point is, in fact, well taken: Esther *does* keep coming into the story, though not always so narcissistically as this. Her very presence creates a problem: she is represented as the embodiment of perfect goodness. But it proves impossible to get this quality across. Esther cannot always be singing her own praises; therefore other people have to do this for her. But since their encomia can

only appear in Esther's own narrative, the combination of rousing
applause and modest disclaimer is liable to sound at odds with itself;
and, in practice, it has been resented.

Ada . . . had a delightful confidence in me when I showed her the keys. . . .
I knew, to be sure, that it was the dear girl's kindness; but I liked to be so
pleasantly cheated.   (Chapter VI)

They all encouraged me; they were determined to do it.   (Chapter IX)

'You are the first friend I ever had, and the best friend I ever can have, and
nobody can respect and love you too much to please me.'
    'Upon my word, Caddy,' said I, 'you are in the general conspiracy to keep
me in a good humour.'   (Chapter XXIII)

This device, as we can see from this, is a tiresome one; and, if Esther's
narrative were entirely couched in such terms, it would have badly
spoiled the book.

But, fortunately, Esther's narrative is not all about Esther. The
satiric mode is not confined to the thirty-two third-person chapters;
it spills over and often drowns out Esther's supposedly undiscerning
voice. The following is very much Dickens, after Carlyle: at any
rate, it is certainly not the voice of an eighteen-year-old female brought
up in nun-like seclusion.

They wanted wearing apparel, they wanted linen rags, they wanted coals,
they wanted soup, they wanted interest, they wanted autographs, they wanted
flannel, they wanted whatever Mr Jarndyce had – or had not . . . Among
the ladies who were most distinguished for this rapacious benevolence (if I
may use the expression), was a Mrs Pardiggle. . . .   (Chapter VIII)

Dickens is using Esther as a camera-eye. And, granted the vision
is angled, the bias is not derived from Esther's own character. Rather,
Dickens is assuming the role of the great director, and his judgment
is implied in the distancing and focus of his shot. In other words,
Esther's convenient presence at (say) a meeting of false philanthropists
allows the author to take the opportunity of caricaturing them.

    In much the same way, Esther's narrative embodies certain elements
of legal satire which, strictly speaking, have nothing to do with her
at all.

The shop had, in several little particulars, the air of being in a legal neigh-
bourhood, and of being, as it were, a dirty hanger-on and disowned relation

of the law. . . . The litter of rags . . . might have been counsellors' bands and gowns torn up. (Chapter V)

One cannot, then, simply detach Esther's narrative from this book, as one can that of Gwendolen Harleth from *Daniel Deronda*. It includes too much integral to the total structure. Here, for instance, we have our first glimpse of the rag-and-bone shop that from beginning to end acts as a deadly caricature of Chancery. Moreover, Esther comes into the presence of a good many characters who are central to the action and who go through much the same paces whether they occur in first-person or in third-person narrative.

Thus, we have at least three varieties of tone in Esther's prose: the authorial voice of satire, the passive camera-eye, and the sentimental/naturalistic voice of the little person herself. And this latter accounts for so little that is crucial to *Bleak House* that it need not trouble us as a disabling factor.

Esther as an actor in this drama is by no means so dominating as the extent of her actual narrative might suggest. For one thing, hers is hardly an active role. She is adopted by an elderly philanthropist, she is befriended by two of his wards, she is married finally to a young doctor – the events in her life are few, and all in the passive voice. And her connection both with Jarndyce and his wards sheds light on them rather than herself. Her real importance in the plot lies in the circumstances of her birth – she is illegitimate – and the fact that her mother does not know her to be alive. But this, too, reflects far more upon her mother. The proud Lady Dedlock – married to a baronet who does not know of her previous lover – occupies the most substantial strand of plot in the book. And though Esther is useful as a trigger to this plot, she does not take much part in it as an active character: for example, she and her mother only meet twice in the entire novel, and only once in the full knowledge their relationship. The central strand of narrative in this complex work is not the life of Esther Summerson but the fall of Lady Dedlock. Her role, too, is a passive one.

This fall is brought about by the machinations of her husband's lawyer, Tulkinghorn. We first see him reading a report of the interminable proceedings of Jarndyce and Jarndyce, a case in which she has an interest. 'Who copied that?' she asks on impulse; and, from that moment, Tulkinghorn begins to hunt her down. He infers, quite correctly, that she has recognized the handwriting, and he traces the transcript through his stationer, Snagsby, back to an obscure law-writer, Nemo. But when he goes to see Nemo at his lodging over the rag-and-bone shop, he finds him dead. Tulkinghorn informs her ladyship of the fact and takes note of her reaction. He continues to watch her and establishes that she has gone on to contact one of the witnesses at the Nemo inquest. He himself talks to this wretch, Poor Jo, and discovers that Lady Dedlock had passed herself off as her own maid and got him to show her the cemetery where Nemo lies buried. Bit by bit, Tulkinghorn pieces together a plausible case: that Lady Dedlock was once engaged to a Captain Hawdon and had a child by him, and that this same Hawdon is in fact the dead and anonymous Nemo.

Meanwhile, there are other lawyers working on the case from another angle. Guppy and Weevle burrow themselves into the confidence of Old Krook, the rag-and-bottle man; and a goblin family of usurers, the Smallweeds, burgeon among his papers after his death. It comes out that the child – whom Lady Dedlock believed to be dead – is Esther Summerson, ward to Mr Jarndyce.

Lady Dedlock learns both of Tulkinghorn's discoveries and those of the Smallweeds. She also learns that the facts are about to be put before her husband. She changes clothes with a bricklayer's wife, flies her home, and is found dead – pressed to the iron gates of Nemo's graveyard, as near to her buried lover as she can get.

Tulkinghorn has no personal need to rake up these old errors and disgraces. But he is presented to us as an embodiment of Law: vigilant, tireless, mechanical, and therefore inimical to the passion that gives birth to a love-child. Esther is Lady Dedlock's daughter in fact, but not in Law. The modern reader may feel that Dickens could have emphasized even more than he did that the conception of Esther was not Lady Dedlock's true sin; rather it was her forsaking a spendthrift officer for a wealthy gentleman whom she deceived into a loveless marriage. Out of what we may assume to have been a passively frigid prudence came the chain of actions that drove Lady Dedlock into her muddy death at the gates of the noisome graveyard. Her ultimate act of reparation is not to us, nor to Sir Leicester, but to her buried lover.

The lawyer, Tulkinghorn, also comes to grief. Making no allowance

for human emotion, he discounts the possibility that the baronet
may be prepared to forgive his lady; may even, genuinely, be in love
with her. He discounts, too, the individuality of the instruments
he uses against her; one of whom, a lady's-maid, kills him in a frenzy
of wounded pride.

This story is told with great power and at considerable speed.
Lady Dedlock is certainly a proud woman brought low from the
gaudy platform where she has acted out a drama of deception, but
she is also an archetypal victim figure. In a striking manner, her
story shows what happens to humanity eroded by the action of Law.
Moreover, the narrative is not of the sentimental, naturalistic kind;
on the contrary, it is handled with considerable skill in manipulating
atmosphere. For example, the essential links with other areas of
the structure are provided by the actual mode of presentation, which
is highly symbolic. The rain, especially, plays a crucial role in the
fashionable world of Lady Dedlock, and it is one of several lines
of imagery that run throughout the book.

> The waters are out in Lincolnshire. An arch of the bridge in the park has
> been sapped and sopped away. The adjacent low-lying ground . . . is a
> stagnant river. . . .   (Chapter II)

> The rain is ever falling, drip, drip, drip, by day and night upon the broad
> flagged terrace-pavement, the Ghost's Walk. The weather is so very bad,
> down in Lincolnshire, that the liveliest imagination can scarcely apprehend
> its ever being fine again. . . .   (Chapter VII)

The waters seem only recently to have retired from the earth after
a deluge; and the Deluge was sent, we may remember, as a punishment for the sins of mankind.

But who is being punished? Sir Leicester Dedlock repeatedly
uses in conversation this figure of speech; that the floodgates of
society have been opened and the landmarks obliterated. He is
certainly right as regards his estate in Lincolnshire, but this is not
what he means. He would be right, too, if he were alluding to the
disgrace that is sweeping over his life – once heavily walled off from
humanity, and now eaten away by the action of Law. But he does
not mean this, either. Rather he is speaking of the dangers of reform;
in franchise, in representation, in class opportunity. In other words,
he himself is an agent of the System that works against the human

individual. In keeping Tulkinghorn, he is honing a knife for his
own throat; just as, in supporting lax government, he is conniving
at the murder of a nation.

Sir Leicester is a baronet, proud, ceremonious and buttoned-up.
One of his enemies declares him to have a head seven hundred years
thick. He exists to a great extent in *oratio obliqua*, as befits a figure
so magisterial. His tone resembles that of Mr Dombey, but of course
Sir Leicester bears a far older name than any city magnate, and
can boast of far more extensive possessions. From time to time
his stiffness and ceremoniousness are expressed in terms of these
possessions: antediluvian forests, frozen family portraits, entwined
iron-work, petrified bowers, obsolete flambeaux which gasp at the
upstart gas. He stands for the ancient landed gentry, and is represented
as a glorious spider stretching strands of relationship in all directions
of Law and Politics. Life for him is an interminable country-house
week-end. But the politicians who foregather at Chesney Wold are
symbolized as a set of ridiculous rhyming names – a parody of their
intricate games of parliamentary intrigue.

There is my Lord Boodle who . . . perceives with astonishment, that supposing
the present government to be overthrown, the limited choice of the Crown,
in the formation of a new Ministry, would lie between Lord Coodle and
Sir Thomas Doodle – supposing it to be impossible for the Duke of Foodle
to act with Goodle, which may be assumed to be the case in consequence
of the breach arising out of that affair with Hoodle. Then, giving the Home
Department and the Leadership of the House of Commons to Joodle, the
Exchequer to Koodle, the Colonies to Loodle, and the Foreign Office to
Moodle, what are you to do with Noodle? You can't offer him the Presidency
of the Counsel; that is reserved for Poodle. You can't put him in the Woods
and Forests; that is hardly good enough for Quoodle. What follows? That
the country is shipwrecked, lost and gone to pieces (as is made manifest to
the patriotism of Sir Leicester Dedlock), because you can't provide for Noodle!

The whole passage turns on this name, Noodle. It is at once a generic
term for a fool and a character in one of Dickens's favourite plays,
Tom Thumb the Great by Henry Fielding. Further, the names that
rhyme with 'Noodle' each have their areas of association. Boodle
is a slang term for money, especially stolen money; Coodle is a kind
of pun on 'coddle'; Doodle is another character in *Tom Thumb*,
and not only does the word signify the scrawling of meaningless

hieroglyphs, but it was a nickname for the incompetent Lord Dudley, Foreign Secretary under Wellington. Foodle puns on 'food'; Goodle suggests hypocrisy; Hoodle, hoodwink and hugger-mugger; Joodle, Judas; Koodle, kudos; Loodle, loot; Moodle, moodiness; Poodle, a tame and fawning lapdog; Quoodle, quid, quod, quid pro quo. And so Sir Leicester Dedlock is in process of helping to form a coddled Cabinet that robs, scribbles, guzzles, cants, hoodwinks, betrays, jockeys, loots, sulks, fawns, and quacks generally. What a prospect!

England has been in a dreadful state for some weeks. Lord Coodle wouldn't go out. Sir Thomas Doodle wouldn't come in, and there being nobody in Great Britain (to speak of) except Coodle and Doodle, there has been no government.

This parodies the chaos that followed the defeat of Lord John Russell in 1851. The country was left without a government for two weeks, until Russell formed another administration even weaker than the one that had collapsed. Dickens saw no hope of social justice arising through political methods of amelioration, and had only contempt for the House of Commons, based, largely, on his own experience of it as a young reporter. He was writing very much in the wake of Carlyle's *Signs of the Times* and *Chartism*, and a good many Radicals shared his pessimistic vision: John Dodds, and the *English Republic* of W. J. Linton, for example. And Dickens, in his turn, makes absolutely clear the responsibility of these laissez-faire politicians for the downfall of the country. The slums in London are a case in point.

These ruined shelters have bred a crowd of foul existence that crawls in and out of gaps in walls and boards; and coils itself to sleep, in maggot numbers, where the rain drips in; and comes and goes, fetching and carrying fever, and something more evil in every footprint than Lord Coodle, and Sir Thomas Doodle, and the Duke of Foodle, and all the fine gentlemen in office down to Zoodle, shall set right in five hundred years – though born expressly to do it.

The slums are particularized as one specific place called Tom-all-Alone's. This was Dickens's first choice as a title for the book, and derives from an empty house near Chatham built by a recluse called Tom Clark. Dickens had a vivid childhood memory of seeing it blown up by explosives. So, behind the ruined semblance, is the sense of impending disaster.

Twice, lately, there has been a crash and a cloud of dust, like the springing of a mine, in Tom-all-Alone's; and, each time, a house has fallen. These accidents have made a paragraph in the newspapers, and have filled a bed or two in the nearest hospital. The gaps remain, and there are not unpopular lodgings among the rubbish. As several more houses are nearly ready to go, the next crash in Tom-all-Alone's may be expected to be a good one.

But there are more ways of coming to grief than being blown up or inundated in ruins. Just as the Dedlocks' place in Lincolnshire is remarkable for incessant rain and consequent flood, so Tom-all-Alone's is characterized chiefly by creeping moisture and resultant disease. There is a close relationship between the vermin breeding on the wretches in this slum and the wretches themselves who infest its tenements. All are deadly parasites. And wherever we see Tom-all-Alone's – and the glimpses throughout the book are numerous – there is this nauseous savour of contagion.

The iron rails peeling away in flakes of rust; the chimneys sinking in; the stone steps to every door (and every door might be Death's Door) turning green. . . .   (Chapter VIII)

With houses looking on, on every side, save where a reeking little tunnel of a court gives access to the iron gate . . . here they lower our dear brother down a foot or two. . . .   (Chapter XI)

For a time there were some dungeon lights burning, as the lamp of life burns in Tom-all-Alone's; heavily, heavily, in the nauseous air, and winking – as that lamp, too, winks in Tom-all-Alone's – at many horrible things.
                                                                (Chapter XLVI)

The whole is subsumed in the nightmare journey where Inspector Bucket at Mr Tulkinghorn's behest takes Snagsby, the law-stationer, deeper and deeper into these nether regions. This journey is based on an actual expedition which Dickens made with Bucket's prototype, Inspector Field, into a place known as St Giles' Rookery. The detective taps villains out of his way, wades through the mud of villainous alleys, draws his companion aside as the fever comes up the street – a corpse borne upon a palanquin; for the 1850s, when Dickens was writing, averaged 20,000 deaths a year in England and Wales alone from cholera and diarrhoea. And Tom-all-Alone's abuts on Nemo's graveyard, where the corpses are so packed that they seem almost to burst through the surface of the slimy ground – again, this is based on such social disgraces as the Drury Lane burial ground, and the one at Spa Fields. But Dickens effects his own synthesis: not only does Lady Dedlock's lover lie in that feverous churchyard, but the detective and the law-stationer are part of the general web of evidence gathering about her. They are looking for the boy at the Inquest, the one that knew Nemo, whose name is Jo. But the people in that hell have relinquished most of their identity.

As few people are known in Tom-all-Alone's by any Christian sign, there is much reference to Mr Snagsby whether he means Carrots, or the Colonel, or Gallows, or Young Chisel, or Terrier Tip, or Lanky, or the Brick. Some think it must be Carrots; some say the Brick. The Colonel is produced, but is not at all near the thing. Whenever Mr Snagsby and his conductors are stationary, the crowd flows round, and from its squalid depths obsequious advice heaves up to Mr Bucket. Whenever they move, and the angry bull's-eyes glare, it fades away, and flits about them up the alleys, and in the ruins, and behind the walls, as before.

This boy Jo is the emanation of Tom-all-Alone's. He is more evocative of squalor than any juvenile character in the whole of Dickens – being very muddy, very hoarse, very ragged. Supremely, he is ignorant. Here he is at the Inquest.

Name, Jo. Nothing else that he knows on. Don't know that everybody has two names. Never heerd of sich a think. Don't know that Jo is short for a longer name. Thinks it long enough for *him*. *He* don't find no fault with it. Spell it? No. *He* can't spell it. No father, no mother, no friends. Never been to school. What's home? Know's a broom's a broom....

The initial idea for Jo may have come from Hood's novel, *Tylney Hall,* which we know Dickens read and admired. There is an accident-prone character in that work called Unlucky Joe who, when asked at *his* trial what he was doing on a given morning, replies that he was starving. A source even nearer home is a case that was reported in January 1850 in both Forster's *Examiner* and the news supplement to Dickens's *Household Words*, the *Household Narrative*. A fourteen-year-old boy, George Ruby – like Jo, a crossing-sweeper – is questioned by Alderman Humphrey.

Alderman Do you know what an oath is?
Boy   No.
Alderman Do you ever say your prayers?

Boy	No, never.
Alderman	Do you know what prayers are?
Boy	No.
Alderman	What do you know?
Boy	I knows how to sweep the crossings.
Alderman	And that is all?
Boy	That's all. I sweeps a crossing.

This factual exchange may very well have inspired Henry Mayhew's section on crossing-sweepers in his *London Labour and the London Poor* (1851) – 'Crossing-sweeping seems to be one of those occupations which are resorted to as an excuse for begging; and indeed as many expressed it to me "it was the last chance left of obtaining an honest crust". In his turn, Mayhew, too, could have been absorbed into Dicken's eventual synthesis, as could other sociological writings like Mary Carpenter's book on reformatory schools – sympathetically reviewed by James Hannah in *Household Words* (30 August 1851); it is especially moving about juvenile vagrants – 'sleeps in carts or landings about four nights a week; father deserted mother 15 years; mother dead 2 years. . .'. For in the 1850s, juvenile vagrancy was standard enough to require a Select Parliamentary Committee to look at it. Dickens himself adapts words he had already used in a speech made at the Metropolitan Sanitary Association a few months earlier, to the voice of the young doctor Woodcourt, getting across the notion that we need to care for the body before we start troubling about the soul.

But, as ever, the final synthesis is, inimitably, Dickens. Jo is the embodiment of ignorance and filth, but he serves a crucial purpose in the book. He is not there to wring tears from us. Rather he links together various groups of characters; partly because he is the victim of lax government, partly because he unwittingly holds the key to Nemo's identity. He acts, also, as a kind of index to various forms of Law. The Church, in the person of Chadband, uses him as a lay figure to be preached over. Chadband's cant, using terms of provision and need, is ironically mocked by the setting: a half-starved boy being addressed by a fat man behind a laden table.

Jo also acts as an index to that form of law invested in the forces of public morality. The police are pragmatists: concerned with the efficient working of society but not with its reform. To Bucket and his myrmidons, Jo is simply a nuisance. This attitude is strikingly embodied in the following exchange.

'This boy,' says the constable, 'although he's repeatedly told to, won't move on –'

'I'm always a moving on, sir,' cries the boy, wiping away his grimy tears with his arm. 'I've always been a moving and a moving on, ever since I was born. Where can I possibly move to, sir, more nor I do move!'

'He won't move on,' says the constable, calmly, with a slight professional hitch of his neck involving its better settlement in his stiff stock, 'although he has been repeatedly cautioned, and therefore I am obliged to take him into custody. He's as obstinate a young gonoph as I know. He WON'T move on.'

'O my eye! Where can I move to!' cries the boy, clutching quite desperately at his hair, and beating his bare feet upon the floor of Mr Snagsby's passage.

'Don't you come none of that, or I shall make blessed short work of you,' says the constable, giving him a passionless shake. 'My instructions are, that you are to move on. I have told you so five hundred times.'

'But where?' cries the boy.

'Well! really constable, you know,' says Mr Snagsby wistfully, and coughing behind his hand his cough of great perplexity and doubt; 'really, that does seem a question. Where, you know?'

'My instructions don't go to that,' replies the constable. 'My instructions are that this boy is to move on.'

The mobility thus enforced upon the meek and suffering Jo gives him a directly technical importance in his role as link character. It means, for one thing, that he need not be represented as static in Tom-all-Alone's.

Nevertheless, wherever he goes, he takes Tom-all-Alone's with him. This is more subtle than at first it seems. Indeed, it is yet a farther example of Jo as Victim of Law. For Tom-all-Alone's is not simply a place neglected through the inattention of politicians. It is also a place fallen into Chancery; a property disputed under the Jarndyce will. As such, it cannot be touched, even for the purpose of repair, until the case in question is resolved. It is a microcosm of England decaying while Noodles dispute. And those who might take a hand in setting things right retreat to the sidelines and beyond. This is the attitude of Mr Jarndyce, who wants to hear nothing about his property – 'a street full of perishing blind houses with their eyes stoned out'. He avoids the law courts, ignores Chancery, immures himself in the country. But though he will not go to Chancery, in the person of Jo, Chancery comes to him.

When driven out of London by the forces of Law – Bucket wishes to prevent his connecting Nemo with Lady Dedlock – Jo is taken ill and befriended by the Jarndyce household. In one night, he manages to infect the place with the fever from Tom-all-Alone's, nearly killing the little maid, Charley, and blighting Esther's good looks for ever. Warned on once more by the omnipresent Bucket, he returns to London and dies – in the arms of Woodcourt, the doctor who is to be Esther's husband.

Law, then, infects and brings down all who come into contact with its terrible System. This is why Jarndyce himself remains a recluse; we see, in a flashback, the example of his great-uncle Tom, the Tom of Tom-all-Alone's – 'It's being ground to bits in a slow mill; it's being roasted at a slow fire; it's being stung to death by single bees; it's being drowned by drops; it's going mad by grains.' Only in one sense does Tom Jarndyce get nearer judgment; he blows his brains out.

This present Jarndyce is a man of disguises. We first see him symbolically wrapped up, and he habitually talks in euphemisms to ward off the evils he cannot resolve – blaming, for example, the ills he sees in society on the east wind – an evasion, since the wind is unaccountable, but one which absolves him from social action. He cannot, therefore, be taken to represent the whole weight of moral evaluation in *Bleak House*. Indeed, it would not do to take Jarndyce as a positive character at all: many of his philanthropies are mistaken – showered upon the heartless confidence man, Skimpole; the incompetent philanthropist, Mrs Jellyby; the overbearing missionary, Mrs Pardiggle – figures satirized mercilessly in Esther's part of the book. And he himself is unable to prevent his young wards from involving themselves in Chancery.

The case that bears his name is a joke and a bye-word; punning drearily on the word 'jaundice'. The Lord Chancellor himself has said, after Falstaff, that it will not finish until the sky rains potatoes. And Jarndyce's own account is clinching.

A certain Jarndyce, in an evil hour, made a great fortune, and made a great Will. In the question how the trusts under that will are to be administered,

the fortune left by the Will is squandered away. . . . Equity sends questions
to Law, Law sends questions back to Equity; Law finds it can't do this,
Equity finds it can't do that. . . .

The authorial comment is not only clinching but raspingly bitter.

The little plaintiff or defendant, who was promised a new rocking-horse
when Jarndyce and Jarndyce should be settled, has grown up, possessed
himself of a real horse, and trotted away into the other world. . . .

The prototypes of this unending case are so numerous that even
the legal historian, Sir William Holdsworth, declines to give examples.
One instance, cited by Edgar Johnson, was the Day case, which at
the time of Dickens's writing had been going on for seventeen years,
had involved at any given time between seventeen and forty lawyers,
and had already incurred costs of £70,000. Even more long-drawn-out
was the Jennings case, which crawled on throughout the nineteenth
century, from seventeen years before Dickens's birth to forty-five
years after he died, amassing as it went, costs of over £250,000! As
far back as the 1820s, the first Chancery Commission had complained
bitterly of the monstrous state of affairs then prevailing, and Lord
Brougham had followed in their wake; this was, roughly, the period
of *Bleak House*, when Lord Lyndhurst had succeeded the reactionary
Eldon. The reason for such slowness of proceeding was that Chancery
insisted on reviewing the whole of each case, no matter how trivial
the point to be decided. Thus, the complexity of juridical procedure
bore no relation to the matter under discussion. No doubt Dickens's
indignation was powered by his own experiences in Chancery: in
1844 he had sued some printers and booksellers for pirating *A
Christmas Carol*, but he suffered heavily in time and pocket for bringing
the suit; and, in any case, the offence was repeated two years later.
This, no doubt, gave Dickens's writing a personal edge; but objections to Chancery were currently being voiced on a national scale.
The Times had renewed the complaints of the Chancery Commission,
and Russell, the Prime Minister, brought out a Bill on the subject;
it proved, however, to be totally inadequate. So Noodle and Doodle
aid and abet the grubbing and grinding lawyers; and they all succeed
in bringing about the state of affairs that includes Poor Jo, Tom-all-
Alone's – and the Wards in Jarndyce.

In spite of their Guardian's pleadings on the subject, these Wards, Richard and Ada Carstone, become embroiled more and more deeply. Richard's counsel and abettor in this hopeless case is one Mr Vholes – another burrowing name for a lawyer – of Symonds Inn. He is one of Dickens's greatest successes. The Inn itself is described as a dustbin consisting of two compartments and a sifter. The way in which the official cat watches a mousehole in Vholes's office is the way – slow, fixed – in which Vholes himself watches Young Richard. He, after all, needs to forage for his cubs – for Vholes, though a symbol, is also a respectable man with three daughters to provide for in an earthy cottage in a damp garden in Kennington; notice the animal implication. One dare not call *him* an unreal character.

Vholes exemplifies the first principle of English law: to make business for itself. But business to the likes of Vholes is penury and misery to the public. As he drives off, carrying Richard at full speed farther and farther into Jarndyce and Jarndyce, the gaunt pale horse drawing them away reminds us of nothing so much as Revelation 6:8 – 'And his name that sat upon him was Death and Hell follows with them. And power was given to them over the fourth part of the earth, to kill with swords, and with hunger, and with death, and with the beasts of the earth'. And such a death is the fate of Jarndyce's ward, Richard.

For, when eventually the missing Will is found in the rag-and-bottle shop by the grubbing Smallweeds, it appears that the entire Jarndyce estate has been consumed in costs; the case lapses; and the young man dies with it.

This case is parodied, but in a minor key, by the man from Shropshire, Gridley. As his name would suggest, his whole life is an acting-out of old Tom Jarndyce's cry 'It's like being roasted on a slow fire'. This episode is based on an actual case sent to Dickens by W. Challinor – on 11 March 1852, by which time one number of *Bleak House* had already appeared and two were already written; one would never guess this, however, from the way in which the case fits into the novel. It tells of a small farmer who disputed a minor point of a will – how much of a legacy his brother had received in advance – and Dickens weaves it in and out of the elaborate fabric of Jarndyce and Jarndyce. For example, he makes the angry country-

man cry out: 'I mustn't look to individuals. It's the system . . . My
Lord knows nothing of it. He sits there to administer the system.'
Simple as this strand of plot is, it exemplifies Dickens's Theme to
perfection. As his imagery shows, Gridley is in process of being
consumed.

> I have been dragged for five-and-twenty years over burning iron, and I have
> lost the habit of treading upon velvet . . . They will tell you the best joke
> they have, is the man from Shropshire . . . It is only by angrily demanding
> the justice I never get, that I am able to keep my wits together . . . There's
> nothing between doing it, and sinking into the smiling state of the poor little
> woman that haunts the court. . . .

The little old woman to whom Gridley refers attends the court every
day; but, while he rages in his heat, she accepts her fate with smiling
calmness. Associated with her is the bird imagery that runs through
the novel. She keeps a number of linnets and larks in cages with
the intention of restoring them to liberty when her judgment should
be given. 'They die in prison, though. Their lives, poor silly
things, are so short in comparison with Chancery proceedings, that,
one by one, the whole collection has died over and over again.'
She has given them names, however: Hope, Joy, Youth, Peace, Rest,
Life, Dust, Ashes, Waste, Want, Ruin, Despair, Madness, Death,
Cunning, Folly, Words, Wigs, Rags, Sheepskin, Plunder, Precedent,
Jargon, Gammon and Spinach. They are caged; they are at risk
to the predatory cat that prowls about them; and, even if released,
they would fall victim to the wild birds outside – the contrast implied
is one between her bird-like utterance and the vulturine squalls of
that 'hideous bird of prey', Grandfather Smallweed. Miss Flite
herself presages that one day she will be found lying stark and sense-
less, as she has found so many birds. And of herself she says, 'I had
youth, and hope. I believe, beauty. It matters very little now'. She
greets the young people she meets at the Court, Ada and Richard,
in much the same way – 'Youth. And hope. And beauty. And Chancery
. . . Pray accept my blessing'. Obviously, the next two birds to be
added to her collection are named 'The Wards in Jarndyce'.

This astonishing portrait was based on a prototype variously
known as Miss Fray or Miss R –. She was described by an anonymous
writer of 1867, well after *Bleak House*, as bearing a reticule in one

hand and, in the other, a paper which she vainly tried to hand to the Lord Chancellor. And another commentator, 'Paul Pry', claimed that she was completely insane, and thought that she was asserting her rights to an estate in Mesopotamia. Another fictive prototype may be a Miss Sant, who used to pay daily visits to Doctors' Commons.

But the bird-like realization of this character is Dickens's own – notice the brief, chirping phrases – and goes along well with the Jarndyce case, that 'scarecrow of a suit'. Moreover, her belief in the possibility of judgment relates more subtly to the attitude of the Man from Shropshire than may at first be apparent. Gridley says, furiously, 'I will accuse the individual workers of that system against me, face to face, before the great eternal bar'. She says, in her bird-like manner, 'I expect a judgment shortly. On the Day of Judgment. I have discovered that the sixth seal mentioned in the Revelation is the Great Seal. It has been open a long time! Pray accept my blessings.' Now the sixth seal is found in Revelation 6:12-17. When it is opened, the kings of the earth and the chief captains and the mighty men will be judged. It is as though, through the uncomprehending voice of this Holy Fool, the little madwoman, Dickens is asserting the claim of the weak and the right of the under-privileged to be heard in the very grinding teeth of Chancery. Law itself is subject to a higher court; Law itself is overdue for Judgment.

Jarndyce, Gridley, Miss Flite are expressions of this theme: they do not exist merely in terms of inner life or personal significance. We are not encouraged to identify ourselves with character or cir-cumstance: the literal enactment is only one level of this drama. Even so, it proves necessary to draw all the strands together in a symbolic representation of the main theme of the book. This is done in the person of Krook, nicknamed the Lord Chancellor, and his rag and bone shop, which is a parody of Chancery.

'You see I have so many things here . . . of so many kinds, and all, as the neighbours think (but *they* know nothing), wasting away and going to rack and ruin, that's why they have given me and my place a christening. And I have so many old parchmentses and papers in my stock. And I have a liking for rust and must and cobwebs. And all's fish that comes to my net. And I can't abear to part with anything I once lay hold of (or so my neighbours think, but what do *they* know?) or to alter anything, or to have any sweeping, nor scouring, nor cleaning, nor repairing going on about me. That's the way I've got the ill name of Chancery. *I* don't mind. I go and see my noble and learned brother every day, when he sits in the Inn . . . There's no great odds betwixt us. We both grub on in a muddle. . . !

Krook has connections with most of the strands of plot: he is landlord to Nemo and Miss Flite, later to Weevle, lives close by Mr Snagsby, is related to the Smallweeds, and meets and talks to Esther Summerson and the hapless Wards in Jarndyce. And, still on the literal plane, Krook is a highly distinctive presence – cadaverous, withered, a stump of a man, frosted with white hairs, a withered root in a fall of snow; a kind of ambulant corpse. He breathes, certainly, but the breath issues from his mouth as though he were on fire within.

This last image is insisted upon throughout the book. Krook is 'A bundle of old clothes, with a spirituous heat smouldering in it . . .'; 'his hot breath seemed to come towards them like a flame . . .'. And the demise of Chancery is prefigured in similar terms – 'If all the injustice it has committed, and all the misery it has caused, could only be locked up with it, and the whole burnt away in a great funeral pyre – why, so much the better. . . .' The feeling is that the very corruption of the law will bring about its destruction. It is as though there were a smouldering fire beneath the dung-hill of Chancery, gradually metamorphosing it from the mud of the earlier chapters to dust – the dust that drives Mr Snagsby to take turns out of doors, that blows in through the windows of Tulkinghorn's chambers and silts his papers up, that settles like a rain of soot upon the ashes and broken bottles in the derelict shop of Lord Chancellor Krook.

Krook's chancery is, like its owner, a closed system, glutted, diseased and noxious. Krook soaks himself in gin until one day he actually sets fire to his guts and explodes, so discharging his corrupt body into the atmosphere; so that the inhabitants of the court where his shop is situated actually smell him and taste him, in some instances touch him, as vapour, soot and grease, through most of a tainted evening.

The atmosphere is built up by an accumulation of unwholesome particulars into an evocation that at last fuses together pestilence and Law. Everyone is ill at ease. The lawyer Weevle is under the illusion that he can trick Krook into letting him burrow through secret documents that he and his friend Guppy think will lead them to the identity of Esther Summerson; but he cannot rest and runs into Snagsby, who is haunting the environs of Krook's shop.

'Airing yourself, as I am doing, before you go to bed?' the stationer inquires.

'Why, there's not very much air to be got here; and what there is, is not very freshening,' Weevle answers, glancing up and down the court.

'Very true, sir. Don't you observe,' says Mr Snagsby, pausing to sniff and taste the air a little; 'don't you observe, Mr Weevle, that you're – not to put too fine a point upon it – that you're rather greasy here, sir?'

'Why, I have noticed myself that there is a queer kind of flavour in the place tonight,' Mr Weevle rejoins. 'I suppose it's chops at the Sol's Arms.'

'Chops, do you think? Oh! – Chops, eh?' Mr Snagsby sniffs and tastes again. 'Well, sir, I suppose it is. But I should say that their cook at the Sol wanted a little thinking after. She has been burning them, sir! And I don't think;' Mr Snagsby sniffs and tastes again, and then spits and wipes his mouth; 'I don't think – not to put too fine a point upon it – that they were quite fresh, when they were shown the gridiron.'

Among other things, this piece of dialogue accomplishes the difficult feat of making an atmosphere tangible – Mr Snagsby *tastes* the air – without over-stressing the detail to the point where it becomes too intense. There is always the element of black comedy playing about the book's horrors. And yet there is great precision, too – chops, overdone, not too fresh in the first place; another sign of the tainting sort of weather.

With the entry of his accomplice, Guppy, Weevle has a confidant to whom he can make clear the horrors falling upon him. The task of waiting on the pleasure of 'the Lord Chancellor' – he is not to know yet that he also has the pleasure of breathing him – is proving too much for his stamina.

'I thought you had gone to Jericho at least, instead of coming here,' says Tony.

'Why, I said about ten.'

'You said about ten,' Tony repeats. 'Yes, so you did say about ten. But, according to my count, it's ten times ten – it's a hundred o'clock. I never had such a night in my life!'

'What has been the matter?'

'That's it!' says Tony. 'Nothing has been the matter. But, here have I been stewing and fuming in this jolly old crib, till I have had the horrors falling on me thick as hail. *There's* a blessed-looking candle!' says Tony, pointing to the heavily-burning taper with a great cabbage head and a long winding-sheet. . . .

The scene appears to be static – consisting merely of the shysters, Weevle and Guppy, waiting for the midnight appointment with Krook that never comes off. And yet the tension continues to rise. For one thing, they are waiting in the room where Nemo died; something of the law-writer's drug-laden atmosphere still exhales from the place, as an exchange between the pair shows – ' "There have been dead men in most rooms" . . . "In most rooms you let them alone and – and they let you alone." ' There is a progression, but it is not best expressed in linear narrative terms. Rather it is a matter of the atmosphere seeming to congeal. From being gaseous – 'see the soot's falling . . . it smears like black fat' – it thickens to a curiously nasty liquid condition. Of course, as the emphasis suggests, it is no ordinary soot that is in question.

Mr Guppy sitting on the window-sill, nodding his head and balancing all these possibilities in his mind, continues thoughtfully to tap it, and clasp it, and measure it with his hand, until he hastily draws his hand away.

'What, in the Devil's name,' he says, 'is this! Look at my fingers!'

A thick, yellow liquor defiles them, which is offensive to the touch and sight, and more offensive to the smell. A stagnant, sickening oil, with some natural repulsion in it that makes them both shudder.

'What have you been doing here? What have you been pouring out of window?'

'I pouring out of window! Nothing, I swear! Never, since I have been here!' cries the lodger.

And yet look here – and look here! When he brings the candle, here, from the corner of the window-sill, it slowly drips and creeps away down the bricks; here, lies in a little thick nauseous pool.

'This is a horrible house,' says Mr Guppy, shutting down the window. 'Give me some water, or I shall cut my hand off.'

The immediate model for this scene would seem to be that of the Macbeths whispering together after the murder of Duncan. Certainly Weevle and Guppy are conspiring to despoil a man – Krook – who is already dead; though, in their case, they do not know it. But the scene is extended to the point where it would fail if it did not admit an element of savage farce – 'Give me some water, or I shall cut my hand off'. The atmosphere continues to congeal as the conspirators venture downstairs to Krook's parlour at the appointed time. Indeed, the atmosphere appears to have degenerated from a liquid state to one that is almost solid, without losing all of its previous modes of existence. Krook is in fact bodily present, but disintegrated into bits and pieces not immediately recognizable for what they are. And yet, even in his state of disintegration, he retains a horrible likeness to what he was in life; showing, perhaps, how far decomposed his body really was, even before he died. For instance, the withered root has become a charred log, and the white hairs are represented by white ashes. And, on its symbolic plane, the disintegration of Krook is the disintegration of Chancery, and, beyond Chancery, the punishing and remorseless Law of man.

The Lord Chancellor of that Court, true to his title in his last act, has died the death of all Lord Chancellors in all Courts, and of all authorities in all places under all names soever, where false pretences are made, and where injustice is done. Call the death by any name Your Highness will, attribute it to whom you will, or say it might have been prevented how you will, it is the same death eternally – inborn, inbred, engendered in the corrupted humours of the vicious body itself, and that only – Spontaneous Combustion, and none other of all the deaths that can be died.

It takes Dickens to portray, in the death of a gin-soaked old man, the explosion of the entire legal system. In spite of all the author's protests, the event could not actually have taken place; it is based upon analogy which, though immensely powerful, can be shown to be false. But the belief in spontaneous combustion was one which writers, especially, were strongly disposed towards. And the antecedents of Dickens's climax in *Bleak House* are curiously rich and complex. One finds a parallel instance in Melville's *Redburn* (1849), where the victim is in an alcoholic stupor, and, unlike the case of Krook, the reader is allowed to witness the actual conflagration – 'crawled over by a swarm of wormlike flames'. And Melville presumably had read Marryat's *Jacob Faithful* (1834), where the hero's mother goes up in smoke, leaving behind a sort of pitchy cinder forming a black mass in the middle of the bed. Both Marryat and Melville would have read Brockden Brown's gothic novel *Wieland* (1798), where the hero's father explodes – his body burned, his clothing charred, in the end putrefying. This seems also to have influenced de Quincey, who speaks, in *Confessions of an English Opium Eater*

(1822) of a man blowing up in the dark without match or candle near him, leaving behind nothing but bones – a result of a vast redundancy of brandy in his body. And another group of sources is behind a case recorded in the *Terrific Register* (Volume II, p.340) – a penny weekly which Dickens devoured as a boy throughout 1824. It is by far the closest in description and method to the rendering in *Bleak House*; naming such properties as a heap of ashes in which the legs and arms could be discerned; and soot covering furniture, tapestry, walls, utensils and food – the latter so contaminated that not even the dogs would touch it. All these, and other details, occur almost word for word in an account of the Countess Cornelia Baudi of Cesena given by the *Gentleman's Magazine* for 1746. The account lays especial weight upon the deliquescent quality of the soot – 'from the lower part of the windows trickled down a greasy, loathsome, yellowish liquor, with an unusual stink. The floor of the chamber was thickly smeared with a gluish moisture, not easily got off.' The diagnosis was that a fire was caused in the Countess's entrails by inflamed effusions of her blood, by fermentation in the stomach, and, especially, by the fiery evaporations from wines and brandies. The whole is drawn from an account by a supposed eye-witness, J. Bianchini.

Yet another probable source centres on Faraday's lectures on physics, which were written up in a popular fashion by Charles Knight in *Household Words* (3 August 1850). Here we have an analogy between the consumption of a candle and our consumption of food; the inference being that, if the food is inflammable, like spirituous liquors, we ourselves are likely to combust. No doubt Knight misunderstood Faraday's analogy; but it is noticeable that most of the cases cited involve drunkards or alcoholics. The consensus appears to have had a very powerful effect upon Dickens's mind.

One might also point to the numerous parallels between the consumption of gin and the disintegration of society that abound in the work of Carlyle, itself an extension of a hint found in Coleridge's *Friend*; or the use made of the smouldering ricks in Disraeli's novel, *Sybil*. The particulars synthesized by Dickens were adapted from a number of sources and involved a physical impossibility; but it is all convincing on the page. Spontaneous Combustion afforded Dickens one of his most powerful allegories.

The sort of objection that might be made to *Bleak House* could
be based, possibly, on the fact that there is no direct equivalent in
the Lord Chancellor's court for Krook's consumption of gin; that
the Lord Chancellor himself is always represented as being urbane
and gentlemanly; that Krook himself, though eccentric and suspicious,
can hardly be credited with the intricate wiles of Chancery. But
in the context of *Bleak House*, Krook and his shop are a powerful
reinforcement of the fog and mud imagery of the Law.

As much mud in the streets, as if the waters had but newly retired from the
face of the earth . . . Smoke lowering down from chimney-pots, making a
soft black drizzle, with flakes of soot in it as big as full-grown snow-flakes
. . . The raw afternoon is rawest and the dense fog is densest, and the muddy
streets are muddiest, near that leaden-headed old obstruction, appropriate
ornament for the threshold of a leaden-headed old corporation; Temple
Bar. And hard by Temple Bar, in Lincoln's Inn Hall, at the very heart of
the fog, sits the Lord Chancellor in his High Court of Chancery.

The symbolic associations of this imagery bring together strands
in the novel that would otherwise have little relationship one with
another. For example, the description of the rain in Lincoln's Inn
Fields irresistibly reminds us of that in the fields of Lincolnshire. It
is not so far from one to the other 'as the crow flies'; apparently
Chancery is all about us, and we are all in Chancery.

The element in the book I have left out of all consideration is
that of the Ironmaster. He has his importance, certainly, as a contrast to Sir Leicester and the Noodles, but he is hardly an organic
part of the whole. The Ironmaster is by no means the first attempt
at a representation of industry in Dickens: one remembers the
ambiguities of the factory town into which Nell and her grandfather
stumble, or the mixture of triumph and fear with which Dickens
regards the railways in *Dombey and Son*. But the proper place for
the Ironmaster – honest, forthright, made by his own efforts – would
have been in Dickens's next novel. No doubt he would so have
figured, but for one thing: the vision has darkened. What Law was
in *Bleak House*, Industry becomes in *Hard Times*.

XVI   Hard Times (1854)

Dickens was not altogether prepared to launch into what ought to have been his great novel of Industry. The statisticians in *The Chimes* and the portrait of the Ironmaster in *Bleak House* certainly show in what direction his thoughts were tending. But the immediate trigger for *Hard Times* was not an imaginative one. The sales of *Household Words* had been falling for some months, and its printers, Bradbury and Evans, urged Dickens to save the magazine by producing a new weekly serial.

He admitted in a letter to Mrs Watson that he began *Hard Times* a full year before he meant to. But he took hold of the subject in much the same way as he had started *Nicholas Nickleby*. At the end of January 1854, he went up to Preston so that he might see at close quarters, not only an industrial town, but also a strike. This visit was written up as a documentary description in *Household Words* ('On Strike', 11 February 1854). And in spite of subsequent denials, it is clear that the Preston strike furnished the novel with much of its background.

However, the complex of industrial action cannot be dealt with simply in terms of a relationship between oppressor and oppressed. The interplay between market, manufactures, trade union and employed man cannot be intermittently thought over and finally clinched by a brief visit to the vital spot. There is no evil in *Hard Times* so clear-cut as Dotheboys Hall. This may be unfortunate, for it must be admitted that, in this novel of ideas, Dickens did not altogether grasp the issues he was reaching towards.

Hard Times succeeded in its immediate task. Through the course of its serialization, *Household Words* doubled, trebled and even,

towards the end, quadrupled its circulation. The novel was radical
in a way intelligent enough to ruffle Macaulay and delight Ruskin
– who, long before Shaw and Leavis, proclaimed it as Dickens's
greatest work. But the obvious influence in the book is Carlyle,
to whom it is dedicated.

Hard Times seeks to link up in one fiction several issues that at
first sight might seem unrelated. These include: the grinding ugliness
of industrial development; the abstract theory of Utilitarianism;
shallow self-interest; the anti-social force of the capitalist; and trade
unionism. We can characterize these themes through various places
or figures in the book itself: Coketown, Gradgrind, Harthouse,
Bounderby and Slackbridge.

The prototype of Coketown is Hanley, and it is established in
much the same way as the foggy Lincoln's Inn Fields of *Bleak House*
or the Marshalsea of *Little Dorrit*. Unfortunately, the difficult
techniques involved in weekly serialization cut down Dickens's
descriptive faculties to the bare bone. What we do see is a town of
red brick and black soot, full of monotonously similar streets, with
interchangeable buildings that could, respectively, be jail, infirmary
or town hall. Coketown on a hot day is hell!

Stokers emerged from low underground doorways, into factory yards, and
sat on steps, and posts, and palings, wiping their swarthy visages, and contemplating coals. The whole town seemed to be frying in oil. There was a
stiflling smell of hot oil everywhere. The steam-engines shone with it, the
dresses of the Hands were soiled with it, the mills throughout their many
stories oozed and trickled it. The atmosphere of those fairy palaces was
like the breath of the simoom: and their inhabitants, wasting with heat,
toiled languidly in the desert. But no temperature made the melancholy mad
elephants more mad or more sane. Their wearisome heads went up and down
at the same rate, in hot weather and cold, wet weather and dry, fair weather
and foul. The measured motion of their shadows on the walls, was the substitute Coketown had to show for the shadows of rustling woods; while,
for the summer hum of insects, it could offer, all the year round, from the
dawn of Monday to the night of Saturday, the whirr of shafts and wheels.

This, in the Carlylean sense of massive assertion, is powerful. But
something is missing – call it the intimate knowledge of a place that
reinforces Dickens's descriptions of law courts and debtors' prisons
with familiar and unexpected detail. And even a descriptive spread

such as the one just quoted is rare in *Hard Times,* so little flexibility
does the tightness of form in a weekly serial allow. For the most
part, Coketown, like any other place in the novel, is seen merely in
passing glimpses.

It is, however, powerfully backed by the figure of Thomas Gradgrind, who links it up with Utilitarianism. This philosophy is based
upon Bentham's dictum concerning social legislation: that government should aim towards the greatest happiness of the greatest
number of people. It is quite plain, on closer scrutiny, that this
argument is open-ended; depending entirely upon who is defining
'greatest' and 'happiness' and from what position in life they are
considering the proposition.

However, the objections that such writers as Dickens and Carlyle
had to Utilitarianism were not based on logical grounds. Rather
they were against the very manner of formulation. Their reaction
was the very temperamental one of the artist who refuses to assess
the qualities of life in terms of quantity. 'The greatest amount of
pleasure', 'the greatest good', 'the satisfaction of more appetencies
rather than fewer' – all these tend to a mechanistic view of human
potential. Value cannot be decided by majority vote; what is left
out of the Bentham-James Mill-Gradgrind formulation is imagination, poetry, sensitivity, discrimination.

It is not what the Utilitarians stand for that is primarily in question.
Gradgrind is not an ogre: at no time does Dickens show him acting
in any other way than sincerely for the best. But his purview of life
is materialist, and therefore limited; certainly too limited for the
moral and social judgments that he permits himself.

'Now, what I want is, Facts. Teach these boys and girls nothing but Facts.
Facts alone are wanted in life. Plant nothing else, and root out everything
else. You can only form the minds of reasoning animals upon Facts: nothing
else will ever be of service to them. This is the principle on which I bring
up my own children, and this is the principle upon which I bring up these
children. Stick to Facts, sir!'

The facts about Gradgrind are that he is a retired manufacturer of
hardware, the Member of Parliament for Coketown, the governor
of a school and the father of five children. One can see why among
the titles Dickens considered for *Hard Times* were *Two and Two
Are Four, Simple Arithmetic* and *A Mere Question of Figures.* As

a public man, it is difficult to bring Gradgrind to account. The aim
of the line of action in which he is the central figure is to discredit
his policies by showing how disastrously they fail in his private life.

In public, certainly, they seem grim enough. A key passage is the
trial lesson given to us in Chapter II. A pale and lifeless boy defines
'horse' – a creature so often taken by writers to exemplify vitality
and virility – as a graminivorous quadruped, shedding its coat in
the spring, requiring to be shod, age known by marks in the mouth,
etc. The boy's name is Bitzer, to typify the fragmentated nature of
his knowledge. These bits of facts stuck together do not amount to
any total realization of a horse. Girl No. 20 – her real name is kept
in abeyance in this classroom – actually belongs to a travelling circus,
Sleary's Horseriding, but she finds herself unable to talk about the
animals with which she is so familiar in the terms of Gradgrind.

Let it not be thought that the Gradgrind system is exaggerated.
Dickens has taken it from the Birkbeck schools, founded by William
Ellis, a Utilitarian and friend of John Stuart Mill. His intention was
to equip the poor for their social function in an industrial society.
These Birkbeck schools were described by Henry Morley in *Household Words*, 25 December 1852. Indeed, in Morley's account there
is even a Bitzer – 'a little fellow, with light flaxen hair . . . was quite
a luminary on all points that were mooted. There was not a question
he did not answer. . . .' The basic method of instruction was the
question-and-answer approach exemplified in Dickens's trial lesson.

'Now, let me ask you girls and boys. Would you paper a room with representations of horses?'

After a pause, one half of the children cried in chorus, 'Yes, sir!' Upon
which the other half, seeing in the gentleman's face that Yes was wrong,
cried out in chorus, 'No, sir!' – as the custom is in these examinations.

'Of course, No. Why wouldn't you? . . .'

'I'll explain to you, then,' said the gentleman, after another and more
dismal pause, 'why you wouldn't paper a room with representations of
horses. Do you ever see horses walking up and down the sides of rooms
in reality – in fact? Do you?'

'Yes, sir!' from one half. 'No, sir!' from the other.

'Of course no,' said the gentleman, with an indignant look at the wrong
half. 'Why then, you are not to see anywhere, what you don't see in fact;
you are not to have anywhere, what you don't have in fact. What is called
Taste, is only another name for Fact.'

The syllabus of the Birkbeck schools was dominated by the science of social economy. In other words, the relationship of man to man was interpreted in terms of the cash-nexus; the applied form of self-interest. So we must not be surprised if it is in such terms that Gradgrind's pupils, Bitzer among them, grew up to see human behaviour.

The imaginative truncation brought about by Gradgrind's system is seen in his children's lives. His daughter has no outlet for her emotional life but her brother. Her brother, in his turn, finds consolation only in compulsive gambling. He robs his employer to pay his debts and lays the blame on an honest working-man. When the theft comes to light, he tells his father that he was governed by the System. 'So many people are employed in positions of trust; so many people, out of so many, will be dishonest. I have heard you talk, a hundred times, of its being a law. How can I help laws?'

So individual responsibility is diminished in favour of conformity to abstract rules of statistics; human choice is limited under the bonds of mechanical determinism. The Gradgrind system would thus claim to judge human behaviour rationally and to hold in check the deflecting force of emotion. Nevertheless, when Bitzer, in Utilitarian maturity, seizes Gradgrind junior for his theft, he finds himself questioned by his old master in terms oddly reminiscent of the lessons at Gradgrind's school.

'Bitzer . . . have you a heart?'

'The circulation, sir,' returned Bitzer, 'couldn't be carried on without one. . . .'

'What motive – even motive in reason – can you have for preventing the escape of this wretched youth,' said Mr Gradgrind, 'and crushing his miserable father? See his sister here. Pity us! . . .'

'I am going to take young Mr Tom back to Coketown, in order to deliver him over to Mr Bounderby. Sir, I have no doubt whatever that Mr Bounderby will then promote me to young Mr Tom's situation. And I wish to have his situation, sir, for it will be a rise to me, and will do me good.'

'If this is solely a question of self-interest with you – 'Mr Gradgrind began.

'I beg your pardon for interrupting, sir,' returned Bitzer; 'but I am sure you know that the whole social system is a question of self-interest. . . .'

The Gradgrind system acts against itself because there is no Utilitarian who at some time does not experience a situation where feeling comes into play. Moreover, self-interest cannot be the sole determining factor if man is to live socially with his fellow-men; and that word 'socially' cannot be acted out merely in terms of economic interest.

A parallel failure is seen in Gradgrind's daughter. The old man can find no reason why she should not marry his friend and Tom's employer, Bounderby. In economic terms, it is a very good match; her lack of feeling for her prospective husband need not disturb it, because her prospective husband requires nothing so immaterial as feeling from her. But the whole match, so rationally conceived, fails disastrously, precisely because Gradgrind has not taken into account this human factor. Louisa returns to her father's house, and all Gradgrind can say is, that he meant to do right.

He said it earnestly, and to do him justice he had. In gauging fathomless depths with his mean little excise-rod, and in staggering over the universe with his rusty stiff-legged compasses, he had meant to do great things. Within the limits of his short tether he had tumbled about, annihilating the flowers of existence with greater simpleness of purpose than many of the blatant personages whose company he kept.

John Stuart Mill thought *Hard Times* a caricature; yet is this really far from his own, totally unironic, description of his gloomily rational father? And in real life we have what at the time of writing Dickens could not possibly know, the fact of the younger Mill's breakdown; so much more dramatic as described in the great Autobiography even than Tom's theft and Louisa's flight from her husband. Moreover, in *Hard Times*, as in life, Utilitarianism opened the door to association with many blatant personages.

One of these is James Harthouse: man about town, would-be Member of Parliament, disaffected from life, enlivening his disaffection by drifting into a near-liaison with Gradgrind's daughter. It is Gradgrind, in fact, who brings him into Coketown, and there is nothing unconvincing about this association in theory. Both men are committed to the doctrine of self-interest. But, in practice, Dickens shows us little of their collaboration. Indeed, there is not one serious conversation recorded between them. Instead, the activities of many months are summarized in terms such as these – 'With the aid of a little more coaching for the political sages . . . he speedily came to be considered of much promise.' The language

here is imprecise; the 'how', 'what' and 'why' of things is evaded.
And such evasiveness renders Harthouse less crucial than he might
have been. The emphasis is placed on his function as instrument
of the plot rather than the Theme; he is seen, that is to say, primarily
as Louisa's potential seducer. But in the latter role, he is easily disposed of. The girl from the circus – No. 20 that was, Sissy that is
– dismisses him in terms that (as Shaw remarked) would have done
credit to a Lord Chief Justice. One can hardly feel that a character
so flimsy was essentially part of the structure of the book; especially
since, without any persuasion from Harthouse, Louisa was already
disaffected from Bounderby.

But Josiah Bounderby is far more relevantly blatant an associate
for Gradgrind; he is, moreover, full of interest in himself. We see
him, alone of all the figures, in truly sensational detail; usually in
terms of a balloon, puffed up, coarse material stretched tight, and
therefore, the inference is, ripe to be deflated. He has, too, a habit
of speaking of himself, even apostrophizing himself, in the third
person, which we recall from another character who affects a bluff
John-Bull pose of frankness, and who has the same initials: Joseph
Bagstock, the choleric major from *Dombey and Son*. But whereas
Bagstock is a gigantically comic irrelevance, Bounderby is integral
to the novel in which he appears; his strand of action the most complex and interesting in the book.

Bounderby is the entrepreneur incarnate: banker, manufacturer,
capitalist, claiming to be that impossibility, a self-made man. He
knows none of the human ties of affection or compassion; for him,
people exist as butts to be bullied or hands to be dismissed. They
are present to his mind only insofar as they are extensions of himself.

Bounderby does not exist with any of our normal associations.
He has cut himself off from time. The future exists only in his will,
the present is that will personified – a boot, to use Orwellian terms,
crashing down upon an unprotected human face – and he has utterly
jettisoned his past. In place of what in a normal human being would
be an autobiographical history, Bounderby has projected a fiction
which is no more than yet another extension of his personality. This
fiction is an account of a past life without – another impossibility
any human contact. He claims to have been deserted by his mother,
turned out of doors by his grandmother, to have slept in the gutter,

lived on rainwater and chance scraps, and to have been glad of an occasional job blacking shoes at a farthing a time.

All this is mere bullying: an attempt to subjugate the outside world to the needs of his ego. When Mr Bounderby's mother fortuitously turns up, she proves to be the decent old proprietress of a village shop who scrimped and saved to send her willing and industrious son through school and into an apprenticeship with a kind master.

Clearly Bounderby's paranoid need to assert himself powered his early efforts: for the son of a village shop to become the richest man in a middle-sized industrial town is a remarkable feat, involving the efforts of many people other than the person most immediately concerned. But his must be the prime effort, and the amount of aggressive energy it required would be extraordinary. It would, in fact, be likely to exceed any possible demand that could be made upon it. Hence Bounderby's impulse to make his success even more remarkable than it is. Hence, too, the distortion of his entire personality. In his effort to represent himself as a truly self-made man, he has cut himself away from all personal relationships: all that he recognizes as connection between himself and others is conceived in terms of power. He has pensioned his mother off on condition that she never comes to see him; he casts his wife off when she asserts herself beyond the role of chattel; he dismisses one of his workmen on arbitrary grounds, even though he knows that this may bring about the man's starvation.

The psychological portrait works very well within the moral framework of Dickens's fable. Bounderby is at once individual capitalist and Capitalism itself personified. Gradgrind may be more clever, but he is a desiccated calculating machine; it is Bounderby who commands the force. He is Utilitarianism in practice. Acting wholly out of self-interest, which for him is not acquisition of money alone but of power, he is able to represent such self-interest in terms of Bentham's 'greatest happiness' principle.

'First of all, you see our smoke. That's meat and drink to us. It's the healthiest thing in the world in all respects, and particularly for the lungs. If you are one of those who wants us to consume it, I differ from you. We are not going to wear the bottoms of our boilers out any faster than we wear 'em out now, for all the humbugging sentiment in Great Britain and Ireland . . . Now you have heard a lot of talk about the work in our mills, no doubt. You have? Very good. I'll state the facts of it to you. It's the pleasantest work there is, and it's the lightest work there is, and it's the best paid work there is. More than that, we couldn't improve the mills themselves, unless we laid down Turkey carpets on the floors. Which we're not a going to do . . . .'

An assertion of will for Bounderby evidently has no satisfaction unless it involves the deprivation or misery of someone else. Put another way; Bounderby cannot see that anyone is in his power unless they are undergoing conditions which no one in their right mind would possibly seek. No doubt Bounderby can justify polluting the atmosphere and misusing the Hands; Utilitarianism is a highly subjectivist creed and can be used to justify almost anything. But Dickens is attacking the capitalist here, as usual with him, on highly personal grounds: this naked assertion of will is part of the over-compensation brought about by a desire to make a place in a world whose dynamic is that of incipient paranoia.

Lest this should be thought an exaggeration, let us consider how quick Bounderby is to over-react at the slightest hint of a difference in opinion. All efforts to meet him nine-tenths of the way are beaten back with surly haste: 'Mr Harthouse would be charmed. "Don't be too sure of that" said Bounderby'; ' "If you will allow me – or whether you will or not, for I am a plain man . . .' " – courtesy is taken to be weakness, the ego resists human contact by treating it as an act of aggression and counter-attacking accordingly.

There is no gap between Bounderby's private and public conduct. The slightest concern among Bounderby's disembodied Hands is instantly and indignantly interpreted as a desire to be set up in a coach and six and fed on turtle soup and venison with a gold spoon. The comic absurdity of this need not blind us to the fact that Bounderby's success in life derives from exaggerating the most transient difference in opinion into a declaration of open war. The native strength of the peasant is allied to a more than native force of character – a character keenly conscious of the opportunities denied it by humble circumstance. It is this that incites the frenetic race towards, and even beyond, the commanding heights. The hardships undergone by peasant generations have made for the weeding out of the weak, so has their constant replenishment of stock by random breeding. Such toughness and endurance went into the bourgeois supplantation of the aristocracy. And by a stroke of genius, Dickens points the fact by providing the robust Bounderby with an aristocratic housekeeper. Mrs Sparsit is physically frail, a hint that she is inbred, and indeed at one point she is practically subsumed into a bad cold. She has been comparatively cushioned from the grosser manifestations of hardship; has certainly never had to work very hard; and was married to an idle and decadent aristocrat, inbred to the last degree, who spent his (inherited) fortune twice over and died of drink at the age of twenty-four. Bounderby, on the other hand, has lived well into his fifties and made enough money to keep her dependent upon him until he chooses to cast her off into penury.

Bounderby and Mrs Sparsit act out this moral fable between them. He represents the ruling class, the bourgeoisie, of the present; she, the ruling classes, the aristocracy, of the past. But what of the proletariat? Not everyone has the ruthless energy of a Bounderby, or the luck to find such willing helpers – a thrifty mother, a kindly master, well-connected friends such as Gradgrind. And, even if such luck were more widespread, it is impossible to imagine what life would be like in a world of Bounderbys. What of the weak, the feeble, the erring; those without Bounderby's advantages?

Here, Dickens is on far less secure ground. The workman, Stephen Blackpool, whom Bounderby dismisses so arbitrarily, is supposed to be a social victim, but we may feel that the odds are biased too heavily against him. Indeed, some of them have nothing directly to do with society at all. It must have been bad enough to be a mill operative in Coketown, without in addition being saddled with a drunken whore for a wife; having, as one's only friend, a woman too virtuous to live with you; who makes you, moreover, promise not to join the Trades Union; that union, in any case, dominated by an insensate bully; having workmates who ostracize you for keeping your promise and staying out of it; and an employer who sacks you, as far as can be ascertained, for being so ostracized. As though this were not enough, Stephen is put under suspicion of perpetrating a robbery, and, in coming forward to clear himself, completes his ill fortune by falling down a disused mine-shaft and breaking his back. We may say that Bounderby, in his faults as in everything else, is a Capitalist; can we honestly say that Stephen is a working man? As his name would suggest, Stephen is a martyr. But I am inclined to think that his martyrdom is a personal rather than a social matter.

There are so many things that Dickens could have done with Stephen. More could have been made of the mine-shaft down which he falls: it ought to have been fenced in after it had been finished with, just as, when in use, its firedamp and propensity towards explosion could have been countered with protective devices; but at no point does Dickens erect it into a social indictment. More could have been made of Stephen's scanty income and conditions of labour at the mill. It is significant that never once in this industrial novel does Dickens show us the day to day life of men in a factory. It would take more than a visit to Preston or Hanley to dramatize this in any depth of detail; yet some such undertaking ought to have been at the heart of the book. Stephen, in fact, is not dramatized as archetypal working man so much as a personification of a victim; not a social victim, either, but the victim of a broken-down marriage. His contrast with Bounderby is not that between master and man; it is rather that between a husband rich enough to free himself of his wife and one too poor to do any such thing.

Stephen, therefore, resembles not so much Jo, in *Bleak House*, as Esther. He stands out of the novel in much the same way and for similar reasons. It is not his case as victim of society we have to consider, but the sentimental tale of a workman and his wife. Stephen's plot is too wildly biased against him to be representative; it cannot act, therefore, as expression of the Theme. Since social satire and human psychology march hand in hand through these later Dickens novels, this thematic failure goes along with Stephen's failure to command respect even as an individual character. Stephen's inappropriateness to the total fiction is at one with his lack of inner life. It is very odd that his wife should turn from a bonny girl to an alcoholic drab, and we might feel in order asking how this came about. But the mere sketch of Stephen's psychology affords no clue. It would be like asking what dialect it is he's supposed to be speaking; or why he agreed to be bound not to join the Union. The hints Dickens gives us are pale and abstract, drawn from Mrs Gaskell, not from life; at odds with each other and with the total structure of the book.

What is a local failure in the character of Stephen becomes disabling when seen at large. Granted Dickens seems to understand pretty

well the bosses; when he comes to the workers he finds himself wildly
at sea.

Oh my friends, the down-trodden operatives of Coketown! Oh my friends
and fellow-countrymen, the slaves of an iron-handed and a grinding des-
potism! Oh, my friends and fellow-sufferers, and fellow-workmen, and
fellow-men! I tell you that the hour is come, when we must rally round one
another as One united power, and crumble into dust the oppressors that too
long have battened upon the plunder of our families, upon the sweat of our
brows, upon the labour of our hands, upon the strength of our sinews, upon
the God-created glorious rights of Humanity, and upon the holy and eternal
privileges of Brotherhood!

Nobody ever spoke like this. The mode of speech does not even
symbolize anything: it is Chadband without the low church behind it.
Dickens deliberately falsified the nature of Trades Unions and their
leaders.

Political bias in itself need not lead to bad fiction; but falsification
and distortion do. It is possible to show the inferiority of this part
of Dickens's novel by referring to what we can ascertain of the raw
material that went into it.

Slackbridge, the speaker here, is much the same person as
Gruffshaw, in Dickens's article 'On Strike'. But the fictional counterpart is allowed much more rein than is Gruffshaw. In the article,
Dickens has the chairman of a meeting call for order when this figure
begins to get inflammatory. And even the documentary figure of
Gruffshaw is caricatured if one turns to his prototype, and that of
Slackbridge, Mortimer Grimshaw. True, Grimshaw was inclined
to colourful oratory, but it has much more sense and less sentimentality than anything you will find in *Hard Times*. 'If our trade cannot prosper, if our commerce cannot flourish, but at the expense
of the comfort and happiness of the operatives of this country, I
will say let trade and commerce perish, and a new order of things be
established' (*The Examiner*, 3 December 1853). This new order
was no wild call for anarchy, but suggestion that the mill be run by
the workers themselves – 'when the manufacturers see our tall
chimneys creeping up, they'll begin to look about them' (*Reynolds's*,
9 April 1854). In other words, Grimshaw's indignation is positive:
he is putting forward a vision of co-operative socialism. Dickens

quite likely would not have liked this idea, but he ought to have given it representation.

But, in any case, such revolutionaries as Grimshaw were marginal to the central points at issue. He was not even regarded as one of the leaders. Far more dominant, in the Preston Strike as elsewhere, were moderates such as George Cowell. This latter impressed even cotton manufacturers such as the Quaker, Henry Ashworth – hardly a friend to trade unionists – with his insight and judgment. Cowell it was who sustained the morale of the strikers throughout a Preston winter without their succumbing to threats or breaking out into violence. In his brilliant article on the subject, Geoffrey Carnall (*Victorian Studies*, 1964) has recreated the personality of this excellent man. It is as well that Carnall did so; for there is no equivalent figure in *Hard Times*.

It is the gap left by the absence of Cowell that makes it possible for Dickens to equate the Trade Union movement with Utilitarianism. And it is true that he caricatures the minor figure of Grimshaw by transmogrifying his appearance (Grimshaw was, unlike Slackbridge, physically imposing), exaggerating his political importance, and castrating him of his ideology. The result is an attempt to make it seem as though the Trades Unions were powered entirely by self-interest. On a naturalistic level, on a political level, on historical, on fictive and stylistic levels, the attempt fails grossly and crassly.

If not Trades Unions, what then? Dickens has a passing moment when he adopts the stance of Carlyle – appealing to the ruling classes over the heads of the workers, and using the Workman's voice, moreover, to do it. How can the social muddle be set to rights? ' 'Tis those as is put ower me, and ower aw the rest of us. What do they tak upon themsels, sir, if not to do't?' It was beyond Dickens, or Carlyle either, to see that in a capitalistic society the interests of employer and workers are unlikely to coincide. And the last thing that either of them was able to visualize was a change in the structure of society. But while Carlyle, after the sharp criticism of his early period, was working out a political ethic that approached perilously close to the fascist concept of *Herrenvolk*, Dickens as a creative writer took refuge in fantasy.

What positive element there is in *Hard Times* is one that takes us back to Astley's in *Sketches by Boz*, the Crummles company in *Nicholas Nickleby*, and Jarley's Waxworks in *The Old Curiosity Shop*. Dickens's antidote to the hard world of fact proves to be tinsel and magic.

'People mutht be amuthed. They can't be alwayth a learning, nor yet they can't be alwayth a working, they ain't made for it. You *mutht* have uth, Thquire. Do the withe thing, and the kind thing, too, and make the betht of uth; not the wurtht!'

Thus, Mr Sleary, of the Horseriding, first and last to Mr Gradgrind. Here we have acrobats, tightrope-walkers, bareback-riders – in fact, all the fun of the fair. But we may feel them to be, not merely idealized, but abstracted. 'Yet there was a remarkable gentleness and childishness about these people, a special inaptitude for any kind of sharp practice, and an untiring readiness to help and pity one another, deserving often of as much respect, and always of as much generous construction, as the every-day virtues of any class of people in the world.' It is a pity that Dickens was not able to show us this in the day-to-day work of a circus. We would require something more substantial than this to stand against the rampart of Utilitarianism and its extensions into politics and industry. Personally I prefer to Sleary's Horseriding the troupe of Mr Crummles, with the attendant jealousies of Mr Folair for the Infant Phenomenon, the vanities of Miss Petowker and Miss Snevellicci, the exaggerated gestures of Old Bricks and Mortar himself; though I should be the first to admit that they have little organic relationship to a theme. Theme indeed there is in *Hard Times*, and plenty of it; but it is Nature, not an Ideal, that needs to be set up as a corrective to Mr Gradgrind. Insofar as Dickens condescends to the authentic details in dealing with Sleary's Horseriding, they turn out to be no more impressive than chit-chat: Mr Sleary is stout and alcoholic; Cupid, out of the ring, is horsey and hoarse-voiced. But circumstances such as these go against Dickens's asseverations of the troupe's gentleness and childishness, and makes us wonder why we should follow them anywhere!

There is nothing, then, in *Hard Times* capable of countering the unholy alliance of Gradgrind and Bounderby. The book therefore seems far grimmer than is strictly necessary for the subject. One cannot exaggerate the distortion in structure caused by the misre-presentation of the Trades Unions and the exaltation of a circus troupe to an implied moral positive. And yet, in spite of these inadequacies, *Hard Times* will stand up to a critical reading far better than any earlier novel of Dickens, *Bleak House* alone excepted. It portrays figures as remarkable for their individuality as any in the whole of Dickens, but, for the most part, they serve the considera-tions of Theme. And the Theme is one capable of engaging serious attention. For Dickens has made a highly serious claim. It is tri-partite in character: that the paranoid temperament fosters a paranoid creed, Utilitarianism, and that this creed extends itself in practice into the irresponsible development of Industry. It is not Industry per se that Dickens is fighting; rather laissez-faire, which polluted the atmosphere, allowed open mine-shafts to fester, employed or starved workers according to the market without any sense of human need or potential. Not industry alone is in question, but the philosophy operating behind it. 'Your sister's training has been pursued according to the system' says the broken Gradgrind; and it is true. *Hard Times*, then, is Dickens's attack upon the System by which the claims of individual human beings are trampled in a general mêlée. Society itself cannot survive under such circumstances. The answers of *Hard Times* may be invalid; the questions it pro-pounds are still with us. It is the most flawed of Dickens's classics, possibly, but it is still a classic.

XVII Little Dorrit (1855-57)

Dickens finished *Hard Times* in July 1854, but did not begin *Little Dorrit* until the end of 1855. In the sixteen months or so intervening, he published little more than a couple of Christmas Stories for *Household Words*. However, he was not lying fallow. Apart from his frenetic activities in the amateur theatre, he had his day-to-day work as editor of a weekly magazine. And he was giving more and more time to social questions and to politics. He was kept busy as a sort of Patronage Secretary to the millionaire philanthropist, Angela Burdett-Coutts. The fraudulence and failure of three banking houses – one of whose directors committed suicide – concerned him deeply. Perhaps most of all, at this period, he was exercised by government maladministration, particularly the disastrous policy of Lord Palmerston, the then Prime Minister, touching the conduct of the Army in the Crimea. Dickens made a brilliant speech to this effect in June 1855, at the third meeting of the newly formed Administrative Reform Association. Of Palmerston, who had attacked his own involvement in amateur drama, he said: 'I will try to give the noble lord the reason of these private theatricals. . . . It is this:- The public theatricals which the noble lord is so condescending as to manage, are so intolerably bad, the machinery is so cumbrous, the parts so ill-distributed, the company so full of "walking gentlemen", the managers have such large families, and are so bent on putting those families into what is theatrically called "first business" – not because of their aptitude for it, but because they *are* their families, that we find ourselves obliged to organize an opposition. We have seen the *Comedy of Errors* played so dismally like a tragedy that we cannot bear it. . .'

Matters such as this served to exacerbate his fury at the England of 1855. It is easy to see how this speech is the matrix, not only of Dickens's political journalism in *Household Words*, but of *Little Dorrit* itself. More, the facts that Dickens observed all around him became identified with several of his own problems, and so the vast terrain of the novel became infused with personal feeling. Society, in this book, is represented as wholly stupid, maladroit and uncomprehending; the only palliative (a poor one) is individual goodness.

Little Dorrit was originally to have been called *Nobody's Fault*. Dickens had told Forster that he was going to have, as a central character, a man who brought about all the mischief in the book, disclaiming responsibility, though, with the formula 'Well, it's a mercy, however, nobody was to blame you know'. Several critics have pointed out that there is no such figure as this in *Little Dorrit*, and that it is impossible to identify anyone in the early chapters who could have been meant to fulfil such a role. But they are wrong in supposing the concept to be jettisoned along with the title.

The attitude implied by 'nobody was to blame' is satirized and acted out through the book. This is not simply a matter of character. It appears as an indictment of irresponsibility, seen in the machinery of government; a series of portraits showing irresponsible or repressive parents; a study of dehumanization in the case of repressed children; the portrayal at once of society in a prison and Society *as* a prison; and indications both at large and in minute particular of an economy hopelessly out of control. But all this makes the book sound more abstract than it is.

The concept of 'nobody's fault' is bodied forth in the powerful symbol of the irresponsible father; from the personal portrait it extends into the dramatization of a prison; and the prison itself extends into the society of which it is part. It is this group of related symbols, turning upon the idea of 'nobody's fault', that gave the book its power. The System *is* somebody's fault; at least it ought to be; but, any more than John Dickens or Mr Micawber, no one is willing to step forward to take the blame and make things better. That is why the book seems like a series of variations on a theme of total despair.

Little Dorrit is a unique blend of the social and personal anguish of Dickens's life. It acts out many of the ideas that were troubling

him. The effort seems to have been to refrain from overt didacticism;
hence, perhaps, the change of title. But such a passage as this, deriving from his speech on Administrative Reform, could have been
an integral part of the novel.

The power of Nobody is becoming so enormous in England, and he alone
is responsible for so many proceedings, both in the way of commission and
omission; he has so much to answer for, and is so constantly called to account;
that a few remarks upon him may not be ill-timed.

The hand which this surprising person had in the late war is amazing to
consider. It was he who left the tents behind, who left the baggage behind,
who chose the worst possible ground for encampments, who provided no
means of transport, who killed the horses, who paralyzed the commissariat,
who knew nothing of the business he professed to know and monopolized,
who decimated the English army. It was Nobody who gave out the famous
unroasted coffee, it was Nobody who made the hospitals more horrible
than language can describe, it was Nobody who occasioned all the dire confusion of Balaklava harbour, it was even Nobody who ordered the fatal
Balaklava cavalry charge. The non-relief of Kars was the work of Nobody,
and Nobody has justly and severely suffered for that infamous transaction.

In civil matters we have Nobody equally active. When a civil office breaks
down, the break-down is sure to be in Nobody's department. I entreat on
my reader, dubious of this proposition to wait until the next break-down
(the reader is certain not to have to wait long), and to observe, whether or
no, it is in Nobody's department. A dispatch of the greatest moment is sent
to a minister abroad, at a most important crisis; Nobody reads it. British
subjects are affronted in a foreign territory; Nobody interferes. Our own
loyal fellow-subjects a few thousand miles away, want to exchange political,
commercial, and domestic intelligence with us; Nobody stops the mail. The
government, with all its mighty means and appliances, is invariably beaten and
outstripped by private enterprise; which we all know to be Nobody's fault.
Something will be the national death of us, some day; and who can doubt that
Nobody will be brought in Guilty?

All this is a clever realization of the fact that the word 'nobody' is
dual in character: it can be a straight negative, but can be used syntac-
tically to refer to a positive entity. Dickens keeps these two irrecon-
cilable senses in play over a fair-sized passage.

But this is exhortation similar to the Boodle-Coodle-Doodle antics
of *Bleak House*. The influence of Carlyle's Latter-Day Pamphlets
is perhaps too near the surface. So, though this passage spells out

the meaning of *Little Dorrit*, it is in fact not part of that novel but an essay in *Household Words* called 'Nobody, Somebody and Everybody'. It appeared on 30 August 1856, or a few weeks after Dickens had written a chapter in *Little Dorrit* called 'A Shoal of Barnacles'. This is in some sense a parallel to the passage I have quoted, but a parallel that takes place in fictional terms. The contrast between them shows clearly that exhortation, rhetoric, verbal horseplay were in future to be siphoned off from the increasingly subtle fictions of Dickens's social novels.

For the Barnacles are not part of some Carlylean denunciation; they are particularized figures adhering to a particularized institution called the Circumlocution Office. There is certainly an appeal from this office and its inhabitants to a general system; but it is important to remember that the generalization is implied through the presentation of specific particulars. The Circumlocution Office is a government department that symbolizes all government departments, indeed, Government itself. It is a network of jobbery and nepotism, mostly a result of intermarriage between the Barnacle and Stiltstalking families, and the assignment of posts to the scions thereof; quite possibly, Dickens had the Stephen family in mind – at any rate, Fitzjames Stephen, replying to *Little Dorrit* in the *Saturday Review*, seems to have thought so. It is in itself a caricature of what the Civil Service was like before the Lewis Order in Council of 1855, but suggests any form of government without personal feel: Dickens's great theme, in fact, of System in lieu of human contact.

But, though all this will indicate that there is a great gap between the hortatory technique of the *Household Words* article and the domestic satire of the Circumlocution Office, there are not only moral but verbal links between the two. According to the article, Nobody knew anything of the business he professed to know and monopolized; worse, it was Nobody who decimated the English army. What of the Circumlocution Office?

Yes, there was Lord Decimus Tite Barnacle, who had risen to official heights on the wings of one indignant idea, and that was, My Lords, that I am yet to be told that it behoves a Minister of this free country to set bounds to the philanthropy, to cramp the charity, to fetter the public spirit, to contrast the enterprise, to damp the independent self-reliance, of its people. . . . On this sublime discovery, in the great art How not to do it, Lord Decimus had long sustained the highest glory of the Barnacle family; and let any ill-advised member of either house but try How to do it by bringing in a Bill to do it, that Bill was as good as dead when Lord Decimus Tite Barnacle rose up in his place, and solemnly said, soaring with indignant majesty as the Circumlocution cheering sounds around him, that he was yet to be told, my Lord, that it behoved him as the Minister of this free country, to set bounds to the philanthropy . . .

Etc., etc., etc. The necessary repetition is kept from being monotonous by the personalization in the concluding sentences of the 'one indignant idea' that had made Lord Decimus great. And we do not need the clue afforded by the essay in *Household Words* to see why Decimus is a singularly appropriate name for the noble Lord. The whole line and purpose of the Circumlocution Office is to exhibit what happens when Nobody runs the country. They have brought one peculiar art to a state of perfection.

It is true that How not to do it was the great study and object of all public departments and professional politicians all round the Circumlocution Office. It is true that every new premier and every new government coming in because they had upheld a certain thing as necessary to be done, were no sooner come in than they applied their utmost faculties discovering How not to do it. It is true that from the moment when a general election was over, every returned man who had been raving on the hustings because it hadn't been done, and who had been asking the friends of the honourable gentleman in the opposite interest on pain of impeachment to tell him why it hadn't been done, and who had been asserting that it must be done, and who had been pledging himself that it should be done, began to devise, How it was not to be done. . .All this is true, but the Circumlocution Office went beyond it.

Because the Circumlocution Office went on mechanically, every day, keeping this wonderful, all-sufficient wheel of statesmanship, How not to do it, in motion. Because the Circumlocution Office was down upon any ill-advised public servant who was going to do it, or who appeared to be by any surprising accident in remote danger of doing it, with a minute, and a memorandum, and a letter of instructions, that extinguished him. It was this spirit of national efficiency in the Circumlocution Office that had gradually led to its having something to do with everything.

Dickens is developing his recognition that it is not the individually wicked man, nor even the corrupt cabal of politicians, that leads to the downfall of the individual. This is a picture of government ministers paralyzed by the inertia of the Civil Service, itself an embodiment of the System. And certainly, in the way it is expressed, this is an acting out of the concept 'Nobody's Fault'. The System, inert, wrong-headed, infiltrates and paralyses all aspects of science, defence, social service, government; even the arts. For one of the laziest and most selfish of these drifters is an amateur artist, in part based on Thackeray, who throws cynical scorn on that which he seems to profess. No wonder Dickens dedicated the novel to one whom he himself sincerely believed to be a great painter: Clarkson Stanfield. Dickens is not content to leave the matter, as Carlyle would, to denunciation, no matter how exalted. He gives us chapter and verse of the Circumlocution Office; how the wretched client waits in halls, glass cases, fire-proof passages where the Department keeps its wind; meets office juniors who know something of some business, but not the one in hand; beards seniors in their squeezed-up airless houses, finding them as stiff and buttoned-up as the prison where they choose to dwell, only to be referred back to the Office, and to find himself ushered from Section to Section – some of which Sections chatter inconsequentially about other matters, others of which inundate that same wretched client with forms, under the irresponsible assurance that nothing anyone does will ever achieve anything. Thus, the Circumlocution Office, while having no inventive ability itself, has the power to strangle any patent at birth by preventing its application to the public use. Thus, once more, it has the power to put a man in prison, but no notion why it has done so, and no intention of doing anything to get him out again.

It is not really Mr Dorrit's fault that he has landed in the Marshalsea – a prison as dark, narrow and airless as the house of Mr Tite Barnacle himself. Probably it is Nobody's fault; but Mr Dorrit is the last person we could go to for an answer.

Necessarily he was going out again directly, because the Marshalsea lock never turned upon a debtor who was not. He brought a portmanteau with him, which he doubted its being worth while to unpack; he was so perfectly clear – like the rest of them, the turnkey on the lock said – that he was going out again directly.

Dorrit has two children, but, as this same disconcertingly realistic turnkey observes, is pretty childish himself; and so is his wife, who has a child coming; and they all live together in a spirit of helpless childishness in a single room with a few sticks of furniture because they think it better that they should not be separated – even for a few weeks. . . .

Meanwhile twenty-three years wear away. The transition in time is managed wonderfully: marked, at first, by the birth of Little Dorrit, the Child of the Marshalsea, but, increasingly, by the prison taint which gradually darkens the veneer of the gentlemanly prisoner.

For the prison proves to be a microcosm of the society outside, with all its euphemism and hypocrisy. The prisoners term themselves Collegians and their cramped common-room a Snuggery. In one sense, they are free: for example, they appear no longer to be harassed by creditors or badgered by business queries. As one old jail-bird, a drunken doctor, says, 'We have got to the bottom, we can't fall, and what have we found? Peace. That's the word for it. Peace.'

Yet this is not strictly true. There is a hierarchy, even within the prison, and it is up this meaningless social ladder that Dorrit mounts, to the great detriment of his spirit. From being a new, still shame-faced debtor, he gradually acquires such distinctions as the Marshalsea can bestow. His wife dies, and the prison confers pity upon him, though he recovers from the blow in a month or so. With the passing years, he acquires the confidence of the turnkeys; indeed, on one or two occasions, has been observed turning the lock of the prison upon himself. And when the oldest turnkey dies, he himself becomes the longest-serving inhabitant of the prison: the Father of the Marshalsea.

And he grew to be proud of the title. If any impostor had tried to claim it, he would have shed tears in resentment of the attempt to deprive him of his rights. A disposition began to be observed in him, to exaggerate the number of years he had been there; it was generally understood that you must deduct a few from his account; he was vain, the fleeting generations of debtors said.

Nowhere before had Dickens achieved such delicacy of irony – the use of words such as 'title' and 'rights' to describe what in fact is a mark only of deprivation of liberty, and the ascription of vanity to what, in a human being, ought to be a sense of degradation – these are two indications chosen at random of the reversal of values operating through the whole chapter, indeed, the whole of the Dorrit strand of action. And this delicacy may be observed, too, in the plasticity of the rhythms, which are not the rhythms of naturalistic prose, but of great poetry. Again, one may indicate such matters in terms of the placing of words: in the last section quoted, the heaviest stress of the whole paragraph comes on the word 'vain', and the dying away of the next phrase – 'the fleeting generations of debtors said' – suggests nothing so much as a mocking echo of whole men departing from a feeble and decaying Father.

By such means is a tension created, between the old debtor's incongruous sense of increasing rank and our sense of his increasing degradation. In time, it becomes a custom for newcomers to the prison to be presented to him; Dickens strikes the note of incongruity when he says that Dorrit receives them with 'a kind of bowed-down beneficence'. It becomes a not unusual circumstance for letters to be put under his door enclosing half-crowns or even the odd half-sovereign – testimonials from departing prisoners to the Father of the Marshalsea. And, lest this correspondence wear itself out, the old man forms the habit of escorting such prisoners to the gate on their departure, as a way of exacting from them what he now believes to be his due. Indeed, when one poor wretch presents him not with the usual silver but with the halfpence which is all he can afford, the Father of the Marshalsea has the face to feel affronted! For the lower he sinks in the scale of beggary, the greater grows his sense of occasion and circumstance.

The Marshalsea itself is as powerfully created as its Father. The authenticity of its presentation is guaranteed by John Howard's factual report of the State of English Prisons, although the experience upon which Dickens was drawing dated from the 1820s of his youth. The prison is emblem rather than documentary. At that time, the squalid houses of the Marshalsea stood back to back, looking outwards to the surrounding narrow paved yard, hemmed in by high walls spiked at the top. Always, on every appearance, what is insisted upon is its darkness.

The night was dark; and the prison lamps in the yard and the candles in the prison windows faintly shining behind many sorts of wry old curtain and blind, had not the air of making it lighter.... *(Chapter VIII)*

The morning light was in no hurry to climb the prison wall and look in at the Snuggery windows.... *(Chapter IX)*

The spikes had never looked so sharp and cruel, nor the bars so heavy, nor
the prison space so gloomy and contracted. . . . *(Chapter XIX)*

The shadow of the Marshalsea was a real darkening influence, and could
be seen on the Dorrit family at any stage of the sun's course. . . . *(Chapter
XXI)*

Little Dorrit, looking musingly down into the dark valley of the prison,
shook her head. . . . *(Chapter XXIV)*

The inhabitants of the Marshalsea are represented as either drunken,
hoarse and puffy or pale, wasted and anaemic. Yet below them there
is an even lower stage – their messengers and hangers-on, shabby
attendants upon shabbiness. 'As they eyed the stranger in passing,
they eyed him with borrowing eyes – hungry, sharp, speculative as to
his softness if they were accredited to him. . .' And Tip, the son of
the Father of the Marshalsea, is of their number; indeed, as one
might expect, becomes their embodiment.

For William Dorrit, whatever he may be to the Marshalsea, is a
poor father to his own children. Weak, dependent, essentially childish,
he affects not to know that his elder daughter supports herself by
dancing and that his younger daughter goes out sewing in the homes
of various ladies. The irony is that this daughter, Little Dorrit,
imputes to such moral evasion the characteristics of nobility. She
says 'It would be a new distress to him even to know that I earn a
little money, and that Fanny earns a little money. He is so anxious
about us, you see, feeling helplessly shut up there. Such a good,
good father!'

In fact, no father could be less responsible. Old Dorrit may be
good at blessing the Marshalsea prisoners in return for their little
Testimonials, but he advises his daughter to encourage the amorous
advances of the turnkey's son as a means of eking out his own slender
privileges. Even Little Dorrit can't see nobility in this. And, degraded
as he has let himself become, the old man is momentarily ashamed
at his suggestion: 'His voice died away, as if she could not bear the
pain of hearing him, and her hand had gradually crept to his lips'
– an ironic parody of his own habitual gesture.

But this moment of shame is the prelude to a bout of megalomania,
ranging from a threnody over his erstwhile good looks, through an
extravagant admonition to all mankind never to lose self-respect, and

into a tearful exultation over the fact that he is the most respected inhabitant of the Marshalsea; the biggest rat, so to speak, in the hole. However, whether bragging or despairing, he is a captive with the jail-rot upon him; the impurity of the prison has darkened whatever is left of his spirit.

The character of Mr Dorrit is in some ways based upon that of Dickens's father, himself a former Marshalsea prisoner: a far more complex and subtle version of Mr Micawber, helplessly clinging on to the decaying shreds of his own gentility. And, in terms of plot, his case has much to do with that of one Henry Allnutt, who spent some years of the eighteenth century in the Marshalsea, and was released on coming into a great fortune. This is exactly what happened to Mr Dorrit: through the action of various intermediaries, it is found that he is really a rich man and his affairs are at last disentangled. The scene when he leaves the prison is one of Dickens's great set-pieces. A banquet is held for the wretches remaining behind; the sometime Father of the Marshalsea passes among them benevolently; and, amidst their plaudits, he leaves in procession with his whole family – with the exception of Little Dorrit, who has fainted in the midst of the excitement, and is consequently forgotten, and left behind.

But there is no freedom for the Dorrit family: wherever they go, they take the darkness of the prison with them. Dorrit cannot – so to speak – get enough air. He travels compulsively. But even his travelling is a form of imprisonment. He is unable to move without an entourage. There is his brother, his son, his daughter, their chaperone; and they are attended by a courier, two footmen, two waiting-maids; together with a corresponding burden of luggage; all borne in a great travelling carriage, a chariot, and a fourgon lumbering along in the rear – a strong body of inconvenience that impedes rather than facilitates progress. It is worth noting that this is one of several links with *Pictures from Italy*, which is in many ways the matrix from which the continental portions of *Little Dorrit* were taken. In that travel book, it is Dickens himself who is scouring the countryside in a carriage of considerable proportions, accompanied not only by the family of whom he is the Head and Chief, but by a courier as well. And just as he, through so much of his life, had suppressed the episode of the blacking factory, so Dorrit vainly tries to conceal the Marshalsea. The family with its numerous attendants rumbles towards the gleaming whiteness of the Alps. It is obvious enough that they are a contrast to the 'dark valley' of the Marshalsea.

The bright morning sun dazzled the eyes, the snow had ceased, the mists had vanished, the mountain air was so clear and light that the new sensation of breathing it was like having entered upon a new existence. To help the delusion, the solid ground itself seemed gone, and the mountain, a shining waste of immense white heaps and masses, to be a region of cloud floating between the blue sky above and the earth far below.

But there is a continual reminder of the Marshalsea, even in the terms of this description. The eyes that are dazzled are those habituated to prison; it is the Dorrit family that has entered on to a new existence; the Dorrits are bewildered by space, as Little Dorrit herself was by the expanse of sky and river seen on her occasional walks upon the Iron Bridge hard by the Marshalsea. Just as the travellers ascend to the looked-for monastery where they are to rest, so 'Darkness and Night were creeping up to the highest ridges of the Alps' – as though they brought their own atmosphere with them. Little Dorrit herself feels that the Marshalsea may be behind some rock; Mr Dorrit sees any space indoors – the monastery itself, for instance – as confined, limited, contracted, monotonous. The shadows of the Marshalsea cannot be left behind so easily. The smallest delay, the slightest blunder, awakes in Old Dorrit a frantic sense of persecution. When a suite of rooms in a country inn is not immediately made available for him, he demands to know why he is not treated like other gentlemen. When his valet fails to understand a more than usually elliptical instruction, he imagines that he is being slighted as a former Marshalsea prisoner. When his past life unexpectedly re-asserts itself, in the person of the turnkey's son with a humble testimonial come to pay him a visit, Dorrit flies into the passion of all time; for he takes this to be a calculated insult.

His instincts, in any case, are not geared to freedom. He had no way of managing his affairs and so got drawn into the toils of the Circumlocution Office; he has no idea of how he got into prison; none, even, of how he got out. And his extreme form and ceremony, got up to conceal an inner incertitude, check and thwart any spontaneity or natural kindness. Indeed, he reproaches Little Dorrit for behaving naturally; accusing her of that for which he himself stands in most need of forgiveness – carrying the prison taint out into Society.

Finally, when he is crumbling and gone senile, he unintentionally gives away the whole of his long-kept secret. There is nothing more dramatic in the whole of Dickens than Dorrit's final exit of all. He is surrounded at a general banquet in Rome by English wealth and English aristocracy, with the usual sprinkling of French and Italian nobility. The table is long; so is the dinner; and the entire company is startled to notice Mr Dorrit lean across to where his daughter is sitting, and call –

'Amy, Amy my child.'

The action was so unusual, to say nothing of his strange eager appearance and strange eager voice, that it instantaneously caused a profound silence.

'Amy, my dear,' he repeated. 'Will you go and see if Bob is on the lock?'

She was at his side, and touching him, but he still perversely supposed her to be in her seat, and called out, still leaning over the table, 'Amy, Amy. I don't feel quite myself. Ha. I don't know what's the matter with me. I particularly wish to see Bob. Ha. Of all the turnkeys, he's as much my friend as yours. See if Bob is in the lodge, and beg him to come to me.'

All the guests were now in confusion, and everybody rose. . . . .

One is irresistibly reminded of Macbeth's disclosure of the murder of Duncan; or of his starting back at the manifestation of Banquo's ghost. Either way, the truth is let out, and the guests rise in confusion. In Dorrit's vision, the banqueting hall of the Roman palace has contracted to the narrow confines of the Marshalsea. And, seeing the number of faces by which he is surrounded, he addresses them with an appropriateness which only seems mistaken if we forget the metaphor that is being acted out, of Society as prison.

Ladies and gentlemen, the duty – ha – devolves upon me of – hum –welcoming you to the Marshalsea. Welcome to the Marshalsea! The space is – ha – limited – the parade might be wider; but you will find it apparently grow larger after a time – a time, ladies and gentlemen – and the air is, all things considered, very good. It blows over the – ha – Surrey hills. Blows over the Surrey hills. This is the Snuggery. Hum. Supported by a small subscription of the – ha – collegiate body. In return for which – hot water – general kitchen – and little domestic advantages. Those who are habituated to the – ha – Marshalsea, are pleased to call me its Father. I am accustomed to be complimented by strangers as the – ha – Father of the Marshalsea. Certainly, if years of residence may establish a claim to so – ha – honourable a title, I may accept the – hum – conferred distinction. Mh child, ladies and gentlemen. My daughter. Born here!...

It has become a – hum – not infrequent custom for my – ha – personal admirers – personal admirers solely – to be pleased to express their desire to acknowledge my semi-official position here, by offering – ha – little tributes, which usually take the form of – ha – Testimonials – pecuniary Testimonials. In the acceptance of those – ha – voluntary recognitions of my humble endeavours to – hum – to uphold a Tone here – a Tone – I beg it to be understood that I do not consider myself compromised. Ha. Not compromised. Ha. Not a beggar. No; I repudiate the title! At the same time far be it from me to – hum – to put upon the fine feelings by which my partial friends are actuated, the slight of scrupling to admit that those offerings are – hum – highly acceptable. On the contrary, they are most acceptable. In my child's name, if not in my own, I make the admission in the fullest manner, at the same time reserving – ha – shall I say my personal dignity? Ladies and gentlemen, God bless you all!

It is as impossible to cut this speech, even for the purposes of quotation, as it would be to cut Macbeth's 'If it were done' or his threnody over his ruined life, 'Tomorrow and tomorrow and tomorrow'. The paradox of Dorrit, the Father turned Child, is here set before us in all its mock dignity and real degradation. The pathos he seeks to invest himself in is false; the tragedy of his seeking after such pathos – that, after all, is genuine. He has, in fact, never left the Marshalsea. The wider Society which he appears to be addressing is a world of prisoners circumscribed within narrow limits. Their titles are figments, like his own, owing their distinction to little but chance and antiquity. They, too, live upon money they have not earned; testimonials to the mockery of position rather than the solid achievement of merit. They, too, put on a show of dignity which conceals all manner of meanness and hypocrisy. Little Dorrit herself muses upon the fact; her meditation is the key to the novel.

This same society in which they lived greatly resembled a superior sort of Marshalsea. Numbers of people seemed to come abroad, pretty much as people had come into the prison; through debt, through idleness, relationship, curiosity, and general unfitness for getting on at home. They were brought into these foreign towns in the custody of couriers and local followers, just as the debtors had been brought into the prison. They prowled about the churches and picture-galleries, much in the old, dreary prison-yard manner. They were usually going away again tomorrow or next week, and rarely knew their own minds, and seldom did what they said they would do, or went where they said they would go: in all this again, very like the prison debtors. They paid high for poor accommodation, and disparaged a place while they pretended to like it; which was exactly the Marshalsea custom. They were envied when they went away, by people left behind feigning not to want to go: and that again was the Marshalsea habit invariably. A certain set of words and phrases, as much belonging to tourists as the College and the Snuggery belonged to the jail, was always in their mouths. They had precisely the same incapacity for settling down to anything, as the prisoners used to do; and they wore untidy dresses, and fell into a slouching way of life; still, always like people in the Marshalsea.

And, just as Dickens demonstrates the failure of the Circumlocution Office to govern the country, so he reveals with emotion ranging from cool irony to burning indignation the failure of Society to set its prisoners free.

It is true, however, that the prisoner may grow into tolerance of his bonds. Mrs General, for example, has found her role in life: she harnesses young ladies to the proprieties. In the present case, the cattle in hand are Mr Dorrit's two daughters. Mrs General – the name is symptomatic of discipline, ushering, rank and ceremony – Mrs General is never dismayed or creased; she makes it her mission to varnish over the uneven surface of life until all is smoothly conformable. She characteristically speaks in aphorisms. Of opinions she remarks: 'Perfect breeding forms none, and is never demonstrative'. Of sight-seeing she says 'It is better not to wonder'. To her charges she remarks, in phraseology that has passed into the language: 'You will find it serviceable, in the formation of a demeanour, if you sometimes say to yourself in company – on entering a room, for instance – Papa, potatoes, poultry, prunes and prism, prunes and prism.' This is symptomatic of the Victorian tendency to sweep problems into a cupboard in the pretence that they don't exist – all in the interests of decorum.

Even more circumscribed than Mrs General is Mrs Merdle, wife to the great financier. Here are some of her views upon Society.

We know it is hollow and conventional and worldly and very shocking, but unless we are Savages in the Tropical Seas (I should have been charmed to be one myself – most delightful life and perfect climate I am told), we must consult it. It is the common lot. . . . Society suppresses us and dominates us. . . . It we could only come to a Millennium, or something of that sort, I for one might have the pleasure of knowing a number of charming and talented persons from whom I am at present excluded. A more primitive state of society would be delicious to me. . . . If a few thousand persons moving in Society could only go and be Indians, I would put my name down directly; but as, moving in Society, we can't be Indians, unfortunately . . .

As to marriage on the part of a man, my dear, Society requires that he should retrieve his fortunes by marriage. Society requires that he should gain by marriage. Society requires that he should found a handsome establishment by marriage. Society does not see, otherwise, what he has to do with marriage. . . . People's sons who have the world before them – they must place themselves in a better position towards Society by marriage, or Society really will not have any patience with their making fools of themselves. Dreadfully worldly all this sounds, does it not. . . . My dear, it is not to be disputed for a moment, because Society has made up its mind on the subject, and there is nothing more to be said. . . .

This particular monologue is spread over two widely separated chapters and diversified by the interpolations of other people; so we do not get Mrs Merdle's views so oppressively as this quotation might suggest. Nevertheless, her attitude is clear: she is an even more willing prisoner of Society than Mr Dorrit was in the Marshalsea when he turned the key upon himself and resolutely refused to take so much as a glance at the street outside. And the voice of Society is represented in the person of Mrs Merdle's parrot, which punctuates her various discourses with satiric gibes. We first see the parrot clinging by its beak on to a golden cage and putting itself into various preposterous attitudes; just like people in Society. When Mrs Merdle speaks of the exactions of Society, the parrot shrieks out its right to those exactions. When she says that we are dominated by Society, the parrot exults in a violent fit of laughter. Whatever she says, in fact, the parrot caricatures in mockery. She is herself, as far as the parrot is concerned, no more than a larger version of the species to which he belongs. Over all Mrs Merdle's conferences this same parrot presides like the judge which he greatly resembles; and can always be relied upon to wind up the exposition with a shriek. The fact that Dickens chose such a symbol to sum up and parody Society carries an ironic weight all of its own.

For Society, the more it comes into evidence, consists of people whose conversation lies in echoing each other's sentiments. It is, for example, generally agreed that Mr Merdle's name is that of the age. Society has conferred its accolade upon him, in fact. But if we try to assess the credentials and integrity of individual members of this Society, we find that they are no more than emblematic projections of their various areas of activity. They are not men but Magnates; and instead of keeping the world on the move, they do their best to trip it up.

Because, about Merdle, they are totally wrong. It is true that Admiralty calls him a wonderful man; that Treasury considers him rich enough to buy up the entire House of Commons; that Bishop is glad that Merdle's wealth is laid out in the best interests of Society. And each and every magnate tries to draw Merdle into his own sphere of interest. Bar knows of an estate Merdle could buy involving both parliamentary seats and ecclesiastical presentations; Bishop knows of missions which could usefully be sent to Africa.

But who is Merdle? Nobody knows where he comes from; nobody knows the extent of his enterprises, or even their nature; nobody knows whether he is worthy of trust or not. Simply, as the Prince of the Church has observed, he lays himself out for Society; and, in return, Society is delighted to receive him into its bonds. There are intimations, however, that all is not well. Merdle suffers from a mysterious Complaint, and not even Physician, a frequent Magnate at the Merdle assemblies, can find out what it is. But as surely as the fact of Mr Dorrit's imprisonment, the dark secret is eventually blown abroad when Merdle himself dies by his own hand in a public bath.

He, the uncouth object of such widespread adulation, the sitter at great men's feasts, the roc's egg of great ladies' assemblies, the subduer of exclusiveness, the leveller of pride, the patron of patrons, the bargain-driver with a Minister for Lordships of the Circumlocution Office, the recipient of more acknowledgment within some ten or fifteen years, at most, than had been bestowed upon all peaceful public benefactors, and upon all the leaders of all the Arts and Sciences, with all their works to testify for them, during two centuries at least – he, the shining wonder, the new constellation to be

followed by the wise men bringing gifts, until it stopped over certain carrion
at the bottom of a bath and disappeared – was simply the greatest Forger
and the greatest Thief that ever cheated the gallows.

It cannot be said that Merdle actively invites confidence. Dupes like
Mr Dorrit literally press their fortunes into his unwilling hands.
The character is based on John Sadleir, the M.P. and company pro-
moter who overreached himself financially and cut his throat one
night on Hampstead Heath; and also on George Hudson, the railway
king who had helped Dickens to launch the *Daily News*, but who had
fled to France in the panic of 1848. Merdle was the name originally
designed for the stepfather of David Copperfield; and, amongst
many other things, it strongly suggests *merde*, which is the French
word for excrement.

Just as Merdle takes Society prisoner, so he himself is imprisoned
within it – one hand holding the other, in characteristic attitude, as
though he had taken himself into custody. And for all the guilty
way in which he slinks through glittering feasts and resplendent
gatherings, not the combined wits of all the Magnates – Admiralty,
Treasury, Bishop, Bar, Physician – is enough to penetrate into the
depths of his fraud. They themselves take no responsibility; once
more, it is Nobody's Fault. Yet every partaker of his lavish entertainments had shared in the plunder of innumerable homes. For,
in the avalanche of Merdle's ruin are buried professions, trades,
pensioners, widows and orphans.

One nobody who is ruined in Mr Merdle's crash is Arthur Clennam.
His debts, too, take him to the Marshalsea. But effectively the man,
like Dorrit, like Merdle, has always been in jail. The Marshalsea
itself is not less inhospitable than the stony aspect of his mother.
She wards off his infant gestures of affection and barricades him
away from the possibility of affection in the outside world. She
blights the timid love of his youth by sending him away into exile
in the Far East. When he breaks transportation, so to speak, by
winding up the business on the death of his father and coming back
to England, he is already forty years of age.

Clennam is the most self-effacing of Dickens's heroes, mainly
because the self has been effaced for him. He is the victim of years
of Calvinist repression, incapable of joy, aggression – indeed most
of the human impulses. But every vital instinct is not lost. Clennam

finds himself attracted by Pet, the beautiful young daughter of a typical Englishman abroad – *his* prototype, too, may be found in *Pictures from Italy*. We see Clennam debating within himself whether or not to fall in love with this girl, so much younger than himself. Notice the form of words: Clennam *debates* whether or not to fall in love. Spontaneity, like so much else, has withered in the Calvinistic jail-house within which his spirit is enclosed. There is no way in which he can come out of his particular prison. So, finding he has a rival, Clennam gives up a sortie in which he was never seriously engaged.

Why should he be vexed or sore at heart? It was not his weakness. It was nobody's weakness within his knowledge, why should it trouble him? And yet it did trouble him. And he thought – who has not thought for a moment, sometimes – that it might be better to flow away monotonously, like the river, and to compound for its insensibility to happiness with its insensibility to pain.

Dickens follows this up, punning on the dual sense of 'nobody'; not in the public manner of Carlyle and the *Household Words* article, but in a sad internal manner. There are a whole series of chapter headings, for instance, that act the melancholy love story out – 'Nobody's Weakness', 'Nobody's Rival', 'Nobody's State of Mind', 'Nobody's Disappearance' – that indicate the sterile ambiguity of Clennam's character; showing, that is to say, his suspension of activity; he is, but he cannot act.

To review his life, was like descending a green tree in fruit and flower, and seeing all the branches wither and drop off one by one, as he came down towards them.

'From the unhappy suppression of my youngest days, through the rigid and unloving home that followed them, through my departure, my long exile, my return, my mother's welcome, my intercourse with her since, down to the afternoon of this day with poor Flora,' said Arthur Clennam, 'what have I found!'

His door was softly opened, and these spoken words startled him, and came as if they were an answer:

'Little Dorrit.'

But just as Dorrit, who makes a slave of his daughter, is himself in confinement; and Merdle, who takes in Society, holds himself, too, in custody; so Mrs Clennam, who has kept her son in an emotional jail all his life, is herself imprisoned. She has been for twelve years unable to leave her room as a result of paralysis. It appears to be hysterical in origin; as Lionel Trilling has remarked, an acting out of the Freudian concept of guilt complex. And certainly the parallel between herself and Old Dorrit is made startlingly clear.

What if his mother had an old reason she well knew for softening to this poor girl! What if the prisoner now sleeping quietly – Heaven grant it! – by the light of the Great Day of Judgment should trace back his fall to her. What if any act of hers, and of his father's, should have even remotely brought the grey heads of those two brothers so low!

A swift thought shot into his mind. In that long imprisonment here, and in her own long confinement to her room, did his mother find a balance to be struck? I admit that I was accessory to that man's captivity. I have suffered for it, in kind. He has decayed in his prison; I in mine. I have paid the penalty.

When all the other thoughts had faded out, this one held possession of him. When he fell asleep, she came before him in her wheeled chair, warding him off with this justification. When he awoke, and sprang up causelessly frightened, the words were in his ears, as if her voice had slowly spoken them at his pillow, to break his rest: 'He withers away in his prison; I wither away in mine; inexorable justice is done; what do I owe on this score!'

In a sense, indeed, Mrs Clennam is ancillary to Dorrit's confinement. She has destroyed the codicil of a will that would have left sufficient money to Dorrit's brother, or, in the event of his death, to his niece, Little Dorrit, to allow for the release of the old man from the Marshalsea prison. Thus the paralysis suffered by Mrs Clennam is in some sense an expiation for the guilt she bears; she has put herself in circumstances parallel to those of the Marshalsea prisoner.

She has suppressed this will because Dorrit's brother was the protector of a dancing girl whom the man thought by the world to be her husband had married secretly. She had only found this out when the girl had a child; that child being Arthur Clennam. Hence the cruel upbringing; hence the self-imposed rigidity – the result of an effort of will which denies criticism, crushes opposition. Mrs Clennam bears a name that she is not entitled to; claims a motherhood she has never experienced. The Bad Mother is judged, not cauterized, by the discovery that she was never, in truth, a mother at all.

But, like the other prisoners of this novel, Mrs Clennam is not wholly constrained by her bonds. She is not one to show much sense of life or curiosity about the world. 'The world has narrowed to these dimensions,' she says, 'It is well for me that I never set my heart upon its hollow vanities'.

The house which she has made her prison is ancient, propped up on half a dozen gigantic crutches. Its exterior is so dingy as to appear black, and the interior seems to be kept in Stygian darkness. The door may be opened by the old clerk, Flintwinch, bearing a single candle; his wife, Affery, cannot be seen for the enshrouding gloom. And the imprisoning atmosphere of this dreadful house is described in terms of death. Its fly-blown pictures, on closer inspection, are seen to depict the Plagues of Egypt. The sideboard is lined with lead, like a coffin in several compartments. The staircase by which we ascend to Mrs Clennam's room is panelled with mourning tablets. And, in her room, on a black bier-like sofa, propped up on a bolster like an executioner's block, sits all day long and every day in her widow's dress the paralysed Mrs Clennam. 'All seasons are alike to me,' she says, 'I know nothing of summer and winter, shut up here. The Lord has been pleased to put me beyond all that.' All physical description of her presents us with a rigid, statue-like being – cold grey hair, immovable face, form stiff as the folds of her stony headdress. She has gone not only beyond the flux of the seasons, but beyond human life itself.

At the end of the book the assassin, Blandois, tries to expose her misdemeanours for the purpose of blackmail. Mrs Clennam overcomes her hysterical paralysis, leaves her bed and actually runs to the Marshalsea. There she throws herself on the mercy of Little Dorrit, and makes a clean breast of the increasingly tortuous web of intrigue that has gathered around her original suppression of the will: my explicit comment brings out, I hope, the implied pun in the novel. It goes along with another: the crutches of that House which has been at once dwelling-place, firm and jail, give way; and the House itself crashes on to the stones of the street at the moment of Mrs Clennam's return. And she falls before it, never to rise or move again: to be, for the remainder of her days, a statue indeed.

Everyone who is imprisoned in *Little Dorrit* is himself a jailer. Mr Dorrit, no less than Mrs Clennam, is the repressive element in the lives of his offspring. And every jailer, by the same token, is himself in prison. No less than Mrs Clennam, Dorrit is confined by past experience within the limits of his own personality. This is one reason why both these characters fail so unutterably as parents. This imprisoning and imprisoned characteristic of Bad Parents is brought out by the contacts between them and the good parents, of whom there are one or two examples in the novel. One contrast with Mrs Clennam is Mr Meagles, the father of Pet, who stands back in order to let his daughter have her will in marrying a polished ruffian, even though he knows it can never in the long run make her happy. At any rate, Pet is to blame, nobody else. And Dorrit, in his turn, contrasts unfavourably with another Good Parent, Mr Nandy; one of Dickens's truly heroic portraits. This feeble old man – whom Dorrit characteristically bullies and patronizes – has chosen to retire to the workhouse rather than be a burden to his daughter, her unemployed husband, and their children. There is a distinct intimation that it was this act of self-sacrifice that got the husband, Plornish, out of the Marshalsea and back into his tenement. But really this is out of one prison and into another.

For the place where Plornish lives is called Bleeding Heart Yard, and it is presented as an embodiment of poverty. The hearts that bleed there are employed at cripplingly low wages, or barely employed at all – the tambour-worker, sempstress, shoe-binder, waistcoat-maker – detritus, it seems, from Marx's chapter in *Capital* on The Working Day. All these people want to work; the lucky ones work all the hours there are; yet they can never make ends meet. Plornish the Plasterer has his opinion, and it is not one acceptably varnished to the taste of Society.

There was old people, after working all their lives, going and being shut up in the workhouse, much worse fed and lodged and treated altogether, than – Mr Plornish said manufacturers, but appeared to mean malefactors. Why, a man didn't know where to turn himself for a crumb of comfort. As to who was to blame for it, Mr Plornish didn't know who was to blame for it. He could tell you who suffered but he couldn't tell you whose fault it was. It wasn't *his* place to find out, and who'd mind what he said, if he did find out? He only know'd that it wasn't put right by them what undertook that line of business, and that it didn't come right of itself.

The echo comes back from *Hard Times*: 'aw a muddle'. Nobody's Fault: that's how things are, and the Circumlocution Office – which ought to know about the plight of these poor prisoners of the muddle – is not going to do anything about it. There is no Marxist vision here, and perhaps we cannot ask this of a creative writer. But it vividly renders the sense of lives that could have been happy and useful being bled away to no purpose whatsoever.

Dickens has got past the stage of blaming such situations upon the individually wicked man. But the paradox of a Society that denies wages while demanding rent is bitterly set down here. The rack-rentier who owns the Yard is Christopher Casby, familiarly known as the Last of the Patriarchs. He takes his turn in the Yard of an evening, with his broad-brimmed hat and flowing grey locks, like a benevolent humming-top. But the jailer, Casby, is himself in tow. The Last of the Patriarchs is always represented as having very little volition of his own. Society permits him to be what he is, and what can be done about that? Heavy, drifting, like an unwieldy ship in the Thames, Casby is kept afloat by the efforts of his agent, Pancks. It is not Casby who is hated by the inhabitants of the Yard, but Pancks, even though it is Casby who pays Pancks to squeeze the Yard dry. With his own unaided efforts, Casby could do little: like all rich men, he is dependent upon his servants. In a rare verbal trope, which, characteristically, he stumbles across rather than coins, Casby informs Pancks 'You are paid to squeeze, and you must squeeze to pay'. In the end, Pancks rebels: knocks off the Patriarch's hat, cuts off his long grey locks, and shows what a blundering booby he really is. But even the collapse of Bleeding Heart Yard into laughter at their now discredited father-figure does not alter our foreboding that this in itself cannot solve the problem of rent demanded and wages denied. As ever, Dickens stopped short at demanding a reconstruction not just of this sector of Society but of Society itself.

The Patriarch who patronized the Yard is just as bad a father to his own daughter as Dorrit was. The evocatively named Flora provoked the first flowering of emotion in Arthur Clennam. But Casby joined with Mrs Clennam in putting an end to this timid and abortive romance, and the girl was married off to a wine-merchant instead; usually referred to as Mr F. It was not ecstasy, remarked Flora, but it was comfort: the slightest hint at any delicate little thing to drink, and it came like magic, in a pint bottle. But, as her constant companion, Mr F.'s Aunt, remarks, there are milestones on the Dover Road. Too much time has gone by: Flora, who was once a lily, is become a peony. She is a pitiful exhibition of girlish mannerisms – those of Copperfield's Dora, let us say – extended artificially into middle age. At one glance the image that Clennam has preserved through an absence of eighteen years falls into pieces. This character was based on Dickens's own re-encounter of his youthful love, Maria Beadnell, but it is very shrewdly worked into the novel as a whole; partly as a symbol of time passing, partly as an exhibition of another child ruined by the irresponsibility of a father; and partly as yet another variation of the prisoner theme – Flora is still living in terms of a past fantasy, her juvenile romance with Clennam.

The area of destruction wrought by the jailers in *Little Dorrit* is seen to be far-reaching. That these jailers are represented as bad fathers – true even of the masculine Mrs Clennam – is not accidental. For behind them all is the abdication of responsibility on the part of Society, alike represented by the Circumlocution Office, by the Marshalsea, and by the circumscribed world of Mrs General, Mrs Merdle, and the Magnates.

Dickens has grown into the bitter realization that the mature man is on his own. All he can turn to is hard work – symbolized by Clennam's partner, the engineer, Doyce – and individual kindliness, as seen in Mr Meagles, Mr Nandy, the Plornishes; so much of it, however, subject to strain and mutability. For all his skill, Doyce falls victim to the Circumlocution Office and later is involved by Clennam in the Merdle crash. Even with her good father, Pet falls on evil days with a bad husband. The self-sacrifice of Nandy can get Plornish out of the Marshalsea, but not out of Bleeding Heart Yard.

And those who have not had even that luck, to be born of good fathers, cannot look to the world for any satisfactory surrogate. Miss Wade is illegitimate, feels rightly or wrongly that this stamps her in the eyes of the world, and takes refuge in a festering and impotent Lesbianism. Tattycoram, also illegitimate, resents the love Mr Meagles shows Pet, runs away with Miss Wade and finds herself jailed by her emotionally. Blandois, the assassin, is proud of belonging nowhere, changes his name to suit the occasion, and is himself imprisoned by the melodramatic roles he adopts in lieu of developing a stable personality. One could go on, but the point, if it is to be made, must be made through the major characters.

Clennam has forty years of undergoing repression before he finds his Little Dorrit: so little, that she seems almost a compensation prize for his youthful dreams of Flora or his hopeless longing for Pet. And Little Dorrit has known none of the joys of childhood: in caring for her thankless family, she has stunted – indeed half-starved – herself. Even when she is rich, she finds herself confused by 'Society' into which she is plunged; poor once more, when her father's money is lost in the Merdle crash, it is no easy life that stretches ahead of her.

Indeed, it is fitting that these two deprived children should come together at last, even though they have been etiolated to no small extent by their struggle. Their mutual diffidence strews endless difficulties in their respective journeys towards a mutual understanding. Clennam thinks of Dorrit as a child; she imagines him still to be in love with Flora. And when in the end they do come together, symbolically under the shadow of the Marshalsea, it is with a very qualified blessing that Dickens sends them out into the world.

They paused for a moment on the steps of the portico, looking at the fresh perspectives of the street in the autumn morning sun's bright rays, and then went down. Went down into a modest life of usefulness and happiness. Went down to give a mother's care in the fullness of time, to Fanny's neglected children no less than to their own, and to leave that lady going into society for ever and a day. Went down to give a tender nurse and friend to Tip for some few years, who was never vexed by the great exactions he made of her, in return for the riches he might have given her if he had ever had them, and who lovingly closed his eyes on the Marshalsea and all its blighted fruits. They went quietly down into the roaring streets, inseparable and blessed; and as they passed along in sunshine and in shade, the noisy and the eager, and the arrogant and the froward and the vain, fretted, and chafed, and made their usual uproar.

We are here a long way from the happiness that blooms for Harry and Rose Maylie, for Kate and Nicholas Nickleby with their respective ciphers of partners, to say nothing of the middle-period novels: Florence with her dashing Walter, David with his angelic Agnes. The darkness has lifted temporarily, but the sun that peers down is that of autumn, and the pleasures to be expected in the remainder of existence are modest ones. The prison walls which could in the earlier novels be scaled by flights into the convention of eighteenth-century picaresque are seen for what they are by the mature artist. The great poet of claustrophobia has refined the tradition in which he works until all that is recognizably left of it is the passive hero enclosed by a situation he is unable to alter. It is a situation that extends back into the past: irrevocably, one is shaped by the circumstances of early youth. Damaging, indeed, they may be; one's grim duty is to redesign what may be left in the way of débris. The deprived child grows up into a maturity in which he recognizes that, if he cries, he cries alone. It is no good waiting for the official visitor or a change in the unfeeling System by which things are run. There is no way, in other words, to extend the bounds of the prison; all one can do is extend a helping hand to the other prisoners.

XVIII   A Tale of Two Cities (1859)

The idea of *A Tale of Two Cities* came to Dickens as far back as 1846, when he was beginning *Dombey and Son* and also engaged in *The Battle of Life*. It was originally conceived as a Christmas Book. He wrote to Forster on 25 July: 'I have been thinking this last day or two that good Christmas characters might be grown out of the idea of a man imprisoned for ten or fifteen years: his imprisonment being the gap between the people and circumstances of the first part and the altered people and circumstances of the second, and his ruin changed mind.' But the idea was crowded out by the tale succeeding *The Battle of Life*, *The Haunted Man*, and a host of other commitments including his projected autobiography. The idea seems to have been re-activated in his mind when he played in Wilkie Collins's melodrama, *The Frozen Deep*, in 1857. The play has no merit, but contains many images of isolation. In its new guise, Dickens seems to have conceived the story as existing in two parts several years separated. 'How as to a story in two periods – with a lapse of time between, like a French Drama? Titles for such a notion. TIME! THE LEAVES OF THE FOREST. SCATTERED LEAVES. THE GREAT WHEEL. ROUND AND ROUND. OLD LEAVES. LONG AGO. FAR APART' etc., etc. But, as these titles indicate, the book does not belong, in execution any more than in conception, to the series of great social novels that marches on through the 1850s and 60s. There would be a good case for relegating *A Tale of Two Cities*, as it eventually came to be called, to an appendix. The main impetus that brought it into being seems to have been the need to provide Dickens's magazine, *All the Year Round*, with a catchpenny serial.

Certainly it has no organic relation with Dickens's other work, and only in one area of its action can it be said to reflect his deeper concerns. Technically, it is a regression. So that what I have already said of *Nicholas Nickleby* and *Martin Chuzzlewit* is true, also, of *A Tale of Two Cities*: the central line of plot is the least important thing about it, and, indeed, carries most of the elements that repel us from the work today. For instance, the hero's dying child says 'Dear papa and mama, I am very sorry to leave you both, and to leave my pretty sister; but I am called, and I must go!' This is the area of Dickens that has receded most from our modern sympathies.

The tale is basically that of a French émigré who is arrested on returning to his native country and sentenced to death. He is rescued by a man who is his double. This man substitutes himself for love of the émigré's wife and goes to the guillotine in his stead. There is no way, other than this, in which a summary could be couched; no account could make the book seem other than melodramatic and sentimental.

There are some possibilities in the concept of the double. One remembers the dual personality of Montague Tigg in *Martin Chuzzlewit*; or of Jonas, in the same book, who returns from his murderous journey half expecting to find himself asleep in his own bed. But Charles Darnay, the émigré, is all camphor and frankincense, while the substitute, Sydney Carton, exists very much in the abstract. We are told of his furious debauches, but all we see of them, apart from a solo bottle of wine and consequent nap, are a couple of late-night sessions with the successful barrister, Stryver, who picks his junior's brains whenever he has to prepare a brief. In fact, Carton appears to be a hard worker and an intelligent man, yet everybody accedes to his denunciation of himself as an idle and dissipated wretch. His scenes with the girl to whom he dares not aspire, Lucie Manette, later married to Darnay, are excruciatingly melodramatic. 'If it had been possible, Miss Manette, that you could have returned the love of a man you see before you – self-flung away, wasted, drunken, poor creature of misuse as you know him to be – he would have been conscious this day and hour, in spite of his happiness, that he would bring you to misery, bring you to sorrow and repentance, blight you, disgrace you, pull you down with him.' This is shrill, abstract, and nerve-racking in its self-pity. In any case his attitude when under pressure is very different: kindly, considerate, unfailingly shrewd – in sharp contrast to Darnay, who sticks his wooden head into every trap prepared for it, and has to rely on various intermediaries to get it out again.

But Carton's famous self-sacrifice at the end of the book has a resonance reminiscent of the stagey attitudinizing of Victorian melodrama, including *The Frozen Deep* itself. 'It is a far, far better thing that I do, than I have ever done; it is a far, far better rest that I go to than I have ever known.' No wonder it made a useful vehicle for the romantic actor-manager, Sir John Martin-Harvey.

One could say that the prose is out of control, unmodulated throughout. In personal crises, the allegiance is mostly to Wilkie Collins and to Lytton – both regular contributors to *All the Year Round*. But the historical narrative derives from Carlyle. However, the influence is very different from that which fertilized *Hard Times*. There the prose was judged; indeed, the economy of the descriptive passages in Dickens's industrial novel forms perhaps the best comment upon Carlyle's characteristic prolixity. But *A Tale of Two Cities*, like *Barnaby Rudge*, tends to rhetorical diffusion. And, unlike *Barnaby Rudge*, historiography in *A Tale of Two Cities* cannot be detached from characterization.

We can dismiss from serious consideration the would-be comic servants, Pross and Cruncher; the cowering spy, John Barsad; and the old bachelor, Jarvis Lorry, except insofar as he is an adjunct to the buried prisoner. Even the pinch-nosed aristocrat, Monseigneur, Darnay's uncle, lacks the selectivity of detail deployed in *Barnaby Rudge*. His interview with Darnay exhibits nothing of the poise and relaxation of the dialogue between Sir John Chester and his son. And the atmosphere of the scene where he is assassinated is laid on with a trowel – his one trait, the pinched nose, is emphasized over and over again, and finally transfers itself to the statues outside his house.

Far better done are the conspirators, Defarge and the three Jacques: we sense the oppressive atmosphere of the little wine shop where conversation ceases as a stranger comes in. Defarge himself, if not inspired, is sturdily achieved, and the third Jacques's finger incessantly traversing his web of facial nerves gives the conspiracy a sinister aspect. In Madame Defarge Dickens here particularizes the line of women inexorably knitting as the tumbrils deposit the hapless aristo-crats at the foot of Mademoiselle Guillotine; she is justly famous. But no real understanding of the political situation is evinced. Madame's implacable hatred of Darnay is made to depend upon a coincidence whereby Darnay, the son-in-law of her husband's old employer, is himself the nephew of a man who raped her sister. The motive is thrust in, with a brevity that makes for confusion, almost as an afterthought. Even the poverty of the French people is done from the outside. Dickens could not include the back streets of Paris, or the starving countryside, in his imaginative landscape as he could Tom-all-Alone's or the night scenes of his social essays.

Some of the crowd sequences are self-imitation – people drinking wine from a burst cask, for instance. This has nothing like the edge and audacity of the burning of the distilleries in *Barnaby Rudge*, when people actually lap up rivers of flaming gin from the gutters. And the storming of the Bastille is, I think, a poor affair; it does not begin to compare with the episode as shown by Carlyle.

'Come, then!' cried Defarge, in a resounding voice. 'Patriots and friends, we are ready! The Bastille!'

With a roar that sounded as if all the breath in France had been shaped into the detested word, the living sea rose, wave on wave, depth on depth, and overflowed the city to that point. Alarm-bells ringing; drums beating, the sea raging and thundering on its new beach, the attack begun. . . .

Cannon, muskets, fire and smoke; but, still the deep ditch, the single draw-bridge, the massive stone walls, and the eight great towers. Slight displace-ments of the raging sea made by the falling wounded. Flashing weapons, blazing torches, smoking waggon-loads of wet straw, hard work at neigh-bouring barricades in all directions, shrieking volleys, execrations, bravery without stint, boom, smash and rattle, and the furious sounding of the living sea; but, still the deep ditch and the single drawbridge, and the massive stone walls, and the eight great towers, and still Defarge of the wine-shop at his gun, grown doubly hot by the service of Four fierce hours.

No doubt this vision of the overturning of order justified Dickens's dedication of the book to the Liberal statesman, Lord John Russell. But how tired, how expected all these adjectives are! – *flashing* wea-pons, *blazing* torches, *smoking* waggon-loads, *hard* work. And the occasional omission of a main verb – 'slight displacements of the raging sea made by the falling wounded' – though possibly meant to mime the terse commentary of a war correspondent, resembles, rather, his rough notes jotted down. The writing falls too easily into mechanical rhythm – even, towards the end, clumsy and needless jingle –

Still the deep ditch and the single drawbridge, and the massive stone walls, and the eight great towers,/And still Defarge of the wine-shop at his gun, grown doubly hot by the service of Four fierce hours.

We have moved from sub-Carlyle to crypto-Longfellow, or worse; the jingle reminds us of nothing so much as the atrocious hymns sung by Brother Hawkyard in Dickens's late short story, 'George Silverman's Explanation'.

All this amounts to one severe criticism: the French Revolution is not at the heart of this book. The events leading up to 1789 were far more complex than the Gordon Riots, so showily dramatized in *Barnaby Rudge*. To describe the political events of the epoch would require an act of imaginative empathy far beyond Dickens's knowledge or range of interest. What one can pick out, though, is the original concept of a man emerging into the world after many years of solitary confinement. Somewhere within the tuppence-coloured landscape of *A Tale of Two Cities* is a short story of remarkable psychological insight called 'Buried Alive'.

What, in fact, I am saying is that the imaginative core of the book centres upon the plight of Doctor Manette. His strand of action, moreover, need not have depended upon the French Revolution. The horror of prolonged solitary confinement and the resultant acting out of irreversible psychological damage was a theme which drew upon the deepest neuroses of the author. Thus Jarvis Lorry meditates:

Now, which of the multitude of faces that showed themselves before him was the true face of the buried person, the shadows of the night did not indicate; but they were all the faces of a man of five-and-forty by years, and they differed principally as the passions they expressed, and in the ghastliness of their worn and wasted state. Pride, contempt, defiance, stubbornness, submission, lamentation, succeeded one another; so did varieties of sunken cheek, cadaverous colour, emaciated hands and figures. But the face was in the main one face, and every head was prematurely white. A hundred times the dozing passenger inquired of this spectre:

'Buried how long?'

The answer was always the same: 'Almost eighteen years.'
'You had abandoned all hope of being dug out?'
'Long ago.'
'You know you are recalled to life?'
'They tell me so.'
'I hope you care to live?'
'I can't say.'

The reality is worse, even, than the imagining. Man is a gregarious animal, as Dickens well knew, and incalculable harm is done by loneliness and neglect. This prisoner, even when excavated from his isolated fastness, has at first to remain locked in his room in case he collapses into hysteria through fear of the world outside. He has to be left alone because for so long he has seen no other person. Though only forty-five, Doctor Manette presents the aspect of an old and white-haired man. He replies to each query with a long silence eventually broken in a voice rusty with disuse. Yet he has one consolation in his solitude. After many years of enforced idleness in his incarceration, some jailer less iron-bound than the rest permitted him a few common tools, some leather, and a bench on which to make shoes – a means of alleviating his agony. This, then, is his fervent occupation: the only bridge between himself and sanity.

We must pass over the scene of recognition between Manette and his daughter. *King Lear* was usually a substitute in Dickens for accurate rendition of feeling: he sees events such as these through a haze of rhetoric, and we uneasily remember the deathbed of Little Nell. No, rather the next effective appearance of Doctor Manette is in an area of Soho seen – as nothing in Paris is seen – with the understanding eye of Dickens's long frequentation. The atmosphere owes much to its topography, which we can identify as No. 1, Greek Street: a large quiet house in a district still, in those days, fairly retired. Here the doctor, still frail but with his memory in part restored, conducts a few ingenious experiments and sees the odd patient. But the sinister reminders of past suffering are still about him. Beyond Lucie's room with her birds and flowers, beyond the Doctor's consulting-chamber, is the Doctor's bedroom – commonplace enough, except that in a corner stands the disused shoemaker's bench and tray of tools. '"I wonder," said Mr Lorry, pausing in his looking about, "that he keeps that reminder of his sufferings about him!"'

We soon find out the reason. At moments of stress, Doctor Manette reverts to his state of mind as a prisoner in solitary confinement. Now, as then, the bench of tools acts as a barrier against total withdrawal from reality. The first relapse comes when Charles Darnay informs him of his love for Lucie. It is temporary; the noise of hammering ceases at the sound of her voice. The second relapse is far more sustained. It occurs after the wedding, when the young couple go away for their honeymoon. He had repressed a good deal during the ceremony, but there is no release when the occasion for repression is gone. Rather, the old lost look comes back, and he retires into his room. After a time, his friends hear the sound of knocking. They find him once more at his bench, with his head bent down, busily at work on a young lady's walking shoe. He is unable to recognize anybody. The light goes, and he sets aside his tools until morning, but he refuses to leave his room. When the light comes again, he resumes his labours at his bench. This goes on right through Lucie's honeymoon. In what is perhaps the finest paragraph in the book, Dickens describes this neurotic action poignantly, but with control and with restraint.

With a hope ever darkening, and with a heart always growing heavier and heavier, Mr Lorry passed through this anxious time. The secret was well kept, and Lucie was unconscious and happy; but he could not fail to observe that the shoemaker, whose hand had been a little out at first, was growing dreadfully skilful, and that he had never been so intent on his work, and that his hands had never been so nimble and expert, as in the dusk of the ninth evening.

One ought to say that Dickens motivates the impending breakdown very strongly, for the man to whom Lucie is to be married is the nephew of Monseigneur who was responsible for Manette's imprisonment. The Doctor, then, is repressing a subject which is too painful for him to express. But, in fact, the situation would work as a fiction without such underpinnings. Any loss, or narrowing of social bounds, let alone the departure of a much-loved daughter, would be likely to provoke stress in a man so damaged.

When Manette comes out of this trance, Lorry urges him – dealing with the case as though it appertained to a third party – to give up his shoemaker's kit. We may doubt whether the advice was good:

right through, Dickens has given us the sense that such simple activity, however meaningless with regard to Manette's professional capabilities, prevented the onset of something far worse, breakdown or dissolution; for no recovery is ever complete. The Doctor does, indeed, show extraordinary energy in getting the passive Darnay released from his first bout of imprisonment in France, but when he is taken again, and this time on evidence which Manette has unwittingly afforded, the old doctor shrieks in hysteria for his vanished bench and tools. Eventually he breaks down into a helpless, inarticulately murmuring, wandering old man. The fact that, in his final prophetic vision on the scaffold, Carton sees him restored and at peace, seems, on the face of it, unlikely. But, as I said, it is impossible to dissociate this line of action from the general farrago of plot in *A Tale of Two Cities*. Though it carries most psychological truth, it cannot exist as a separate story. And the context in which it occurs cannot do more than obfuscate the dramatic line of a psyche's disintegration. It is no wonder that those who do not like Dickens praise this particular book. Its predominant melodrama and sentimentality do not belong to the Dickens progress through the great satires on Law, Industry, Prison, Class and Money. Rather its place is with the sensational serials of Wilkie Collins and the cloud-cuckoo-land of the Christmas Stories.

XIX   Great Expectations (1861)

This, the grimmest of Dickens's books, was conceived as a comic extravaganza. 'For a little piece I have been writing – or am writing; for I hope to finish it today – such a very fine, new, and grotesque idea has opened upon me, that I begin to doubt whether I had not better cancel the little paper, and reserve the notion for a new book.' Even when the 'little paper' had opened out into a new serial, he sent the first instalment to John Forster, saying, 'I have made the opening, I hope, in its general effect exceedingly droll. I have put a child and a good-natured foolish man, in relations that seem to me very funny.' It is symptomatic of the emotional depths beneath the literal plot of this book that Dickens could have so misrepresented its meaning.

Even the impetus behind the writing seemed to be dictated by commercial motives. The sales of *All the Year Round* were declining beneath the weight of a tedious serial by Charles Lever, *A Day's Ride*. The ride actually lasted nine months. After the first four, Dickens found it necessary to launch *Great Expectations* as yet another of his attempts at rescue. That was in December 1861.

But it turned out very differently from its author's anticipation. So far from being a comic novel, the new work was full of the distilled wisdom of maturity. *Great Expectations* – no book of Dickens is better named – warns us to put no trust in the surface illusions of class and caste. Our basic personality is shaped in youth and can never change. All we can do is learn from experience how best to deploy such talents and weaknesses as we are born with. Every hope of altering his condition that Pip, the central character, ever entertained is smashed over his head. The only thing that survives is the affection of those who love him, not for what he aspires to be, but for what he is. The extent of his development can be measured by the degree in which he finds his world picture inadequate, and himself in the wrong.

Apart from *David Copperfield*, no one of Dickens's novels is so centred upon a single entity. But whereas, in the earlier book, Dickens was concerned to defend himself against a world he felt had been unfair to him, in *Great Expectations* he puts Pip on trial and finds him sadly wanting.

All action in this novel moves either towards or away from its central character. We can extrapolate, if we please, and define the various strands of plot. There is Pip in relation to patronage; Pip in relation to the social world; Pip and heartbreak; Pip at first rejecting, then learning to accept, a fellow-being; Pip winning acceptance, first on potential, then – after bitter trials – on achievement; Pip recognizing the hollowness of Class and the true nature of being a gentleman. Each of these strands is dominated by a single character, and may be distinguished in terms of Miss Havisham, Mr Jaggers, Estell a, the convict, Pocket (perhaps Wemmick, too), and Joe Gargery, the blacksmith.

Furthermore, the novel is interspersed with parodies of the central figure which act out an ironic commentary upon his pretensions. Beyond all these is the remarkable prose in which the narrative is couched. At every juncture, we have a dual point of view. While the immediate present is acted out, the central character's older self recounts his youthful follies with the judging eye of disillusioned, though not embittered, middle age.

One uses, in these circumstances, the author's life to indicate why his work took this particular shape and no other. In such terms, *Great Expectations* appears as a sustained exercise in self-castigation. The trait in Pip most often remarked by critics as social snobbery in fact goes far deeper than that. Just as Dickens buried beneath his extrovert personality the blacking factory in which he worked as a boy, so Pip gilds over his laborious youth as a blacksmith; just as Dickens preferred to forget the lowly antecedents of his family, so Pip, in his affluence, turns his back on his friends. Just as Dickens moved in, but was never part of, a glittering social milieu, so Pip, in polite society, skates over profound social unease.

Seen in retrospect, it appears that Dickens attacked in his villains that which he doubted in himself. Was Pecksniff hypocritical?

Tigg, double-faced? Old Dorrit in retreat from a past he would rather forget? All these traits are found, not in a middle-aged monster, but in the figure of a personable young man; with, moreover, the dominant strain of a social snobbery seen with a clarity utterly new in Dickens. Self-flagellation could no farther go.

Even so, certain allowances must be made. There is, in the young Pip, a predisposition towards discontent with his lot. There he is, living in the featureless marshes, adopted by his sister, bullied by her friends, with only the gentle blacksmith, her husband, to protect him from her wrath. Her eternal boast is that, when orphaned young, she brought him up 'by hand'. That is to say, he was bottle-fed: no better emblem for his starved need to assert himself could be found. Add to this, that she habitually wears an apron stuck full of needles and pins, and we see how vain any attempt would be to seek solace at her bony breast. In lieu of affection or caress, Pip is belaboured with a cane ironically called 'Tickler'. Thus, to lay down some residual ground for sympathy with a character who does not turn out well, Dickens provides a background which embodies aspects inimical to him.

Since Pip is a blacksmith's boy living in a cut-off village, it is obvious he cannot see Society. But, in the form of a whole procession of emissaries, Society impinges upon him. The first, and highly traumatic, experience is a chance encounter with an escaped convict, shivering with ague and starving, adrift on the marshes. He scares the boy into stealing him some food and drink. No real compassion on the boy's part enters into this; it is an experience which Pip prefers to forget. And, though there are sundry reminders of the episode through the book, one can hardly say that it continues at the forefront of the action. Neither Pip nor the reader realizes how central this event will turn out to be.

The nature of Pip's existence renders him curiously vulnerable to overtures from other spheres. The most powerful of these comes from Miss Havisham, a recluse who lives near by and whom no one has seen for decades. Her immediate motive is to find a boy to play with her lovely young ward. But the effect of this upon Pip is out of all proportion to her original motive. For Miss Havisham presents no ordinary spectacle. She sits eternally in a dressing-room shut off from the light of day. Wax candles illumine half-packed trunks, a disarray of dresses, decayed flowers, the whole covered over with dust. And she herself, though old, is dressed like a bride.

I saw that the bride within the bridal dress had withered like the dress, and like the flowers, and had no brightness left but the brightness of her sunken eyes. I saw that the dress had been put upon the rounded figure of a young woman, and that the figure upon which it now hung loose, had shrunk to skin and bone. Once, I had been taken to see some ghastly waxwork at the Fair, representing I know not what impossible personage lying in state. Once, I had been taken to one of our old marsh churches to see a skeleton in the ashes of a rich dress, that had been dug out of a vault under the church pavement. Now, waxwork and skeleton seemed to have dark eyes that moved and looked at me. I should have cried out, if I could.

The simple fact is that Miss Havisham was jilted on what was to have been her wedding day. All this self-torment is part of a vendetta directed not only at herself but outwards, as well, against the world. With keen psychological insight, Dickens renders the blacksmith's boy so bewildered by this extraordinary apparition that he has no way of describing it. Instead, he falls back on a fantasy involving flags, dogs, coaches – extravagant enough, no doubt, but conformable to a child's power of expression in a way that the living death of Miss Havisham certainly isn't. 'A skeleton in the ashes of a rich dress that had been dug out of a vault under the church pavement' – that sounds authentic. And scholars have been at pains to search out possible prototypes for this character. Both Miss Donnithorne of Sydney and Miss Dick of Ventnor spent their lives after being jilted existing in seclusion amidst the mouldering ruins of their wedding feasts. And Dickens recorded, in a *Household Words* essay of 1853, his childhood memory of an old woman in white to be seen picking her way through the crowds of Oxford Street to the church where a rich Quaker was once to marry her. This same character had been used by Charles Mathews, the actor Dickens so admired, in a sketch of the 1830s. There an old lady named Miss Mildew called daily at the Expectation Office, dressed in her wedding clothes, to find out what had become of her long-lost love. All of which suggests that Miss Havisham was not so far-fetched after all. Like many of Dickens's great eccentrics, her portrayal is a faithful representation of one psychological fact: that the human psyche will make great sacrifices in order to avoid total disintegration.

And, for all her oddity, Miss Havisham shows Pip a glimpse of Society beyond his previous life. It is one to which, with all its falsity, he begins to aspire. Miss Havisham's accent is different, her manner is different; she has a beautiful young ward who treats Pip with disdain. All this goes to make him aware of his common origins. In these weird surroundings, anything natural seems uncouth. Miss Havisham has turned day into night, and love into hate. By projecting outwards her own sense of frustration she has transmogrified the world into Society.

And is this so different from the moral distortion of Society itself? It puts on a show for the spectator far removed from natural work or hours, and runs even to the most cold-blooded hypocrisy. For Miss Havisham allows Pip to make his great and unfounded assumption: that she is the Patron destined to remove him from his class. And, circumstanced as he is, Pip is only too ready to be her dupe. He permits her ward to fascinate him, and this is only a preliminary to Estella's adult extension of Miss Havisham's vengeance into Society itself. Miss Havisham has shaped in Estella an instrument for destruction – as she herself has been destroyed.

'Let me see you play cards with this boy.'
   'With this boy? Why, he is a common labouring-boy!' . . .
   'Well? You can break his heart.'
   'What do you play, boy?' asked Estella of myself, with the greatest disdain.
   'Nothing but beggar my neighbour, miss.'
   'Beggar him,' said Miss Havisham.

Pip, then, is made discontented, and not just with his home. He feels nothing but disgust for his trade, his indentures and his kindly master, the blacksmith. The encounter with Miss Havisham and her disdainful ward opens him still further to receive yet another emissary from Society; one, this time, with the power to transport him beyond his context completely. And this is Mr Jaggers, the lawyer from London.

Jaggers has already been seen, once, briefly, standing on the stairs at Miss Havisham's. This is enough to establish some sort of alliance with the superannuated bride. But his true incursion is into the peaceful scene at the local tavern, The Jolly Bargemen, where the yokels are peacefully smoking and enjoying the paper. Jaggers appears strikingly incongruous there, with his large head, large watch-chain, scented soap, creaking boots and great, dominating forefinger. Having reduced the company to terror and imbecility, he summons the blacksmith and his apprentice out and informs them – what is the turning-point in the plot – that he is the bearer of a communication. And that communication tells us that the boy is the heir to Great Expectations. Jaggers explains to the astonished Pip that henceforth he is to live as a gentleman. He is to be brought to London, clothed, fed, educated, and given an allowance – which is all in preparation for receiving a great estate at the behest of a patron whose name he cannot reveal.

Pip's world has suddenly changed. He arrives in London and finds it – not the immensity he had supposed, but, on the whole, ugly, crooked, narrow, dirty. Much, in fact, like the office of Mr Jaggers. It is the assertive Jaggers who is now his guardian, and not the gentle Joe; Jaggers, whose life is his work, whose work is other people's secrets, whose office is crowded with needy suppliants, shady criminals, suborned witnesses – and who walks among the suppliants, criminals and witnesses of Society's upper echelons, with equal ease. He is not only the lawyer of One-eyed Mike but of the remote Miss Havisham; and worse Clients than that are to appear on the horizon. Jaggers, then, is a kind of emanation of the Society which Pip has entered. Its sullying effect is shown, emblematically as is Dickens's wont, by the lawyer's obsessive cleanliness. He washes his clients off, as though he were a surgeon or a dentist, by scrubbing his hands in scented soap and drying them all over a huge towel in a washroom specially kept for the purpose in his office. After a case of unusually dark complexion, he gargles and scrapes out the dirt from under his fingernails as well. How different, one feels, from the clinker and coal-dust in the forge of Joe Gargery.

What is the role this figure plays in the book? Some critics have called Jaggers kindly; others, wicked. In fact, he is neither. He repeatedly refers to himself as an agent paid for his services, and this is, in fact, the case. He has no real home: he inhabits, rather than lives in, a house, little of which is used, and those rooms in use are given over to books and papers – as though his work overflowed and flooded even there. There is a passing hint (see Chapter LI) that he once had his dreams; but what we see is the man of business, the neutral repository of confidences, the go-between linking up various factions.

For when Pip's new Society comes into evidence, it proves to be no less dusty and tortuous than the office of Jaggers himself. Pip begins his London life in a dingy collection of ash-ridden squeezed-up buildings. How different from the mist and rain of the marshes! Even when, after his majority, Pip moves out, he still is at the mercy of a thieving laundress and a page whom he calls the Avenger. There is no way it seems of having a home in mid-London. His life is one of idleness and increasing debt, awaiting the advent of his Patron. He wastes time in pointless chat and occasional brawling in a foolish club for young gentlemen – the Finches of the Grove. Above all, he dances perpetual attendance on Estella. She is the luminary of his desires, and he circulates sadly about her, a moth around a flame – as she herself says. And Pip –

I saw her often at Richmond, I heard of her often in town, and I used often to take her and the Brandleys on the water; there were picnics, fête days, plays, operas, concerts, parties, all sorts of pleasures, through which I pursued her – and they were all miseries to me. I never had one hour's happiness in her society, and yet my mind all round the four-and-twenty hours was harping on the happiness of having her with me unto death.

Estella is an element not just in the book but in the work of Dickens as a whole. She is, in a sense, the heroine for which all his novels were waiting. In Estella, we have his first effective presentation of a sexually attractive girl. One finds hints of this in David Copperfield's courtship of Dora, or Clennam in *Little Dorrit* yearning with all the hopelessness of middle age for Pet. But Estella as a creation wholly transcends all these.

She is based upon the Irish actress, Ellen Ternan, who eventually became Dickens's mistress. Legend has it that he first saw her backstage at the Haymarket when she was making her début in Francis Talfourd's *Atalanta*, and that she was distressed at having to appear on the boards in chiton and tights. The acquaintance was certainly made in April 1857, and it ripened rapidly. We find Dickens employing her in a production of Wilkie Collins's melodrama *The Frozen Deep*: she played in a revival in Manchester in the August of that year. The relationship was intensified by circumstance. Dickens himself played Wardour, a man who has missed his chance in love. By all accounts, his was a highly emotional performance. And it coincided with Dickens's growing disaffection from his wife. Rumours began to circulate – one, apparently, spread by his mother-in-law, Mrs Hogarth, and his sister-in-law, Helen. With characteristic precipitancy, Dickens took the extraordinary step of announcing his separation from Catherine in public – in the columns of the *Household Words* for 12 June 1858. The tone of this letter suggests that intimacy between Dickens and Ellen had not yet begun. But, by October, he had set her up in a flat near Oxford Street, later moving her to Camden Town; and he seems to have spent a life of torment thereafter. Ironically enough, a key line spoken by Dickens in *The Frozen Deep* was 'The only hopeless wretchedness in the world is the wretchedness that women cause'.

Ellen represented a glamour that had hitherto been absent from Dickens's laborious life. And this seems to have been the raw material, not only for Pip's dazzlement, but also his unappeasable desire. The narrator – Pip in his later days – judges the fatality of the attraction sadly enough. And yet there are signs that he does not wholly understand it. This, strangely, enhances the presentation. Estella's whole power is in her effect upon Pip. He admits he never had one happy moment in her company. Yet some masochistic need in him is satisfied by being kept at bay. There is in his makeup fear of sexual fulfilment. And Pip persists in this cold, unfruitful courtship of disaster. For Estella – as she admits – has nothing to give. She is the beckoning fair one; the sphinx without a secret. Pip projects his own rays upon this enigma. We will look in vain through *Great Expectations* for Estella's insight or wit. She is not so much a flame for a moth, perhaps, as a mirror against which a butterfly beats in vain.

However enigmatic Estella may have been to his hero, Dickens takes some pains to motivate her in the book. Much of what she says as a young girl is coarse and unfeeling – precisely the traits she attributes to the young Pip. But her comments on Pip's lack of caste gain a bitter irony in retrospect. For her own antecedents – even though she is unaware of them – are appalling. Her father is the convict whom Pip tries to help on the marshes. Her mother is a murderess rescued by Jaggers's forensic skill. So her heredity embraces vagrancy, adultery, murder. Farther: she has been reared from childhood by a woman locked in neurosis. And her own personality has been deliberately warped so as to carry Miss Havisham's grudge on into a new generation.

What could be expected from such a heredity and such an environment? It is true that, as Estella grows older, she learns control. But the control takes the form of abnegating personality. Estella knows she is beautiful; she lets her beauty do the work. Habitually, she speaks of herself and Pip as puppets. 'We have no choice, you and I, but to obey our instructions. We are not free to follow our own devices, you and I.' Characteristically, the sexual game she plays is what Eric Berne calls 'Stocking'. That is to say, she puts her goods on display without meaning to part with them. A keener edge is given to the game by her apparent refusal to lead Pip on.

'Pip, Pip,' she said one evening coming to such a check, when we sat apart at a darkening window of the house in Richmond; 'will you never take warning?'
  'Of what?'
  'Of me.'
  'Warning not to be attracted by you, do you mean, Estella?'
  'Do I mean! If you don't know what I mean, you are blind.'

Even the apparent rebuff is tantalizing. Whether he meant to or not, Dickens has painted a portrait of classical frigidity.

Fate, who has fulfilled so many of Pip's foolish aspirations, spares him none of the resultant misery. He lives to see Estella fall into the hands of the reductio ad absurdum of all those gentlemanly ideals. She becomes the wife of the dullest of all the Finches in that dreadful Grove: the loutish Bentley Drummle, immensely wealthy heir to a long line of thick-headed baronets. The logical extreme, in other words, of Pip's erroneous concept of a gentleman.

Right through the novel, the word 'gentleman' rings out like a keynote. It occurs literally scores of times through the text. Pip raises it when a boy –

'The beautiful young lady at Miss Havisham's, and she's more beautiful than anybody ever was, and I admire her dreadfully, and I want to be a gentleman on her acount. . . .'

Mr Jaggers uses it as a weapon against Joe when announcing Pip's expectations –

'Well, Mr Pip, I think the sooner you leave here – as you are to be a gentle-man – the better. . .'

Pip broods over it in connection with the Estella of his early man-hood –

Truly it was impossible to dissociate her presence from all those wretched hankerings after money and gentility that had disturbed my boyhood. . . .

And all such occurrences of 'gentleman' and 'gentility' can be seen as foreshadowings of the traumatic scene where the founder of Pip's fortunes finally stands revealed – not as weird Miss Havisham, for-gotten relic of a glittering Society, but as the Convict whom Pip had helped on the marshes: an event so far back in the book and so little touched upon since that I doubt whether any reader could honestly say that he guessed, at first reading, the source of Pip's Expectations. The fountain-head of gentility stands in Pip's presence at last – weather-ed, furrowed, bald, slouched, even his foot dragging a little as if still trailing his fetters; Provis, from New South Wales, born Abel Magwitch. This is the architect of Pip's fortunes, who has lifted him clear of Joe and the blacksmith's forge and rendered him fit to in-habit nothing but a Society of vain hopes.

'Yes, Pip, dear boy, I've made a gentleman on you . . .! I lived rough that you should live smooth; I worked hard that you should be above work. . . . I tell it, for you to know as that there hunted dunghill dog wot you kept life in, got his head so high that he could make a gentleman – and, Pip, you're him. . . .'

' "Lord strike me dead!" I says each time – and I goes out in the open air to say it under the open heavens – "but wot, if I gets liberty and money, I'll make that boy a gentleman!" And I done it. . . .'

'And then, dear boy, it was a recompense to me, look 'ee here, to know in secret that I was making a gentleman. The blood horses of them colonists might fling the dust over me as I was walking; what do I say? I says to my-self, "I'm making a better gentleman nor ever you'll be!" . . . I says to my-self, "If I ain't a gentleman, nor ain't got no learning, I'm the owner of such." '

But Pip's friend, Herbert Pocket, has learned something from his father, an otherwise unsuccessful tutor; and he says that no man who was not a true gentleman at heart, ever was, since the world began, a true gentleman in manner. He says that no varnish can hide the grain of the wood, and that the more varnish you put on, the more the grain will express itself. This truth is seen, at its ugliest, in Estella's beau, Bentley Drummle, who expresses *his* grain in crudity and violence. It is also seen in Pip's own career: some ugly grain still shows through all the varnishing until it is planed away by the attrition of a hard life. If Pip does become a gentleman, it is by means not envisaged by his patrons, real or pretended.

One way in which he grows in stature is by tending this Convict. At first he feels nothing but disgust for the man and his revolting habits. The Convict tears at his food with a jack-knife, gobbles it lop-sidedly with his few remaining fangs, wipes the last morsel of bread on his fingers before he swallows it down. But Pip has been the Convict's charge, and now the roles are reversed. The man has been sentenced for unnamed crimes, has been transported for life, and has risked that life to come back to see his gentleman. The whole is powered by – perhaps what relates to his compulsive eating habits – a fearful craving for affection. But we see a painful contrast between the joy the Convict has in beholding Pip, on the one hand, and, on the other, the revulsion Pip feels for the Convict. And yet Pip disguises him, hides him, lays plans for smuggling him out of the country. Despite himself, he comes to feel pity for him, if it is only the feeling one has for a suffering creature. So little aware is he of his emotion that he describes it in terms of a softening of the Convict's manner. In fact, however, he is beginning to make allowances for Abel – the Convict is, at least, not Cain – as he has for few others in his life.

The attempt to smuggle the Convict away fails, and the man is severely injured in his recapture. Pip sits by his bed – at last, beginning to grow into a gentleman.

For now my repugnance to him had all melted away, and in the hunted wounded shackled creature who held my hand in his, I only saw a man who had meant to be my benefactor, and who had felt affectionately, gratefully, and generously, towards me with great constancy through a series of years. I only saw in him a much better man than I had been to Joe.

Mercifully, though condemned, the Convict dies before his execution. And, as a convicted felon, his possessions are forfeit to the Crown. So Pip, having been rescued from an honest trade, in good earnest has to look about him. As he confides to his friend, 'I am heavily in debt – very heavily for me, who have now no expectations – and I have been bred to no calling, and I am fit for nothing.' In recognizing this, he has at last learned the beginnings of purpose and self-respect.

Nevertheless, well before this, there were those who could recognize in Pip the lineaments of the man he eventually became. It is a poor creature indeed who has not at least one friend prepared to take him on trust. What Traddles is to Copperfield, Herbert Pocket is to Pip – with this distinction. Though the young Pip feels superior to his idealistic friend, as Copperfield does to Traddles, the older Pip who tells the story recognizes – as the older Copperfield does not – the superiority in tolerance and kindness in the man he once had the temerity to patronize.

Presumably Herbert was as much aware of Pip's shortcomings at the dinner-table as – allowing for degree – Pip is aware of those in the Convict. But what Pip recoils from in horror, Herbert takes in hand with a delicate humour of his own.

Let me introduce the topic by mentioning that in London it is not the custom to put the knife in the mouth – for fear of accidents – and that while the fork is reserved for that use, it is not put further in than necessary . . . Take another glass of wine, and excuse my mentioning that society as a body does not expect one to be so strictly conscientious in emptying one's glass, as to turn it bottom upwards with the rim on one's nose. . . .

Herbert, in many ways, is the gentleman Pip ought to have been; but, with him, gentility comes by nature. Symptomatically, whereas Pip hangs around Estella as though she were a symbol of class aspiration, Herbert defies his own far more snobbish milieu by engaging himself to a penniless girl who is nothing more than the daughter of an invalided ship's purser. The young Pip laughs at Herbert's expectations, and certainly they are cloudy enough. Herbert believes that, by sitting in a counting-house and looking about him in the City, he will begin by insuring ships, go on to trade in silk with the East Indies and in sugar with the West, and end up trafficking in elephants' tusks with Ceylon. But at least these expectations can only be fulfilled through his own exertions; he does not, like Pip, hang upon the whim of a mysterious patron.

At first, the friendship of the two young men is very much a one-way affair. Pip does little for Herbert, except run him into debt. The older Pip, telling the story, admits that he contracted increasingly luxurious ways of living – 'My lavish habits led his easy nature into expenses that he could not afford, corrupted the simplicity of his life, and disturbed his peace with anxieties and regrets.' Pip's way of compensating for this – and perhaps for covering up an underlying guilt – is to bully him in words such as these: 'Be firm, Herbert . . . look into your affairs. Stare them out of countenance.' To which the unfortunate Herbert replies, quite truthfully, that they are staring *him* out of countenance. But, just as one sign of Pip's maturing into a gentleman is the pity he increasingly takes upon the Convict, so an early sign of his softening nature is seen in his engaging some part of his income in helping Herbert to a partnership in a shipping firm. His expectations did, at least, that amount of good to somebody, it seems. And, indirectly, this unselfish action turned to his own advantage, though it was an advantage he could never have foreseen. For, all his Expectations crushed, Pip seeks and gains employment in Herbert's firm. Like Arthur Clennam in *Little Dorrit*, his path through life is destined to be modest, but useful.

It is a sign of incipient grace in Pip, that even in his cub-like days, he was able to gain Herbert's friendship. Another friend in the novel is even less likely; none other than a clerk to Jaggers, the wooden John Wemmick. When we first see Wemmick, he appears as an adjunct to his master: hard, dry, with a mouth in form and character like that of a post-box – adept at receiving information, but allowing none to be prised out. Yet, even in this first description, there are signs of a more malleable personality. The dints in his wooden face, had its texture been softer, might well have been dimples. And it turns out that Wemmick away from the office is a very different person at home. One day he takes Pip with him out of the London dust and into the market gardens of Walworth. There he has built a cottage that truly is an Englishman's castle. Its roof is cut into little battlements; it is surrounded by a tiny moat, crossed by a minuscule drawbridge. Behind these fortifications repose the antidotes to Wemmick's Society of Jaggers and law – his aged father, his lady friend, his garden, his miniature pond, his pig. Walking home each night from London, he changes in stages from the lawyer's clerk to the dutiful son and cheerful – if decorous – lover. Modest though the little property is, it bears witness to its owner's ingenuity. Admission is guarded – Jaggers has never heard of it – and Pip's entry shows – as with Herbert

– that a true friend has discerned in the young cub incipient signs of grace. And the fact that eventually Wemmick marries his faithful Miss Skiffins suggests that the dints may turn out to be dimples after all. Once past the blunders of youth, we have some idea of the terrain ahead and have a map and a few trading-posts, if only we can summon up the courage to rely upon them.

The index of Pip's maturity is the extent to which he can feel for others, and this – so runs the burden of the book – is what truly makes a gentleman. Hence, perhaps, the dedication of *Great Expectations* to Dickens's humble friend, the Reverend Chauncey Hare Townshend. And, throughout, the standard of gentility is set in a quarter which, to the young Pip, is most unexpected. In his boyhood he is made unhappy by Mrs Gargery, ambitious by Miss Havisham, frustrated by Estella, and finally enticed away by Mr Jaggers and his talk of Great Expectations. But what he is enticed from is what in the end he has to recognize as the embodiment of true gentility. And this is seen in the life of Joe, the blacksmith.

The relationship between Joe Gargery and the child Pip is built up in stages. Retrospectively, we have a composite impression of them sitting side by side in the chimney corner gazing at the fire and chatting. In practice, however, such communion occurs as intermittent oases in a generally disruptive atmosphere. Joe and Pip, it is true, have various games: for instance, every evening, each holds up his slice of bread and butter to show how far he has got with it. But, although Dickens gives us the sense that this has happened time and time again, the first occasion on which we see it is the night when Pip steals the food for the Convict. Amongst other things, this involves putting a slice of bread down his trousers and pretending he has swallowed it whole.

'I say, you know!' muttered Joe, shaking his head at me in a very serious remonstrance. 'Pip, old chap! You'll do yourself a mischief. It'll stick somewhere. You can't have chawed it, Pip. . . If you can cough any trifle of it up, Pip, I'd recommend you to do it,' said Joe all aghast. 'Manners is manners, but still your elth's your elth.'

Their intercommunication is constantly interrupted by Pip's sister, Joe's wife, who is perpetually on the Rampage about one thing or another. She treats them both very much alike, as backward children, pulling Joe's whiskers and dosing Pip with tar-water. There is a moving passage when Joe explains to Pip – seriously, but on the level of a child – the reason why he doesn't rise up against such treatment.

My father, Pip, he were given to drink, and when he were overtook with drink, he hammered away at my mother most onmerciful. It were a'most the only hammering he did, indeed, 'xcepting at myself. And he hammered at me with a wigour only to be equalled by the wigour with which he didn't hammer at his anwil. – You're a listening and understanding, Pip? . . . Well, your sister's a master-mind . . . And I ain't a master-mind . . . And last of all, Pip – and this I want to say very serious to you, old chap – I see so much of my poor mother, of a woman drudging and slaving, and breaking her honest heart and never getting no peace in her mortal days, that I'm dead afeerd of going wrong in the way of not doing what's right by a woman, and I'd fur rather of the two go wrong t'other way, and be a little ill-conwenienced myself.

The true gentleman is not recognized by varnish; certainly Joe has none. Instead, he has a deep consideration for others. More, he has his place in the world, and fulfils it admirably. He is slow to learn the lessons that Pip tries to teach him, but it is Pip, not he, who is ashamed of his lack of learning. He says, with unconscious irony, 'I'm so awful dull. I'm only master of my own trade.' Pip has to grow up into the realization that he himself has been transplanted out of an honest calling into a set of false hopes in a hollow Society and is consequently fit for nothing. How much better, then, to be master of a trade!

Dickens is wholly successful in portraying Joe's skill as a blacksmith. It is to be remembered that this was even then a dying industry: with his usual atavism, Dickens scores more heavily here than he can with the more advanced technology of Stephen Blackpool in *Hard Times* or Daniel Doyce in *Little Dorrit.* Like Langland's Piers Plowman or Wordsworth's Michael, Joe is an embodiment of the dignity of labour; that labour Pip so despised when he hankered after leaving the forge.

Joe can only appear incongruous when seen out of his natural habitat. In his work-clothes, Joe is a well-knit blacksmith; dressed up in his Sunday suit, he looks like a scarecrow. But he only wears such garb when going into sophisticated surroundings, and Dickens turns this oddity to advantage, using it as a means of showing up the limits of sophistication. It is a criticism of Estella that she takes Joe to be a laughing-stock; an even worse criticism of Pip that he feels ashamed of Joe and not of Estella who laughs at him. Who in this situation is the lady, and who the gentleman? It is a criticism not of Joe but of Miss Havisham that, on their one encounter, he is unable to address her directly. Once more Pip is embarrassed by his serio-comic oratio obliqua; but who is in the more ridiculous circumstances, the superannuated bride or the blacksmith in Sunday dress? When Joe steadfastly refuses to accept Jaggers's money in lieu of Pip's services, the lawyer from London regards him as a village idiot. But who is the more intelligent – he who puts a price on human affection or he who knows it as a gift, not to be bartered or sold? In every single encounter with sophisticated Society, Joe's lack of congruity with his interlocutors shows that they are at fault, not he. The fact that Joe is everything Pip wants to leave, and the Society of Estella everything he wants to gain, is the greatest criticism of all Pip's aspirations.

It is Joe in this book, not Pip, not Drummle, who is the true gentleman. The strength of the blacksmith is immense, and not only in his daily labours. We see him lose his temper just twice in the book. Once, when his wife is insulted, he knocks his journeyman into the coal-dust; and once, when his love for Pip is impugned, he turns on the domineering Jaggers and frightens him – the only person who ever succeeds in doing this. It is characteristic of this gentleman that he stands up in defiance only twice: once on behalf of a woman, the other on behalf of a child.

And, like a true gentleman, he knows how to be gentle. Dickens compares his touch with that of a steam-hammer which is capable of smashing a skull or patting an egg. He visits Pip the first time in London: in a comic, yet exquisitely poignant scene. Joe does not know how to address the adult Pip, and Pip is impatient with him because he perpetually drops his hat and exhibits other signs of embarrassment. It does not occur to Pip that, were he easier with Joe, Joe – out of his common surroundings – would be easier with him. He leaves Pip's lodgings, never to return until Pip is brought low – by the Convict, by Estella, by debt, by fever – and nurses him back into health with a touch, as Dickens says, like an angel's wing.

When Pip comes finally round, he finds Joe has retired to his true métier: the marshes, and the forge.

Along with Joe, in every sense, goes Biddy. She, the most successful of Dickens's household angels, is a triumph of underassertion. Though she says little, what she says makes sense. We see her first as a teacher at a dame school, and then as the housekeeper at Joe's when his wife is struck down by an unknown hand. There is no verbal encounter with Pip in which she does not get the better of him: not because she wants to score a point, but because what she says is true. When he tells Biddy he wants to be a gentleman on Estella's account, she says:

'Do you want to be a gentleman, to spite her or to gain her over?' . . .

'I don't know,' I moodily answered.

'Because if it is to spite her,' Biddy pursued, 'I should think – but you know best – that might be better and more independently done by caring nothing for her words. And if it is to gain her over, I should think – but you know best – she was not worth gaining over.'

Biddy's steady realism stands as a reproach to Pip's narcissistic romanticism, and the young Pip resents it. He is driven, in default of reply – for he does *not* know best – to the pettish wilfulness of a child. Of Biddy's wisdom there is no doubt: the rapidity with which she picks up an education, the unobtrusive efficiency with which she runs Joe's home – how different from Mrs Gargery's rampaging – are external witness to the strength of the character within.

In each of her encounters with Pip, she makes that definite point: that a gentleman fulfils his place in the world and shows consideration to others. At an early stage of his life, Pip is callow and unfeeling enough to tell Biddy that he could have loved her had it not been for his aspirations. Years later, burnt and purged by his various trials, he grows into an awareness of her true nature. But this damaged gentleman can never return to the forge. Pip does, absurdly enough, attempt the pilgrimage back; he means to claim Joe as his friend, and Biddy as his wife. But Biddy's steady recognition of what makes a gentleman has earned her the right to be a fitting mate for Joe; and Pip arrives only in time to see them married.

Yet even out of this comes a mild hope. They have a son whom they call Pip, and he occupies – like the Pip of old – the fireside chair, protected by Joe's great thigh. The implication is that *this* Pip will not be driven by a shrewish mother-surrogate to be tempted by an elusive wraith and so seek the anodyne of vain expectation. In little, here is the hope that Joe's son may turn out to become the man Pip might have been.

The whole action is judged as it unfolds. One such mode of judgment occurs as a form of comic relief, seen especially in parodies of Pip and his pretensions. For example, when Pip goes back to his home village to visit Miss Havisham, he carefully avoids seeing Joe. The meanness of this is parodied by the tailor's apprentice, who has witnessed in his master's shop Pip's transformation from blacksmith to dandy.

He wore the blue-bag in the manner of my great-coat, and was strutting along the pavement towards me on the opposite side of the street, attended by a company of delighted young friends to whom he from time to time exclaimed, with a wave of his hand, 'Don't know yah!' Words cannot state the amount of aggravation and injury wreaked upon me by Trabb's boy, when, passing abreast of me, he pulled up his shirt collar, twined his side-hair, stuck an arm akimbo, and smirked extravagantly by, wriggling his elbows and body, and drawling to his attendants, 'Don't know yah, don't know yah, pon my soul don't know yah!'

Wopsle, too, the church clerk who takes to the stage, curiously parodies Pip's career throughout. In the village he is tolerated for his sonorous responses in church, his recitations at parties and the graphic way in which he reads the newspaper to the customers of The Jolly Bargemen every evening. Deluded by ambition, he seeks his fortune upon the London stage, making his début as Hamlet, no less. But his forehead and curls are improbable, his hat is too small, the audience greet him with jeers, orange-peel and occasional cries of 'Amen', and altogether it soon becomes apparent that he has aimed his sights too high. A moderately gifted amateur in his native setting, he appears only too ridiculous before a larger public. All this is quite authentic: stage-struck gentlemen were in the habit of paying private theatres in order to let them tread the boards: clearly Wopsle blows his savings on a Shakespearian lead! The raw material for this can be found in Dickens's article, 'Gaslight Fairies' (*Household Words*, 10 February 1855).

The inference is obvious: Pip even dreams that it is he who is playing Hamlet to Miss Havisham's Ghost, without knowing the words of his part. And, like those of Pip, Wopsle's expectations inexorably decline. He is heard of, through playbills, as a faithful Black, a comic Tartar, and eventually ends up as a species of Sorcerer's Apprentice; presumably his money has run out. And the parts he plays suggest the main theme of the book: certainly this is true of the last one. Like Pip, he has allowed his belief in himself to outstrip any talent he had.

Yet another parody figure can be seen in Joe's journeyman, Orlick. He slouches out of the coal-dust, and carries about him a distinct aura of forge. It is he who is presumed to have struck down Pip's sister. Indeed, this has the effect of knocking some humility into her, but Orlick learns nothing from her christian forgiveness. He – in a rather extraneous episode – attempts Pip's life, but escapes. Orlick represents the brute that Pip himself was anxious to leave behind, but there is no character in the book he resembles more than Gentleman Drummle. Varnished or unvarnished, the grain shows all too clear. In the end he is imprisoned for robbing another of Pip's false patrons, Uncle Pumblechook. In a strange way, this latter figure reminds us of Miss Havisham, implicitly laying claim to have founded Pip's fortunes, and, like Miss Havisham, having a physical downfall. His being tied up and choked is a comic parody of the fire that consumes Pip's pseudo-patroness. More remotely, Compeyson, the Monks-figure who steals through the book, is another parody. He it is who encourages the Convict into crime and eventually serves as the agent who hunts him down. And it is he – the false gentleman – who has, in that remote past, jilted Miss Havisham. But he is never allowed directly to confront us, and so leads a shadowy existence, not as a character, but as an agent of the plot.

All these parodies would count for little were it not for the tone of the prose. This is remarkably flexible, able to convey the sharp Dickensian present with a commentary, implied or explicit, that hints at retrospective judgment. It is as though the past, present and future of the central protagonist is, at any given moment, held in the Narrator's mind. And here we must emphasize once more that the Narrator is not the young Pip but the middle-aged Mr Pirrip, saddened and purged by his young self's adventures and failures.

It all makes for a complexity of effect far more satisfying than the brisk, cinematic narrative of *David Copperfield.*

Analysis shows that this flexibility of tone is gained in three distinct ways. The first is apparent from quotations already used: the presentation of events in such a manner as to imply a judgment upon them. But there is an interim stage where the judgment is made more explicitly: tied to events, it is true, but emerging out of them by way of parenthesis. For instance, when Pip accuses Biddy of envying his good fortune, the reader may feel that it is he himself who is in dire need of forgiveness. Pip ambiguously tells Biddy that this is a bad side of human nature: the Narrator picks up the ambiguity, and extends it thus: 'In which sentiment, waiving its application, I have since seen reason to think I was right'. The language of these interspersions is distinct from that of the dramatic narrative: notably, the vocabulary is weightier, as here – 'sentiment', 'reason'. Also, there is a distinct sense of time having gone by since the scenes portrayed were experienced.

The third way in which Dickens suggests the presence of an older Narrator, and hence of judgment more mature than that which may be expected of the young Pip, is by making explicit comments on the action. These avoid the flatness of mere statement by being rooted deeply in context. Such comments as the older Pip passes upon his infatuation for Estella take on a *gravitas* worthy of Dr Johnson himself.

Whatever her tone with me happened to be, I could put no trust in it, and hold no hope in it; and yet I went on against trust and against hope. Why repeat it a thousand times? So it always was. . . .

As the time wore on, an impression settled heavily upon me that Estella was married. Fearful of having it confirmed, though it was all but a conviction, I avoided the newspaper. . . . Why I hoarded up this last little wretched rag of hope that was rent and given to the wind, how do I know? Why did you who read this, commit that not dissimilar inconsistency of your own, last year, last month, last week?

It is as though the Narrator were appealing over the heads of his characters to the reader himself. Yet this is not the moralistic detachment we find in Fielding and Thackeray, for it is the central character speaking, aged and purged by the experience that he relates.

Gradually, through the book, as expectation after expectation comes to nothing, the protagonist grows up to the gravity of tone deployed by his Narrator. One cannot, in the later stages, so readily separate the young Pip from his older self. One remembers the scene when he forgives Miss Havisham her duplicity –

Could I look upon her without compassion, seeing her punishment in the ruin she was, in her profound unfitness for the earth on which she was placed, in the vanity of sorrow which had become a master mania, like the vanity of penitence, the vanity of remorse, the vanity of unworthiness, and other monstrous vanities that have been curses in this world?

A similar effect is gained, this time through dialogue, when Pip asks forgiveness of Joe. Perhaps that is how one attains to be a gentleman: to undergo the humility of forgiving and being forgiven. But the penalty exacted is great, and on Pip's return to the forge after many years in the East the narrative fabric begins to show signs of a flaw. The lapse comes after the question Biddy puts to Pip about his lost love – 'You are sure you don't fret for her?' In the text as we have it, Pip replies hesitantly, that he thinks not. There follows a scene when he revisits Miss Havisham's house and fortuitously meets a widowed Estella. The implication of their meeting is that they will come together again and get married. But this is a revision suggested by Bulwer Lytton, and incorporated at proof stage. And it is a falsification of all that has taken place in the book. For it is clear that, after what he has suffered, Pip has a heart to compassionate and forgive; all spontaneity of love, however, has been beaten out of him. A union with Estella is wildly out of key with the previous narrative tone. However, one prerogative the reader can permit himself is to choose to read the best of the author's existing drafts. In this case it seems to me that Dickens's first thoughts were superior to his revision. If we revert to Pip's original reply to Biddy's question, we shall find the book draw on to its grave, inevitable conclusion.

'Dear Pip,' said Biddy, 'you are sure you don't fret for her?'
    'I am sure and certain, Biddy.'
    It was two years more, before I saw herself. I had heard of her as leading a most unhappy life, and as being separated from her husband who had used her with great cruelty, and who had become quite renowned as a compound of pride, brutality and meanness. I had heard of the death of her husband (from an accident consequent on ill-treating a horse) and of her

being married again to a Shropshire doctor, who, against his interest, had once very manfully interposed, on an occasion when he was in professional attendance on Mr Drummle, and had witnessed some outrageous treatment of her. I had heard that the Shropshire doctor was not rich, and that they lived on her own personal fortune. I was in England again – in London, and walking along Piccadilly with little Pip – when a servant came running after me to ask would I step back to a lady in a carriage who wished to speak to me. It was a little pony carriage, which the lady was driving; and the lady and I looked sadly enough on one another. 'I am greatly changed, I know; but I thought you would like to shake hands with Estella too, Pip. Lift up that pretty child and let me kiss it! (She supposed the child, I think, to be my child.) I was very glad to have had the interview; for, in her face, and in her voice, and in her touch, she gave me the assurance, that suffering had been much stronger than Miss Havisham's teaching, and had given her a heart to understand what my heart used to be.

That 'used to be' – there is the tone of the Narrator throughout, the tone into which Pip has to grow. For he has not been born a gentleman, as Joe and Herbert and Wemmick were; and to grow into one means a great sacrifice of selfish inclination which will bring about a corresponding loss of passion and drive. Yet this is one way of beating the Class System. It is with gravity and sadness that Pirrip surveys his younger self; and this puts him, as narrator, in the category of the great repressed figures of Dickens's later books; in particular, Clennam of *Little Dorrit* and Rokesmith of *Our Mutual Friend*. If young Pip sets out to London as a picaresque adventurer, old Pirrip comes home to the marshes as a defeated hero.

XX   Our Mutual Friend (1864-65)

Apart from *Barnaby Rudge*, no one of Dickens's novels had more trouble getting off to a start than *Our Mutual Friend*. Yet the one is almost the worst of his books and the other arguably the best. In the latter case, the difficulties are obvious. Dickens was beginning to feel his age – fifty-two. The readings which he gave up and down the country were taking toll of his time and health, and it was only a disappointment with the second of these tours that forced him into leisure sufficient to begin writing again. His liaison with Ellen Ternan was an emotional drain: what little we know of it from the outside suggests she was both coquettish and unresponsive, perhaps because she had been virtually forced into acquiescence; and this is amply borne out by the internal evidence of the books. The social strain, too, must have been considerable: Dickens was keeping a relationship known to intimate friends out of the popular press and the view of the reading public. Moreover, the exuberant freshness of his early inspiration was gone – a fact marked by critics with predilections as different as those of Henry James and G. K. Chesterton.

This last may not have been such a bad thing after all. It meant that Dickens had to plan his books more carefully. He could no longer rely upon a sudden burst of invention to tide him over an awkward place. And, while this meant his readers were denied any equivalent to the madman in *Nicholas Nickleby*, Charley the Pawnbroker in *David Copperfield*, or the more fanciful capers of Quilp, it equally meant that they were spared the passages of Tennysonian blank verse that – as in the story of Martha in *Copperfield* – did office in lieu of planning and structure. More, it meant that the action was consonant with the underlying theme of the book, and not aligned away from it as is the case with certain incidents in the earlier novels, and, in two or three of those novels, certain of the plots. There is hardly a page in *Our Mutual Friend* which does not develop the theme in some way, and hardly a page could be written by any author other than Dickens. The early influences of Shakespeare and Smollett have been fully absorbed into the mature author's art. And there are scenes enacted and emotions projected which surpass anything Dickens had written before; no doubt because, for all their apparent objectivity, they derived from sources peculiarly close to his inward being.

The title was thought of as early as 1861, and Dickens had held to it through all the objections of his friends. Between that year and the actual beginning of the book, Dickens had time to meditate his leading motifs. In their raw form, they seem clumsy. The three strands of action, as Dickens first envisaged them, are these: a young man feigns death and is present as an onlooker at the activities of his friends and connections after that supposed event; an impecunious impostor, feigning wealth, marries a woman whom he takes to be wealthy and who proves to be as poor – and as much as an impostor – as himself; an uneducated father finds life difficult living with his educated son. The first of these strands proved to be the book's mainstay. The second, in writing, receded into the general fabric of narration, while the third grew out of all recognition into the love-story of a working-class girl and a fine gentleman. And, even in planning, these isolated strands came together to form a whole far more impressive than had been foreseen in the original conception. Dickens had determined not to publish a line until he had at least five episodes in hand, and he maintained, for the most part, this lead over the printer. The book ran serially from May 1864 until November 1865, and built up a telling amalgam, not only of strands of plot, but of cohesive symbolism. *Our Mutual Friend* remains a trenchant attack upon that part of the System that most subjugates the needs of the individual: Money, and especially money for its own sake, the wrong use of money. One would expect some poignant writing from one who had been deprived of its benefits in youth and whose major triumph in middle age had been the circumvention of its want.

Our Mutual Friend could well be subtitled 'The Voice of Society'. The presiding spirit is dead before the book begins, but remains a malignant influence throughout, almost until the end. Old Harmon is a miser, and exists mostly in the comments of those who knew him or who have heard of his malevolent exploits through hearsay. Thus Mortimer, acceptable guest at beanfeasts in High Society, strikingly describes him as

a tremendous old rascal who made his money by dust. . . . By which means, or by others, he grew rich as a Dust Contractor, and lived in a hollow in a hilly country entirely composed of Dust. On his own small estate the growling old vagabond threw up his own mountain range, and its geological formation was Dust. Coal-dust, vegetable-dust, bone-dust, crockery-dust, rough dust and sifted dust – all manner of Dust.

In this way, one of the leading lines of symbolism is suggested to us, and we get the impression of a particularly vindictive mole in a cellarage of his own vile construction. Harmon lived, if that is the word, in a dwellinghouse at the foot of these same dust-mounds. It was called, in the words of another witness, Harmony Jail – 'they give it the name on account of Old Harmon living solitary there,' says a hoarse gentleman in a donkey-cart, 'on account of his never agreeing with nobody'. The place itself, even when cleaned up after his death, presents the aspect of desolation. It is a gloomy house, bare of paint, furniture, experience of human life; bearing, too, signs of having wasted more from desuetude than from use.

The bedroom where the clutching old man had lost his grip on life was left as he had left it. There was the old grisly four-post bedstead, without hangings, and with a jail-like upper rim of iron and spikes; and there was the old patch-work counterpane. There was the tight-clenched old bureau, receding atop like a bad and secret forehead; there was the cumbersome old table with twisted legs, at the bedside; and there was the box upon it where the Will had lain. . . . A hard family likeness was upon all these things.

The whole place, one notices, is described in terms of clutching and clawing, until even the Miser's seemingly inexorable grasp on existence is shaken off. Yet, as we shall see, he retains his grip on the lives of those who survived him.

Some did not survive. Old Harmon fully lived up to his nickname of the Jailer. Another witness, an old family servant, tells us 'when

his son was a little child, it was up and down these stairs that he
mostly came and went to his father. He was very timid of his father.
I've seen him sit on these stairs, in his shy way, poor child, many
a time'. Even the childish scrawl on the wall two or three steps up
the staircase, where the boy and his sister measured each other's
height, remains as a memento of blighted childhood. 'Too many
a time,' says yet another witness, 'had I seen him sitting lonely, when
he was a poor child to be pitied, heart and hand! Too many a time
had I seen him in need of being brightened up with a comforting
word!' The house is haunted with these images of its desolate past
– in the servant's testimony, 'all in a moment I felt there was a face
growing out of the dark. . . . For a moment it was the old man's,
and then it got younger. For a moment it was a strange face, and
then it was all the faces. . . . I even felt they were in the yard behind
the side-door, and on the little staircase, floating away into the
yard. . . .'

Even Mortimer's cool Voice of Society finds itself, if it were at
all possible, having to restrain a rising tide of indignation at the
hatred of free activity which is the driving force behind the custodian
of Harmony Jail.

The moral being – I believe that's the right expression – of this exemplary
person derived its highest gratification from anathematizing his nearest
relations and turning them out of doors. Having begun (as was natural)
by rendering those attentions to the wife of his bosom, he next found himself
at leisure to bestow a similar recognition on the claims of his daughter. He
chose a husband for her, entirely to his own satisfaction, and not in the least
to hers, and proceeded to settle on her, as a marriage portion, I don't know
how much dust, but something immense. At this stage of the affair the poor
girl respectfully intimated that she was secretly engaged to that popular
character whom the novelists and versifiers call Another, and that such a
marriage would make Dust of her heart and Dust of her life – in short, would
set her up, on a very extensive scale, in her father's business. Immediately,
the venerable parent – on a cold winter's night, it is said – anathematized and
turned her out.

This is a remarkable document to come from the pen of an author
who, six years previously, had turned his own wife out of doors.
But such comments, from such divergent sources, dispersed throughout the book, give us the idea of this presiding figure as a baleful

influence, corrupt in itself and corrupting others. It is the very spirit of Money, and Money seen, moreover, in terms of dust. And it can be purged and refined only through suffering.

The key figure is the old man's son, John Harmon – he who has been described as shuddering on the stairs, plucking up courage to meet his malevolent father. He was sent away to be educated on the cheap in Brussels – rather like Dickens's own boys – and this, too, is reported, long after the event, as a poignant scene.

He was a child of seven year old. He was going away, all alone and forlorn, to that foreign school, and he come into our place . . . to have a warm at our fire. There was his little scanty travelling clothes upon him. There was his little scanty box outside in the shivering wind, which I was going to carry for him down to the steamboat, as the old man wouldn't hear of allowing a sixpence coach-money . . . Then, when the old man calls, he says 'I must go! God bless you!' . . . and looks up at both of us, as if it was in pain – in agony. Such a look. . . .

It was while the boy was at school in Brussels that his sister, like his mother, was turned out of doors. Somehow he got across to England and to the Jail to plead his sister's cause. His intercession was met with the ferocity that might have been expected, and, like his sister, he was dismissed. Old Harmon, like Dickens himself, took divergence of opinion to entail the outbreak of hostility. Shocked and terrified, the boy nevertheless managed to work his way as a common seaman before the mast to the Cape of Good Hope, where he eventually set up as a wine-grower in a small way. But when the old man died, the will that was found proved to have left young Harmon the whole range of dust-mountains, except for one which went to the old servants. There was, however, a blighting condition – as there always would be with Harmon's will. The inheritance was subject to the son marrying a girl – a grown woman when the novel proper begins – whom the old man had encountered years previously when she had been a mere child. This in itself is an instance of the Miser's malevolence clutching at live young people from the grave itself. For the girl's fate is decided by a will outside her own in a matter in which only her own will can operate. One would hardly expect a marriage, so instituted, to be a success. But the girl's family is so irretrievably poverty-stricken that she herself has very little choice in the matter.

Old Harmon's will has an even darker motivation than appears
on the surface. Here is the voice of yet one more witness – the girl's
own, fatally innocent, father. When Old Harmon first saw them,
he tells his daughter, 'you were stamping your little foot, my dear,
and screaming with your little voice, and laying into me with your
little bonnet, which you had snatched off for the purpose . . . you
were doing this one Sunday morning when I took you out, because
I didn't go the exact way you wanted, when the old gentleman, sitting
on a seat near, said, "That's a nice girl; that's a *very* nice girl; pro-
mising girl!"' What, obviously, the spoiled brat promised to be
was a termagant and a virago, and this is what the Miser destined
for his wretched son, so that, when his own father was no longer
there to torment him, he should have a plague and a torment for
a wife.

But, even from the grave, Harmon overreached himself. This
was only one of the wills that the unhappy miser – divided even in
his modes of malice – left behind him. The other wills remain
undisclosed until later in the novel. One, in a flat tin box discovered
in the yard of Harmony Jail, leaves everything except the smallest
mound, to the Crown – 'inasmuch as he has never made friends
and has ever had a rebellious family'. Another, of still later date,
has been concealed in a Dutch bottle inside one of the mounds: the
document reviles his family with an even higher degree of explicitness
– though by then the mother and sister were dead – and left everything
unconditionally to the old man's servants, the Boffins; probably in
the hope that their simplicity would become corrupted by sudden
wealth. It is important to remember that, *de jure* as well as *de facto*,
Boffin is the true owner of the mounds of dust.

There is nothing inherently improbable about this: it was an age
of arbitrary and overbearing paternalism. And we ourselves live
in a century in which malevolence such as Harmon's has extended
itself from dominion over families to the subjugation of entire nations.
Nor is there any exaggeration in the value of the mounds of dust.
Humphry House has pointed out that, in the days before such matters
were taken over by the municipalities, refuse collection was a rich
source of revenue to the private contractor. An article by R. H.
Horne had appeared in *Household Words* on 13 July 1850 – fourteen
years before the novel was published – describing what fortunes

could be made out of Dust. It relates that, in 1820, the Marylebone Dust-heap produced between four or five thousand pounds, and that one dust-contractor had offered to settle upon his daughter as a marriage-portion a mound that was later sold for £40,000. What this would come to at today's prices is unthinkable. The value of such mounds inhered partly in the precious objects which were occasionally found in them, but mainly in their basic contents. There were ashes, which were useful for making bricks; soot, which could be used in lieu of manure; and decaying human excrement, which was much in demand as a fertilizer. It will be seen what power there is in Dickens's decision to make such mounds, throughout the book, a symbol for accumulated wealth. This is a dramatic extension of the pun contained within the name of the overblown financier of *Little Dorrit*, Merdle, and a dynamic representation of the psychological factors involved in hoarding.

No wonder that, with such a fiancée and such an inheritance, young John Harmon plans to lie low and observe both his putative wife and Boffin, the caretaker of the Mounds, before he comes to be embroiled with them. He confides his plan to one Radfoot, a mate on the ship on his journey home. In some ways, this Radfoot is a simulacrum of what young Harmon could be with such a heredity: grasping and treacherous. For Radfoot causes Harmon to be drugged in order to facilitate the murder that will be necessary to rob him of the capital derived from the sale of his farm in South Africa. Radfoot contrives to change clothes with Harmon, presumably to render his prospective victim unidentifiable after death. However, the murder is never put into action. For a fortuitous resemblance, made very close indeed by their exchange of garments, leads to Radfoot's being killed in mistake for Harmon by two of his accomplices – a passenger and a steward who had been on board that same ship. And both Radfoot and young Harmon are thrown into the river as dead. The corpse of Radfoot is found, dressed in Harmon's clothes, and the body is identified as that of the heir to the Mounds. That is how the first strand of Dickens's plot is brought into play; because all this is told in snippets and disclosures through the book. The action itself begins with Harmon's escape.

We first see him when he begins to move among past and future associates, though his true identity remains unknown to them. First he makes sure that Radfoot is truly dead. In going to view the corpse, he calls himself by a pseudonym which retains his own initials: Julius Handford. The play on the two names – *Hand*ford, Rad*foot* – is obvious, and shows how the dead man is a counterpart of what he himself might have turned out to be. Not quite so obvious is the corollary: the would-be assassin has been caught red-handed, but so, in a sense, has his intended victim. Without friends, almost without clothes, Harmon undergoes a further transformation, into the stranger, Rokesmith. This name, too, has symbolic connotations; not least clearly seen when he – so to speak – buries his original identity under the Mounds of Dust. It is like a live man shovelling mould over a corpse.

He went down to his room, and buried John Harmon many additional fathoms deep. He took his hat and he walked out, and, as he went to Holloway or anywhere else – not at all minding where – heaped mounds upon mounds of earth over John Harmon's grave. His walking did not bring him home until the dawn of day. And so busy had he been all night, piling and piling weights upon weights of earth above John Harmon's grave, that by that time John Harmon lay buried under a whole Alpine range; and still the Sexton Rokesmith accumulated mountains over him, lightening his labours with the dirge, 'Cover him, crush him, keep him down!'

So Dickens himself had buried his past in the blacking factory, the menial occupation of his grandparents, his parents themselves in his vain attempt to keep them exiled from London – uselessly, for the secret breaks out in his works, if nowhere else. Harmon may have buried his identity, but, as the imagery here suggests, he is not free of the contaminating influence of the dust. But the resource that brought him from Brussels to Harmony Jail, and took him from the Jail to South Africa, and that kept him afloat while Radfoot perished, has never crumbled. He gets lodgings with the family of the wife his father willed to him, the better to observe the character of the girl, Bella; he finds employment as Secretary to Boffin, the old servant who succeeded to the Mounds, in order to see him, too, at close quarters. Thus he walks in their midst, unknown and undetected.

Yet there is a cloud on his face, a shadow in his manner. 'It has been written of men who have undergone a cruel captivity, or who have passed through a terrible strait, or who in self-preservation have killed a defenceless fellow-creature, that the record thereof has never faded from their countenance until they died.' Even kindly Mrs Boffin remarks to him, 'Sometimes you have a kind of kept-down manner with you, which is not like your age.' Who can wonder at it, with such a history, and such a secret?

But his resolution, though kept down, so to speak, remains constant, and serves him in good stead. For it is his misfortune to see the Dust that corrupted his father act for the worse upon his destined wife, Bella, and upon Boffin, the present custodian of the Mounds.

With what at first seem the best intentions, the Boffins seek to adopt the young girl – widow without ever having been wife – in order to turn her loose upon a fashionable world; a world in its way as corrupt as the contents of the Mounds themselves. But the seeds of corruption are already immanent in Bella. Retrospectively, we have heard how, as a little girl, she flogged her father with her bonnet; grown up, we expect her to treat the male sex with the same disdain. Perhaps there is more than the passing resemblance of name to link Bella Wilfer with Dickens's mistress, Ellen Ternan. There seems to be a personal emphasis – a joining of the narration with young Harmon – in viewing her mercenary folly with a sigh. Bella's wilful destructiveness – symbolized in her name and in her continual tearing away and biting at her curls – is expressed most definitely in a constant repining against her lot – 'I hate to be poor, and we are degradingly poor, offensively poor, miserably poor, beastly poor'. One would have thought that Harmon's Will would have been one way out of such discontent; but no – she protests of her prospective husband, 'how *could* I like him, left to him in a will, like a dozen of spoons, with everything cut and dried beforehand, like orange chips'. In which case one would think that the circumstance of the young man's (supposed) death would make her feel free; but this is not so. 'What a glimpse of wealth I had, and how it melted away, and how I am here in this ridiculous mourning – which I hate! – a kind of widow who never was married.' In other words, Bella is quite prepared to make the worst of everything, without ever attempting to find a positive way out. No doubt any one of the possibilities she has been subjected to is unpleasant; but repining is no solution. In representing this trait of character, Dickens is being very percipient; it is worth remarking that Ellen Ternan's mother and her sister were both failed actresses, and Bella's mother appears a kind of off-stage tragedy queen, while her snappish young sister, Lavinia, personifies the family's unpleasant qualities without any of Bella's saving graces.

These graces are far to seek, and it takes some effort to bring them to light. Bella's one positive relationship in the early pages of the book is that with her father. This inadequate gentleman is nicknamed 'Rumty' after the chorus of a comic song Dickens had read as a child in *The Humourist's Miscellany*; it had been one favoured by facetious Mr Chick within the solemn portals of Dombey and Son. Dickens takes care to represent this Rumty as never having properly grown up. He is described as a chubby little cherub whose continuing progeny have come, rather like Dickens's own, as something of a surprise to him. But Bella is undoubtedly his favourite, and spoiled as only such a psychologically immature father could spoil her. The favour is returned – in its way. Bella may bite and tear at her own hair, but she brushes and curls his. It is apparent that the Parent-Child roles have got themselves reversed –

Bella . . . had already taken him by the chin, pulled his hat off, and begun to stick his hair up in her old way. . . .

Back came her father, more like a boy than ever, in his release from school. . . .

There was water in the foolish little fellow's eyes, but she kissed them dry. . . .

Any doubt about whether this relationship is to be criticised should be dispelled when we consider how wickedly it is parodied within the same novel. A similar, though more sordid, reversal of roles is seen in that crypto-adult, the crippled Dolls' Dressmaker, derived from Mayhew, and her childish inebriate of a parent, 'Mr Dolls'.

But no more conducive to a development into maturity than her shabby life at home is Bella's transplantation to the glittering halls of her surrogate parents, Mr and Mrs Boffin. They plan to adopt her because of what they deem to be her cruel disappointment in the loss of her intended husband; intended, even though only by Old Harmon's Will. It is significant that the other child they adopt, to remind them of young John Harmon, is a genuine orphan who dies almost as soon as he is received into their fostering arms. Unhappy as Bella is in each of her metamorphoses – having first been poor, next richly affianced, and then released from her golden obligation – her migration to the glorious dung-heap of society suits her least of all. One may query whether Ellen Ternan was really happy in her West End apartment. It is not Bella's body that is in danger of dying, but her spirit.

Gradually Bella becomes infected. We find her strolling in the fields reading a novel 'more about money than anything else'. She has to be reminded by the ever-watchful Harmon in his guise as Boffin's secretary that it is a long time since she saw her family. 'So insolent, so trivial, so mercenary, so careless, so hard to touch, so hard to turn,' he muses to himself, 'and yet so pretty, so pretty' – a sigh from the heart and, one cannot help feeling, backed by the full authority of the narrator.

The progress of Bella's disease is indicated by the growing arrogance with which she treats the man whom she takes to be Boffin's humble secretary. Of his reminder that a social call to her family might be welcome, she says 'I beg leave to ask you, Mr Rokesmith, why you took that liberty?' When he makes it clear that he is attracted by her, she does not merely intimate that his advances are unwelcome – which she is entitled to do – but rejects them brutally, with 'Preposterous! I have far other views in life'.

Her views have been made plain enough. She tells her astonished little father, 'I must have money, Pa. I feel that I can't beg it, borrow it, or steal it; and so I have resolved that I must marry it . . . In consequence of which I am always looking out for money to captivate.'

But Bella is skating on the thinnest possible ice. She is taken in hand by an amateur matchmaker, Mrs Lammle; whose performance in that area has been prefigured by an attempt, that nearly came off, to sell a wretched little debutante to a churlish moneylender. Moreover, at Miss Bella's time of life, it is not to be expected that she should examine herself very closely on the congruity or stability of her position in the Boffin household. There are certain oddities there that are hinted at even upon Mr Boffin's very first appearance – 'a broad, round-shouldered, onesided old fellow in mourning . . . Both as to his dress and to himself, he was of an overlapping rhinoceros build, with folds in his cheeks, and his forehead, and his eyelids, and his lips, and his ears.'

It is a well-known fact that rhinoceroses attract and harbour parasites. However, they are not noted for sensitivity. Long before Boffin's explicit outbreak into miserhood, there are signs of his coming corruption. The lawyer's clerk tells him that Mortimer had given him an appointment, only to receive a crude reply: – 'I don't want him to give it, you know. I'll pay my way, my boy.' Later, he shows sympathy with his wife's idea of fashion: 'When we worked like the neighbours, we suited one another. Now we have left off work, we have left off suiting one another.' They have come into a great fortune – the Mounds – and they must act up to it. As this new fortune coarsens him, Boffin becomes blusterous in the face of his Secretary's education: 'I ain't a scholar in much, Rokesmith, but I'm a pretty fair scholar in dust.' And, later still, we see the beginnings of true miserliness when he makes the Secretary work hard to get him into his new house: 'When you *do* pay people for looking alive, it's as well to know that they *are* looking alive.'

The gradual deterioration of Boffin is made all the more convincing because certain avenues of escape from his miserliness are left open: his genial treatment of Bella, for instance, his evident affection for his wife. But these avenues gradually contract: Bella is treated more and more like a doll, while Mrs Boffin suffers sharp checks when she shows signs of interfering in her husband's increasingly tendentious attitudinising.

As with Bella, so with Boffin: the index of deterioration is seen most clearly in relation to the Secretary. When the latter suggests that the time has come to fix his salary, Boffin rebukes him testily: 'Don't be above calling it wages, man. What the deuce! I never talked of *my* salary when I was in service.' The matter is discussed, brutally enough, in public; and Boffin makes it clear that he wants the Secretary to dance attendance on him whether there is anything that particularly needs to be done or not. Boffin even boasts of this assertiveness and brutality: 'Our old selves weren't people of fortune; our new selves are.' It is all, apparently, a part of acting up to new riches.

As with Bella, so with Boffin. His ambition grows to meet his fortune; he is becoming the type and figure of a parvenu. Once he would have been content with only one of the Mounds of Dust – 'but we hadn't tried what it was to have the rest then'. And even the avenue of escape from this bluster and bullying, his relation to Bella, becomes calcined with questions of commerce. More and more he reduces her from a person to a commodity. He indulges in such compliments as 'You have no call to be told to value yourself, my dear' and 'You'll make money of your good looks'.

The whole thing blows up ferociously when Boffin discovers the Secretary's interest, however hopeless it may be, in his mercenary little ward. 'What are you, I should like to know? . . . This young lady was looking about the market for a good bid; she wasn't in it to be snapped up by fellows who had no money to lay out; nothing to buy with.' The Secretary – Harmon, we must remember – stands before this onslaught with calm dignity, and claims his human right to do what he can to win her affection and possess her heart. The ferocity of the Miser's reply brings Old Harmon's exploits vividly to our memory – 'Win her affection and possess her heart! Mew says the cat, Quack-quack says the duck, Bow-wow-wow says the dog' – reducing all human intimacy to farmyard coupling and animal struggle for supremacy. This is patriarchalism run mad into domestic tyranny. 'What is due to this young lady is Money, and this young lady right well knows it . . . I know this young lady, and we all three know that it's Money she makes a stand for – money, money, money . . .'

This key line echoes throughout the book. The remorseful Bella, who recognises all too clearly the truth in this description of what she has become, must recall her previous colloquy with her father: 'the whole life I place before myself is money, money, money'. One thinks, too, of the ferocious tune to which Boffin's caretaker, the truncated Wegg, sets his master as he stumps along: piano with his real foot, forte with his wooden leg: 'He's GROWN too FOND of MONEY for THAT, he's GROWN too FOND of MONEY.' And, closer still, the gloomy refrain of the Jewish moneylender, Riah – in reality a front for the 'Christian' Fledgeby – intoned to one of his wilting clients: 'Trust nothing to me, Sir. Money, money, money.'

And this money is equated with dust throughout the book. The world has, in effect, contracted to an enclosed space where certain tall mounds rise high against the sky. And the air is fouler than that even of the other social novels – the grating wind saws, rather than blows, and carries with it dust and débris that is compared with mysterious paper currency; and the natural creatures and vegetation wilt before it. Human beings blink, wheeze and choke; the city itself has become one disgusting Mound enfolding a gigantic catarrh.

The misers whose deplorable lives Boffin consults as working models – many of them enshrined in Merryweather's *Lives and Anecdotes*, a book Dickens had in his own library – make the same equation: they hide their wealth in filth: 'One of Mr Dancer's richest escritoires was found to be a dung-heap in the cowhouse; a sum but little short of two thousand five hundred pounds was contained in this rich piece of manure. . . .' A miniature Mound, in fact! And the researches of Captain Holmes, fortunate heir to the Dancers, are aped on a larger scale by the unutterable Wegg, creeping and slithering up and down, sticking his wooden leg into heavens knows what, in his avid efforts to possess himself of the wealth he believes to be secreted in the Harmon Mounds – 'My lords and gentlemen and honourable boards, when you in the course of your dust-shovelling and cinder-raking have piled up a mountain of pretentious failure, you must off with your honourable coats for the removal of it, and fall to the work with the power of all the queen's horses and all the queen's men, or it will come rushing down and bury you alive . . .' So, in his comment, Dickens portrays not only the rotting and corrupting character of the Great Money System, but also its power to crush the very life out of the individual. It is not by accident that Boffin engages himself deeply in *The Decline and Fall of the Roman Empire*.

The equation of gold with dust is made even in the shocked Bella's rejection of Boffin as father-surrogate: she declares she would rather the Secretary thought well of her 'though he swept the streets for bread, than that you did, though you splashed the mud upon him from the wheels of a chariot of pure gold.' This foreshadows the liberal conclusion of the book – it is not a Marxist novel – in suggesting that there is a proper way of handling dust, if only to sweep it into places where it would be appropriate. And from this moment, the reform of Bella begins. She leaves the Boffin mounds and declares her love for Rokesmith, the humble Secretary. Once one has recognised that gold is dust, one can proceed, it seems, to make dust into gold. The Secretary, awaiting Bella at Greenwich, sees the steamer bringing in his bride, not as 'coaly' but as 'gold-dusty'. When Bella settles down as his wife in a modest little house on Black-heath, he sees her as never being worth less than all the gold in the world to him – as he had hoped in the days even of her surface corruption, 'true golden gold at heart'. When he asks her whether she could wish to be rich – as rich as Boffin – she answers 'Was he much the better for his wealth? Was I much the better for the little part I once had in it?' She finds wealth in her suburban paradise and wealth in the child she eventually bears. This domesticity was the life that Dickens forsook – 'Blow Domestic Hearth! I should like to go on all over the Kingdom, acting everywhere'.

So Bella does not stay at the domestic hearth. But the erstwhile Secretary has to prepare her for the great revelation: that he is the veritable John Harmon returned from the dead, and that they are both to be immeasurably rich. As it happens, the revelation – long delayed in their modest domestic happiness – precipitates itself by accident; and is followed by the discovery that, what Bella took to be the corruption of Boffin, was no more than a monstrous charade, performed for the express benefit of herself.

The reader may not know quite how to take this. For one thing, each and every manifestation of Boffin's miserhood is convincing at the time – he wrinkles his face into a map of curves and corners, he confidentially confabulates with his own nose – and we could be inclined to doubt whether Boffin could act convincingly such scenes as the denunciation of the Secretary in the face of his friends and relations. More likely Dickens changed his mind in mid-novel, working the ferocious indictment of material wealth into a softer conclusion – that wealth can be beneficial in the right hands; one remembers that Dickens advised on the charities supported by the wealthy Baroness Coutts. Dickens, in fact, attacks not so much private property as the abuses to which it is put. This may not lead to the stern resolution that could have been desired, but at least it is not a gross inconsistency. Bella's rejection of her old self, of the Mounds, of Boffin's miserhood, makes the Harmon gold 'turn bright after a long, long rust in the dark'. Or as the reformed Boffin agrees, watching Bella and her infant in their fairytale palace – an aquarium of golden fish, a nursery garnished with rainbows: 'It looks as if the old man's spirit had found rest at last.'

But nothing can efface the impression of Boffin's character. What we most remember in *Our Mutual Friend* is not the panacea of individual kindliness, but the corruption of Boffin, real or feigned, and the relentless struggle for possession of the mounds of dust.

And now, in the blooming summer days, behold Mr and Mrs Boffin established in the eminently aristocratic family mansions, and behold all manner of crawling, creeping, fluttering and buzzing creatures, attracted by the gold dust of the Golden Dustman.

The old rhinoceros certainly has attracted his parasites. Boffin becomes as much fêted as the successful novelist, his author, himself. Cards are left by the Veneerings, by old Lady Tippins, by dried-up Mr Twemlow, even by the portentous Podsnaps. And who are all these people who buzz and creep around the Harmon Mounds and the Golden Dustman?

They are the several Voices of Society – we do not know quite which is the true one – that act as a kind of chorus throughout the novel. The Veneerings, as their name would suggest, are Society's bright dressing: people who have burgeoned from nowhere, with neither antecedents nor future. They give entertainments like something out of the Arabian Nights, conjured up without the aid of money. But such entertainments are really arid – the plate that carries fruit, flowers, candles, salt across the acres of Veneering table, is, significantly, worked into semblances of camels crossing the desert. And the guests are seen in the great mirror which overhangs the sideboard as flimsy and insubstantial. Veneering himself is a veiled prophet, not prophesying; Mrs Veneering is discernible only in terms of her jewels; Twemlow, a gentleman in reduced circumstances, who goes wherever he is invited, looks desiccated; horrible, malicious old Lady Tippins, affecting the graces of a young girl, shows up as artificial, put together for the occasion by her maid. Even the younger members of the company – Mortimer, Eugene – appear as chronically tired of life. The company is still farther stuffed with meaningless buffers, old and young, to prevent collision between incompatible guests; and, as Veneering's interests expand through the novel into airier and airier gold, the list of guests itself thins out to include Directors, Contractors, Bankers and Chairmen of companies.

Only the Podsnaps remain ineradicably solid. This is true of their presence in the glittering and insubstantial Veneering mansion; it is still more true when we see them at home. The house of Mr Podsnap is solid, gross, late-Victorian; seeming as immovable as the Harmon Mounds. The drawing-room is described in terms of its massive adjuncts – a corpulent straddling platform of silver in the midst of the table, heavy silver wine-coolers, massive silver spoons and forks designed to thrust the Podsnap opinions down the throats of the company along with his solid, heavy food. If at Veneering's the guests are seen filmily reflected in the dining-room mirror, at Podsnap's they are thoroughly weighed down, and assessed like so much plate.

Mr Podsnap's horizon is limited to what he himself sees. Foreign countries are dismissed as being un-English. His world gets up at eight, shaves (closely) at a quarter past, breakfasts at nine, goes to the City at ten, comes home at half past five, and dines at seven. In other words, Podsnap represents England, though England seen in doubtful company – society in decline and about to fall. It is interesting to think that Dickens drew some of the most damning traits of this figure from his insular and dogmatic friend, John Forster.

In the course of things, Mr Podsnap has found himself a wife: one with a great quantity of bone, handsome enough to be hung with various decorations and marks of esteem, appearing spirited like a rocking-horse, and, like a rocking-horse, not actually going anywhere. And these two have a daughter, who is woebegone and anaemic and flat in refusing to be anything like a horse; even the semblance of one. Still, she has her uses. When Podsnap begins to be cornered in conversation, he sweeps the distasteful topic away with a characteristic gesture of his arm; and if the interlocutor persists, he declares that the conversation is not one to be continued in front of the Young Person. It is popularly surmised that young Miss Podsnap is the Person in question; and that her cheek is peculiarly liable to the blush.

Common to the feasts both of the Veneerings and the Podsnaps are the mature young gentlemen and the mature young lady. They can be seen in Veneering's mirror, artlessly flirting with each other; but, in fact, they are in process of taking one another in. The golden surface of their honeymoon – symbolized by the cliffs of Shanklin, Isle of Wight – becomes damp earth; another passing reference to the Mounds. For Lammle has found his apparently rich wife to be penniless, while she now knows him as an impecunious fortune-hunter. They have successfully deceived each other.

But they make a compact to wage war against the world at large. They successfully charm Mr Podsnap's baby rocking-horse as part of an attempt to sell her to the mean-minded usurer, Fledgeby. When this scheme fails, indeed, it is to Bella they turn their attention; Mrs Lammle seeks to supplant her in Boffin's affections, while Mr Lammle, in his turn, tries to fill the place of the Secretary. This scheme also fails. The tone of the Lammle episode is more like that of Thackeray than anything else in Dickens – how to live well on nothing a year – but in a gloomier, less exuberant key. And it is clear that the Lammles do not play the part in the action originally envisaged. Rather they are part of the general ruck of Veneerings, Podsnaps and their even more sinister camp-followers.

The effect of the whole is choric. We first see these Voices of Society commenting on Mortimer's narrative of the Harmon Will and its aftermath: what is tragedy in private life affords Society endless opportunity for flippancy and sarcasm. At the end of the novel, we see them holding up to ridicule the marriage of Eugene Wrayburn to the boatman's daughter, Lizzie; thus both main strands of plot pass before Society's purview. But the idea of a gentleman marrying so far out of his sphere convulses the chorus with mirth. Mortimer finds himself once more in the role of narrator; he, after all, was the only member of Society present at the wedding. But Society treats him as though he had just returned from some primitive ritual. This passage allows Dickens to sum up its leading members in turn and also to show us the marriage – which even he does not directly dramatise – in different perspectives.

'Say, how did you leave the savages?' asks Lady Tippins.

'They were becoming civilized when I left Juan Fernandez,' says Mortimer. 'At least they were eating one another, which looked like it.' ...

'How was the bride dressed ... I hope she steered herself, skiffed herself, paddled herself and starboarded herself, or whatever the technical term may be, to the ceremony?'

'However she got to it, she graced it,' says Mortimer.

Lady Tippins with a skittish little scream, attracts the general attention. 'Graced it! Take care of me if I faint, Veneering. He means to tell us, that a horrid female waterman is graceful!' ...

'But excuse me,' says Podsnap, with his temper and his shirt-collar about equally rumpled; 'was this young woman ever a female waterman?'

'Never. But she sometimes rowed in a boat with her father, I believe.'

General sensation against the young woman. Brewer shakes his head. Boots shakes his head. Buffer shakes his head. . . .

'Then all I have to say is,' returns Podsnap, putting the thing away with his right arm, 'that my gorge rises against such a marriage – that it offends and disgusts me – that it makes me sick – and that I desire to know no more about it.'

('Now I wonder,' thinks Mortimer, amused, 'whether you are the Voice of Society!') . . .

Mrs Podsnap is of opinion that in these matters 'there should be an equality of station and fortune, and that a man accustomed to Society should look out for a woman accustomed to Society and capable of bearing her part in it with – an ease and elegance of carriage – that.' Mrs Podsnap stops there, delicately intimating that every such man should look out for a fine woman as nearly resembling herself as he may hope to discover.

('Now I wonder,' thinks Mortimer, 'whether *you* are the Voice!') . . .

Good gracious! My Twemlow forgotten! My dearest! My own! What is his vote? Twemlow has the air of being ill-at-ease, as he takes his hand from his forehead and replies. 'I am disposed to think,' says he, 'that this is a question of the feelings of a gentleman . . . If this gentleman's feelings of gratitude, of respect, of admiration, and affection, induced him (as I presume they did) to marry this lady –'

'This lady!' echoes Podsnap.

'Sir,' returns Twemlow, '*you* repeat the word; I repeat the word. This lady. What else would you call her if the gentleman were present? . . . if such feelings on the part of this gentleman, induced this gentleman to marry this lady, I think he is the greater gentleman for the action, and makes her the greater lady. . . .'

So it turns out that Twemlow, the decayed gentleman, is the true Voice of Society. This – considering his weakness and poverty – does not bode too well for Society's future. But the other voices that sneer and bully – as we have seen in this instance – chorically through the book, are vulgar and overbearing, devoid of antecedent or grace.

It is significant that Mortimer's friend Eugene, elsewhere so articulate, is usually found to be speechless in the House of Death which is the Veneerings' or the Podsnaps' residence, leaving Mortimer to voice his peculiar brand of irony in his stead. For Eugene makes a point of not engaging in life to any serious extent, and he views all actions, including his own, as utterly meaningless. Thus, his pursuit of the boatman's daughter can be called neither a serious courtship nor a frivolous attempt at seduction. It is clear that, as he himself says, he doesn't know his own motives. But they are dubious enough to rouse fear in the girl at her anomalous position in close proximity to the gentleman. So she runs away into the country, and it is only by bribery and stratagem that Eugene can find out where she is.

Now, Eugene may be taken as the type of a fine gentleman: elegant, impecunious, but master of whatever situation he happens to find himself in; very much the beau ideal of the socially uneasy Dickens. While Lizzie is of the low, lowly: the daughter of Hexam, a man who scavenges the river for corpses; the epitome of what Dickens feared he might become in the blacking factory. The antithesis is a little blurred because of the resolutely middle-class accents in which this working-class girl speaks. But we may defend her speech, perhaps, in terms of its stylization; occasionally it does rise to a real eloquence in dealing with what, for her, is an impossible social relationship: 'How can I think of you as being on equal terms with me? If my mind could put you on equal terms with me, you could not be yourself.' It can, in fact, be said that Lizzie is carried by the situation. The genuineness of her difficulty and Eugene's has been seen in the satiric remarks that the social chorus makes upon their marriage. And indeed, it takes a good deal to bring this marriage about.

Lizzie has a younger brother who is represented as the epitome of hard, slogging selfishness, all through the book. He raises himself with ambition and effort from illiteracy to professional status as a schoolmaster. His guide and friend through all this struggle has been another schoolmaster, one Bradley Headstone. And Headstone has some claim to be considered as the darkest character in the whole of Dickens.

On the surface, Headstone is a decent young man: the propriety of his garb and demeanour is stressed throughout. This is a matter of restraint: below the surface, he is a maelstrom of heaving passions. He becomes fixated upon Lizzie and she runs from him, as from the fine gentleman. There is, however, an important distinction to be made here. In the case of Eugene, Lizzie is afraid of betraying herself;

she is not repelled by the careless manner of the fine gentleman. But she is by the schoolmaster's passionate intensity.

There are two key scenes that reveal the turmoil in Headstone. One shows him to his great disadvantage in verbal contest with the gentleman. Eugene twits him with his profession, calling him Schoolmaster instead of his rightful name, interrupting his halting logic with insolent irrelevancies.

The other scene is even more revealing. It shows Headstone's attempt to propose marriage to Lizzie. Never was so faltering and awkward an approach – 'I said . . . when I saw you last, that there was something unexplained, which might perhaps influence you. I have come this evening to explain it. I hope you will not judge of me by my hesitating manner when I speak to you. You see me at my greatest disadvantage . . . '

This is the approach of a man devoid of that inner confidence we must all possess if we are ever to grow into adults. Headstone – the name is ominous – is diffident on the surface because he is still childishly avid within. He is not, properly speaking, a man: it may be that his initial attraction towards Lizzie has something to do with her being his pupil's sister – certainly his relationship with Charley seems over-intense. As Eugene remarks, he is too passionate to be a good schoolmaster.

In his approach to Lizzie, he considers her only in relation to himself; as an extension of his own personality; as an object. 'You are the ruin – the ruin – the ruin of me. I have no resources in myself, I have no confidence in myself, I have no government of myself, when you are near me or in my thoughts.'

What motivates Headstone is a devouring paranoia. No doubt he would be useless in any capacity to either sex: the first person singular occurs all too frequently in his discourse. This may be a result of his consciousness of illegitimacy: perhaps he *has* no rightful name. And, though in his efforts to make a name for himself, he has disciplined his faculties to years of arduous toil, this, too, has taken irrecoverable toll. The discipline necessary to suppress his passions through a penurious and toilsome life has blocked the passages of egress necessary to his animal nature. No wonder that, when the thwarted emotion erupts, it does so like a volcano.

All this goes along with a keen sense of unworthiness: perhaps he has not only subjugated, but been ashamed of, his natural proclivities. He is curiously vulnerable, in his lowliness, to the voice of authority. This might explain not only his helplessness before Eugene's ridicule, but his awkwardness in relation to Lizzie. Anything to which Headstone aspires is, by definition, too good for him. In any case, what is the nature of his aspiration? Supposing the object of his desire yielded to it, would that not be a condemnation of that object? In other words, Headstone has trapped himself. By reaching out to what is too good for him, he condemns himself for not succeeding, and would, if he had succeeded, have condemned the prize of his success for yielding to him. In either case, he has insufficiently apprehended the other person concerned, and would, in either case, be a dangerous partner. Lizzie's sure instinct sees this: it is, in fact, acted out vividly in Headstone's gestures. When he should be talking gently to the girl, he shouts, strikes at the air, tears at a wall, and, finally, lays his knuckles open by pummelling it.

The only other outlet for such thwarted passion is violence. Headstone does his best to murder Eugene, and, in fact, succeeds in maiming him. It is, as Orwell remarks, a damaged gentleman that Lizzie finally marries. But Headstone is not present at the wedding. The only ring he achieves is a ring of iron determination – the same that got him through his struggles and studies – in which he holds and drowns the brute Riderhood, the brute who sought to hunt him down and blackmail him. In drowning Riderhood, he drowns the brute in himself.

For the river sweeps through the book in a sequence of images that runs directly counter to that of the Mounds. Characteristically, the river destroys those who are evil and baptizes those who are good. It may even allow a second chance. For example, with this Riderhood who has previously almost drowned –

Doctor examines the dank carcase, and pronounces, not hopefully, that it is worth while trying to animate the same ... He is struggling to come back. Now he is almost here, now he is far away again. Now he is struggling harder to get back. And yet – like us all, when we swoon – like us all, every day of our lives when we wake – he is instinctively unwilling to be restored to the consciousness of his existence, and would be left dormant, if he could. ... The low, bad, unimpressionable face is coming up from the depths of the river, or what other depths, to the surface again. ... 'Many a better man', moralises Tom Tootle, with a gloomy shake of his head, 'ain't had his luck.'

'It's to be hoped he'll make a better use of his life,' says Bob Glamour. . . .

But he doesn't; and meets his nemesis in the inexorable Headstone. The two men struggle together on the edge of Plashwater Mill Lock:

'Let go!' said Riderhood. 'Stop! What are you trying at? You can't drown Me! Ain't I told you that the man as has come through drowning can never be drowned? I can't be drowned.'

'I can be!' returned Bradley, in a desperate clenched voice. 'I am resolved to be. I'll hold you living, and I'll hold you dead. Come down!'

Riderhood went over into the smooth pit, backward, and Bradley Headstone upon him. When the two were found, lying under the ooze and scum behind one of the rotting gates, Riderhood's hold had relaxed, probably in falling, and his eyes were staring upwards. But he was girdled still with Bradley's iron ring, and the rivets of the ring held tight.

But the river also acts as an instrument of purgation. Headstone's vicious assault upon Eugene's life helps the fine gentleman to cleanse himself of his old frivolity. He crashes into the river, and nearly drowns – 'a bloody face turned upwards towards the moon, and drifting away'. But the same crisis purges Lizzie of her shame at being a boatman's daughter. She puts her skill to powerful use –

A sure touch of her old practised hand, a sure step of her old practised foot, a sure light balance of her body, and she was in the boat . . . Intently over her shoulder, without slackening speed, she looked ahead for the driving face. She passed the scene of the struggle – yonder it was, on her left, well over the boat's stern . . . looking as the boat drove everywhere, everywhere, for the floating face. . . .

Firm of look, and firm of purpose, she intently watched its coming on, until it was very near; then, with a touch unshipped her sculls, and crept after in the boat, between kneeling and crouching. Once, she let the body evade her, not being sure of her grasp. Twice, and she had seized it by its bloody hair . . . As if possessed by supernatural spirit and strength, she lashed it safe, resumed her seat, and rowed in, desperately, for the nearest shallow water where she might run the boat aground. Desperately, but not wildly, for she knew that if she lost distinctness of intention, all was lost and gone. . . .

These are only excerpts from one of the most dramatic and surely managed passages in the whole of Dickens. This is a superb relating of past and present: showing how the Scavenger's craft could be turned to a good use. Eugene's fight back to life is compared with that of a drowning man, rising and sinking. His marriage to Lizzie is the first decisive step back to life: after this, he begins to recover. It is indeed a damaged gentleman that Lizzie marries; both have learned a great deal from the action of the river.

So, too, has John Harmon. It is not too much to say that his immersion in the river cleanses him of his father's evil spirit –

'This is John Harmon drowning! John Harmon, struggle for your life. John Harmon, call on Heaven and save yourself!' I think I cried it aloud in a great agony, and then a heavy horrid unintelligible something vanished, and it was I who was struggling there alone in the water. . . .

Drowned corpses, struggling bodies, drift through this gloomy and tempestuous book. It begins with old Hexam, the scavenger, keeping an eager lookout and towing in the dead that 'lunged at him sometimes in an awful manner when the boat was checked'. It is the corpse of Radfoot who would have murdered Harmon and who is punished for this by the river. The river deals a like fate to Hexam, who himself lurches overboard, to be towed to his death by his own boat, entangled, in every sense of the phrase, in his own line. It would be tempting indeed to show how the river is used as a social leveller, to strip rich men of their pride and poor men of their shame. The crime itself takes on the aspect of its victim –

Thus, like the tides on which it had been borne to the knowledge of men, the Harmon Murder – as it came to be popularly called – went up and down, and ebbed and flowed, now in the town, now in the country, now among palaces, now among hovels, now among lords and ladies and gentlefolks, now among labourers and hammerers and ballast-heavers, until at last, after a long interval of slack water, it got out to sea and drifted away.

The surface of the river may be as filthy as that of the Mounds, but, unlike these, the river is flexuous in motion and broadens out to sea.

The symbolism of the book is an integral part of the plot, and the plot itself is a working out of Dickens's Theme. Nowhere do we get very far from the concept of Money, and Money operating as the instrument of a System. Lack of money debars Lizzie from Eugene and helps to render Headstone diffident and awkward. How little part it ought to play in human desires is shown by the pertinacity of Harmon's pursuit of Bella and of the inexorable way in which he weans her from the claims of commerce. Nowhere in Dickens, except in *Little Dorrit*, is there so subtle a blend of the personal and the social in the great terrain of interwoven character and symbolism spread out before us.

One must not underestimate the extent to which, in launching his assault upon the economics of society, Dickens gave of his own personal substance. Old Harmon, the will of steel and domestic tyrant, presides over the book, and it is clear that the fortunes of four characters are central: John Harmon, Bella Wilfer, Eugene Wrayburn, Lizzie Hexam. Each and every one relates intimately to Dickens's own life. John Harmon is the man who suppresses his past, concealing his arrogant identity under a mask of subservience which, seen from a different angle, might well take us within striking distance of Heep; and it must be remembered that Dickens, in his public role, was also a servant, and took pains to cover over much that his public might have found distasteful. Bella, the jilt and flirt, can at first be won, but only with money; and that was how, according to Edgar Johnson, Ellen was worn down into acquiescence during Dickens's stormy courtship. Eugene, in his turn, is something Dickens would have liked to be: the gentleman born, so certain of his place in Society as to be able to treat it with disdain. At the same time, beneath his nonchalance, he is haunted by lack of ready money and fear of disaffection from his class. While Lizzie, the least alive of the quartet, has at least worked hard in a struggle towards literacy, and is painfully conscious of the limiting nature of her social origins; she can only be saved by the altruistic practice of her craft.

But the figure most close to Dickens is Headstone; not a member of the central quartet. Perhaps he makes his presence too much felt for the scheme of the book. This is not a matter of space given over to presentation but to quality in the writing. It is Headstone who has most to conceal; who is least socially safe; who is imbued with passions his author dare not own; who lives in order to subjugate another to his will; who therefore comes across like a blast from the Inferno of his author's secret life.

Truly, the infantile syndrome of Dickens's humble origins, childhood illness, detention in the blacking factory, irresponsible parents, cast a long shadow into the adult world. For all his achievement, Dickens is a study in deprivation. Paradoxically, in dramatising this, he reaches his greatest heights. In understanding the nature of his defeat, he won against the System his final victory.

XXI   The Mystery of Edwin Drood (1870)

Five years elapsed between the publication of *Our Mutual Friend* and that of Dickens's last, and uncompleted, novel, *Edwin Drood*. From 1858 onwards, Dickens's publications had become increasingly intermittent, mostly owing to the great demands that his reading tours made on him.

Dickens had always been drawn to public performance. Even after he had begun his career as a journalist, he had taken drama lessons and applied to the celebrated monologuist, Charles Mathews, for an audition. As a young man, he indulged in romps and entertainments with the Beadnell girls and, later, with the family of George Hogarth. And in his thirties, taking advantage of the pause after *Martin Chuzzlewit* which saw also the first of the Christmas Books, Dickens decided to direct a revival of *Every Man in his Humour* at the private theatre of a dramatic school run by the retired actress, Miss Kelly. The production took place on 20 September 1845.

Dickens's choice of play seems significant. The humours of his childhood mentor, Henry Fielding, can be traced through that author's early plays back to Restoration comedy, in its turn profoundly influenced by the genius of Ben Jonson. And it is interesting that it was Jonson's earliest play, albeit in a revised version, that Dickens chose to put on; rather, that is to say, than the more subtle and complex *Volpone* or *The Alchemist*. As it was, Dickens assembled a cast which was distinguished, if not in the theatre, certainly in the world of painting and letters. Most of the actors were contributors to *Punch*: Mark Lemon, its editor, played Brainworm; Henry Mayhew, Old Knowell; Douglas Jerrold, Master Stephen; John Leech, Master Mathew; John Forster, Kitely. Dickens himself played the braggadocio Captain Bobadill – a slender figure, abundantly mustachioed, with a tremendous voice; as one spectator said, glorious in conceit and frothy pomp. Audience reaction varied, but Macready, the great professional, was only mildly ironic about this amateur enterprise.

This was the first of several productions, mostly for charity, which were staged, in the provinces as well as London, between 1845 and 1857. The social connections of the various casts ensured that they drew glittering audiences. To an astonishing extent, Dickens kept his little company of busy professional men together. Clarkson Stanfield, dedicatee of *Little Dorrit*, did most of the settings, while Mark Lemon played Falstaff to Dickens's Shallow in *The Merry Wives of Windsor* (produced, 1848) and collaborated with Dickens in writing the farce of *Mr Nightingale's Diary* (1851) in which Dickens personated one Gabblewig, undertaking five different disguises, including one reminiscent of Mrs Gamp herself. Wilkie Collins, too, bulked large in these theatricals, as he did in Dickens's own life, enlarging his social range with many backstage introductions around the West End theatres. It was in 1857, on one of these greenroom expeditions, that Dickens first met Ellen Ternan, and, in the same year, that she played opposite him in the Manchester revival of Collins's melodrama, *The Frozen Deep*. The production was staged for the benefit of the widow and orphans of one of these amateur stalwarts, Douglas Jerrold, and it proved to be Dickens's last appearance as an amateur. This may partly have been the result of meeting Ellen Ternan, but a contingent influence was that of the business manager of the show, Arthur Smith. It was at his suggestion that Dickens was henceforward to employ his dramatic talents by appearing as a solo artist reading his own work.

Dickens had already done much in the way of reading aloud. He was wont to try out new chapters from his books on relatives and close friends. Occasionally – as when he travelled from Switzerland in 1845 to read *The Chimes* to a select gathering in London – these recitals were semi-public performances. He had also appeared before the more general public, reading *A Christmas Carol* several times over between 1853 and 1858, for charity. So his basic technique had developed well before he undertook his first reading tour. He knew how to give his slight figure the effect of imposing presence on a concert platform; he knew, too, how to employ to advantage a voice naturally deep and resonant, making full use of pause and rubato to render his meaning plain. Whatever tendencies towards extravagance in makeup or action he had indulged in as an amateur player were severely curbed when there were no other actors to crowd him on the stage and when it was his own work that was to be performed. The accent was upon economy of means: he allowed himself no costume other than simple evening dress, no properties other than a reading-desk and a book. He gave himself complete rein only when bodying forth a central character, a Scrooge or a Gamp; otherwise he characterized fairly lightly, suggesting, rather than impersonating, the minor figures of a tale. And he played for twelve years in Britain and America to packed houses.

The first tour, under the management of Arthur Smith, consisted of 129 appearances in forty-nine different towns, in Scotland and Ireland as well as England. The tour lasted from April 1858 to February 1859, with an extra group of readings in the October of the latter year. So it will be seen that Dickens's readings were not isolated appearances or occasional presentations: he was on that rostrum an average of five nights a week with frequent matinees, usually taking in a different town every night. There was, however, a gap of two and a half years between this tour and the next, during which he wrote *A Tale of Two Cities* and *Great Expectations* and instituted *The Uncommercial Traveller*.

The second tour lasted from October 1861 to June 1862, with a break in the February of the latter year; there had also been a preliminary group of readings in March 1861, in London. This made fifty-seven performances in all, in twenty-three different towns. Arthur Smith had made the preliminary arrangements for this tour, but his death in September 1861 left the day-to-day management in the far less capable hands of Headland, his assistant. The hardworking Reader found added to his artistic burden incidents provoked by the issue of undated tickets, by overbooking, by delayed or inaccurate publicity. Such annoyances as these were enough to make Dickens abandon all thought of professional tours for nearly four years – the years of *Our Mutual Friend* and the second series of Uncommercial Travels.

And, when Dickens did resume his readings, they were handled by the music publishers and promoters of concerts, Messrs Chappell and Co., in the person of their executive, George Dolby. The first contract was for thirty readings: Chappell and Co. made all the arrangements, defrayed all expenses and gave Dickens a fee of fifty pounds clear per reading. And his first contract was followed by another, this time for fifty readings at an increased fee of sixty pounds each. So the tour as a whole consisted of eighty readings and Dickens made £4,500 out of them – a staggering figure if one takes into account the greater value of money in those days. We must remember that Dickens still had several children dependent upon him, was accustomed himself to live in a lavish style, and was maintaining three households: his own, his wife's and that of Ellen Ternan. However, it was not merely the desire for money that drove him on. The deprived child longing for recognition was achingly present in the achieved man. All his life Dickens had sought an especially close relationship with the reading public; in his Readings, he found it. But, no question, the money helped, and later tours were even more profitable. The seventy-six performances arranged by Dolby for the American tour netted Dickens £19,000. The tour lasted from December 1867 to April 1868; it was based on New York and covered such provincial capitals as Boston, Philadelphia and Baltimore. And for the final series of readings, beginning 6 October 1868, Chappell offered Dickens £7,500 for a hundred performances; that is to say, seventy-five pounds per reading. They were confident that they could offer this and still make a substantial profit. In fact, only seventy-five readings were given, though Dickens compensated Chappell with an extra twelve performances in London. The strain of the tour was too great, and Dickens collapsed before it was finished, never fully again to be himself. If one considers the gruelling itinerary, the reasons for his breakdown at Bolton on 20 April will not be far to seek.

1869

Tuesday	30 March	London	St James's Hall
Wednesday	31 March	Sheffield	Music Hall
Thursday	1 April	Birmingham	Town Hall
Friday	2 April	Birmingham	Town Hall
Monday	5 April	Liverpool	Theatre Royal
Tuesday	6 April	Liverpool	Theatre Royal
Thursday	8 April	Liverpool	Theatre Royal

Friday	9 April	Liverpool	Theatre Royal
Tuesday	13 April	London	St James's Hall
Friday	16 April	Leeds	Mechanics' Institute
Monday	19 April	Blackburn	Exchange Assembly Rooms
Tuesday	20 April	Bolton	Temperance Hall

It must not be imagined that Dickens used his major works for these readings. Rather he drew upon his Christmas Stories and the more accessible scenes from his early novels as texts for performance. It seemed as though he was quite content to follow the public's own estimation of his work; an estimation which rested largely on such pieces as *A Christmas Carol*, *The Chimes*, *The Cricket on the Hearth*, 'The'Poor Traveller', 'Boots at the Holly Tree Inn', 'Mrs Gamp', 'Little Dombey' and 'The Trial' from *Pickwick Papers*. These, in fact, were the works upon which the first tour was based. Items that were brought in later look equally like recital pieces rather than serious fiction; they included 'Bob Sawyer's Party' from *Pickwick Papers;* 'Mr Chops the Dwarf' from 'A House to Let'; and the later Christmas Stories, 'Doctor Marigold', 'Barbox Brothers' and 'The Boy from Mugby Junction'. It is a world of phantasmagoria and sensation, far removed from the symbolic drama of the social novels. It associates itself rather with the more fanciful Christmas Stories, and also looks forward towards the macabre imaginings of *Edwin Drood*. Almost the only work of social incident included was 'Dotheboys Hall' and a farrago of events from *David Copperfield*. And even these were played for humour and pathos rather than as straight criticism of society. Of the density of texture and weightiness of theme manifest in the later novels there is not a sign.

Matters such as Bob Sawyer, Mr Chops *et al.* required the voice and presence of the narrator to project them. Indeed, it might be as well to think of the Readings, and not the texts on which they depend, as works of art in themselves. This is true even of the last item to be added: 'Sikes and Nancy'. It is not the straight excerpt from *Oliver Twist* that might have been anticipated. For one thing, the text is cut and heightened to make for increased speed and excitement. For another, the voice and manner of the middle-aged narrator on the rostrum was widely different from the sanguine young author who had penned the original novel. Behind Dickens in 1868 was a broken marriage, the beginning and continuance of the affair with Ellen Ternan, his self-imposed torments of a working life, Jonas Chuzzlewit, John Rokesmith, Bradley Headstone; and before him loomed the shadowy figure of John Jasper in pursuit of Edwin Drood. It would seem that Dickens, in that reading, had a good deal to kill. Against all the advice of his physicians and his friends, he performed the murder of Nancy up and down the country. It ended up by nearly killing him.

But the collapse at Bolton that prematurely ended the Farewell Reading Tour may well have been a blessing in disguise. For over four years, since *Our Mutual Friend*, Dickens had neglected his writing to project himself into these frenetic readings. Now he was forcibly thrust back upon himself. And, in July 1869, within three months of his collapse, we find him writing to Forster about his idea for a new novel. He was contemplating a plot concerning two young people who, from a very early age, had been pledged to each other. The interest, he said, was to lie in the tracing of their separate ways and the impossibility of predicting the direction in which they would tend. The odd thing is that Dickens does not seem to have realized that he had done precisely that in *Our Mutual Friend*. The idea of turning this sketch for a plot into a murder story was adumbrated, again to Forster, in a letter of 6 August. Other elements were built into the scheme. Dickens followed up this last letter by telling Forster that his new novel was to concern the murder of a nephew by his uncle. And he hinted, not only to Forster but to his son, Charley, his daughter, Kate, his son-in-law, Charles Collins, and his illustrator, Luke Fildes, that the novel was to contain a 'very curious new idea'. Mysteriously, he informed this intimate circle of people that he was not at liberty to divulge this idea 'or the interest of the book would be gone'.

The murder was enhanced in its strangeness by being set in the dreamy atmosphere of an ancient cathedral city. This draws for its colouring on Dickens's memories of his youth in Rochester; its nostalgic tone reminds us of certain reminiscent pages in *The Uncommercial Traveller*.

For sufficient reasons, which this narrative will itself unfold as it advances, a fictitious name must be bestowed upon the old cathedral town. Let it stand in these pages as Cloisterham. It was once possibly known to the

Druids by another name, and certainly to the Romans by another, and to the Saxons by another, and to the Normans by another; and a name more or less in the course of many centuries can be of little moment to its dusty chronicles.

Notice that Dickens writes, not of a fictitious cathedral town, but of one with 'a fictitious name'. And truly, whether termed Doubryf, Durobrivis, Hrofesceastes or Roucestre, it is the Rochester of Dickens's boyhood that is set so evocatively before us here.

An ancient city, Cloisterham, and no meet dwelling-place for anyone with hankerings after the noisy world. A monotonous, silent city, deriving an earthy flavour throughout from its cathedral crypt, and so abounding in vestiges of monastic graves, that the children grow small salad in the dust of abbots and abbesses, and make dirt-pies of nuns and friars. . . In a word, a city of another and a bygone time is Cloisterham, with its hoarse cathedral bell, its hoarse rooks hovering about the cathedral tower, its hoarser and less distant rooks in the stalls far beneath. Fragments of old wall, saint's chapel, chapter-house, convent and monastery, have got incongruously or obstructively built into many of its houses and gardens. . . . .

The work is akin not only to the more fanciful Christmas Stories but also to the flights into fantasy that often prefigured impending exhaustion in *Nicholas Nickleby* and *The Old Curiosity Shop*. The work is devoid of Dickens's deeper social concerns; but, for all that, it represents, in this incongruously peaceful setting, an exploration into the darker regions of morbid psychology that had fascinated him ever since the Madman's Manuscript of *Pickwick Papers* and the story called 'A Confession' which he published in *Master Humphrey's Clock*. Both these case-histories bear more than a passing resemblance to the fictions of Jonas Chuzzlewit and Bradley Headstone; and the latter, in his turn, leads us infallibly on to the brooding figure of John Jasper, outwardly respectable choirmaster, inwardly hopeless opium-addict and real or potential murderer.

Mr Jasper is a dark man of some six-and-twenty, with thick, lustrous, well-arranged black hair, and whiskers. He looks older than he is, as dark men often do. His voice is deep and good, his face and figure are good, his manner is a little sombre. His room is a little sombre, and may have had its influence in forming his manner. It is mostly in shadow. . . .

'The cramped monotony of my existence grinds me away.by the grain. . . . The echoes of my own voice among the arches seems to mock me with my

daily drudging round. No wretched monk who droned his life away in that
gloomy place, before me, can have been more tired of it than I am. He could
take for relief (and did take) to carving demons out of the stalls and seats
and desks. What shall I do? Must I take to carving them out of my heart?'

Perhaps an additional stimulus to creativity was Dickens's desire to
outdo Wilkie Collins, his tireless collaborator in many Christmas
numbers of his magazines, on the younger man's own ground; though
any just assessment would consider that in this the great social novelist
was demeaning himself.

But, if such was Dickens's aim, he succeeded in it. The critics,
who scolded Dickens throughout his lifetime for simplistic characterization and obvious narratives, have not ceased through the
hundred years of its existence trying to solve *The Mystery of Edwin
Drood*. The book remains unsolved: eternally tantalizing because,
being unfinished, its theme was destined never to be played out.
Dickens wrote the book in spasms through guttering exhaustion and
creeping paralysis, and his death in mid-novel was the most convincing answer the critics could have received as to whether or not
their author was simple-minded.

About certain matters the Droodists, or an overwhelming pre-
ponderance of them, are agreed. *Edwin Drood* is far removed from
the modern whodunit. In fact, we know exactly who did it, or meant
to do it: the sinister choirmaster, Jasper. It is pretty clear, for example,
that Jasper tries to throw suspicion upon Neville Landless, a young
stranger in the town, who has a devoted sister, Helena. And his
interest in Edwin's fiancée, Rosa Budd – pledged to Edwin from
childhood – is also plainly evident. What we do not know is how
he was to be exposed. The mystery of *Edwin Drood* lies not in exposition but in denouement.

But, since we do not possess the denouement, on all issues concerning it, dissension runs pretty deep. For example, there is a difficulty about what ought to have been a perfectly clear point: whether
or not a murder has been committed. The intention to commit
murder is there, certainly, plainly set before us; and certainly Jasper's
nephew, Edwin Drood, disappears. But this need not mean that he
is done to death. Some of the early commentators followed Richard
Proctor's famous continuation of the book, *Watched by the Dead*,
and saw *Edwin Drood* as a story about a man, thought deceased, in

reality looking upon the passes of his putative murderer. This view, held by Gillan Vase, Henry Woollen and W. Ridley Kent, among others, has had currency in more recent times mainly in stage and screen versions of the book. Malcolm Morley, for example, quotes plays setting out this view by Will King, Ethel Raithby and Edward Purchase. And certainly, if the childhood betrothal motif from *Our Mutual Friend* is present, 'watched by the dead', its related theme, could be present also. Though modern criticism has tended to reject this interpretation, there are instances in which a persuasive case has been made. William Bleifuss, for example, suggests that, after all Jasper's plotting and planning to do away with his nephew, the success of his scheme would constitute an anti-climax. So Bleifuss sees Edwin as marrying Rosa in the final denouement: following Woollen, he regards the disappearance of the young man as something of a love-test.

Droodiana stretches far and wide, including novels, plays, films, essays and even reports from spiritualist séances. Of the sixty-five solutions to the mystery with which I am personally acquainted, twenty-three believe Drood to be alive – though there is no agreement as to his whereabouts – and forty-two would have Drood dead.

With two exceptions, those who believe Drood dead take Jasper to have murdered him. Since there can be little mystery about so bald a circumstance, much interest attaches to Jasper's motivation. F. J. Cross suggests that he wanted to inherit the Drood estate; Lady Pansy Pakenham suggests that his dynamic was a passion for Rosa; Katherine Kelly says that Jasper was a fanatic who killed Drood in order to save Rosa from an unhappy marriage; Eustace Conway has it that the murder was owing to a drug-induced fit of temporary insanity; Aubrey Boyd puts Jasper down as a Svengali-like mesmerist; Howard Duffield as a strangler or thug.

Some circumstantial detail attaches to each one of these interpretations. For instance, the last is reinforced by the fact that Jasper is seen wearing a black silk scarf akin to the rumal, the fragment of the gown of Kali with which the Thugs traditionally did their work. Some Droodists have even agreed that Jasper is not what he seems: Mary Kavanagh puts him down as an impostor, Jasper's Eurasian half-brother come to impersonate him. Such an air of mystery surrounds the man that even far-fetched interpretations like this attract a following. But it is noticeable that attempts in forecasting the development of Jasper's character and the probable nature of his exposure vary wildly.

Matters are complicated by the presence of several elements in the novel that look uncommonly like sets of clues. Much the most striking of these is the entry of a very peculiar character as late as Chapter 18. Critics and playwrights alike have had considerable fun in trying to guess the purpose and identity of Dick Datchery. All in all, he is perhaps the most mysterious feature of the book. He suddenly appears in Cloisterham, claiming to be no more than an idle buffer drifting through life on his means; but his appearance is odd, to say the least of it. He has an unusually large head, a shock of white hair, black eyebrows, and gives a general impression of going about in heavy disguise. But if Datchery is in disguise, who is he in real life? Out of a sample of fifty-three answers to this question, I find no less than thirteen different opinions vouchsafed. Dickens would appear to have laid his clues very ambiguously.

Datchery is taken to be Drood in heavy disguise by those who believe that the young man is alive – there are exceptions to this, as to anything else in Drood literature, but such is the general rule. Eight of my sample put the interpretation forward. Now this would be a satisfactory acting out of the motif, 'watched by the dead'; though it is worth mentioning that Datchery is a highly conspicuous watcher, and, indeed, seems at times to be doing his best to draw attention to himself.

So, when he had done his dinner, he was duly directed to the spot and sallied out for it. But the Crozier being an hotel of a most retiring disposition, and the waiter's directions being fatally precise, he soon became bewildered, and went boggling about and about the cathedral tower. . . .

. . .an ancient vaulted room, in which a large-headed, grey-haired gentleman is writing, under the odd circumstances of sitting open to the thoroughfare and eyeing all who pass, as if he were toll-taker of the gateway. . . .

Another set of opinions – six out of the fifty-three – suggest that Datchery is Helena Landless, devoted sister of the young man who falls under suspicion of Edwin's murder. J. Cuming Walters is the chief proponent of this point of view, and has argued with some force that Helena is represented as being emotionally committed against

Jasper; that she is of strong will; that, in childhood, she four times ran away from home dressed as a boy, and so was used to male impersonation; and that no other person in the drama has the motivation or the ability to act such a part.

Unfortunately, it is equally possible to argue in favour of Lieutenant Tartar, who, like Datchery, appears late in the book, and who appears to be strongly committed on the side of Drood's fiancée, Rosa Budd. Five people opt for Tartar, including such solid Droodists as Willoughby Matchett, G. F. Gadd, and Percy Carden. The last-named finds various verbal similarities between Tartar and Datchery; for example the repeated 'I beg pardon' which is common to them both and to no other character in the book. Each case, as we examine it, has points in its favour; and it is only when we compare one group of cases with another group that our uneasiness rises in proportion to the critics' certainty.

Six more interpretations including one by Andrew Lang opt for Neville Landless. Certainly his name falls heavily under suspicion, and, in the fragment of the novel left to us, he is not shown as doing very much by way of clearing it. But I ought to say that this particular solution is one chiefly adopted by playwrights – Morley quotes W. H. Stephens as an early example – and what is satisfactorily histrionic on the stage might not necessarily do for a novel.

Only four solutions in my sample see Datchery as Grewgious, Rosa's eccentric and high-minded guardian. But among the solutions is one by Richard Baker, who of all recent scholars has given *Edwin Drood* most attention. His case, no less than those of Proctor or Walters or Carden for *their* respective choices, is formidable. Grewgious has an attention to detail that is remarkably like that of Datchery; Datchery and Grewgious follow similar procedures in taking out lodgings; Grewgious's flat crop of sandy hair would – as the narrative itself remarks – be admirable for the wearing of a wig. And certainly it is noticeable, as other critics point out, that there are parallel instances of Grewgious continually stroking his hair while Datchery perpetually shakes out *his*.

We might be convinced, if an even heavier weight of opinion did not put forward Grewgious's clerk, Bazzard, as the real Dick Datchery: thirteen people in all, including Dickens's own daughter, Kate Perugini, opted for this solution. There is the fact that Bazzard is of a histrionic temperament and is author of a tragedy; there is the additional fact that he is closely associated with the person (Grewgious) who throughout the novel shows most hostility to Jasper; there is, moreover, the extraordinary amount of space given to details of his life and hard times – extraordinary, if he had no part to play more than being Grewgious's clerk. A good deal depends on whether the author sees him, like J. Cuming Walters, in the failed-poet tradition of Snodgrass and Knag, or whether he sees him, like William Bleifuss, as a shrewd eccentric in the line of Noggs and Wemmick.

There are not wanting, either, those who believe Datchery to be none other than himself. A minority point of view, led by Lady Pansy Pakenham, suggests he is not in disguise at all, but is a genuinely new character. Gavin Brend takes him to be a member of the Drood family; S. J. Rust to be Drood's true guardian for whom Jasper was only a delegate; Montague Saunders sees him as a member of the firm of solicitors to whom Grewgious gave his legal work; Wilmot Corfield as the China Shepherdess's clerical brother-in-law; Lehmann-Haupt as Poker, a character who exists only in a rejected draft of an earlier chapter.

Clearly, this is stalemate. The critics should confess themselves baffled. Dickens, after all, was quite capable of laying an entirely false trail of clues. In other words, though Datchery may *look* disguised, it is possible that he has made us the victim of a double bluff: hence the conspicuousness of his mannerisms. Or again: the theatrical manner of Bazzard may be a diversion away from the profounder motivation of a more central character. But that character need not be Helena: figures other than Datchery have been suggested as subjects for her talents of impersonation, and those talents themselves may be something of a red herring. The fact that so many views of Datchery can be so persuasively argued suggests strongly that there is no possibility of a consensus at all.

And this, too, is true of the book. It is all too easy for critics and writers to read their own fictions into Dickens's fragment. Thus, in a quite distinguished series of essays, Felix Aylmer argues that Jasper is to be taken at his face value as the friend and protector of Edwin; that his life, and Edwin's, are threatened by a mysterious Visitor from the East; that an attempt on both their lives is taken by Edwin as an assault upon himself by Jasper; in consequence of which, he disappears. This is a fabric of circumstance, remarkable for its ingenuity, but founded upon not the slightest hint in the book of any such Visitor. It seems that the unfinished Fragment calls forth answering sparks of fantasy in the critics' imaginations. Instances suggest themselves: Helena is variously taken to reappear as her brother ('F.C.B.'), as Drood (Carden), as Drood's ghost (Jamieson and Rosenthal), as a Chinaman (Ellis), as a lascar (Jones-Evans and Morford); while Mary Kavanagh believes that Edwin himself reappears in the guise of Lieutenant Tartar. But even when such fantasies as these are discounted, the book remains a mystery, and a hopelessly puzzling one, at that.

All the various interpretations of the Droodists do is cast a backward light upon the events of the book as we have it. Thus, those who believe Drood to be alive and well and watching developments in Cloisterham will take the novel as being in shape something of a revenge drama: its hero, wrongly presumed dead, moving among the living; there are parallels for this not only in Harmon in *Our Mutual Friend* but in Meltham in 'Hunted Down', a story Dickens had written in 1859. Those who believe Drood to be dead, however, will see the book less as a revenge drama than as a psychological study: a gradual stripping away of the layers of pretence which cloak the central figure of Jasper. In much the same way, to have a leading protagonist of the book such as Drood himself or Helena in disguise as Datchery, will naturally put far more weight on that character's part in the plot than if he is a Nadgett-like agent, whether it be Bazzard the clerk or a figure not in any disguise at all. In other words, each and every attempt to finish the trajectory which Dickens left uncompleted will indicate only the way in which the interpreter views what we already have of that trajectory.

Dickens's clues, after all, have a way of seeming meaningful only to hindsight. It is not frivolous to remind the Droodists that, halfway through a reading of *Nicholas Nickleby* or *Barnaby Rudge*, it would be a shrewd reader indeed who could relate Smike and Hugh to their respective fathers. The point is more seriously true of *Great Expectations*: we can detect, on re-reading the novel, those clues that lead on to the revelation of Pip's benefactor. But, on first reading, such matters as the stranger who gives Pip two pounds seem explanatory rather than satisfactory. Much the same may be true of certain pointers in *Edwin Drood*. An immense amount of weight is laid on the Sapsea tomb; our attention is forcibly drawn to the mound of quicklime in the stonemason's yard; the name Deputy – applied to a hideous small boy – also seems significant; so does the malignity of the Opium Woman – a striking yet inexplicable presence in the novel; but significant of what?

It may very well be that Dickens was keeping various options open: laying at one and the same time alternative sets of clues. There are plenty of examples of Dickens backing himself both ways: the miserliness of Boffin – real or pretended? – is only one example that springs to mind. Or he may have laid one line of clues so far along the printed text – say, those that point to Drood being dead – and switched at a given point to some other line; in which case I do not see how any solution could be tenable. It is even possible that, as Wills declared, Dickens changed his mind half-way through. We can believe the testimony of Dickens's son that, when he began the novel, he intended to kill Drood; but that intention need not have remained constant, any more than Dickens remained constant to his idea of the degradation of Walter Gay or the bachelorhood of Philip Pirrip. And if Wills is right, and Dickens's change of mind got him into endless difficulties, what would be the effect of such a change on the reader?

Exhaustion, as we have seen throughout Dickens's career, often projected the great author into his most brilliant fantasies. Hence almost any set of clues in our possession makes sense; hence the extreme persuasiveness of the various interpretations. What is certain, however, is that no *two* sets of clues are going to work; reconciliation among the Droodists has proved impossible. Any interpretation will seem plausible only until it is compared with a different, but equally plausible, interpretation.

And so, all we can do with the vast body of Droodiana is to make use of it, as we do other criticism, not to judge intention, but to gauge effect. It is not for the critic to complete an unfinished work but to throw light upon the fragment actually in his possession. *Edwin Drood*, with its atmospherics and phantasmagoria, belongs to the hallucinatory world of Christmas Stories, of Quilp and Gamp, of the mesmeric Readings themselves. It has no place in the canon of major novels. We may regret that Dickens left behind him a work so brilliant in its various parts, so irresoluble in its meaning as a whole. Yet it is fitting that the great artist should quit this life with a book that was living testimony, in the teeth of the critics' censure, to the unpredictability of his art. His fellow-writers may rejoice that Dickens finally drove his critics not merely to pronounce upon his efforts but to make frenetic attempts to write a reply. And how much superior is Dickens's fragmentation to their self-sufficiency! Their failure at exegesis is his final triumph.

Appendices

Selective Bibliography

Index

Appendix I

The Mudfog Papers (1837-39)
Sketches of Young Gentlemen (1838)
Sketches of Young Couples (1840)

There are areas of Dickens's work that seem hardly to have been commented upon. Reading them, one begins to see why. *The Mudfog Papers*, the *Sketches of Young Gentlemen* and the *Sketches of Young Couples* are no more than pot-boilers. As such, they have no organic connection with the rest of Dickens and this is why they are relegated to an appendix. But, for the sake of completeness, some note should be taken of them.

The Mudfog Papers were written as fillers for *Bentley's Miscellany*. They follow in composition the first and weakest chapter of *Pickwick Papers*: the one which records a debate of the Pickwick Club. It has been surmised that the Club was a parody of the newly-founded British Association; without question this is true of 'The Mudfog Association for the Advancement of Everything'.

It is an unengaging spectacle to see a man of letters scoffing at that which he patently does not understand. Satire is founded upon empathy; the weakest part of *Gulliver's Travels* is the section that shows Swift mocking the science of his time – there is a particularly unfortunate take-off of Leuwenhoek. In the case of Dickens, the British Association need not trouble to duck. This is the letter of his humour; the facetious, rather than the inimitable, Boz. We cannot be moved to mirth by the spectacle of a correspondent to Section A (Zoology and Botany) reporting an attempt to educate fleas; or by Doctor Kutankumagen (Moscow) reporting to Section B (Anatomy and Medicine) his attempt to quell a patient's tendency to excessive laughter by reducing his diet and condemning him to perpetual abstinence. Those who are interested may find links with Dickens's other novels: the pig-faced lady, with whom Mrs Nickleby

was to compare herself in a moment of indignation, makes a momentary appearance; and Mr Slug's attack on juvenile reading (Section
C – Statistics) in its crude way anticipates Mr Gradgrind's insistence
on facts. But neither these, nor the accounts of a learned professor's
discomfort at Mudfog and perilous journey the year after to Oldcastle
can redeem the work from tedium. And in any case the institution
mocked is, as we all know, a beneficial instrument in the development
of knowledge.

Still less can be said about *Sketches of Young Gentlemen,* a pot-
boiler done for Chapman and Hall in a month. Its slipshod quality
may be understood when we say that the same month saw the editing
of Grimaldi's autobiography, the writing of a sizable portion of
Oliver Twist and the editorial concerns of *Bentley's Miscellany.* It is
by way of being an answer to *Sketches of Young Ladies* by 'Quiz',
otherwise known as E. Caswell. It has the unique claim to be interesting
because of Phiz's illustrations rather than Dickens's text. Briefly,
Dickens sketches various types of young men under such heads as
'The Bashful Young Gentleman', 'The Very Friendly Young Gentleman', 'The Domestic Young Gentleman', etc. Insofar as the sketches
gain interest, they do so when there is some slight semblance of plot.
Thus, 'The Domestic Young Gentleman' begins –

Let us make a slight sketch of our amiable friend, Mr Felix Nixon. We are
strongly disposed to think that if we put him in this place, he will answer
our purpose without another word of comment.

Felix, then, is a young gentleman who lives at home with his mother, just
within the twopenny-post office circle of three miles from St Martin le Grand.
He wears India-rubber goloshes when the weather is at all damp, and always
has a silk handkerchief neatly folded up in the right-hand pocket of his great-
coat, to tie over his mouth when he goes home at night; moreover, being
rather near-sighted, he carries spectacles for particular occasions, and has
a weakish tremulous voice, of which he makes great use, for he talks as much
as any old lady breathing.

But, except as an odd foreshadowing of Conan Doyle's mythical
Hosmer Angel in the Sherlock Holmes stories, of what use is this?
Even the skin of fiction cannot disguise the fact that fundamentally
it is just as much an example, and therefore a walking cliché, as the
Bashful Young Gentleman, who has not a shadow of personalization
– 'If the bashful young gentleman, in turning a street corner, chances

to stumble suddenly upon two or three young ladies of his acquaintance, nothing can exceed his confusion and agitation'. Etc.

In much the same style are the *Sketches of Young Couples*, also written as a pot-boiler for Chapman and Hall. There are the Young Couple, the Formal Couple, the Couple who Coddle Themselves – 'Mrs Merrywinkle's maiden name was Chopper. She was the only child of Mr and Mrs Chopper. Her father died when she was, as the playbooks express it, "yet an infant"; and so old Mrs Chopper, when her daughter married, made the house of her son-in-law her home from that time henceforward, and set up her staff of rest with Mr and Mrs Merrywinkle.' This is tedium personified, like the weakest passages in *Sketches by Boz*; and the detail expended upon such excursions as Mr Merrywinkle's getting to the office is not compensated for by any acute or extraordinary observation of hypochondria.

The main interest of these productions is that they are by Dickens, and now and again we see a characteristic touch or notion. But the emphasis must be that they are slight examples of word-spinning: the most flagrant example is 'Mr Robert Bolton' which has not even an excuse of a plot and seems designed to fill up an odd space. Yet they are remarkably hard to come by – I have found them reprinted in Arthur Waugh's 'Biographical' edition of the works of Dickens – and, for the sake of completeness, they require mention by the critic as much as inclusion by the editor.

Appendix II

The Life of Our Lord (1849)
A Child's History of England (1853)

In 1849, Dickens finished a version of the Gospels for his children. It had been begun in 1846, and is largely based on St Luke. He had no thought of publishing it, and its manuscript descended, via his sister-in-law, Georgina, to Dickens's son, Sir Henry. The will of this latter provided that, if the majority of his family were in favour of publication, *The Life of Our Lord* should be given to the world after his death. Accordingly, it was first published in 1934.

We shall look in vain for any of the characteristic Dickens panache in this little production. As may be gathered from his various comments to clergymen and others, and from the simple-minded pietism of his will, Dickens was neither theologian nor biblical critic, and had no desire to go very deeply into what were, for him, matters of faith. His Christianity, in fact, was more or less identical with that of Thomas Arnold, and is remarkable only for laying no stress on the Divinity of Christ or the virginity of Mary. It is interesting that he manages to couple his instinctive Radicalism with his profession of Christianity in such passages as the following:

That there might be some good men to go about with him, teaching the people, Jesus Christ chose Twelve poor men to be his companions. These twelve are called *The apostles* or *Disciples*, and he chose them from among Poor Men in order that the Poor might know – always after that; in all years to come – that Heaven was made for them as well as for the rich, and that God makes no difference between those who wear good clothes and those who go barefoot and in rags. The most miserable, the most ugly, deformed, wretched creatures that live, will be brightest Angels in Heaven if they are good here on earth. Never forget this, when you are grown up. . . .

We need not doubt Dickens's sincerity here. It is amply borne out by his labours on behalf of multifarious charitable ventures: these persisted throughout his life. Nevertheless, the point is made far more powerfully in the graphic figures of Dan Peggotty and Joe Gargery, those true gentlemen of his novels. And it is to be regretted that Dickens's piety allows no spark of the authentic Boz in his dialogue here, or virtually monosyllabic narration.

A Child's History of England is a livelier performance altogether. It appeared irregularly in *Household Words* from 25 January 1851 onwards. Dickens did not concentrate too much upon this performance. Indeed it was dictated, in such moments as he had spare from amateur acting, editing his magazine, and working to establish a Guild of Literature and Art, to Georgina Hogarth. Moreover, it depends very heavily for its facts and their arrangement upon Keightley's *History of England* (1837). Some of Dickens's interpretations are his own, and the style, certainly, is not derivative. This can be seen if we make a comparison between the respective accounts of Henry VIII. Keightley disapproves, but shrouds his rancour in an academic historical style, while Dickens sizzles and splutters like a fire-bomb.

The new monarch was just eighteen years of age, handsome in person and popular in manners. The claims of the White and Red Roses were united in him, so that all chances of a disputed title were removed. The unpopularity of the late king, through his avarice, made men look with joyful anticipation to the reign of a young and gallant prince; and the treasures amassed by that avarice enabled him to fulfil these expectations. . . The early deaths of his offspring, who had but blossomed to die, probably led him to reflect on the nature of his marriage; he consulted the pages of the Angelic Doctor, and there found that the pope has not the power to dispense with the laws of God . . . Hitherto he had treated Catherine with all due respect as his queen; but when she could not be induced to withdraw her appeal to Rome, it was signified to her that she must leave Windsor. . . . She replied, 'that to whatever place she might remove nothing could remove her from being the King's lawful wife. . . .'

In contrast to Keightley's stately and cautious periods, Dickens takes violent sides, shows a colourful partisanship, and harangues Henry with a zest that recalls his famous letter about Squeers to Master Hughes (12 December 1838).

We now come to King Henry the Eighth, whom it has been too much the fashion to call 'Bluff King Hal,' and 'Burly King Harry,' and other fine names; but whom I shall take the liberty to call, plainly, one of the most detestable villains that ever drew breath. You will be able to judge, long before we come to the end of his life, whether he deserves the character.

He was just eighteen years of age when he came to the throne. People said he was handsome then; but I don't believe it. He was a big, burly, noisy, small-eyed, large-faced, double-chinned, swinish-looking fellow in later life (as we know from the likenesses of him, painted by the famous Hans Holbein), and it is not easy to believe that so bad a character can ever have been veiled under a prepossessing appearance.

He was anxious to make himself popular, and the people, who had long disliked the late King, were very willing to believe that he deserved to be so. He was extremely fond of show and display, and so were they. . . . Now Queen Catherine was no longer young or handsome, and it is likely that she was not particularly good-tempered; having been always rather melancholy, and having been made more so by the deaths of four of her children when they were very young. So, the King fell in love with the fair Anne Boleyn, and said to himself, 'How can I be best rid of my own troublesome wife whom I am tired of, and marry Anne?'

You recollect that Queen Catherine had been the wife of Henry's brother. What does the King do, after thinking it over, but calls his favourite priests about him, and says O! his mind is in such a dreadful state, and he is so frightfully uneasy, because he is afraid it was not lawful for him to marry the Queen!. . . they all said, Ah! that was very true, and it was a serious business; and perhaps the best way to make it right would be for his Majesty to be divorced. . . . Being now quite resolved to get rid of Queen Catherine, and to marry Anne Boleyn without more ado, the King made Cranmer Archbishop of Canterbury, and directed Queen Catherine to leave the Court. She obeyed; but replied that wherever she went, she was Queen of England still, and would remain so, to the last. . . .

Of course, this is something of a high-spot in Dickens's *Child's History*. He always had a special dislike of Henry VIII, and makes one of his most detestable characters, Mrs Skewton in *Dombey and Son*, refer to him with enthusiasm. So when he calls him 'a blot of blood and grease upon the History of England', we can feel his sympathies are engaged. Unfortunately, the *Child's History* does not keep up that lively style of polemic throughout. As the book wears on, it is noticeable that Dickens depends more and more heavily on Keightley. As usual, the arrangement of the factual matter follows Keightley closely, but even the wording of Dickens's account of James II's reign is almost identical. Even that bored him, so he stopped abruptly at that point, to give us a brisk résumé of the reigns of subsequent monarchs, all in a single chapter, ending at the accession of Queen Victoria. Clearly, after 125,000 words of dictation, the enterprise had outworn its charm.

The History is mostly an account of kings and battles; we would look in vain for any of Dickens's social insight in these pages. It is significant that the prime influence upon the book was Keightley rather than (say) Carlyle. For Dickens was an historian, though of a very minor kind, and, in his account of the Gordon Riots (see *Barnaby Rudge*) he has left us a piece of colourful narration infinitely better than anything of the kind in *A Child's History of England*.

Appendix III

Hunted Down (1859)
No Thoroughfare (1867)
George Silverman's Explanation (1868)
A Holiday Romance (1868)

In the *Reprinted Pieces* we may find four Christmas Stories that do not follow the usual pattern: 'The Poor Relation's Story', 'The Child's Story', 'The Schoolboy's Story', 'Nobody's Story'. They were all written before Dickens set up the collaborative method for the Christmas numbers of *Household Words* and *All the Year Round*. There were, however, two issues which read like straight novelettes: 'The Perils of Certain English Prisoners' (*Household Words*, 1857), and 'No Thoroughfare' (*All the Year Round*, 1867). Both were written in collaboration with Wilkie Collins. The first is, like 'The Wreck of the Golden Mary' (*Household Words*, 1856), a blood-and-thunder Captain Marryat affair, with a dash of tears thrown in at the end as the Old Soldier confesses how he had always loved the Lady. 'No Thoroughfare' is larger-scale altogether, but virtually indistinguishable from Collins's usual work. It is memorable, if at all, for its portrait of the bulky and pathetic wine-merchant, Wilding, with his clouding vision and muzzy head. 'No Thoroughfare' was the very last of the *Christmas Stories*, though it is seldom printed with them: it came out in 1867.

Dickens wrote only three stories in his later years unconnected with the Christmas series. Two of them are of slight interest. 'Hunted Down' (1859) is a piece of melodramatic claptrap written as a result of a tempting offer from Robert Bonner of the *New York Ledger*. Dickens was at work on *A Tale of Two Cities* at the time. The only thing worth recording about this story is its physical description of Slinkton, with his path of white scalp as a centre parting his sleek black hair. It is said to be based upon the forger, Thomas Wainewright. 'A Holiday Romance' appeared in a children's magazine in

1868, also resulting from an American offer. It is a charming trifle, giving four different accounts, each purporting to be written by one of four children, of the same adventure.

'George Silverman's Explanation' (1868), written for *The Atlantic Monthly,* presents considerably more interest. It is full of a pervading self-disgust that links its central figure with that of other repressed heroes – Clennam and Rokesmith, in particular. It begins with scenes of abject poverty, heavily influenced by the Mrs Gaskell of *Mary Barton,* but with a raw drama of Dickens's own – sharpened by being seen through the eyes of a child, albeit one so neglected that he is little better than a wild beast. It affords, too, the last of Dickens's Calvinistic portraits. Brother Hawkyard aptly winds up the line begun with Stiggins and continued through Pecksniff, Murdstone, Miss Barbary, Chadband and Mrs Clennam. He is a distinctive creation, with his 'I have been the best servant the Lord has had in his service for this five-and-thirty year (oh, I have!); and he knows the value of such a servant as I have been to him (oh yes, he does!)'

But there is an ambiguity running all through this story of how a timid little vicar aids an elopement. So much of the action has little to do with the manifest plot, and so much of the self-blame seems to be laid on in the manner of a dramatic monologue. So that we are not sure where we stand in relation to the person described, or even whether we should believe his Explanation. It seems as though there is experience here Dickens is unable to work into a satisfactory correlative, either through an unwillingness to face up to it or through the adoption of confines too limited for the purpose. 'George Silverman's Explanation' remains a sport and a curiosity in Dickens's output. Explanatory it may be; but it is not satisfactory.

A Selective Bibliography

I have listed only those works which I myself found useful. An asterisk indicates when I found a given work indispensable.

GENERAL

Axton, William, *Circle of Fire* (Lexington, Kentucky, 1966)
———, '"Keystone" Structure in Dickens' Serial Novels', *University of Toronto Quarterly*, Vol. 36 (1967), p.31
Blount, Trevor, *Dickens: The Early Novels* (London, 1968)
* Butt, John and Tillotson, K., *Dickens at Work* (London, 1957)
Cockshut, A.O.J., *The Imagination of Charles Dickens* (London, 1961)
* Collins, Philip, *Dickens and Crime* (London, 1962)
* ———, *Dickens and Education* (London, 1963)
———, (ed.) *The Critical Heritage* (London, 1970)
* Dabney, Ross H., *Love and Property in the Novels of Charles Dickens* (Berkeley, California, 1967)
Daleski, H.M., *Dickens and the Art of Analogy* (London, 1970)
Davis, Earle, *The Flint and the Flame* (London, 1964)
Dyson, A.E., *The Inimitable Dickens* (London, 1970)
Engel, Monroe, *The Maturity of Dickens* (Cambridge, Mass., 1959)
Ford, George H., *Dickens and his Readers* (Princeton, N.J., 1955)
* Forster, John, *The Life of Charles Dickens* (London, 1872-74)
Futrell, Michael, 'Dickens and Dostoyevsky', *English Miscellany*, Vol. 7 (1956), p.48
Garis, Robert, *The Dickens Theatre* (Oxford, 1965)
Ghent, Dorothy Van, 'The Dickens World: A View from Todgers's', *Sewanee Review*, Vol. 68 (1950), p.419
Hardy, Barbara, *The Moral Art of Charles Dickens* (London, 1970)
* House, Humphry, *The Dickens World* (London, 1942)
* Johnson, Edgar, *Charles Dickens: His Tragedy and Triumph* (London, 1953)
Leavis, F.R. and Q.D., *Dickens the Novelist* (London, 1970)

Lindsay, Jack, *Charles Dickens* (London, 1950)

Lucas, John, *The Melancholy Man* (London, 1970)

* Marcus, Steven, *Dickens: from Pickwick to Dombey* (London, 1965)

Marshall, William, *The World of the Victorian Novel* (South Brunswick, N.J., 1967)

* Miller, J. Hillis, *Charles Dickens: The World of his Novels* (Cambridge, Mass., 1958)

Orwell, George, 'Charles Dickens'. In *Inside the Whale* (London, 1940)

* Spilka, Mark, *Dickens and Kafka* (London, 1967)

Stoehr, Taylor, *The Dreamer's Stance* (Ithaca, N.Y., 1965)

Sucksmith, H.P., *The Narrative Art of Charles Dickens* (Oxford 1970)

Trilling, Lionel, 'The Dickens of Our Day'. In *A Gathering of Fugitives* (Boston, 1956)

* Wierstra, F.D., *Smollett and Dickens* (Den Helder, Holland, 1928)

Wilson, Angus, 'Charles Dickens: A Haunting'. *Critical Quarterly*, Vol. 2 (1960), p.101

———, 'The Heroes and Heroines of Charles Dickens'. In *Dickens and the Twentieth Century*, ed. Gross and Pearson (London, 1962)

* Wilson, Edmund, 'The Two Scrooges'. In *The Wound and the Bow* (Cambridge, Mass., 1941)

I Sketches by Boz

* Browning, Robert, 'Sketches by Boz'. In *Dickens and the Twentieth Century*, ed. Gross and Pearson (London, 1962)

Carlton, William J., '"The Old Lady" in *Sketches by Boz*,' *The Dickensian*, Vol. 49 (1953), p.149

———, 'Captain Holland Identified', *The Dickensian*, Vol. 57 (1961), p.69

Darton, F.J. Harvey, 'Dickens: The Beginner', *Quarterly Review*, Vol. 262 (1934), p.52

* Dexter, Walter, 'Charles Dickens: Journalist', *Nineteenth Century*, Vol. 65 (1934), p.705

* ———, 'The Genesis of *Sketches by Boz*', *The Dickensian*, Vol. 30 (1934), p.105

———, 'Dickens's First Contribution to the Morning Chronicle', *The Dickensian*, Vol. 31 (1935), p.5

Grubb, Gerald G., 'Dickens's First Experience as a Parliamentary Reporter', *The Dickensian*, Vol. 36 (1940), p.211

Lascelles, T.S., 'Transport in the Dickensian Era', *The Dickensian*, Vol. 58 (1962), p.50

McNulty, J.H., 'First and Last', *The Dickensian*, Vol. 47 (1951), p.82

Morley, Malcolm, 'Revelry by Night', *The Dickensian* (1964), p.97

Nielsen, Helmer, 'Some Observations on *Sketches by Boz*', *The Dickensian*, Vol. 34 (1938), p.243

Pearce, Talbot, 'Dickens – An Early Influence', *The Dickensian*, Vol. 64 (1965), p.157

Tillotson, Kathleen, 'Dickens and a Story by John Poole', *The Dickensian*, Vol. 52 (1955), p.69

II PICKWICK PAPERS

Benington, David, 'Seasonal Relevance in Pickwick Papers', *Nineteenth Century Fiction*, Vol. 16 (1961), p.219

Bovill, E.W., 'Tony Weller's Trade', *Notes and Queries* (1956), pp.324, 527

Brown, F.J., 'Those Dickens Christmases', *The Dickensian*, Vol. 60 (1964), p.17

* Carlton, W.J., 'Serjeant Buzfuz', *The Dickensian*, Vol. 45 (1949), p.21

Carter, John Archer, 'Memories of Charley Wag', *The Dickensian*, Vol. 64 (1966), p.147 (Review of *Souvenirs of Charles Dickens* by J.H. Siddons)

* Clark, Olney, 'Caroline Norton to Lord Melbourne', *Victorian Studies*, Vol. 8 (1965), p.255

Eason, Angus, 'Imprisonment for Debt in *Pickwick Papers*', *The Dickensian*, Vol. 64 (1968), p.106, p.111

Easton, Edward Raymond, MD, 'Doctors in Dickens', *The Dickensian*, Vol. 41 (1945), p.150

Hall, Hammond, 'Some Pickwickian Parallels', *Chambers's Journal*, April 1929, p.257 (especially interesting on Hogarth)

* Hill, H. Wallace, 'Jingle and Boswell', *New Statesman*, 24 January 1953, p.95

* Holdsworth, Sir William, *Dickens as a Legal Historian* (New Haven, Conn., 1928), Chapter 4

Killham, John, 'Pickwick: Dickens and the Art of Fiction'. In *Dickens and the Twentieth Century*, ed. Gross and Pearson (London, 1962)

Patten, Robert L. 'Interpolated Tales in *Pickwick Papers*', *Dickens Studies*, Vol. 1. (1965), p.86

———, 'The Art of Dickens' Interpolated Tales', *ELH*, Vol. 34 (1967) p.349

———, 'The Unpropitious Muse: Pickwick's Interpolated Tales', *Dickens Studies Newsletter*, Vol. 1. (1970), p.7

Reinhold, Heinz, 'The Stroller's Tale in *Pickwick*', *The Dickensian*, Vol. 64 (1968), p.143

Scrutton, T.B., 'The State of the Prisons as seen by John Howard and Charles Dickens', *The Dickensian*, Vol. 64 (1966), p.112

Stevenson, Lionel, 'Names in *Pickwick*', *The Dickensian*, Vol. 32 (1936), p.241

Wierstra, F.D., *Smollett and Dickens* (Den Helder, Holland, 1928)

Wood, Frederick T., 'Sam Weller's Cockneyisms', *Notes and Queries* (1946), p.234

III OLIVER TWIST

Gibson, Frank A., 'Hard on the Lawyers', *The Dickensian*, Vol. 59 (1963), p.160

Hamilton, Marie, 'The Indebtedness of *Oliver Twist* to Defoe's *History of the Devil'*, *PMLA*, Vol. 40 (1925), p.892

* Kettle, Arnold, 'Oliver Twist'. In *An Introduction to the English Novel* (London, 1951)

Lane, Lauriat, 'The Devil in *Oliver Twist'*, *The Dickensian*, Vol. 52 (1956), p.132

―――, 'Dickens's Archetypal Jew', *PMLA*, Vol. 73 (1958), p.94

Lucas, Alec, '*Oliver Twist* and the Newgate Novel', *The Dalhousie Review*, Vol. 34 (1954), p.381

* Marcus, Steven, 'The Wise Child'. In *Dickens: from Pickwick to Dombey* (London, 1965)

Phillips, George Lewis, 'Dickens and the Chimney Sweepers', *The Dickensian*, Vol. 59 (1963), p.28

* Stone, Harry, 'From Fagin to Riah', *Midstream*, Vol. 6 (1960), p.21

―――, 'Dark Corners of the Mind', *The Horn Book Magazine*, Vol. 39 (1963), p.306

Tobias, J.J., 'Ikey Solomons', *The Dickensian*, Vol. 65 (1969), p.171

Williamson, Colin, 'Two Missing Links in *Oliver Twist'*, *Nineteenth Century Fiction*, Vol. 22 (1967), p.225

IV NICHOLAS NICKLEBY

Adrian, Arthur H., '*Nicholas Nickleby* and Education Reform', *Nineteenth Century Fiction*, Vol. 4 (1946), p.237

* Carter, John Archer, 'The World of Squeers and the World of Crummles', *The Dickensian*, Vol. 58 (1962), p.50

* Clinton-Baddeley, V.C., 'Benevolent Teachers of Youth', *The Cornhill Magazine*, Vol. 170 (1957), p.361

―――, 'Snevellicci', *The Dickensian*, Vol. 57 (1961), p.43

Davies, Edith M., 'The Cock Lane Ghost', *The Dickensian*, Vol. 25 (1939), p.10

Greaves, John, 'The Thirsty Woman of Tutbury', *The Dickensian*, Vol. 61 (1965), p.51 (and see p.180)

Hill, T.W., 'Notes on *Nicholas Nickleby'*, *The Dickensian*, Vol. 46 (1950), p.99

Kreutz, Irving R., 'Sly of Manner, Sharp of Tooth: A Study of Dickens' Villains', *Nineteenth Century Fiction*, Vol. 22 (1968), p.331

Langton, Robert, 'The Brothers Cheeryble and the Grant Brothers', *Manchester Quarterly*, January 1886

* Morley, Malcolm, 'When Crummles Played', *The Dickensian*, Vol. 58 (1962), p.23

———, 'More about Crummles', *The Dickensian*, Vol. 59 (1963), p.51

Wierstra, F.D., *Smollett and Dickens* (Den Helder, Holland, 1928)

Wing, G.D., 'A Part to Tear a Cat in', *The Dickensian*, Vol. 64 (1968), p.10

V THE OLD CURIOSITY SHOP

Bennett, William Crosby, 'The Mystery of the Marchioness', *The Dickensian*, Vol. 36 (1941), p.205

Carlton, W.J., 'The Death of Mary Hogarth', *The Dickensian*, Vol. 63 (1967), p.68

'Cranfield, Lionel' (Edward Sackville-West), 'Books in General', *New Statesman*, 10 February 1945

Futrell, Michael, 'Dostoevsky and Dickens', *English Miscellany*, Vol. 7 (1956), p.48

Gibson, Frank A., 'A Seventeenth Century Kit Nubbles', *The Dickensian*, Vol. 53 (1957), p.12

* Marcus, Steven, 'The Myth of Nell'. In *Dickens: from Pickwick to Dombey* (1965)

Pearson, Gabriel, '*The Old Curiosity Shop*'. In *Dickens and the Twentieth Century*, ed. Gross and Pearson (London, 1962)

Raleigh, J.H., 'The Novel and the City', *Victorian Studies*, Vol. 11 (1968), p.291

Reid, J.C., *The Hidden World of Charles Dickens* (Auckland, N.Z., 1961) (An answer to K.J. Fielding, *Dickens: A Critical Introduction*, 1958, p.52)

* Steig, Michael, 'The Central Action of *The Old Curiosity Shop*', *Literature and Psychology*, Vol. 15 (1965), p.162

VI BARNABY RUDGE

Blount, Trevor, *Dickens: The Early Novels* (London, 1968)

Gibson, Frank A., 'A Note on George Gordon', *The Dickensian*, Vol. 57 (1961), p.81

Gray, W. Forbes, 'The Prototype of Gashford in *Barnaby Rudge*', *The Dickensian*, Vol. 29 (1933), p.175

Grubb, Gerald G., 'The Personal and Literary Relationships of Dickens and Poe', *Nineteenth Century Fiction*, Vol. 5 (1950), p.209

Lindsay, Jack, 'Barnaby Rudge'. In Dickens and the Twentieth Century, ed. Gross and Pearson (London, 1962)

Monod, Sylvère, 'Rebel with a Cause: Hugh of the Maypole', Dickens Studies, Vol. 1 (1965), p.4

Pearson, E. Kendell, 'Facts about the Gordon Riots', The Dickensian, Vol. 30 (1934), p.43

Ziegler, Arnold U., 'A Barnaby Rudge Source,' The Dickensian, Vol. 54 (1958), p.80

VII AMERICAN NOTES

MARTIN CHUZZLEWIT, CH. XV-XVII, XXI-XXIV, XXXIII-XXXIV

Baetzhold, R.G., 'What place was the model for Martin Chuzzlewit's Eden?' The Dickensian, Vol. 55 (1959), p.169

* Heilman, R.B., 'The New World in Dickens's Writings', The Trollopian, Vol. 1 (1947), p.11

* Stone, Harry, 'Dickens's Use of his American Experiences in Martin Chuzzlewit', PMLA, Vol. 72 (1957), p.464

——, 'Dickens and Melville go to Chapel', The Dickensian, Vol. 54 (1958), p.50

VIII MARTIN CHUZZLEWIT

Brogunier, Joseph, 'The Dreams of Montague Tigg, and Jonas Chuzzlewit', The Dickensian, Vol. 58 (1962), p.165

Churchill, R.C., 'Dickens, Drama and Tradition', Scrutiny, Vol. 10 (1942), p.366

Dyson, A.E., 'Howls the Sublime', Critical Quarterly, Vol. 9 (1967), p.234

* Furbank, P.N., Introduction and Notes to the Penguin Edition of Martin Chuzzlewit (Harmondsworth, Middx, 1968)

Hardy, Barbara, 'Martin Chuzzlewit'. In Dickens and the Twentieth Century, ed. Gross and Pearson (London, 1962)

IX CHRISTMAS BOOKS

Brown, F.J., 'Those Dickens Christmases', The Dickensian, Vol. 60 (1964), p.17

Gibson, Frank A., 'Nature's Possible', The Dickensian, Vol. 58 (1962), p.43 (on The Battle of Life)

McMaster, R.D., 'Dickens and the Horrific', Dalhousie Review, Vol. 38 (1958), p.18

Morris, William G., 'The Conversion of Scrooge', Studies in Short Fiction, Vol. 3 (1965), p.46

Slater, Michael, 'The Christmas Books', *The Dickensian*, Vol. 65 (1969), p.17

* Stone, Harry, 'Dickens' Artistry and the Haunted Man', *South Atlantic Quarterly*, Vol. 61 (1962), p.492

X Letters on Social Questions
  Pictures from Italy

* Brice, Alec, 'Ignorance and its Victims', *The Dickensian*, Vol. 63 (1967), p.143
* ———,'A Truly British Judge', *The Dickensian*, Vol. 66 (1970), p.30.
  ———, and Fielding, K.J., 'Charles Dickens on the Exclusion of Evidence', *The Dickensian*, Vol. 64 (1968), p.131
* ———,'The Tooting Disaster', *Victorian Studies*, Vol. 12 (1968), p.227
  Carlton, William J., 'Dickens Studies Italian', *The Dickensian*, Vol. 62 (1966), p.108
  Collins, Philip, 'Dickens and Popular Amusements', *The Dickensian*, Vol. 61 (1965), p.7
  Grubb, Gerald G., 'Dickens and the *Daily News*', *Nineteenth Century Fiction*, Vols. 6 and 7 (1951-53)
  Staples, Leslie C., 'Pictures from Genoa', *The Dickensian*, Vol. 46 (1950), p.84
  Tillotson, Kathleen and Burgis, Nina, 'Dickens at Drury Lane', *The Dickensian*, Vol. 65 (1969), p.81

XI Dombey and Son

Atthill, Robin, 'Dickens and the Railway', *English*, Vol. 13 (1961), p.130
Axton, William, 'Tonal Unity in *Dombey and Son*', *PMLA*, Vol. 78 (1963), p.341
Billington, J.D., 'Mr Dombey travels by rail', *The Dickensian*, Vol. 28 (1932), p.206
Carlton, William J., 'A Note on Captain Cuttle', *The Dickensian*, Vol. 64 (1968), p.152
Futrell, Michael, 'Dickens and Dostoyevsky', *English Miscellany*, Vol. 7 (1956), p.48
Lascelles, T.S., 'Transport in the Dickensian Era', *The Dickensian*, Vol. 58 (1962), p.75
Leavis, F.R., '*Dombey and Son*', *Sewanee Review*, Vol. 70 (1962), p.177
Lucas, John, '*Dombey and Son*'. In *Tradition and Tolerance in Nineteenth Century Fiction*, ed. Howard, Lucas and Good (London, 1966)

Macdonald, Robert H., 'The Dog Diogenes', *Notes and Queries*, Vol. 210 (1965), p.59

* Moynahan, Julian, 'Dealings with the Firm of Dombey and Son'. In *Dickens and the Twentieth Century*, ed. Gross and Pearson (1962), p.121

Spielmann, Mabel H., 'Florence Dombey's Tears', *The Dickensian*, Vol. 21 (1925), p.57 (and see N. Key, *ibid.*, p.219)

* Stone, Harry, 'Music-Staircase Imagery in *Dombey and Son*', *College English* Vol. 25 (1963), p.217

XII DAVID COPPERFIELD

Anon., 'David Copperfield and Dialect', *TLS*, 30 April, 1949

* Blount, Trevor, Introduction to the Penguin edition of *David Copperfield* (Harmondsworth, Middx, 1966)

Carlton, W.J., '"The Deed" in *David Copperfield*', *The Dickensian*, Vol. 48 (1952), p.101

Collins, Philip, 'Dickens' Reading', *The Dickensian*, Vol. 60 (1964), p.136

Gard, Roger, '*David Copperfield*', *Essays in Criticism*, Vol. 15 (1965), p.313

Futrell, Michael, 'Dostoyevsky and Dickens', *English Miscellany*, Vol. 7 (1956), p.48

Jones, John, '*David Copperfield*'. In *Dickens and the Twentieth Century*, ed. Gross and Pearson (London, 1962)

Kincaid, James, 'The Structure of *David Copperfield*', *Dickens Studies*, Vol. 2 (1966), p.74

* Manheim, Leonard, 'Floras and Doras: Women in Dickens' novels', *Texas Studies in Literature and Language* (1965), p.181

Needham, Gwendolyn, 'The Undisciplined Heart of David Copperfield', *Nineteenth Century Fiction*, Vol. 9 (1954), p.81

Sharrock, Roger, 'A Reminiscence of *In Memoriam* in *David Copperfield*', *Notes and Queries*, Vol. 201 (1956), p.502

* Spilka, Mark, '*David Copperfield* as Psychological Fiction', *Critical Quarterly*, Vol. 1 (1959), p.292

Wierstra, F.D., *Smollett and Dickens* (Den Helder, Holland, 1928)

XIII HOUSEHOLD WORDS, ETC.

Carlton, William J., 'Dickens' Forgotten Retreat in France', *The Dickensian*, Vol. 62 (1966), p.69

* Collins, Philip, 'Keep *Household Words* Imaginative', *The Dickensian*, Vol. 52 (1956), p.117

* ———, 'Dickens as Editor', *The Dickensian*, Vol. 56 (1960), p.85

* ———, 'The Significance of Dickens' Periodicals', *Review of English Literature*, Vol. II (1961), p.55

———, 'To Lose no Drop of that Immortal Man', *The Dickensian*, Vol. 66 (1970), p.43. (A review of Harry Stone's edition of the *Uncollected Writings*, 1968.)

Hardwick, Mollie, 'Born under Aquarius', *The Dickensian*, Vol. 62 (1966), p.92 (Especial reference to 'Our English Watering Place', 'Our French Watering Place')

Heath, Rt. Hon. Edward, 'The Dickens Conference Banquet', *The Dickensian*, Vol. 64 (1968), p.192 (Especial reference to 'Our English Watering Place')

Stone, Harry, 'Dark Corners of the Mind', *Horn Book Magazine*, Vol. 39 (1963), p.306 (Especial reference to Captain Murderer)

* ———,'Dickens "Conducts" *Household Words*', *The Dickensian*, Vol. 64 (1968), p.82

* ———, Introduction and Notes to the *Uncollected Writings of Charles Dickens* (Harmondsworth, Middx, 1968)

XIV CHRISTMAS STORIES

Brown, F.J., 'Those Dickens Christmases', *The Dickensian*, Vol. 60 (1964), p.17

Lascelles, T.S., 'The Signalman's Story', *The Dickensian*, Vol. 56 (1960), p.84

———, 'Transport in the Dickensian Era', *The Dickensian*, Vol. 58 (1962), p.152 (Esp. ref. 'Mugby Junction')

Stone, Harry, 'Dark Corners of the Mind', *Horn Book Magazine*, Vol. 39 (1963), p.306

XV BLEAK HOUSE

* Adrian, Arthur H., 'Dickens and the Brick-and-Mortar Sects', *Nineteenth Century Fiction*, Vol. 10 (1955)

Anon., *Gentleman's Magazine*, Vol. 16 (1746), p.368

Anon., 'Doctors' Commons', *The Dickensian*, Vol. 21 (1925), p.27

Axton, William F., 'The Trouble with Esther', *Modern Language Quarterly*, Vol. 26 (1965), p.545

———, 'Esther's Nicknames', *The Dickensian*, Vol. 62 (1966), p.158

* ———,'Religious and Scientific Imagery in *Bleak House*', *Nineteenth Century Fiction*, Vol. 22 (1968), p.349

Blount, Trevor, 'A revised Image in the opening chapter of *Bleak House*', *Notes and Queries*, Vol. 207 (1962), p.303

* ———, 'The Graveyard Satire of *Bleak House*, in the Context of 1850', *Review of English Studies*, Vol. 14 (1963), p.370

* ———, 'The Chadbands and Dickens's View of Dissenters', *Modern Language Quarterly*, Vol. 25 (1964), p.295

* ———, 'The Ironmaster and the New Acquisitiveness', *Essays in Criticism*, Vol. 15 (1965), p.414

* ———, 'Dickens's Slum Satire in *Bleak House*', *Modern Language Review*, Vol. 60 (1965), p.340

* ———, 'Chancery as Evil and Challenge in *Bleak House*', *Dickens Studies*, Vol. 1 (1965), p.112

* ———, 'Poor Jo, Education and the problems of juvenile delinquency', *Modern Philology*, Vol. 62 (1965), p.325

* ———, 'The Importance of Place in *Bleak House*', *The Dickensian*, Vol. 61 (1965), p.140

* ———, 'The Documentary Symbolism of Chancery in *Bleak House*', *The Dickensian*, Vol. 62 (1966), pp.47, 106, 170

* ———, 'Sir Leicester Dedlock and "Deportment" Turveydrop: some aspects of Dickens' use of parallelism', *Nineteenth Century Fiction*, Vol. 21 (1966), p.141

* ———, '*Bleak House* and the Sloane Scandal of 1850', *Dickens Studies*, Vol. 3 (1967), p.63

* Brice, Alec and Fielding, K.J., 'The Tooting Disaster', *Victorian Studies*, Vol. 12 (1968), p.227

* Butt, John, '*Bleak House* in the Context of 1851', *Nineteenth Century Fiction*, Vol. 10 (1955), p.1

* ———, '*Bleak House* Once More', *Critical Quarterly*, Vol. 1 (1959), p.302

Carlton, William J., 'Miss Fray and Miss Flite', *Notes and Queries*, Vol. 196 (1951), p.521

* Collins, Philip, '*Bleak House* and Dickens' Household Narrative', *Nineteenth Century Fiction*, Vol. 14 (1960), p.345

Cooperman, Stanley, 'Dickens and the Secular Blasphemy', *College English*, Vol. 22 (1960), p.156

Dettelbach, Cynthia, 'Bird Imagery in *Bleak House*', *The Dickensian*, Vol. 59 (1963), p.177

Engel, Monroe, 'The Politics of Dickens' Novels', *PMLA*, Vol. 71 (1956), p.945

Galvin, Thomas, 'Mr Vholes of Symonds' Inn', *The Dickensian*, Vol. 64 (1968), p.22

Gill, Stephen, 'Allusion in *Bleak House*', *Nineteenth Century Fiction*, Vol. 22 (1967), p.145

Harris, Wendell V., 'Jo at the Inquest', *The Dickensian*, Vol. 64 (1968), p.48

Holdsworth, Sir William, *Dickens as a Legal Historian* (New Haven, Conn., 1928), Chapter 3

Kenney, Blair G., 'Carlyle and *Bleak House*', *The Dickensian*, Vol. 66 (1970), p.36

* Kettle, Arnold, 'Dickens and the Popular Tradition', *Zeitschrift für Anglistik und Amerikanistik*, Vol. 9 (1961), p.229

* McMaster, R.D., 'Dickens and the Horrific', *Dalhousie Review*, Vol. 38 (1958), p.18

Monod, Sylvère, 'Esther Summerson, Charles Dickens and the Reader in *Bleak House*', *Dickens Studies*, Vol. 5 (1969), p.5

Morley, Malcolm, 'Revelry by Night', *The Dickensian*, Vol. 60 (1964), p.100

Perkins, George, 'Death by Spontaneous Combustion', *The Dickensian*, Vol. 60 (1964), p.57

'Pry, Paul', *Oddities of London Life* (London, 1838)

Sørensen, Knud, 'Subjective Narration in *Bleak House*', *English Studies*, Vol. 40 (1959), p.431

Staples, Leslie, 'Borrioboola-Gha', *The Dickensian*, Vol. 57 (1961), p.10

* Sucksmith, H.P., 'Dickens at Work in *Bleak House*', *Renaissance and Modern Studies*, Vol. 9 (1965), p.47

Whitley, Alvin, 'Two Hints for *Bleak House*', *The Dickensian*, Vol. 52 (1956), p.183

Wiley, Elizabeth, 'Four Strange Cases', *The Dickensian*, Vol. 58 (1962), p.120

* Wilkinson, Amy, '*Bleak House*: From Faraday to Judgment Day', *ELH*, Vol. 34 (1967), p.224

Worth, George J., 'The Genesis of the Crossing Sweeper', *JEGP*, Vol. 60 (1961), p.44

Zabel, Morton D., 'Introduction to *Bleak House*', (1956) rep. *The Dickens Critics*, ed. Ford and Lane (Ithaca, N.Y. 1961), p.325

XVI HARD TIMES

* Carnall, Geoffrey, 'Dickens, Mrs Gaskell and the Preston Strike', *Victorian Studies*, Vol. 8 (1964), p.31

Christian, Mildred, 'Carlyle's Influence upon the Social Theory of Dickens', *Nineteenth Century Fiction*, Vol. 1 (1947), p.27

Cooperman, Stanley, 'Dickens and the Secular Blasphemy', *College English*, Vol. 22 (1960), p.156

Dunn, Richard J., 'Skimpole and Harthouse: The Dickens Character in Transition', *Dickens Studies*, Vol. 3 (1965), p.121

* Gilmour, Robin, 'The Gradgrind School', *Victorian Studies*, Vol. 11 (1967),

p.207 (in part, a reply to John Holloway, in *Dickens and the Twentieth Century*, ed. Gross and Pearson, 1962)

Leavis, F.R., '*Hard Times*'. In *The Great Tradition* (London, 1948)

Lucas, John, 'Mrs Gaskell and Brotherhood'. In *Tradition and Tolerance in Nineteenth Century Fiction*, ed. Howard, Lucas and Good (London, 1966)

Ruskin, John, '*Hard Times*' (1860). In *Unto this Last* (1862). Rep. *The Dickens Critics*, ed. Ford and Lane (Ithaca, N.Y., 1961), p.47

* Shaw, G.B., Introduction to *Hard Times* (1912). Rep. *The Dickens Critics*, ed. Ford and Lane (Ithaca, N.Y., 1961), p.125

* Williams, Raymond, 'Social Criticism in Dickens', *Critical Quarterly*, Vol. 6 (1964), p.214

Voss, A.E., 'A Note on Theme and Structure in *Hard Times*', *Theoria* (South Africa), No. 23 (1964), p.35

XVII Little Dorrit

Bell, Vereen M., 'Mrs General's Victorian England', *Nineteenth Century Fiction*, Vol. 20 (1965), p.177

* Cooperman, Stanley, 'Dickens and the Secular Blasphemy', *College English*, Vol. 22 (1960), p.156

Gervais, David, 'The Poetry of *Little Dorrit*', *Cambridge Quarterly*, Vol. 4 (1968), p.38

Howard, John, *The State of the Prisons* (1777). Rep. Everyman's Library, No. 835

Leavis, Q.D., 'A Note on Literary Indebtedness – Dickens, George Eliot, Henry James', *Hudson Review*, Vol. 8 (1956), p.423

McMaster, R.D., '*Little Dorrit*: Experience and Design', *Queen's Quarterly*, Vol. 67, p.530

* Manheim, Leonard, 'Floras and Doras: The Women in Dickens' Novels', *Texas Studies in Literature and Language* (1965), p.182

Nethercot, Arthur, 'Prunes and Miss Prism', *Modern Drama*, Vol. 6 (1963), p.112

Reid, J.C., *The Hidden World of Charles Dickens* (Auckland, N.Z., 1962)

Scrutton, T.B., 'The State of the Prisons as seen by John Howard and Charles Dickens', *The Dickensian*, Vol. 62 (1966), p.112

* Trilling, Lionel, Introduction to *Little Dorrit*. Rep. *The Opposing Self* (Boston, 1955)

* Williams, Raymond, 'Social Criticism in Dickens', *Critical Quarterly*, Vol. 6 (1964), p.214

Woolliams, W.P., 'Jarndyce and Jarndyce', *The Dickensian*, Vol. 41 (1944), p.26 (for description of debtors' prisons)

XVIII A Tale of Two Cities

Carlton, William M., 'Dickens Studies French', *The Dickensian*, Vol. 59 (1963), p.21

Lindsay, Jack, '*Barnaby Rudge*'. In *Dickens and the Twentieth Century*, ed. Gross and Pearson (London, 1962) (an aside on *A Tale of Two Cities*)

McCelvey, George, '*A Tale of Two Cities* and Gin-Drinking', *Notes and Queries*, March 1961, p.96

McMaster, R.D., 'Dickens and the Horrific', *Dalhousie Review*, Vol. 38 (1958), p.18

Reffield, A.E., 'Dr Manette in Soho', *The Dickensian*, Vol. 59 (1963), p.172

Ryan, J.S., '*A Tale of Two Cities*', *Dickens Studies*, Vol. 2 (1966), p.147

XIX Great Expectations

Axton, William, '"Keystone" Structure in Dickens's Serial Novels', *University of Toronto Quarterly*, Vol. 37 (1967), p.31

Bart, Barry D., 'Trabb's Boy and Orlick', *Victorian Newsletter*, No. 29 (1966), p.27

Bell, Vereen M., 'Parents and Children in *Great Expectations*', *Victorian Newsletter*, Vol. 30 (1968), p.5

Clinton-Baddeley, V.C., 'Wopsle', *The Dickensian*, Vol. 57 (1961), p.150

Finkel, Robert J., 'Another Boy brought up by hand', *Nineteenth Century Fiction*, Vol. 20 (1966), p.389

Goldfarb, Russell M., 'The Menu of *Great Expectations*', *Victorian Newsletter*, No. 21 (1962), p.18

Hagan, J.H., 'Structural Patterns in Dickens's *Great Expectations*', *ELH* Vol. 21 (1954), p.54

Hallan, Clifford B., 'The Structure of *Great Expectations*', *Dickens Studies*, Vol. 2 (1966), p.26

Hill, T.W., 'Notes on *Great Expectations*', *The Dickensian*, Vol. 53 (1957), pp.119, 184; Vol. 54 (1958), pp.53, 123, 185; Vol.55 (1959), pp.57, 121

House, Humphry, 'G.B.S. on *Great Expectations*'. Rep. *All in Due Time* (1955)

Hutchings, Richard J., 'Dickens at Bonchurch', *The Dickensian*, Vol. 62 (1965), p.97

Meisel, Martin, 'The Ending of *Great Expectations*', *Essays in Criticism*, Vol. 15 (1965), p.326

— ——, 'Miss Havisham Brought to Book', *PMLA*, Vol. 81 (1966), p.278

* Moynahan, Julian, 'The Hero's Guilt: The Case of *Great Expectations*', *Essays in Criticism*, Vol. 10 (1960), p.60

Nisbet, Ada, *Dickens and Ellen Ternan* (Berkeley, California, 1952)

* Partlow, Robert B., 'The Moving I: A Study of the Point of View in *Great Expectations*', *College English*, Vol. 23 (1961), p.122

Peyrouton, N.C., 'John Wemmick: Enigma', *Dickens Studies*, Vol. 1 (1965), p.39

Ryan, J.S., 'A Possible Australian Source for Miss Havisham', *Australian Literary Studies*, Vol. 1 (1963), p.134

* Shaw, G.B., Introduction to *Great Expectations* (1937). Rep. *Charles Dickens*, ed. Stephen Wall (Harmondsworth, Middx, 1970)

* Stone, Harry, 'Fire, Hand and Gate', *Kenyon Review*, Vol. 24 (1962), p.662

———, 'Dickens' Woman in White', *Victorian Newsletter*, No. 30 (1968)

Wentersdorf, Karl P., 'Mirror Images in *Great Expectations*', *Nineteenth Century Fiction*, Vol. 2 (1966), p.203

XX OUR MUTUAL FRIEND

* Barnard, Robert, 'The Choral Symphony', *Review of English Literature*, Vol. 2 (1961), p.89

Hardy, Barbara, '*Martin Chuzzlewit*' (for an aside on *Our Mutual Friend*). In *Dickens and the Twentieth Century*, ed. Gross and Pearson (London, 1962)

Hobsbaum, Philip, 'The Critics and *Our Mutual Friend*', *Essays in Criticism*, Vol. 13 (1963), p.231

McMaster, R.D., 'Birds of Prey', *Dalhousie Review*, Vol. 40 (1960), p.372

Miyoshi, Masao, 'Resolution of Identity in *Our Mutual Friend*', *Victorian Newsletter*, No. 26 (1964), p.5

Morgan, William de, Introduction to *Our Mutual Friend* (Waverley Edition, London, 1912).

Nelson, Harland S., 'Dickens's *Our Mutual Friend* and Henry Mayhew's *London Labour and the London Poor*', *Nineteenth Century Fiction*, Vol. 20 (1965), p.207

Sharp, Sister Corona, 'The Archetypal Feminine', *University of Kansas City Review*, Vol. 27 (1961), p.307

Stone, Harry, 'From Fagin to Riah', *Midstream*, Vol. 6 (1960), p.21

Trilling, Lionel, 'The Dickens of Our Day'. Rep. *A Gathering of Fugitives* (Boston, 1956)

Young, G.F., 'Noddy Boffin's Misers', *The Dickensian*, Vol. 43 (1946), p.14

XXI EDWIN DROOD (i)

Ainger, Alfred, 'Mr Dickens' Amateur Theatricals', *Macmillan's Magazine*, January 1871. Rep. *The Dickensian*, Vol. 36 (1940), p.203

Anon., *The Times*, 1 July 1857. Rep. *The Dickensian*, Vol. 37 (1941), p.171

Anon., *Town Talk*, 5 January 1858. Rep. *The Dickensian*, Vol. 37 (1941), p.223

* Dexter, Walter, 'For One Night Only: Dickens's Appearances as an Amateur Actor', *The Dickensian*, Vol. 35 (1939), p.231; Vol. 36 (1940), pp.20, 195

————, 'Dickens as an Amateur Actor', *The Dickensian*, Vol. 37 (1941), p.10

* ————, 'Mr Charles Dickens Will Read', *The Dickensian*, Vol. 37 (1941), pp.107, 133, 201; Vol. 38 (1941), pp.41, 158, 231; Vol. 39 (1943), p.93

Dolby, George, *Charles Dickens as I knew Him* (London, 1885)

Kent, Charles, *Charles Dickens as a Reader* (1872)

Pine, Walter, 'Dickens' Readings at Portsmouth', *The Dickensian*, Vol. 35, (1939), p.205

(ii)

Aylmer, Felix, 'The Drood Case Re-Opened', *The Dickensian*, Vol. 20 (1924), p.192

———— 'The Sapsea Tomb', *The Dickensian*, Vol. 23 (1927), p.177

———— 'First-Aid for the "Drood" Audience', *The Dickensian*, Vol. 55 (1959), p.133

———— *The Drood Case* (London, 1964)

'B., F.C.' *Cambridge Review*, 25 January 1906, p.185

* Baker, Richard, *The Drood Murder Case* (Berkeley, California, 1951)

Bilham, D.M., '*Edwin Drood* – To Resolve a Mystery', *The Dickensian*, Vol. 57 (1966), p.181

* Bleifuss, William W., 'The Re-Examination of *Edwin Drood*', *The Dickensian*, Vol. 51 (1954), pp.110, 176

Boyd, Aubrey, *A New Angle on the Drood Mystery* (Washington, 1922)

Brend, Gavin, 'A Re-Examination of *Edwin Drood*', *The Dickensian*, Vol. 51 (1954), p.87

Carden, Percy T., 'The Case for Tartar Re-Stated', *The Dickensian*, Vol. 15 (1919), p.189

————, *The Murder of Edwin Drood* (London, 1920)

————, 'A New Angle on the Drood Mystery', *The Dickensian*, Vol. 20 (1924), p.38

Collins, Charles Allston, *The Dickensian*, Vol. 15 (1919), p.196. And see Joseph Daly, below

Collins, Philip, 'Dickens and the Whiston Case', *The Dickensian*, Vol. 58 (1962), p.47

* ————, 'Inspector Bucket Visits the Princess Puffer', *The Dickensian*, Vol. 60 (1964), p.88

Conway, Eustace, *Anthony Munday, and other essays* (privately printed, New York, 1927)

Corfield, Wilmot, 'The Drood Mystery', *The Dickensian*, Vol. 29 (1933), p.96

Cox, Arthur J., 'The Drood Remains', *Dickens Studies*, Vol. 2 (1966), p.33

Cross, F.J., '*Edwin Drood* Again', *The Dickensian*, Vol. 24 (1927), p.61

Daly, Joseph, *Life of Augustin Daly* (London, 1917). See esp. pp. 107-8 (for the views of Charles Allston Collins)

Dickens, Jr., Charles, Introduction to *The Mystery of Edwin Drood* (London, 1923)

* Duffield, Howard, 'John Jasper – Strangler', *The Bookman* (USA), Vol. 70 (1930), p.581

Ellis, M.A., '"The Chinaman" in *The Mystery of Edwin Drood*',*The Dickensian*, Vol. 17 (1921), p.138

Fildes, Sir Luke, Letter to *The Times*, 3 November 1905

Gadd, G.F., 'Datchery the Enigma', *The Dickensian*, Vol. 2 (1906), p.13

————, '*The Mystery of Edwin Drood*', *The Dickensian*, Vol. 29 (1933), p.238

Hill, T.W., 'Drood Time in Cloisterham', *The Dickensian*, Vol. 39 (1943), p.113

————, 'Notes on *The Mystery of Edwin Drood*', *The Dickensian*, Vol. 40 (1944), p.198

Jamieson, H.W. and Rosenthal, F.M.B., '*The Mystery of Edwin Drood*', *The Dickensian*, Vol. 25 (1929), pp.28, 100

Jones-Evans, Eric, *John Jasper's Secret* (London, 1951). Adapted as a play from Morford, *q.v.*

Kavanagh, Mary, *A New Solution to The Mystery of Edwin Drood* (London, 1919)

Kelly, Katherine, 'John Jasper', *The Dickensian*, Vol. 19 (1923), p.34

————, 'The Drood Case Re-Opened', *The Dickensian*, Vol. 21 (1925), p.20

Kent, W.Ridley, '*Edwin Drood*', *The Dickensian*, Vol. 9 (1913), p.20

Lang, Andrew, *The Puzzle of Dickens' Last Plot* (London, 1905)

* Lehmann-Haupt, C.F., 'New Facts Concerning *Edwin Drood*', *The Dickensian*, Vol. 25 (1929), p.165

, 'Studies in *Edwin Drood*',*The Dickensian*, Vol. 31 (1935), p.299; Vol. 32 (1936), pp.29, 57, 135, 219, 301

Matchett, Willoughby, 'The Eternal Problem', *The Dickensian*, Vol. 8 (1912), p.320

————, 'Datchery', *The Dickensian*, Vol. 10 (1914), p.133

Morford, Henry, *John Jasper's Secret* (1871). And see Jones-Evans (above) for theatrical adaptation

* Morley, Malcolm, 'Stage Solutions to the Mystery', *The Dickensian*, Vol. 53 (1957), pp.46, 93, 180

Nicoll, Sir W.Robertson, *The Problem of Edwin Drood* (London, 1912)

Pakenham, Lady Pansy, 'The Memorandum Book, Forster and *Edwin Drood*', *The Dickensian*, Vol. 51 (1955), p.117

Perugini, Kate, '*Edwin Drood* and the Last Days of Dickens', *Pall Mall Gazette*, January 1906, p.643

Proctor, Richard, *Watched by the Dead* (London, 1887)

Rust, S.J. '*The Mystery of Edwin Drood*', *The Dickensian*, Vol. 29 (1933), p.96

Sanders, E.L., 'The Technique of *Edwin Drood*', *The Dickensian*, Vol. 28 (1932), p.190

Saunders, Montagu, *The Mystery in the Drood Family* (London, 1914)

———, 'Dickens, Drood and Datchery', *The Dickensian*, Vol. 15 (1919), p.182

Shore, W.Teignmouth, 'A Light on the Drood Mystery', *The Dickensian*, Vol. 22 (1926), p.62

Squire, Sir J.C., 'The Drood Mystery Insoluble', *The Dickensian*, Vol. 15 (1919), p.195

Vase, Gillan, *The Great Mystery Solved* (London, 1878)

Walters, J. Cuming, *The Complete Mystery of Edwin Drood* (London, 1912)

———, 'Mr Knag and his Brethren', *The Dickensian*, Vol. 24 (1928), p.140

———, 'The Bazzard Burlesque', *The Dickensian*, Vol. 24 (1928), p.279

Woollen, Henry, '*Edwin Drood*', *The Dickensian*, Vol. 9 (1913), p.74

APPENDIX I: THE MUDFOG PAPERS, ETC.

Easton, Edward Raymond, M.D., 'Doctors in Dickens', *The Dickensian*, Vol. 41 (1945), p.150

APPENDIX II: THE LIFE OF OUR LORD, ETC.

Peyrouton, N.C., 'Life of Our Lord', *The Dickensian*, Vol. 59 (1963), p.102

Sokolsky, G.E., 'We Jews', *The Dickensian*, Vol. 33 (1937), p.66

APPENDIX III: GEORGE SILVERMAN, ETC.

* Adrian, Arthur H., 'Dickens and the Brick-and-Mortar Sects', *Nineteenth Century Fiction*, Vol. 10 (1955), p.188

Bart, Barry T., 'George Silverman's Explanation', *The Dickensian*, Vol. 60 (1964), p.48

Bradby, M.K., 'An Explanation of "George Silverman's Explanation"', *The Dickensian*, Vol. 36 (1940), p.13

Flamm, Dudley, 'The Prosecutor Within', *The Dickensian*, Vol. 66 (1970), p.16

Leavis, Q.D., *Dickens the Novelist* (London, 1970), pp.282-7
Stone, Harry, 'Dickens' Tragic Universe: "George Silverman's Explanation"',
    Studies in Philology, Vol. 55 (1958), p.86
———, 'Dark Corners of the Mind', *Horn Book Magazine*, Vol. 39 (1963),
    p.306

Index